THE ANNUAL
OF
PSYCHOANALYSIS

THE ANNUAL
OF PSYCHOANALYSIS

A Publication of the
Institute for Psychoanalysis
Chicago

Volume XX

THE ANALYTIC PRESS

1992   Hillsdale, NJ   London

Published by The Analytic Press, Hillsdale, NJ.

Typeset in Baskerville
by Lind Graphics, Upper Saddle River, NJ

ISSN 0092-5055
ISBN 0-88163-133-7

Printed in the United States of America
10 9 8 7 6 5 4 3 2 1

This, the twentieth volume of *The Annual of Psychoanalysis,* is the first under my editorship. Although highly identified with Chicago, *The Annual* has throughout the years published work by major psychoanalytic contributors from across the United States and other countries as well. *The Annual of Psychoanalysis* approaches its third decade committed to excellence rather than to any particular school of psychoanalytic thought.

Jerome A. Winer, M.D.

Contents

I

THEORETICAL STUDIES

II

CLINICAL STUDIES

III

APPLIED PSYCHOANALYSIS

IV

PSYCHOANALYSIS AND PHILOSOPHY

Contributors

Richard Almond, M.D., Faculty, San Francisco Psychoanalytic Institute; Clinical Professor of Psychiatry, Stanford University School of Medicine.

Andrew Brook, D. Phil., Professor of Philosophy, Carleton University, Ottawa; Faculty, Toronto Institute for Contemporary Psychoanalysis.

James C. Cowan, Ph.D., Adjunct Professor of English, University of North Carolina, Chapel Hill; author, *D. H. Lawrence and the Trembling Balance* (1990).

Robert Galatzer-Levy, M.D., Lecturer in Psychiatry, University of Chicago; Training and Supervising Analyst, and Child and Adolescent Supervising Analyst, Institute for Psychoanalysis, Chicago.

John E. Gedo, M.D., Author, *The Mind in Disorder* (1988), *The Biology of Clinical Encounters* (1991), and (with Mark Gehrie) *Impasse and Innovation in Psychoanalysis* (forthcoming).

Gary N. Goldsmith, M.D., Faculty, Psychoanalytic Institute of New England, East; Clinical Instructor in Psychiatry, Harvard Medical School; Associate in Psychiatry, Beth Israel Hospital.

Mayer I. Gruber, Ph.D., Senior Lecturer, Department of Bible and Ancient Near East, Ben-Gurion University of the Negev, Beersheva, Israel.

Sudhir Kakar, Ph.D., Visiting Professor, Department of Psychology, University of Chicago.

Annette Lachmann, M.A., Adjunct Lecturer, Borough of Manhattan Community College, John Jay College of Criminal Law, New York.

Frank M. Lachmann, Ph.D., Core Faculty, Institute for the Psychoanalytic Study of Subjectivity; Training Analyst, Postgraduate Center for Mental Health, New York.

George F. Mahl, Ph.D., Professor Emeritus of Psychiatry and Psychology, Yale University.

W. W. Meissner, S.J., M.D., University Professor of Psychoanalysis, Boston College; Training and Supervising Analyst, Boston Psychoanalytic Institute.

Arnold H. Modell, M.D., Clinical Professor of Psychiatry, Harvard Medical School, Beth Israel Hospital; Training and Supervising Analyst, Boston Psychoanalytic Institute.

Kenneth M. Newman, M.D., Training and Supervising Analyst, Institute for Psychoanalysis, Chicago.

Henry F. Smith, M.D., Faculty, Psychoanalytic Institute of New England, East; Assistant Clinical Professor of Psychiatry, Harvard Medical School.

Alice Rosen Soref, M.A., Member, Infant Research Study Group of the Boston Psychoanalytic Society and Institute; private practice of psychoanalytic psychotherapy, New Centre, MA.

David M. Terman, M.D., Training and Supervising Analyst, Institute for Psychoanalysis, Chicago.

Ernest S. Wolf, M.D., Faculty, Training and Supervising Analyst, Institute for Psychoanalysis, Chicago; Assistant Professor of Psychiatry, Northwestern University Medical School.

I

THEORETICAL STUDIES

The Private Self and Private Space

ARNOLD H. MODELL

My thinking about the self has been guided by the fact that the self is fundamentally and deeply paradoxical. When we begin to formulate our ideas regarding the self, we are confronted with both clinical and conceptual paradoxes. In this chapter I focus on two such paradoxes, namely, that aspects of the self are simultaneously both public and private and that the self is simultaneously both dependent and autonomous.

There is another paradox concerning the self that will prove to be only an apparent paradox. There is a core of the self that remains the same over time; this is not to claim an absolute sameness but a recognizable sameness, an ability to recover one's identity despite whatever happens to oneself. This continuity of being is vital for our psychological health, yet the experience of self is also coterminous with an ever-changing flux of consciousness. Accordingly, the self has been described both as a psychic structure and as a state of consciousness.

Our reaction to paradox is probably a matter of temperament. Some of us love paradox while others seek to eliminate it by coming down hard on one wing of a paradox to the exclusion of the other. Sometimes entire literatures develop in this fashion and end up by not communicating with each other. For example, the paradox that the self is both structure and consciousness has led to very different literatures, which rarely keep both aspects of the paradox in view. One well aware of paradox was William James (1890), who wrestled with the problem of how a sustained sense of identity is possible if the self is experienced within the flux of consciousness. This paradox nearly drove him to distraction, and he was to struggle with this enigma until the end of his life (Myers, 1986).

Freud hardly addressed the problem of the self; when he did consider

1

it, he thought of it as a psychic structure and did not comment on the Jamesian self as consciousness. Among Freud's contemporaries, Paul Federn (1952), who introduced the concept of ego boundaries, was the first psychoanalyst—and for many years the only psychoanalyst—who systematically observed the self as consciousness. The majority of psychoanalysts, following Freud's example, considered the self only in the context of psychic structure. For many years the problem of the self was therefore seen exclusively as the problem of identity.

There is another paradox with regard to the self that needs to be mentioned. Here the paradox, a puzzle that has engaged philosophers for centuries, is more conceptual or epistemological. This is the seemingly insoluble problem of objectifying the subjective experience of self (for a recent review of this issue see Taylor, 1989). Freud dealt with this paradox by alternately describing the "I" in anthropomorphic (i.e., personal) terms—as if the relation between the ego and the superego were that of a child and a punitive or sometimes loving parent—and describing the ego in purely objective, impersonal language as a structure formed as the consequence of the neutralization of instinctual energy. Hartmann (1950) chose the latter, impersonal, option with the introduction of the term *self-representation*, preserving the Cartesian distinction between the object of perception and its representation in the mind. He intended to avoid Freud's anthropomorphism by assuming that forming a representation of the self in the mind is no different in kind from a representation in the mind of any other object of perception. From this point of view, observing one's self or another's self is not fundamentally different from observing trees or clouds or any other object in the external world.

Kohut's self psychology can be seen as a radical attempt to solve this epistemological paradox. When I first encountered self psychology, it seemed to me that Kohut rediscovered certain aspects of the phenomenology of the self that were absent in classical psychoanalysis. Disorders of the self were, however, well known to those psychoanalysts, such as followers of the British school of object relations, who worked with sicker patients (Modell, 1986). I therefore remained somewhat skeptical of Kohut's claim that self psychology represented a radically new psychology that could not be integrated into Freudian psychoanalysis. I have come to realize that I had then not yet understood something fundamental about self psychology. *What is radical in self psychology and totally original, at least within the psychoanalytic tradition, is its philosophical position with regard to the problem of objectifying the experience of the self.* For Kohut, the primacy of empathic understanding, defined as a vicarious introspection, is an irreducible given. Kohut therefore shunned all attempts to "objectify" the experience of self, as illustrated by ego psychology's use of the third party concept of self-representation. His stance is not unlike that of William James, for whom the subjective experience of consciousness required no further objectification. Kohut could therefore be described as a radical phenomenologist. However, phenomenology itself introduces fresh problems and difficulties.

With regard to the paradox of the private and social self, self psychology has focused almost exclusively on the social self. I don't question the heuristic value of what self psychology describes as the self–selfobject relationship, nor do I question our lifelong need for affirming selfobjects. But this only accounts for the social self and does not do justice to that aspect of the self that is experienced in solitude, in experiences that may never be shared with others. The self from this point of view is not dependent on others but is an independent agent, the source of autonomy. As Winnicott noted (1963), there is a part of the self that we never communicate to others and that must not be influenced by others. Self psychology, on the other hand, is essentially a psychology of relatedness. You will recall that Kohut (1980) often likened the need for affirming selfobjects to the need for oxygen. I would counter with the assertion that we cannot remain psychologically alive without the preservation of private space, that is, the preservation of a psychological space within which we can refuel ourselves.

Private experiences that originate in isolation may or may not be shared. And, as Winnicott observed, there are aspects of the private self that are never communicated. Within the private self one can replicate and model the external world and thus obtain some freedom from the "tyranny of real time" (Edelman, 1989). One thinks, for example, of Freud's description of the child's game where the child symbolically recreates the trauma of his mother's departure by throwing and retrieving a spool over the side of his cot (Freud, 1920). Freud interpreted this as a great cultural achievement inasmuch as the child, through symbolic action, was able to achieve an instinctual renunciation. One may interpret this "cultural achievement" from another direction and see it as the child's capacity to model, within the self, those events occurring in real time and thus emancipate himself from environmental inputs.

The private self is also the site where one can experience the joys of mastery, and in this sense it is the place where one can be fueled from within. The private self is also the seat of authenticity, of personal morality, and of vital personal interests. For those who face dreadful environments, private space is the place in which one can retreat to alternative worlds of fantasy, worlds that may guarantee psychic survival in a nonsupportive environment.

The idea of a private self is ancient as it is embodied to some extent in the religious idea of a soul that is known only to its possessor and communicates to no one but God. Before Christianity, Aristotle observed that the soul is the seat of our moral choices and that the tyrant can put one's body in chains but can never conquer one's soul (Taylor, 1989).

You will have recognized that the *private self* very nearly corresponds to Winnicott's (1960) true self. I prefer to speak of the private self since the term *true self* suggests a reified entity, although that was not Winnicott's intent. Ideally, we need an adjective that encompasses the notion of both privacy and authenticity. By choosing the term *true self*, Winnicott emphasized the authentic aspect of this inner self and highlighted the contrast between the authenticity, the affective wholeness, of the inner self and the false compliance of the social self. While not depreciating the importance of affective authenticity, I prefer the term *private self* since it highlights the contrast between the autonomy of this inner self and the dependence of the social self. As you know, in disturbances of the self we can observe both the need to preserve the privacy of the self and an inauthenticity—what can be called a decentering of the self—wherein the individual becomes estranged from his own affective core.

Winnicott's true self is a bodily self, the site of creativity and psychic aliveness. Preservation of the true self provides the assurance of the continuity of being. Contact with this inner self enables the individual to be alone, but, as Winnicott (1958) observed, the child's capacity to be alone, paradoxically, requires the presence of the mother. In order to enjoy private space, the continuity of being must be provided for by the human environment. Winnicott (1988) believed that the creative apperception of the world begins in states of nonrelatedness, where the child is symbolically held by a maternal presence. Within this private world the child can transform the pain of external reality and thus achieve some measure of autonomy. Winnicott viewed the false self as a shell of social compliance that enables the individual to keep this inner psychic reality hidden and protected.

Winnicott recognized the vital need for privacy and withdrawal, the need for time-out from relatedness. Winnicott's intuitive apprehension of the infant's need for unintruded private time has been confirmed by scientific studies of infant behavior (see Soref, this volume). Investigators have noted that the infant is able to regulate its interactions with the mother so that periods of relatedness are interspersed with periods of nonrelatedness. Sander (1983) refers to this private time as an "open space." He and his collaborators observed newborn infants in their interaction with their mothers in a continuous (around-the-clock) longitudinal study. By the third week of life the mother responds to the infant's needs by providing the infant with periods of relative disengagement.

Sander sees this as the infant's opportunity to exercise an "individually idiosyncratic and selective volitional initiative." The infant is free to follow his own *interests,* which may involve self-exploration or responding to low-level stimuli. Sander makes the significant point that *"disengagement has a place of equal importance with engagement." I would further suggest that this natural rhythm of a balance between alternate periods of relatedness and disengagement persists throughout life.*

As all observers of children and animals have noted, there is joy in those activities that result in an experience of mastery. White (1963) called this experience one of *efficacy* and competence. It is important to recognize that this source of pleasure is different from the pleasure of relatedness or the pleasure of such consummatory activities as sexuality or a good feed. Brazelton (1980) calls this capacity to find joy from within, through mastery, "fueling the system from within." I believe that this capacity remains as a core of the private self. When present, the self feels strong; when absent, the self feels weak and depleted.

The idea that contact with this inner core of the self enables the individual to achieve a relative autonomy from the environment finds some support from contemporary neuroscience. To the best of my knowledge, Gerald Edelman (1989), a Nobel laureate for his work in immunology, was the first to propose a model of the self as an evolutionary structure whose adaptive function is to free the individual from the tyranny of real time. In my recent book, *Other Times, Other Realities* (Modell, 1990), I have indicated how Edelman's theory of categorical memory is similar to Freud's important, but insufficiently recognized, concept of *nachträglichkeit,* a retranscription of memory. I have found Edelman's model of the brain to be immediately relevant to such basic psychoanalytic phenomena as the transference. In *The Remembered Present* Edelman (1989) offers a model of the biological self that is also congruent with the idea of an inner core of the self that confers a measure of autonomy from the environment.

Edelman believes that it has not been sufficiently recognized that there are two systems within the central nervous system that differ radically in their evolutionary history. One is the system that provides the neural basis for the experience of self; it is oriented internally and is based upon introception. Structures that mediate the perception of the external world differ anatomically and have a different evolutionary history. A striking adaptive advantage is given to those species that have an awareness of self, for this awareness is linked to the capacity to create a model of the world free of real time (Edelman, 1989, p. 92). This modeling, of course, takes a quantum leap with the capacity for symbolization and language. Edelman's model of the biological self resolves the paradox of the continuity of the self in the midst of the constant flux of conscious perception, the paradox that William James found to be insoluble. The continuity of the self is preserved by virtue of the self's linkage with the homeostatic brain systems; the flux of perceptions occurring in real time are recategorized through a "matching" with the value-laden memories of former states. I would interpret Edelman's term *value-laden memories* to include reference to the memories of motivational affective states, both positive and negative. Edelman's (1987) theory suggests an inner self that is self-generating: "It would not be surprising if, to some extent, every perception were considered to be an act of creation and every memory an act of imagination" (p. 329).

What is the psychoanalytic evidence for the existence of a private self? One short answer is that its existence can be inferred from the extreme and intensive measures that some patients take to preserve it from intrusion. The preservation of private space is an important motive for defense and resistance. In many psychoanalyses one can observe in the opening phase that a variety of attempts are made to defend the privacy of the self. For many patients the fundamental rule of psychoanalysis is an impossible injunction since it threatens the very survival of the private self. Some patients apparently comply with this injunction and fill the hours with talk. But if the talk is delivered in an unvarying monotone, talk from which the affective charge has been removed, the analyst may feel lost in a sea of words. In the absence of authenticity there cannot be a psychoanalytic dialogue. In some cases intense feelings appear to be communicated, but the analyst may find later that the affects are inauthentic in that they are exaggerated or false (Modell, 1984). To communicate genuine feeling is also an expression of need, so that the communication of authentic affects is intrinsically object-seeking. The converse is also true: the noncommunication of affect is a communication that one does not need anything from the other; it is a communication of self-sufficiency (Modell, 1980). In this case the fundamental rule and the growing dependency upon the analyst, fostered by the psychoanalytic setting, are perceived as threats to self-sufficiency; in some instances patients fear that they will lose their individuality as a result of the psychoanalytic process.

It can be argued that the private self is not threatened in health, that it is only when the self is experienced as fragile and vulnerable that such defenses are in evidence in psychoanalytic treatment. But who among us are so healthy that they feel no need to preserve the privacy of the self? Psychopathology enhances theory in that it exaggerates normal processes so that they can be more easily observed, and the vulnerability of the private self can be observed most clearly in individuals who suffer from a disorder of the self.

I shall present a brief vignette of a patient whom I think of as schizoid. Others might describe her as suffering from some form of a narcissistic personality or from a social phobia. I find these terms to be quite arbitrary; her diagnosis need not trouble us as I can assure you that she is neither a borderline nor a psychotic patient. I shall concentrate on the phenomenology of her experience of self; for our purposes a fuller description of the psychoanalytic process is not necessary. Understand, however, that she was able to communicate these experiences only after several years of psychoanalysis, during which time aspects of a negative father transference were successfully analyzed. Prior to this period there were times when portions of the self were dissociated and splitoff, leading to distinct episodes of projective identification. With the consolidation of her sense of self and the development of a trusting relationship with me, the patient has had no further episodes of projective identification.

The patient suffered from a severe form of social anxiety in that she felt as if her sense of self could be completely sucked out and obliterated by the other person. As a child she had the fantasy that the octopus used its tentacles to suck out the inner contents of its victims, and, in analogous fashion, she believed that her sense of identity could be thus sucked out by others. Her sense of self was not threatened when she was alone, but she always felt vulnerable in the presence of others, especially if they were strangers. She felt that to be in the presence of another person exposed her to risk, that the continued existence of her self was held hostage to the response of others.

My patient's octopus fantasy involved the belief that the core of herself could be connected to another unknown self by some secret passage, as if her present self occupied a *known* universe but a future self could occupy a different *unknown* universe. She visualized this concretely as a self occupying a sphere that was connected by a mysterious or hidden passage to the other, unknown, sphere. She believed that when she was in the presence of another person, her known self was at risk in that it could be drained into this other, unknown, sphere and that she thus could be transformed into a different person.

My patient referred to her private self as a "core" that could be controlled by "popping" it in or out. She could "pop out" this inner core to preserve the private self from intrusion or humiliation. When her inner core was "popped out," what remained was a "false self" (her words), which she believed to be thin, stiff, and shallow, lacking authentic affects. My patient was aware, however, that when the inner core of her personality was absent, social contact was not quite adequate in that she appeared to other people as distant and flat. She felt that she "resided" within this inner core and that without it she was not truly there. If the inner core was breached, it felt to her like a rape or like someone breaking into her house. "Popping out" this core was analogous to removing her valuables to a safer place.

This inner core of her self, if breached by the other, became vulnerable to the pain of humiliation, which my patient felt to be nearly unbearable. She believed that, in a sense, she could be psychically "raped." The orifice through which this rape might occur was not the genitals but the eyes. It is through one's eyes that one makes social contact; the eyes are the guardian of the soul. One glimpses the soul through the eyes; the expression of the eyes reveal authentic affective states that can otherwise be masked by the face. My patient, therefore, had great difficulty in having others look into her eyes, and she generally averted her glance. The prospect of an ophthalmic examination sent her into a panic. Yet she liked observing other people's eyes to obtain knowledge of their psychic states: she believed, for example, that those who held their gaze were psychically present and those who were shifty-eyed, psychically absent. She classified people accordingly as having either "good" or "bad" eyes. The eyes were for her an early warning system.

The patient began psychoanalysis after a period of psychotherapy. When her treatment was shifted from a face-to-face setup to the use of the couch, she felt much more comfortable since I could not see her eyes and she was relieved of the burden of having to read my eyes. When I asked her what she feared the other person would see in her eyes, she responded that the other person would see chaos, which would be unbearably humiliating, as if a defect of the self were exposed, as if she were hiding a tail. To be humiliated by others meant that one was controlled by the other person and could be infinitely exploited. She associated to the abuses practiced by leaders of cults; she felt such abuses were akin to the control of a subject by a hypnotist.

When this patient was caught off-guard, when the unexpected happened, she was unable to regulate the ideal distance from others. Her sense of self was thus vulnerable not only to the unempathic response of others but simply as a consequence of being known to others. She was someone for whom empathy could be threatening; to be immediately understood by a stranger was very frightening to her. Also, her own empathic understanding placed her self in jeopardy: for example, when she felt an empathic connection with another person, she felt merged with that person. And if she felt merged, she then feared that she would lose her sense of self. Merging with another threatened her sense of intactness and continuity of the self. She experienced her sense of self as intermittent, as if she were a still camera, whose shutter clicks intermittently, rather than a movie camera, which records continuously.

This patient illustrates that the ultimate threat to the private, inner self is its loss of continuity. You will recall that in naming this inner self I chose to emphasize privacy rather than authenticity. Let us now return to the problem of authenticity. Our work with the so-called narcissistic disorders has taught us that these patients, in their effort to safeguard the privacy of the self, may inadvertently lose contact with their own inner affective core. We can describe this as a decentering of the self. Where the child's private space is habitually violated, habitual defenses are erected. It seems as if the defenses used against the intruder are unfortunately turned upon the self; *the methods employed to protect private space against intrusion by others are inevitably turned against the self.* Such individuals become estranged from their own affective core and are as false and inauthentic within themselves as they are with others. In the struggle to preserve private space they therefore achieve a tragic pyrrhic victory. Ironically, the fight to protect the private self continues even after the individual has lost contact with it; he is like a householder who maintains a burglar alarm long after misplacing the family jewels. *In closing oneself off from others, one inadvertently closes oneself off from oneself.*

It is very common today for psychotherapists and psychoanalysts to note a characteristic initial complaint: an inability to commit oneself either to a love relationship or to work. This fear of commitment is sometimes accompanied by an inner sense of deadness, a sense of futility and emptiness, a lack of psychic aliveness. Patients with this complaint feel that their lives are unfocused and lacking in purpose and direction. I interpret these symptoms as an indication that such individuals have lost contact with an inner core of themselves so that they do not know what they really desire.

There is widespread agreement that the inner core of the self is an affective core. Whether or not one still believes in Freud's instinct theory, the id can be thought of as the locus of impersonal impulses that are somatic in origin. In this regard, Winnicott (1958) made an interesting observation: with the help of an empathic and in-tune mother the infant is able to transform the impulses of the id into personal impulses. You will recognize that this idea has been much elaborated by others (e.g., Stern, 1985); it is consistent with the observation that mothers who are in affective attunement with their child enable the child to both accept and identify his affects. The infant, Winnicott (1958) says, rediscovers the *personal* impulse: "The individual who has developed the capacity to be alone is constantly able to rediscover the personal impulse and the personal impulse is not wasted because the state of being alone is something which (though paradoxically) always implies that someone else is there" (p. 34). Feelings and impulses are experienced as intrusions if they are felt to originate from an area outside of private space; it is as if such impulses are treated as part of an external environment.

These ideas suggest a reinterpretation of one of Freud's most quoted aphorisms: *Wo Es war, soll Ich werden,* "where id was there shall ego be" (1933, p. 80). Although I am not a Lacanian (I really don't understand him), I found his retranslation of this aphorism to be attractive. Lacan (1977) reinterpreted and retranslated the aphorism to read: "Where *it* was there shall *I* be (p. 128). Seen in this light, one aim of psychoanalytic treatment is to extend the domain of the personal over the impersonal, to extend the domain of self over the impersonal. The opposition between the ego and the id is not so much between a rational self and irrational passions as between the personal and the impersonal.

There are at least three aspects to the private self that have evident clinical implications. First, by definition, private space is space that is not to be intruded upon. Second, some experiences within the private self must not be communicated to others. Third, this inner self is the site of self-sufficiency and self-generation.

The therapeutic principle of nonintrusion has a long history in psychoanalysis. Nonintrusion is essentially a recognition of personhood. Ferenczi (1933) warned that parental insensitivity regarding the child's personhood would have profound consequences for the child's sense of self and his relation to reality. The therapeutic principle of nonintrusion was subsequently made quite explicit by Balint (1968). Winnicott (1971) appears to have arrived at the same idea independently; he warned that therapists should not be too clever and thus rob their patients of their creativity. And he went even further: he stated that mothers who rob their children of their creativity do something worse than castration. The principle of nonintrusion has also, as is well known, been emphasized by Kohut (1977) as an aspect of empathic sensitivity.

As I have indicated, in order to preserve the privacy of the self some patients become noncommunicative and apparently unrelated. I have described this as a defense in a two-person context, in contrast to the more customary view of defense as a purely intrapsychic process (Modell, 1984). More recently, I have come to realize that to view this process only as a defense omits another significant aspect. This is, to be sure, a defense, but, paradoxically, it is a defense that promotes therapeutic change. For many patients psychoanalysis represents the first opportunity they have ever had to reconnect with their private self in an environment that is relatively safe. The continuity of the self is assured by the holding function of the psychoanalytic setting while, at the same time, the patient is encased within his own private space. The therapeutic setting is the larger sphere in which the smaller sphere of the private self is held incommunicado. Because patients are relatively noncommunicative and apparently affectively disengaged, they do not provide the analyst with the necessary clues to make interpretations; from the analyst's point of view, this process is a resistance. Accordingly, analysts may be surprised to observe that clinical improvement has occurred without any specific interventions on their part; in fact, it is the absence of intrusive interventions that is an agent of the therapeutic action (Modell, 1976). This observation is similar to that of Gedo (1979) in *Beyond Interpretation,* namely, that the analyst can assist the patient's introspective work by lending his presence as an impartial witness without further intruding on the analysand (p. 18).

The therapeutic setting can be thought of as an outer shell or a second skin that protects the analysand from the external world while allowing the preservation of his private construction of reality. When there is environmental failure, this private self is necessary for survival. The safety of the therapeutic environment may, for some, offer a second chance, a chance to create an inner world that is not an emergency measure, that is, a response to an environmental danger. Therapy is a chance to discover one's personal life, to have one's own thoughts in a protected environment. Analysts note progress when their patients appear to be increasingly there, to be more present, to be more in the room with them. With the increasing communication of genuine affects the patient seems more psychically alive and, in a certain sense, more human. When patients gradually come into better contact with their own inner affective core, they are more secure and, in turn, able to allow their private space to become more permeable to outside influences.

The analyst, initially, is part of the environment, a necessary presence but more of a bystander than a fully engaged participant. After the analyst has met the patient's test (Weiss and Sampson, 1986) and has established the safety of the psychoanalytic setting, it is important for the patient to simply be. One patient, whose treatment I supervised, described this process as dancing by oneself. He engaged his therapist to the extent of admiring his dancing; she was his audience, not his partner. Dancing together would occur later.

The analyst can be supported in these therapeutic noninterventions by the theoretical considerations that I described earlier, stemming from the recognition that the private self is the site of self-generation. I believe that in this respect there is a difference between my views and those of some self psychologists. For example, Kohut (1984) conceived of the fundamental pathology of the self in the so-called narcissistic disorders as consisting of a self that is "defective, a self prone to fragmentation, weakness and disharmony" (p. 70). In his recent book *Treating the Self,* Ernst Wolf (1988) affirms Kohut's position: "Certain principles should be restated. A weakened self stands at the center of all self object relation disorders" (p. 95). This is an accurate phenomenological description of the social self in so-called narcissistic disorders. But we encounter here one of the limitations of phenomenology, for a patient who experiences the self as weak and defective, as did my patient, may not necessarily present this picture to an outside observer who perceives the patient's resilience and resourcefulness. I don't question the existence of developmental disorders that result in functional deficiencies, but the patient's experience of a defect or deficiency may not correspond to the "objective" view of an outside observer. It is also important that the analyst recognize the patient's self-generative capacities; in some cases what the patient experiences as a defect of the self may not be irreversible but may, instead, represent a dissociation from this inner generative self.

We are faced again with the unsolved problem of the objectification of the experience of self. If we are guided simply by the patient's experience of a weak and defective self, we may not recognize that a potential source of healing resides in the patient and not in ourselves. Further, if the analyst does not grasp the paradoxical nature of the self, if he sees only the dependent social self and believes it is only the analyst who possesses the means to heal the patient's defective and weakened self, he places the patient in a too passive position.

I am suggesting that these theoretical assumptions have a certain influence upon technique. I recognize, however, that when I compare my technique to the way other colleagues practice analysis, I am treading on thin ice. For the differences may reside in the way we talk about analysis and not in the way we actually practice analysis. One can only judge things from the outside, by what appears in print. Some self psychologists seem to suggest that it is the analyst who provides, though a mature selfobject relation, that which is missing in the patient's experience. I claim that this addresses only the social self and not the private self. If the theory of the social self is balanced by a theory of the private self, this will undoubtedly have an influence upon technique. If the analyst conceives of a self that generates itself from within, he sees his role as not only a provider of that which is missing but as a facilitator or a midwife who will, initially at least, supply the setting that enables the patient to experience a protected, companionable solitude. This is a solitude in which the analysand remains within his own private space while being held by the presence of the analyst. It is in this protected solitude that I believe the patient extends the domain of the personal.

References

Balint, M. (1968), *The Basic Fault.* London: Tavistock.

Brazelton, T. B. (1980), Neonatal assessment. In: *The Course of Life, Vol. 1,* ed. S. Greenspan & G. Pollock. Washington: US Department of Health and Human Services, pp. 203–233.

Edelman, G. (1987), *Neural Darwinism.* New York: Basic Books.

—— (1989), *The Remembered Present.* New York: Basic Books.

Federn, P. (1952), *Ego Psychology and the Psychoses.* New York: Basic Books.

Ferenczi, S. (1933). Confusion of tongues between adults and the child. In: *Final Contributions to the Problems and Methods of Psychoanalysis.* New York: Brunner/Mazel, 1955, pp. 156–167.

Freud, S. (1920), Beyond the pleasure principle. *Standard Edition,* 18:7–64. London: Hogarth Press, 1955.

—— (1933), The new introductory lectures. *Standard Edition,* 22:5–182. London: Hogarth Press, 1964.

Gedo, J. (1979), *Beyond Interpretation.* New York: International Universities Press.

Hartmann, H. (1950), Comments on the psychoanalytic theory of the ego. *The Psychoanalytic Study of the Child,* 5:74–96. New York: International Universities Press.

James, W. (1890), *The Principles of Psychology, Vol. 1.* New York: Dover, 1950.

Kohut, H. (1977), *The Restoration of the Self.* New York: International Universities Press.

—— (1980), Two letters. In: *Advances in Self Psychology,* ed. A. Goldberg. New York: International Universities Press, pp. 449–469.

—— (1984), *How Does Analysis Cure?,* ed. A. Goldberg & P. Stepansky. Chicago: University of Chicago Press.

Lacan, J. (1977), *Écrits.* New York: W. W. Norton.

Modell, A. (1976), "The holding environment" and the therapeutic action of psychoanalysis. *J. Amer. Psychoanal. Assn.,* 24:285–307.

—— (1980), Affects and their non-communication. *Internat. J. Psycho-Anal.,* 61:259–267.

—— (1984), *Psychoanalysis in a New Context.* New York: International Universities Press.

—— (1986), The missing elements in Kohut's cure. *Psychoanal. Inq.,* 6:367–385.

—— (1990), *Other Times, Other Realities.* Cambridge, MA: Harvard University Press.

Myers, G. (1986), *William James.* New Haven, CT: Yale University Press.

Sander, L. (1983), Polarity, paradox and the organizing process of development. In: *Frontiers of Infant Psychiatry,* ed. J. D. Call, E. Galenson & R. Tyson. New York: Basic Books, pp. 334–346.

Stern, D. (1985), *The Interpersonal World of the Infant.* New York: Basic Books.

Taylor, C. (1989), *Sources of the Self.* Cambridge, MA: Harvard University Press.

Weiss, J. & H. Sampson (1986), *The Psychoanalytic Process.* New York: Guilford Press.

White, R. W. (1963), Ego and reality in psychoanalytic theory. *Psychological Issues.* Monogr. 11. New York: International Universities Press.

Winnicott, D. W. (1958), The capacity to be alone. In: *The Maturational Processes and the Facilitating Environment.* New York: International Universities Press, 1965, pp. 29–36.

—— (1960), Ego distortion in terms of true and false self. In: *The Maturational Processes and the Facilitating Environment.* New York: International Universities Press, 1965, pp. 140–152.

_____ (1963), Communicating and not communicating leading to a study of certain opposites. In: *The Maturational Processes and the Facilitating Environment.* New York: International Universities Press, 1965, pp. 179–192.

_____ (1971), Playing. In: *Playing and Reality.* New York: Basic Books, pp. 38–52.

_____ (1988), The concept of health using instinct theory. In: *Human Nature.* New York: Schocken Books, pp. 51–64.

Wolf, E. (1988), *Treating the Self.* New York: Guilford Press.

Discussion of Arnold Modell's "The Private Self and Private Space"

JOHN E. GEDO

Arnold Modell has, in the past 30 years, established himself as one of the half-dozen American psychoanalysts whose writings have expressed an original, internally consistent theoretical and clinical viewpoint. Whenever I have been asked for the names of colleagues whose conceptual work I most respect, I have more often than not singled out Modell because, despite numerous differences in style and detail, I have found the widest agreement between his understanding of our discipline and my own and because I have found in his writings the kind of regard for accuracy, logical rigor, respect for the contributions of those who adhere to schools of thought different from his own, and attention to the overall requirements of psychoanalytic theory that are lacking in the works of colleagues whose work is merely fashionable.

In his chapter Modell has, in one sense, returned to the theme of his enormously influential paper of 1965, namely, the difficulties of carving out an autonomous existence — what he now calls a "private space." When he wrote "On the Right to a Life," Modell (1965) was engaged in preparing his first book, *Object Love and Reality*, (1968) a work that deals with the crucial role of object relations in personality development and is a major statement about the essential vicissitudes of human bonding for adaptation. Thus, from the beginning of his career as a psychoanalytic theorist, Modell gave equal weight to both aspects of what he calls the "paradoxical" human need for simultaneous dependency and autonomy. Perhaps this balance in his thinking has, in the interval, been to some extent screened by his consistent espousal of object relations theory in a succession of publications that (in my eyes) has earned him the mantle of Winnicott's most important successor.

In his chapter, Modell presents a position statement in which he outlines in a lucid manner the clinical and conceptual limitations of a psychoanalytic viewpoint *confined* to a theory of object relations. Let me state, to begin with, that his success in doing so is a major accomplishment: I know how difficult such an achievement is because a dozen years ago I tried to reach the same goal, with indifferent success, in what I called a "metapsychological assessment" of object relations theories (Gedo, 1979a). Even more important than this acknowledgment of Modell's persuasiveness is the obligation to recognize that in his chapter he has transcended the Winnicottian framework of much of his own past work. In turning to neurobiology for clues about the regulation of behavior, Modell has clarified his more fundamental allegiance to the Freudian tradition — to what the historian Frank Sulloway called being a "biologist of the mind." I suspect it is my own commitment to that viewpoint that caused me to find an underlying kinship between Modell's ideas and my own.

The most obvious *difference* between Modell and me lies in the manner we tend to use to present our ideas. I am fond of bluntness and irony, Arnold is courteous, tactful, almost elliptical. He has written for an audience including many adherents of "self psychology," and he has been careful to discuss their beliefs in an empathic mode. As I hear Modell's message, however, he is stating the opinion I have been shouting from any available rooftop for almost 20 years: however valuable Kohut's clinical discoveries about the transference constellations he originally called "narcissistic" have proved to be, the theoretical system he erected on these foundations — the psychology of relations between self and selfobject — is unacceptably reductionistic (see Gedo, 1989). In my judgment, Modell is absolutely correct in classifying Kohut's theory as a subspecies of the broader category of object relations theories.

Modell has muted his critique of Kohutian theories by focusing not so much on their shortcomings as on their value, if understood as applicable in certain specific contexts. Without pretending to expertise in this area of philosophy, I sense that Modell's characterization of Kohut's ultimate approach as that of a "radical phenomenologist" is well chosen. This categorization clarifies that Kohut's psychoanalytic antecedents are to be sought in the concepts of Federn (1952), specifically, in the idea of *"Ich Gefühl,"* often translated as the "sense of self," which is the purely subjective aspect of identity. For me, this clarification helps to explain why Kohut eventually discussed the characteristics of "self" in purely adjectival terms, such as "enfeebled" or "vigorous." It also illuminates the oddity that self psychology is, in practical terms, most concerned about fluctuations in self-esteem — in the vocabulary Kohut used until around

1972, about issues of narcissism. As Modell rightly points out, such a focus leaves the matter of psychic structure out of account. The subjective sense of self is, however, obviously *most* dependent on changes in self-esteem.

I have paid all this attention to the implications of Modell's chapter for our evaluation of Kohut's contributions because the latter have become known, in brief, as "*self* psychology." I have for some time regarded that designation as a misnomer; that was my reason for specifying, from 1979 onward, that my own *structural* conceptualizations of "self" should be referred to as dealing with the "self-organization." My earlier endorsement of Kohut's theoretical proposals had been based on the misapprehension that by "self" Kohut also meant a psychic structure. My confusion illustrates one of the paradoxes that Modell mentioned, that of the simultaneous "public" and "private" aspects of the self. At the same time, I believe it shows that the seeming paradox is actually the result of a semantic muddle: the term *self* simply has more than one meaning. Hence, in scientific discourse, it would be best to avoid it altogether; in its place we would do well consistently to use the more precise terms *sense of self* and *self-organization,* whichever is appropriate.

Modell is aware that our reactions to paradox are matters of temperament. Clearly, he *enjoys* disentangling these conceptual knots. I, too, am convinced that an apparent paradox betrays the fact that we have been thinking about a problem in terms of categories poorly applicable to it. Like Modell, I am neither complacent about living with paradoxes nor wish magically to eliminate them by ignoring the dilemma. Thus, I also believe that we can transcend the issue that Modell singles out as most troubling; we should be able to answer how a sustained sense of identity is possible despite the continual flux of consciousness. I think the solution can be found in the realization that the self-organization, in contrast to the sense of self, remains largely inaccessible to consciousness. I say "largely" instead of speaking more categorically about this because we do become aware of any *mis*match between our authentic, private motivations and the feedback we receive from our milieu. However, even in these circumstances of heightened "self-consciousness," it is not the precise nature of our hierarchy of aims that comes into our awareness but the signal that one has been misidentified.

From this vantage point, I have some question about Modell's assumption that there is a fundamental difference between self-observation and perception of the external world. As Modell himself states elsewhere in his chapter, the "paradox" is resolved by a biological approach to the problem. Introception relies relatively little on the sensory modalities through which we apprehend the external world, and only a fraction of the information gathered by means of proprioception, kinesthesia, or the registration of affects reaches the level of consciousness. As Fred Levin (1990) reports in his recent book, *Mapping the Mind,* a model of "self-in-the-world" is established, probably in the cerebellum, very early in life; there is no reason to believe that such a core of the bodily self ordinarily impinges on consciousness. In this sense, Modell may be too harsh in his critique of Hartmann's concept of "self-representation"—this term never did refer to the subjective sense of self; insofar as it is understood as a functional capacity beyond consciousness, it is potentially capable of objectification.

What I find unsatisfactory about Hartmann's conceptualization is not its attempt to objectify but its failure to grasp that a mental model of one's person is not only a *content* of the mind (i.e., a store of information) but, in a more essential sense, a guide to future action. In my view, what Freud called "repetition compulsion" is the effect of the vital need to maintain continuity in behavior and the inevitable correlate of such constancy, adequate organization. This is accomplished by means of slowing potential change in behavior to a rate the person can encompass or assimilate; a model of self-in-the-world is essential to provide the standard against which new behavior can be measured.

In contrast to this point of slight disagreement, I am enthusiastic about Modell's emphasis on the fact that much of human experience, though communicable to others, occurs in solitude. Modell actually prefers the term *privacy,* but I submit this word is somewhat misleading, for the essence of any experience, however it may involve someone else, is its private aspect. It has been said that one can only live one's life inside one's own skin. Clearly, this self-evident truth is not what Modell is concerned with: even when he talks about a "social self," he never loses the intrapsychic frame of reference that, in my opinion, differentiates the psychoanalytic point of view from other psychologies. I believe Modell intends to tell us that just as babies quickly learn to model the events that they witness "in real time," they are enabled, pari passu, to construct models of whatever occurs in their "interpersonal space." Such models of object relations, Modell tells us, form but one part, albeit a crucial one, of human experience—yet equally vital experiences, like those of mastery, may occur in solitude.

I am heartily in agreement with Modell's preference for the term *private self* over Winnicott's (1954) choice of *true self.* I have always been unhappy with the latter, because the behaviors Winnicott classified as the "false self" are just as genuinely part of an individual's repertoire as are the noncompliant behaviors he mistakenly called "true." As you doubtless know, if we succeed in helping a person overcome such a dichotomy in assessing personal goals, that individual does not lose the capacity to make use of what used to be "false self"; improvement has taken place when it becomes possible to employ these behaviors whenever one chooses, that is, *volitionally,* instead of being forced to resort to them because of anxiety or guilt. Hence, I have always wished for a better terminological solution. Of course, I do prefer Hartmannian objectification, so I shall continue to use my own term, *self-organization;* but I believe Modell's *private self* represents a conceptual advance in the direction I have advocated.

As many of you know, I have repeatedly criticized self psychology precisely because it completely ignores all experience that takes place outside an interpersonal framework (see Gedo, 1986, chapters 7 and 8). Although Modell now expresses the same criticism, he does so much more mildly than I have done because he is willing to grant that Kohut's conception of self–selfobject transactions is fully valid. The extent of its validity is, of course, an empirical question about which we do not as yet have enough evidence to entitle us to speak with certainty. My own tentative impression is that Kohut strongly overstated the nature of the need for selfobjects (and, as an inevitable consequence, he overlooked the crucial importance of autonomous competence). Kohut compared the need for selfobjects to the imperative necessity for the availability of oxygen. Even if we grant that idealizable caretakers who offer reliable information are certainly very much needed, the question of how much affirmation a child needs, and how promptly remains unanswered. Perhaps selfobjects are not as imperatively necessary as is oxygen. About this issue I am tempted to propose an analogy concerning the need for vitamins: long-term deprivation will make one ill, but one can survive avitaminosis for considerable periods.

Nor does Modell drive home the very excellent point he has made about the potentiality of human beings, once they have consolidated a "private self," to subsist on their own resources, to be "self-generating," as he puts it. This viewpoint directly contradicts Kohut's arbitrary dictum that we are forever dependent on selfobjects — and his astonishing claim that the ambition to be self-sufficient is per se pathological. About this matter, I feel Modell has carried tact beyond the limits of its usefulness: the real implication of his conclusion is that Kohut's recommendations about the appropriate aims of psychoanalytic treatment threaten to undermine the need for autonomy by inducing "separation guilt" within the transference.

It is also possible that Modell is not being merely tactful; perhaps this is one matter in which he has not yet separated himself from his Winnicottian loyalties! Although he states that Winnicott recognized the infant's need for solitude, he gives greater emphasis to Winnicott's reiteration of the importance of the continuing availability of the mother. Of course, there is nothing wrong with these statements, except that Winnicott put them in somewhat sentimental terms. It seems to me that the caretaker's presence is essential *not* to provide "symbolic holding" (albeit it does do that!); *I* would say that the caretaker is needed in order to assist the child to regulate stimulation in a manner that will make possible the organization of information (i.e., of experience) into reliable psychic models. This regulation of stimulation is what the affective attunement Daniel Stern (1985) has brought to our attention does much to accomplish. At any rate, I believe Modell's argument implies that a permanent reliance on selfobjects is bound to undermine the individual's sense of mastery and competence. Granting that our autonomy is never better than relative, permanent reliance on selfobjects is a matter about which, in agreement with Modell, I hold the following opinion: the closer one gets to self-sufficiency, the better.

Modell and I are also in agreement about the fact that the neurobiological evidence (he refers to the work of Edelman, 1987; in my previous writings, I relied on that of Levin) points in a direction necessitating a conception of a basic mental function mapping the individual's relation to the world. I have advocated this kind of psycho-analytic conceptualization for some years, starting with my book, *Beyond Interpretation* (Gedo, 1979b). Although he has used a somewhat different vocabulary, Michael Basch (1976) has also proposed very similar concepts. I can only welcome Modell into the ranks of those who organize psychoanalytic ideas on such a basis. As the fascinating case he has summarized for us demonstrates, neither libido theory nor object relations theories are as suitable for organizing certain data as is a theory of self-organization.

I hope I am not quibbling if I mention one omission in Modell's thesis that may represent an interesting difference of opinion between us. As I read his account of Edelman's hypotheses, I understand Modell to say that a self-generating structured model of oneself is a universal develop-mental achievement. If that is what he means, I must beg to differ. In my clinical experience, a fair number of people have sought assistance precisely because their earliest memories of affective states presented such a bewildering mélange that they never succeeded in integrating them in a coherent way. These individuals presented themselves in analysis with unintegrated subsets of memories; the split in their self-organization was not defensively motivated but had persisted unchanged from their infancy. I have referred to structural conditions of this kind as disorders in self-cohesion. Parenthetically, I should like to note that nowhere in his writings did Kohut consider psychopathology of this kind.

Another point concerning which I take issue with Modell is his continued reliance on a putative nosological category he calls "disorders of the self"; if we take the general thrust of his argument seriously, it has rendered this conception meaningless. I do not intend to imply that the self-organization cannot be viewed as having its pathologies—quite the contrary! My point is that once we place the "private self" into its proper position for our theories of mental functioning, no psychopathology can be posited that is *not* a reflection of some disorder of that structure. Modell was absolutely right not to concern himself with a psychiatric diagnosis for the analysand he used as his clinical illustration; from a psychoanalytic perspective, her problems could be understood in terms of a structural description. This is another way of saying that adequate comprehension of psychological maladaptation is always possible if one uses a developmental scheme centered on self-organization, such as the hierarchical model I proposed, in collaboration with Goldberg, some 20 years ago (Gedo and Goldberg, 1973). Of course, it is impossible to prove this claim by showing that it is valid for specific cases; I can only urge the reader to take it seriously because for more than 20 years I have never encountered clinical material—whether my own or that reported by others—for which it was untrue.

At this point, let me turn to the therapeutic consequences of Modell's theory, so nicely illustrated by the case summary he has presented. He begins by telling us that his analysand was neither psychotic nor borderline; in other words, consideration of the structural organization of "self," the necessity for which is demonstrated in the remainder of this chapter, can be just as important for understanding better adapted personalities as it is in cases generally seen as more primitive. We are told that in the early phases of analysis the patient presented aspects of behavior that were split off from each other and that these hitherto isolated portions of the personality were consolidated as a result of the successful analysis of transference manifestations Modell calls "negative." In my vocabulary, this therapeutic activity is that of "unification"—a necessity in dealing with archaic issues (those of mode II in the Gedo and Goldberg hierarchical model of 1973). As I understand it, we are being told that Modell initially focuses his technical resources on dealing with the most archaic issues among those that confront him. I am in wholehearted agreement with this therapeutic strategy.

Although Modell's account is not entirely explicit on this score, I assume that unification was accomplished by showing the analysand that what she perceived to be bad in the analytic interpersonal space originated within herself. At least, this is how I would have approached the problem of dealing with the repeated occurrence of "projective identification." This point merits emphasis because many clinicians, under the influence of self psychology, are afraid to assist patients to "own" their unacceptable behaviors lest they injure the latters' fragile self-esteem. Such therapeutic inhibitions actually constitute errors both in empathy and in diagnosis: they are based on the mistaken belief that the presenting problem is organized in a more advanced mode (mode III of the 1973 hierarchical model) than actually happens to be the case.

Modell goes on to tell us that even after unification has been accomplished, the analysand's "ego boundaries" (to resurrect Federn's, 1952, imprecise but evocative term about the subjective sense of self) remained inconstant. She expressed these fluctuations in *"Ich Gefühl"* by means of fantasies based on childlike concretizations of her psychic experience, such as being drained of her identity through the suction of octopus-like creatures. She talked of "popping out" her inner core to defend herself against such disorganizing intrusions; clearly, this image refers to a regressive state wherein she once again instituted a defensive split to safeguard her private experience. Insightfully, this patient was able to state that this defense protected her from *humiliation;* I regard this as an indication that she preferred regression to the possibility of injuries to her self-esteem. Ultimately, of course, self-esteem could not be maintained precisely because she was so tempted to engage in fantasies of merging with more powerful others. These temptations must have constituted her specific readiness to form an archaic transference. In other words, the subjective loss of continuity in *Ich Gefühl* is a consequence of her own disavowed wishes, and her inability to acknowledge all aspects of her personality is one result of having to stop the depletion of her self-esteem that would follow from continuous acknowledgment of these infantile impulses. As Modell put this, his analysand had to lose "contact with [her] inner core."

Another way to state the nature of this patient's dilemma is that she was ever tempted to give up self-sufficiency in favor of symbiosis with a selfobject. It hardly matters whether one thinks of this as a need to protect a private space (as Modell prefers to do) or as a desire to surrender the privilege of solitude in favor of a return to some infantile pattern of obligatory psychic merger. For many years now, Modell has successfully dealt with such problems by scrupulously avoiding intrusiveness; as he tells us, in this regard he is following in the footsteps of Balint (and, by implication, those of Ferenczi). Formerly, Modell referred to the need for solitude as the provision of a "cocoon"—a lovely metaphor, replaced in *this* chapter by an explication in terms of a structural conceptualization.

Although I fully agree that in certain contingencies it is optimal for the analyst to be nonintrusive, thus allowing the analysand's resources to be mobilized to achieve mastery in self-understanding, I would like to reiterate that in *this* instance Modell actively disposed of the negative transference before the issue of solitude became focal. He helped to achieve the consolidation of self-organization, presumably by focusing on the discontinuities in self-experience, in preference to commenting on specifics of mental content. Moreover, one cannot assume that if the analysis provides a safe milieu by avoiding intrusiveness, every analysand will automatically improve as a consequence, eventually permitting the analyst to exercise some influence over the transaction. Many patients experience nonintrusiveness as traumatically unhelpful, despite their intolerance of our interventions: we are damned if we do and damned if we don't!

Thus, the theoretical considerations Modell has brought to our attention cannot be used to justify any single course of action in terms of practical therapeutics. The way of nonintrusiveness may be optimal for therapists of a certain personality type who (like Winnicott's, 1960, good-enough mothers) are always able to make their benign presence felt, however passively they stay on the sidelines. More aloof individuals, like myself, are less successful in applying the tactics Modell has outlined and have tried to find ways more consonant with their own assets and liabilities. Instead of describing the methods I have developed for myself, let me state the obvious: *analytic* results will be obtained only if we are successful in understanding, in collaboration with the analysand, what precise effect our technical procedures have had and why. It is in that task that the theory Modell advocates should be enormously helpful.

Incidentally, the same principle applies to the technical management of the issue of psychological deficits: we do not necessarily confirm patients' worst fears by accurately identifying their missing skills, for such a diagnosis can be conveyed in a manner that amounts to a hopeful challenge to learn better ways. Let me repeat, therefore, that it is not so much our primary interventions that prove to be crucial; rather, it is the manner in which we process their consequences and reverberations that will be decisive in the analytic arena.

Let me conclude by affirming that Arnold Modell has, once again, produced a work that expands our psychoanalytic horizons and provides better ways to understand our clinical successes and failures than we have possessed in the past. For this writing and for the opportunity to follow the evolution of his work in the course of a lifetime, we owe Arnold many thanks.

References

Basch, M. (1976), Psychoanalysis and communication science. *The Annual of Psychoanalysis,* 4:385–422, New York: International Universities Press.

Edelman, G. (1987), *Neural Darwinism.* New York: Basic Books.

Federn, P. (1952), *Ego Psychology and the Psychoses,* ed. E. Weiss. New York: Basic Books.

Gedo, J. (1979a), Theories of object relations: A metapsychological assessment. *J. Amer. Psychoanal. Assoc.,* 27:361–374.

_____ (1979b), *Beyond Interpretation.* New York: International Universities Press.

_____ (1986), *Conceptual Issues in Psychoanalysis.* Hillsdale, NJ: The Analytic Press.

_____ (1989), Self psychology: A post-Kohutian view. In: *Self Psychology: Comparisons and Contrasts,* ed. D. Detrick & S. Detrick. Hillsdale, NJ: The Analytic Press.

_____ & Goldberg, A. (1973), *Models of the Mind.* Chicago: University of Chicago Press.

Levin, F. (1990), *Mapping the Mind.* Hillsdale, NJ: The Analytic Press.

Modell, A. (1965), On having a right to a life: An aspect of the superego's development. *Internat. J. Psycho-Anal.,* 46:323–331.

_____ (1968), *Object Love and Reality.* New York: International Universities Press.

Stern, D. (1985), *The Interpersonal World of the Infant.* New York: Basic Books.

Winnicott, D. (1954), Metapsychological and clinical aspects of regression within the psychoanalytical set-up. In: *Collected Papers,* New York: Basic Books, 1958, pp. 278–294.

_____ (1960), The theory of the parent-infant relationship. In: *The Maturational Processes and the Facilitating Environment.* New York: International Universities Press, 1965, pp. 37–55.

The Self, In and Out of Relatedness

ALICE ROSEN SOREF

The past few decades have witnessed a dramatic increase in infant, neonatal, and intrauterine research. The resulting revisions in the traditional view of the infant come at a time when psychoanalysis is also revising and broadening its theoretical base along lines that parallel infant research. Analytic initiatives in the areas of object relations and the study of the self dovetail with research findings on the infant's interaction with caregivers and its adaptive prowess. There has been a trend among those who have produced or studied infant research to upgrade the infant's status from autistic to realistic, helpless to adaptive, passive to active, and from *tabula rasa* to shaper of its environment. This shift arises from the new data, but perhaps it also reflects differences in the clinical versus the research population. Developmentalists, looking at the "Before" group, are impressed by the newborn's unexpected competence. Clinicians, who deal with the "After" group, have been impressed by the infant's relative helplessness in the face of long-term pathogenic influences.

Many psychoanalytic thinkers have welcomed the new empirical base and have already begun to explore its implications for psychoanalytic theory and clinical work with adults. This chapter is an effort to contribute to that task. Infant data are uniquely valuable in that they are fundamental, normative, and largely uncontaminated by the environment. As such, they provide a basic architectural design of human psychology. Although profound transformations and discontinuities mark the growth process, certain basic developmental agendas, guide-

I gratefully acknowledge the critical assistance of Drs. Gerald Adler, Dan Buie, Peter Chubinsky, and Anton Kris.

lines, and motivations that are present at birth continue throughout life, in both health and pathology. If we can identify these continuities, infant research can anchor psychoanalytic theory to the *terra firma* of a normative "baseline." In this chapter I postulate and explore certain aspects of lifelong functioning in the areas of innate motivation and self-protective regulatory processes.

Much of this thinking is based on theoretical revisions of early development that have been suggested by infant research. One change that is particularly important to the concepts offered here is the modification of the Mahlerian theory of infantile fusion. This concept has now been challenged by several developmentalists and clinicians (Peterfreund, 1978; Klein, 1981; Horner, 1985; Stern, 1985; Harrison, 1986; Sander, 1987; Lichtenberg, 1989). Pine (1986) makes an informed effort to integrate the fusion concept with current research; it founders, I believe, on an unwarranted assumption that certain events in the infant's life are experienced by him as merger.

Despite the increasing repudiation of the thesis of infantile merger, so far we do not have a clearly elaborated substitute for it. This chapter offers and explores an alternative model, along with its potential contributions to psychoanalytic theory and adult clinical practice. I propose a two-track model of psychological life in which self and relatedness comprise two distinguishable, yet highly interdependent, lifelong lines of development.[1] Self and relatedness also comprise two complementary spheres of experience that promote self-integration and self-expansion, respectively. This formulation offers an organizational framework for research and clinical data that is more consistent with both. The model diverges from both ends of the Mahlerian path by emphasizing the active role of the infant's emerging self from birth and the ongoing importance of relatedness in later life. A central thesis of this chapter is the proposal of a lifelong need for self-inviolacy and self-sovereignty, which are seen here as vital to cohesiveness and healthy self-development. The abrogation of this need is a common feature of psychopathology that cuts across the diagnostic spectrum. The proposed need will be explored from fetal through adult manifestations.

In the interests of space, I shall confine myself to those features of relatedness and those aspects of development that are most relevant to the aforementioned themes. Also, I hope the reader will bear with a somewhat exaggerated dividing line between self and relatedness. I have emphasized the division partly for clarity and also to underscore an additional perspective on the current theoretical overemphasis on relatedness.

---

[1]Grotstein's (1980) "dual track" differs in that it refers to separateness and *fusion* rather than separateness and *relatedness* (p. 394).

Other authors have spoken of self and relatedness as two distinguishable issues in development but have not made the distinction a focal point for further elaboration and development in their work (Stechler and Kaplan, 1980; Sander, 1983; Stern, 1985; Demos and Kaplan, 1986). Klein (1976) delineates "I" and "We" as components of identity that refer to self and group consciousness (p. 178). The duality in the present discussion refers to interactive versus noninteractive experience, rather than identity. I use the terms *noninteractive, self,* and *alone* to refer to the uniqueness of each organism as well as a condition of nonengagement with external objects. Demos (1987) points out a widespread tendency to deemphasize self-functioning, even though the great majority of the infant's experience is noninteractive. As an example, Demos and Kaplan (1986) have described the successful self-organization and regulation achieved by two 5½-week-old infants while they were alone. A more detailed discussion of the self and its functioning outside of external relatedness has been contributed by Storr (1988).

The term *self* applied to the newborn refers to a point on a continuum of lifelong self-development. Stern (1989) defines self as "a subjective organizing perspective that attempts to make order out of lived experience at whatever level such experience is registered and organized. Infants begin to make subjective order of their experiences . . . from the moment they are born . . ." (p. 169). This definition frees the term from its traditional reference to self-reflection or self-awareness, which do not appear until 18 months. A lifespan perspective of self-development is currently shared by many developmental theorists (Emde, 1983; Stern, 1985; Sander, 1987; Beebe and Lachmann, 1988; Lichtenberg, 1989).

In keeping with this view of the self, I shall attempt to specify some of the parallels between infant and adult functioning, particularly as they bear on three related theses: (1) self and relatedness are two distinguishable, yet interdependent, lines of development and spheres of functioning; (2) the self is innately differentiated and fundamentally motivated to pursue growth and protect its intactness throughout life; and (3) infant research pertaining to these themes has implications for our understanding of the adult, in treatment and in everyday life. A running theme of this chapter is that clinical and theoretical issues can be better understood by a more balanced consideration of both the self and the interplay of self-and-other.

The Two-Track Theory

A lifetime journey along the two tracks of self and relatedness is initiated at birth, with precursors in the uterus. The fetus actively contributes to its survival and adaptation (Graves, 1980; Hofer, 1988; Smotherman and Robinson, 1988). Early *anlages* of relatedness also appear. Research indicates that the fetus entrains to mother's circadian rhythms (Reppert and Weaver, 1988) and gains familiarity with her voice (Fifer and Moon, 1988). The newborn is motivated to survive and develop, both in and out of its important relationships. The primary caregiving relationship furnishes the soil in which these motivations may either flourish or wither.

Although the infant–caregiver relationship is a powerful shaper of the infant's self-development, it is not its creator. This point may be a statement of the obvious, but I think it needs to be emphasized at this time. In recent years, the infant has been awash in theories of its emergence "out of" the "infant–mother matrix" or of its gradual coalescence from a state of dual unity. Object relations theory, particularly Mahler's postulates, while deepening our understanding of the primary caregiving relationship, have tended to obscure the infant's distinct role in its development. In addition, the area of attachment theory in the infant literature has tended to underscore this obfuscation of the infant's self as an entity: for example: "The self emerges from early relationships . . . [and] is a social creation" (Sroufe, 1989, p. 71). Although this literature clearly articulates the mutuality of the system, the role of the infant tends to be diminished as an artifact of the relational focus.

What does each member contribute? The infant brings to the caregiving relationship an innate adaptational system that includes inherited characteristics, temperament, reflexes, and intrauterine experience. The infant's contributions partially account for such phenomena as the presence of one healthy child out of several disturbed siblings or the nonconcordence rate of schizophrenia in twins. Infants can impede nurturing responses by such factors as hypersensitivity, limited consolability, and poor state control, all of which can limit the infant's capacity to engage with the caregiver. Analogously, adult patients differ in their treatability based on such capacities as trust, frustration tolerance, and perseverance. The caregiver, or analyst, contributes a similar amalgam of inherited and learned predispositions to the encounter. The relationship of a particular patient–therapist or infant–caregiver pair is uniquely shaped by the characteristics of each individual. In turn, the interaction they produce will, over time, change each of them. The most thorough understanding of this system would require studying the contributions of each individual as well as the relationship they form. An exclusive focus on either self or relatedness produces an incomplete or inaccurate picture of human psychology.

The notion that relationships exist from birth is not new. However, tracing a sense of self back to birth is a more recent, and still somewhat controversial, contribution. Its most persuasive support comes from Stern's (1985) synthesis of pertinent infant research. His argument against infantile fusion is twofold: (1) From birth, the infant begins to build perceptual, cognitive, and affective experience of the existence of self and other. (This experience is presymbolic and preconceptual.) (2) The infant does not confuse his experience, behavior, or affect with mother's. A delusional perception of merger would not be possible before the onset of symbolic processes, during the second year of life. Until that time, the infant is essentially a realist.

Stern's seminal contribution, along with the research of the 1970s on infant–mother interaction, suggests that the infant dwells in two different worlds—the world of self and of relatedness. These worlds constitute paths of development as well as realms of experience. Researchers such as Brazelton, Koslowski, and Main (1974); Stern (1974); Trevarthen (1977); Beebe and Stern (1977); and Tronick, Als, and Adamson (1979) have performed microanalyses of infant–mother behaviors by focusing one camera on each, producing a split-screen image that could subsequently be reviewed frame by frame.

The most striking (and unanimous) finding, in terms of the present thesis, was that the experiences of self and of relatedness were both in evidence from early on. Brazelton, Koslowski, and Main (1974) laid particular emphasis on this observation. Their stop-frame analysis revealed that infants, 4–20 weeks old, alternated between engagement and disengagement with mother in rhythmic cycles occurring 4.4 times per minute. The cycles were initiated and terminated by the infant. This finding is consistent with previous data on approach–withdrawal cycles in both humans and animals (Schneirla, 1965; Kimberly, 1970). The biological roots of this pattern are suggested by the presence of rest–activity cycles (Hofer, 1988) and rapid eye movements in utero, (Stern, 1974) and a burst–pause pattern of sucking characteristic of nursing (Kaye, 1977). There is speculation that such cycles also prepare a pattern of conversational turn taking. When the mother was able to conform to the infant's attentional rhythm, an optimal regulation of the infant's stimulation and affective arousal was achieved. This smooth mutual alternation of engagement and disengagement, known as "synchrony," maintains the infant's homeostatic balance (Stechler and Carpenter, 1967; Brazelton, Koslowski, and Main, 1974; Stern, 1974). Sander (1987) has reported similar infant–mother coordination in other areas of regulation.

Sensory regulation is a prerequisite to safety and organization. Inappropriate or intrusive stimulation can disorganize and overwhelm an

infant's immature systems, compromising his developing sense of boundaries and inviolacy. The infant's needs for organization are of fundamental, possibly paramount, importance. Very brief engagement cycles
have been observed as early as one week (Brazelton, Koslowski, and
Main, 1974) and, more recently, at birth (Censullo, Lester, and
Hoffman, 1985). Work by Stern (1974) indicates that mothers continually modify the length and quality of their interaction, allowing the infant
to experience a wide variety of stimulation and affective arousal; the
infant's control over visual gaze is his vehicle for keeping inputs within his
"optimal range" (p. 207).

In my opinion, the early pattern of moving in and out of interaction
constitutes a physical and psychological bedrock and is a prototype of
lifelong human functioning. From early on, the infant experiences life as
a separate entity *and* as a member of a relating team. Soon the
requirement for rhythmicity subsides; nevertheless, time for solitude and
time for external relatedness both remain vital to equilibrium and
organization throughout life.

Some Theoretical Implications of the Differentiated Infant

It is interesting to note that the concept of the infant as a distinct entity
from birth is consistent with its biological history. The cell and division
of cells in the embryo constitute an organically distinct unit, surviving
through a parasitic dependence on its host. After conception, there is no
biological precedent for fusion as a developmental phase. The separateness and dependency seen at a physiological level in intrauterine life are
consistent with their dual emergence at a psychological level after birth.

Despite growing criticism of the theory of infantile fusion, delusional
merger is still attributed rather broadly to the experience of adults, even
though the existence of the phenomenon is questionable outside of
psychosis. By merger I mean an involuntary subjective experience of
fusion from which one cannot emerge at will. Harrison (1986) traced the
tenuous history of merger as a concept: it emerged largely from
observations of psychotics and is absent in Freud's thinking. Harrison
decries the tendency to regard merger illusions as factual and/or normal
(or even desirable) regressions.

In my opinion, merger is largely a misnomer, or metaphor, for other
phenomena. It has been mistakenly equated with *wishes* for and *fantasies*
of merger, with dependency, and with deep intimacy. In intimacy, there
exists a capacity to shift attentional focus away from, or suspend
awareness of, self–other boundaries. It is a mistake to classify this

phenomenon as merger. "Oneness" (Silverman, Lachmann, and Milich, 1982) and the "oceanic feeling" can also be explained in terms of suspended awareness. Whether delusional merger accompanies these feelings has not been demonstrated, to my knowledge.

In the severe psychopathologies—psychosis and severe personality disorders—the illusion of merger may give way to a delusion of merger, but this bears no relation to mature intimacy. In fact, those individuals who lack or lose differentiation are incapable of the attunement, resonance, and closeness that characterizes genuine intimacy for the very reason that their tenuous ego boundaries make human connection an annihilatory threat.

One example of this semantic error in regard to intimacy has been the assumption that merger is a feature of "primary maternal preoccupation" (Winnicott, 1956, p. 300). Although mothers may describe their intimacy with the infant in terms of fusion, the term is more likely metaphorical than literal. Sander (1976) argues for a necessary balance between a mother's empathy and "objectivity in viewing [the infant] as an object apart from her own projections and displacements" (p. 132). Sander's perspective is echoed by Bergman (1985), who, though she retains the traditional theory of infantile merger, describes mother's role as a "bridge between the subjective and objective world" (p. 171). In my view, in order to form this bridge, it is necessary to be empathically with (but not fused with) the infant in his world, to attune and respond to communications at his developmental level, and then to walk with him into the more consensual world of later communication.

Fusion also tends to be mistaken for dependency. Kohut (1984) invoked merger to characterize the archaic self–selfobject transference in borderline and narcissistic pathology. (The aspect of merger has been dropped by some of his followers.) In fact, what he describes is dependency rather than fusion. Merger has served as a natural metaphor for dependency because the visual image of merger epitomizes dependency gratifications. The image precludes being alone, out of another's thoughts, or faced with limits or differences. At its extreme, dependency may include reluctance, or even refusal, on the part of a patient to live his own life, along with an insistence that it be lived by the analyst. This insistence is often accompanied by the wish to dominate or "own" the analyst, to prohibit him from having a life, or a self, of his own. Here, at the deepest levels of dependency, the wish is that the selfobject function almost as a self-substitute. But the force behind this requirement betrays an unmistakably distinct and powerful will. Even the most passively dependent patients will, on some level, abhor intrusion, appropriation, or any other threat to the intactness or freedom of their individual selves. Moreover, if the selfobject were merged with the self, then the selfobject would likely be tarred with the same devaluations, such as worthlessness, that are directed at the self. The selfobject would then lose its effectiveness in providing a distinct and untarnished reference point for mirroring, idealization, and twinship.

Another development that has been linked with fusion is Winnicott's (1953) transitional object. This phenomenon also has more to do with dependence and independence than with merger and differentiation. The development of the "capacity to be alone" in childhood (Winnicott, 1958, p. 29) depends on concretized fantasies of interaction. These constitute a blurring of the boundary between fantasy and reality, rather than self and object. The wish is, "Mommy is with me whenever I need her." The fantasied compromise provided by the transitional object eases the transition to autonomy more directly than would an experience of, or wish for, fusion.

If we repudiate merger in the infant's early experience, then separation is no longer his task. It is a given. This finding revises the prevailing theory that differentiation originates as an unwelcome and ineluctable alternative to symbiosis, that symbiotic frustration is its precondition. This traditional theory deemphasizes the infant's self-motivated pursuit of autonomous growth. By the same token, differentiation need not stem from the inadequacies of the hallucinated breast (Freud, 1900, p. 566). Instead, motivations for autonomy can be traced to the *pursuit* of, rather than the *frustration* of, fundamental needs. These needs (which are being formulated in the current literature) would include motivations for independent achievement, assertiveness, exploration, and mastery. (Although frustration does not inaugurate the development of autonomy, it plays a vital role in it—but only if combined with substantial gratification [Demos, 1983].)

Motivation for Development of the Differentiated Self

The biological and psychological motivation for differentiated survival and growth is primary and, therefore, not easily thwarted. Both inborn and environmental perturbations of these pursuits are met by powerful "self-righting tendencies." Later versions of these motivations may explain the valiant struggle we see in many adult patients to retrieve selfhood from the residue of an early environment that threatened to extinguish it. These essential motivations were noted well before contemporary research. Bibring (1937) spoke of biologically based "natural forces of cure" (p. 188), and Anna Freud (1965) drew attention to "the urge to complete development" (p. 28). Kohut (1977) has also regarded self-development as an overriding and innate motivation.

Another manifestation of the early investment in differentiated growth might be inferred from the infant's constructive responses to appropriate levels of frustration. Murphy and Moriarty (1976) have suggested that "total acceptance [of the infant's developmental pace] may leave him without challenge, without any necessity for making an effort" (p. 146). An example of such frustration would be the disruptions that have been noted in infant–mother synchrony. Gianino and Tronick (1988) have found that the infant's and mother's engagement–withdrawal rhythm is frequently derailed by brief miscoordinations. Such mismatches generate distress in the infant. The infant's need to regulate this distress mobilizes coping behavior, largely directed at restoring synchrony. In the average situation the infant's efforts will meet with repeated success, given a sufficient base of synchrony, the caregiver's close collaboration in the reparative effort, and a manageable level of stress. These experiences of recapturing synchrony foster a sense of self-competence along with trust in the caregiver. The phenomenon is analogous to "optimal frustration" (Kohut, 1984, p. 98).

Another example of a fundamental motivation for individual development is the pursuit of mastery, described by Hendrick (1942) and White (1959). We see clear examples of this motivation at eight weeks when the infant learns that he can control aspects of the external environment. When a mobile placed above his crib is connected so that a voluntary leg movement can make it turn, the infant takes a much more animated interest in the mobile. As he makes it move, he smiles, coos, relaxes, and laughs, expressing what many authors consider to be a joy in competence (Hunt and Uzgiris, 1964; Watson, 1972; Papoušek and Papoušek, 1975; Bower, 1977). Mastery motivation has also been documented in two-day-old neonates, who learned to alter their sucking rhythms so that they could hear a recording of a woman singing (DeCasper and Carstens, 1981). Synchrony represents the epitome of contingent responding. In this vein, researchers have found that adults prefer the company of people who match their interactional rhythm (see review paper by Feldstein and Welkowitz, 1978). Effectance pleasure may also contribute to the elation of the practicing subphase, described by Mahler, Pine, and Bergman, (1975).

Recently proposed motivational systems also lend support to the hypothesis of an innate investment in individual growth. The system proposed by Lichtenberg (1989) includes needs for assertion and exploration. Emde's (1988) basic motives include activity, self-regulation, and affective monitoring. The inclusion of these self-initiated pursuits is one of the ways in which these motivational systems contrast with drive theory, in which the self is too occupied with instinctual and societal pressures to pursue self-development for its own sake.

Motivation for Self-Protection and Inviolacy

The human organism has a vital, lifelong need to maintain the intactness, boundedness, and government of its distinct self. These matters are central to healthy development. Problems in these areas are found in both neurotic and character pathology. Although the vicissitudes of the need vary with maturation, its presence is traceable throughout the lifespan. Innate needs for sensory regulation are analogous to the adult's needs for organization and integration. In order to relate to others, it is necessary to have one's "house in order," that is, that intactness is assured. Many contemporary conceptualizations of the developmental phases of infancy postulate self-regulation, homeostasis, or organization as the first phase (Sander, 1983; Stern, 1985; Greenspan, 1988; Emde, 1988). These conditions, which support physiological and psychological intactness, are prerequisites to both infant and adult interaction.

The intact self has a biological history of protective boundedness, beginning with the uterine wall and the amniotic sack. These physical boundaries are soon augmented by self-protective fetal reflexes. At 7½ weeks gestational age, the fetus develops the capacity to withdraw. The fact that this capacity predates the capacity to approach by three weeks may indicate that it is more fundamental to the organism's survival. Graves (1980) states that the reflex to withdraw is the "more effective [response] in the approach–withdrawal paradigm" (p. 239). An innate capacity for withdrawal is also noted by Lichtenberg (1989, p. 173). Later, the fetus supplements withdrawal with habituation, an additional capacity to reduce the impact of stimulation. At birth the healthy neonate adds to these faculties the ability to self-soothe by bringing his hand up to his mouth (Brazelton, 1983). These activities deflect external stimuli, and they also begin the formation of an endogenous, functional boundary that holds the self inside and intact. The effectiveness of this boundary depends on a great deal of supplementation by the primary caregiver. This concept differs from Freud's (1920) stimulus barrier in that it is self-initiated rather than a biological given. The hypothesis of a self-regulated boundary, as opposed to an impermeable barrier, is consistent with newer findings on the infant's *needs* for stimulation. Another difference is that the functions of the self-initiated boundary extend throughout life whereas the stimulus barrier was seen as time-limited to early infancy.

Along with self-soothing, the neonate adds disengagement and attentional cycles to his budding arsenal of self-protection. When engagement is overstimulating, he will avert his gaze, habituate, or "shut down." Beebe and Stern (1977) provide a graphic example of withdrawal responses to intrusive stimulation: "The mother chased the infant . . . pulling his arm or hand . . . even attempting to force the infant's head in her direction. . . . The infant could duck, move back, turn away, pull away, or become limp" (p. 45). In addition, during the first week of life, the infant manifests a looming response when an object or person approaches his face or eyes: he will pull his head back and interpose his hands between his face and the object (Bower, 1977). Later milestones in the development of inviolacy would include the "No" at age two (Spitz, 1957); the later interest in secret sanctuaries, such as private tree houses, pet houses, and doll houses; the adolescent's "No," and, finally, the achievement of autonomy in mature adulthood. Autonomy provides the greatest degree of inviolacy by substantially reducing the adult's vulnerability to interpersonal and environmental stress. One of the requirements for this achievement is an adult version of the disengagement and rest that were necessary to the infant.

Others who have studied self-inviolacy have also related it to disengagement. Winnicott (1963) proposed the concept of an "isolated core" of the true self, which requires utter isolation and privacy, in infancy and throughout life: "This core never communicates with the world of perceived objects [and] must never be communicated with . . ." (p. 187). He asserted that communication with the isolated core constitutes an "impingement" that annihilates the true self and forces the inauguration of a false self (1960, p. 46). Emde's (1983) "affective core" refers to continuous aspects of the self (p. 165). Winnicott's core differs from Emde's in that it refers to authenticity, is not explicitly related to affectivity, and *is* subject to transformation. Winnicott's isolated core gains some research support in the infant's aversive responses to maternal intrusion. Meares (1988) recognizes a comparable need in adult psychoanalysis; he cautions that "brilliant and accurate guesses about . . . inner states [can lead to] a feeling of violation or of theft of part of the core experiences of self" (p. 247). Stern's (1977) observation of "interpersonal space" (a customary physical distance of about two feet that adults maintain between them in our culture), may represent a concrete manifestation of Winnicott's concept (p. 20). Stern (1977) traces this phenomenon to the looming response.

I essentially agree with Winnicott's thesis, but I think it needs to be integrated with (and tempered by) his and others' concepts about relationships. First, it is important to note that by "isolated core,"

Winnicott means being "alone . . . in the presence of mother" (1958, p. 30). Second, the need to *share* aspects of the core self is also essential to the development of the true self, a concept Winnicott (1967) expresses elsewhere. "Isolation" is needed for the initiation and integration of the true self, but interaction is equally necessary to allow these self attributes to become manifest and therefore known to the self and to the generative object (Winnicott, 1967; Emde, 1983; Kohut, 1984; Buie, 1985; Stern, 1985; Sander, 1987). Bringing the self into active commerce with others permits self-recognition and self-expansion, functions that can then be processed and consolidated in periods of disengagement. In order for generative relationships to protect the core self, they must meet two conditions. One is that the individual be accorded complete control over which portions of core self will be shared and with whom. Protection and promotion of the individual's function as "gatekeeper" of his core self are particularly critical in psychoanalysis. Secondly, it is essential that responses of the caregiver or the analyst be nonimpinging. It is more the *nature* of the object's response than the fact of responding that can help or hurt true self-development. These responses will be explored further later in this chapter.

Sander (1983) has further delineated Winnicott's isolated core in calling attention to the "open space," which begins in early infancy. This is a time when the infant is not engaged in social interaction and is also not distracted by unmet needs or distress. He proposes that when internal and interpersonal states of equilibrium coincide, the infant has the ideal circumstance for the organization of self and surround and for the emergence of initiative. These conditions permit an undiluted focus on the "spontaneous gesture" (Winnicott, 1960, p. 146). If the infant makes a sound or moves his hand, he can perceive these gestures as "own" and "real" because the perception is not associated with other variables, such as an interaction or the satisfaction of a bodily need (Winnicott, 1958, p. 34). In a similar vein, Murphy and Moriarty (1976) have noted that "the baby needs not only attention (with the interaction it involves) but sufficient time to himself for his own cognitive processes to work at organizing his perceptions [and that] excessive intrusive activity . . . deprives the baby of the freedom and . . . processing time needed for optimal coping" (p. 145).

I am in full agreement with these observations; however, as with Winnicott's construct, I think it is important to emphasize the role of relatedness in the open space. For Sander (1983), the occurrence of the open space is dependent upon a caregiving relationship that is so well-coordinated that the infant's attention to it can be temporarily suspended. I would add to this concept that relatedness colors and expands the material to be organized in the open space; the resulting increment in organization then enhances relatedness. Development and mature functioning proceed optimally when circumstances permit an interspersing of disengagement and interaction. The need for both conditions is present throughout life, in both normality and pathology.

Self and Relatedness in Adulthood

The two tracks of self and relatedness play a complementary role, promoting self-integration and self-expansion, respectively. As noted earlier, autonomy is a key factor in determining the degree to which these complementary functions will be effective.

RELATEDNESS (INTERACTIVE EXPERIENCE)

Throughout life, relationships promote the recognition, expansion, and enhancement of the self. Autonomy (based upon internal representations of nurturing relationships) allows adult relationships to play the role of buttressing self-sustaining structure, rather than supplying it. This structure requires the support of loving and validating relationships; however, it can sustain viability without them for prolonged periods, if necessary. (A notable exception would be a regressive loss of structure in response to unusual stress or a significant loss. At such times, important relationships serve both to fill in for lost functions and to shore up intact ones.) But, for the most part, autonomy permits the functions of relationships to shift from life support to life enhancement. Unlike the Mahlerian goal of separation, autonomy does not *diminish* the need for relatedness; in a sense, it is a *prerequisite* for it. Only when relationships are no longer bent to the purpose of maintaining the self can they reach their potential of genuine connectedness, without distortion or danger, as true self relating to true other. In this view, autonomy changes the nature of the reliance rather then supplanting it.

Adult relationships furnish an arena for self-realization and enlivenment. Without relatedness, we cannot be all that we are. Each relationship is an interpersonal system more than, and different from, the sum of its participants. It therefore elicits elements of personality and relating style that are unique to that relationship. Different people can vivify new aspects of one's self by joining different sectors of the self. After the death of a significant other, the feeling that part of the self has died is a reality. Although we retain a portion of what the other awakened, part of it returns to dormancy when it is no longer contacted.

The process is similar to resonating to a foreign culture during a trip and then losing much of that "feel" after returning home.

People with a sense of humor elicit our comedic talents; sharing ideas allows us to find out what we think; teaching allows us to learn what we almost knew. Relationships refine identity and endow experience with a greater sense of reality. In sum, relationships contribute to the sense of realness, scope, and meaning of one's self and one's experience.

As the other's personality influences which sectors of our personality will emerge, his state of mind also impacts the exchange. Just as mother–infant interaction requires mutual feedback, mature relating also depends upon a mutual interactional structure. If one member of the dyad is unable or unwilling to participate actively in the communication, the other will experience the opposite of the aforementioned enlivenment and self-expansion. Interactive readiness seems to wax and wane for reasons that are not always clear. Even though the inaccessible member may sound as if he is participating, the other's experience is one of sending out a line of communication into a vacuum, like throwing a ball that does not get caught or returned. Something analogous, but much more extreme, is experienced in the infant's lifeless withdrawal from the "still-faced," or depressed, mother (Tronick et al., 1978). The experience of no relational "place to be" quickly constricts and deadens the self, causing depression and degrees of incapacity, for example, blocking, failures of memory, inability to find the right word (or any word), having nothing to say, and needing to escape through sleepiness or other forms of withdrawal. Sleepiness has been noted by many clinicians in response to a patient's affective withdrawal. One cannot retrieve one's liveliness by withdrawing into self because when two people confront each other, they must interact in some fashion (Watzlawick, Beavin, and Jackson, 1967). For this reason, even a short period of nonsubstantive conversation is inordinately draining. In analytic work, some patients' inaccessibility can persist for months or years at a time.

When autonomy is underdeveloped, relationships can provide degrees of self-recognition, expansion, and enlivenment. However, these functions are limited by the danger that relating poses to the "isolated core" (Winnicott, 1963, p. 187). As long as an individual lacks autonomy, he cannot maintain self-inviolacy. His self-boundary must remain highly permeable to external influence in order to admit needed supplies, and this permeability limits his capacity to maintain the privacy and intactness of the core self. In addition, the contributions of relatedness are constrained by the necessity to skew objects in a direction that supports pathological structure. Among its other functions, psychopathology provides a holding environment, with its familiar organization of the self and the environment. As organization is crucial to the intactness of the self, one's psychic structure, or "theory of reality" (Epstein, 1987) is preserved almost as tenaciously as life itself (p. 45). This adherence to the present organization is consistent with the neurological finding that the preservation of the familiar is more fundamental than the pursuit of pleasure (Hadley, 1989). These biasing factors curtail the enhancing potential of genuine object relating.

SELF-TIME (NONINTERACTIVE EXPERIENCE)

As in infancy, disengagement tends to be marked by reduced stimulation, a condition that fosters self-integration and initiative. Autonomy changes self-experience from being alone to being "with" oneself, as well as with one's internalized objects, in a nice internal "home." This environment is a relatively secure and comfortable internal surround where one's actions receive a loving (or at least predictable) reception. Noninteractive experience tends, therefore, to be more protected than relatedness. Without autonomy, self-experience can leave the individual unnurtured and adrift in a dysphoric inner world. Even in these conditions, self-experience still allows significant integrative processes to take place.

Time away from relatedness is truly "free" time in many regards. One is free from the work of relating, for example, the narrowing of cognition and affect into communication channels that "fit" the object and the task of selecting which portions of self to bring into the interaction. While relatedness requires a continued alert state, noninteractive time allows one to experience the full spectrum of cognitive, affective, and physical states of consciousness. These range from sleep to activities that approach the liveliness of interaction. Noninteractive experience functions optimally when it includes the full range. Quiet self-experience, such as watching a body of water or other landscape for a protracted period, offers the kind of rest and calm associated with the infant's experience of being alone "in the presence of [the] mother" (Winnicott, 1958, p. 30). A more active level of relaxation can occur with low-level or nontaxing stimuli, such as music or the company of companion with whom talk is not essential. Activities at the more active end of the spectrum would include going to a movie or concert or working on a creative project. Without adequate self-sustaining structure, relaxation may be limited to a narrow portion of the range or may not be possible at all. Quiet self-experience may feel too alone or unsafe.

Along with rest, reduced stimulation, freedom from interactive channeling and from state restrictions, time with oneself also permits free access to preverbal realms of experience. Stern (1985) describes early preverbal experience (birth to two months) as a sensorially rich world in which global aspects of sensory experience from different modalities become linked, a process that begins to organize the world. The preverbal world might be thought of as more experience-near than the world of language. Words partially distort reality since they restrict meaning to that which can be labeled, setting aside the other sensory attributes of the experience that fall outside the label. Stern states that creativity depends upon access to this early flow. If I understand him correctly, these cross-modal integrations would give a poet the facility to integrate sound, image, rhythm, and meaning or allow a scientist to abstract his thinking from customary connections in order to explore a new connection.

Creativity and thinking often proceed best if one is by oneself (Storr, 1988). Ultimately the self-well runs dry, and external stimulation is necessary to replenish it. One can see in any sort of creative endeavor the meshing of individual thought with influences from the work of others. Psychoanalytic writings, for example, so clearly illustrate the flow between a rootedness in and a departure from the preexisting literature.

An insufficiency of "time-out" tends to lead to irritability, disorganization, and disorientation, in pathology or health. An unbroken, long-term overload of stimulation can produce intense stimulus sensitivity that can culminate in a need for complete shutdown. It is as if the boundary that protects self-intactness gets worn down by protracted bombardment. Time-out allows the boundary to reconstitute. After a vacation, formerly stressful stimuli are more likely to "bounce off"; organization and cohesiveness are restored and are more easily maintained. In the vernacular, self-time is heralded as a chance to, "get my head together," "get hold of myself," "collect my thoughts," or "get it together." If there has been a good-enough opportunity for rest and integration, a return to increased stimulation and interaction is welcome. This cycle of self-time and interactional time, foreshadowed in the infant's experience, is necessary to maintain equilibrium and to experience the unique content and coloration afforded by each sphere.

Implications for Adult Psychoanalytic Treatment

The concepts outlined here provide perspectives that are useful in analytic work. The two-track model, in place of the theory of primary fusion, can offer more freedom and optimism to work with personality disorders. The therapeutic task can be defined as uncovering, rather than generating, a basic motivation for differentiated growth. This model also reduces the concern that in-depth work with nonpsychotic patients poses a risk of regression to dedifferentiation. While merger wishes may arise, they are less inured than they would be if merger were a primary life experience. As Stern (1989) has put it, "All wishes and fears of union are secondary" (p. 172). A recognition of the primacy of the patient's motivation for growth can also reduce some of the adversarial features of the work, since it underscores the patient's and therapist's fundamental alignment.

The premise of innate differentiation also adds clarity to the principle of abstinence. It helps distinguish useful from antitherapeutic types of gratification. Particularly with personality disorders, certain gratifications are necessary to build the elements of self-maintaining structure, for example, self-esteem, self-love, and security. (The ways these functions are fostered in treatment have been reviewed by Buie, 1985.) Gratifications that build autonomy serve the patient's "entitlement to survive" a phrase contributed by Buie and Adler, 1972, (p. 95), as distinct from his narcissistic entitlement. The generative versus regressive potential of gratification requires ongoing appraisal in each case.

The notion of lifelong growth motivation suggests that certain parallels may be drawn between the infant–caregiver and the patient–therapist relationship. These are highlighted in the following example of interactive synchrony provided by Brazelton, Koslowski, and Main (1974):

> One of our mothers was particularly striking in her capacity to subside as [her baby] decreased his attention to her. She relaxed back in her chair smiling softly, reducing other activity such as vocalizing and moving, waiting for him to return. When he did look back, she began slowly to add behavior on behavior, as if she were feeling out how much he could master. She also sensed his need to reciprocate. She vocalized, then waited for his response. When she smiled, she waited until he smiled before she began to build up her own smiling again. Her moving in close to him was paced sensitively to coincide with his body cycling, and if he became excited or jerky in his movement, she subsided back into her chair [p. 67].

This mother provided space for and accessibility during the infant's withdrawal, as well as an engagement that encouraged his "spontaneous gesture" (Winnicott, 1960, p. 145). She respected his nascent self-regulatory capacities by deferring to his engagement–disengagement rhythms. She also sensed and promoted his initiative, for example, his needs to come and go and to reciprocate. In short, she offered a holding environment that did not intrude, one that did not appropriate, ignore, or assault the infant's emerging self. The infant's periods of disengagement were supported by "being alone . . . in the presence of mother"

(Winnicott, 1958, p. 30). Researchers have observed that mothers tend to continue to watch, or "frame," the infant during his disengagement. This observation is borne out in the films of Brazelton, Koslowski, and Main (1974) in which the infant keeps mother in peripheral vision during his withdrawal and turns back quickly if she, "turns her head, closes her eyes, or leans back in her chair" (p. 58). Mahler, Pine, and Bergman (1975) refer to a similar phenomenon in terms of the mother's remaining "quietly available" during the comings and goings of the rapprochement phase (p. 79). This nonintrusive availability has much in common with the free-associative method. Like the mother, the analyst is there all the time, adjusting his level of activity to the developmental needs of the patient.

To the extent that the caregiver is not sensitive to the infant's and child's self-regulatory needs and capacities, subsequent development of these functions may be limited. Many of our patients have experienced this insensitivity. They may therefore require explicit encouragement to regulate their engagement in the contact and in the work, to avoid overloading and to augment their sense of self-sovereignty. Disengagement is not only reparative; it also promotes initiative, integration, and consolidation of what is learned in treatment. Outside treatment hours there is often a less defended drifting over the analytic material that yields certain associations, connections, and insights that may not arise in the therapist's or analyst's presence. In treatment hours the patient's needs for distance may emerge as heightened resistance, flattened affect, regressions, missed appointments, or negativity. The analyst can help by accepting these strategies as well as by encouraging the development of more direct ones, such as the patient's telling the analyst that he needs to be quiet — or that he needs the analyst to be quiet — or that he needs to confine his own productions to extra-analytical material until he feels less tenuous.

Some patients adopt a predictable alternation between therapeutic engagement and withdrawal, reminiscent of the infant's rhythmic attentional cycles. The therapist also needs to honor his own regulatory needs; he may unconsciously provide private time in the therapeutic hour by breaking eye contact or cognitive-affective contact with the patient. The occasional therapy patient who stares at us fixedly produces exhaustion and irritability. We can infer that Freud (1913) was aware of the need for regulation from his ingenious explanation for the use of the couch.

The analytic technique of following the patient's material parallels the sensitive mother's tendency to follow her infant's lead. She adjusts and "times" her own "material" in accord with his developmental level, and this protects his intactness and organization. This protection is much more complex yet no less crucial in analytic treatment, since it has so often been deficient in our patients' histories.

For many patients such protection requires the utmost analytic vigilance. Life experience has eroded their "right" to privacy, dignity, and control over what they choose to share. In early infancy these "rights" may not have been nurtured in interactive and noninteractive experience. One way the open space can be provided in the analytic setting is by a tolerance for uncertainty (Sander, 1983). Our comfort with the unknowns, with the transitional space, and with the many uncertainties of the clinical situation offers the patient a clear opening for the emergence and elaboration of his true self.

In some instances it is helpful to refrain from all interventions. For example, nonverbal communication, which can be worked with to great benefit with some patients, can feel violating or produce unworkable degrees of shame and self-consciousness in others. With many patients, certain commonly used words can be experienced as appropriations of the self, such as the word *must* in "That must have made you angry." Many interventions can be more safely expressed as questions rather than statements. Certain moments of deep affectivity can be moments in which intactness is at risk. In these instances, the most protective way to transmit that one has "gotten" the experience may be with a simple affective acknowledgment like, "Yeah." The particular need for restraint in the early phases of treatment is consistent with Kohut's (1977) concept of "empathic immersion" (p. xxii).

A history of repeated invasive stimulation can result in therapeutic impasse owing to the patient's terror and consequent commitment to avoidance. The resultant defensive hiding can include de-animation, extreme guardedness, or even dissembling. Anger and narcissistic entitlement may be heightened to avoid closeness. This childhood trauma may be signaled by schizoidlike withdrawal, ideas of reference, and/or pervasive anxiety.

One patient expressed incursions of self and their sequelae with unusual clarity. She described being unable to keep people out: "They get inside, and I disappear." In childhood her mother had habitually violated the patient's core self by breaking into quiet times in her room with tongue-lashings about not doing enough housework. The patient could not relax or daydream for fear of one of these unpredictable invasions. She also described her sense of panic on the occasions when she let her guard down in the company of other children and her mother would walk in the room and "catch" a spontaneous expression on her face before she could erase it. In her adult life she suffered from marked ideas of reference and fears of being emotionally exposed. She was able to relax her false-self conformity and think freely only when by herself. One exception was the occasional treatment hour where she felt less permeable, sensing "a circle" around herself.

This patient required more than usual restraint regarding which material could be brought to her attention. She had a pronounced defense against the transference and disavowed her transference needs. Just before my return from a vacation, she had two successive dreams involving a man who loved her for herself and wanted to be with her all the time. These dreams brought her relief and greater organization after what had been an unusually troubled separation. I felt it was important at this time to not interpret her barely disguised relief that I would be back soon to restore her experience of being valued and cared for. Such an interpretation probably would have been experienced as "catching" her in an unguarded expression.

In conclusion, infant research supports a two-track model of self and relatedness. It is postulated that both tracks are present throughout life as distinguishable lines of development and complementary spheres of experience that are highly interdependent. In accord with this model, an empirically based theory of innate differentiation suggests that the pursuit of self-development is lifelong. I have focused here on self-regulation, self-inviolacy, and self-sovereignty as fundamental aspects of that development and have explored the ways in which these needs of the self interdigitate with relationships in both infancy and adult life. The primary nature of these needs has been demonstrated in fetal and infant research. I would speculate that their abrogation, from infancy through early childhood, plays a central role in psychopathology. I have explored some of the implications of these perspectives for adult psychoanalytic treatment and theory.

References

Beebe, B. & Lachmann, F. M. (1988), Mother–infant mutual influence and precursors of psychic structure. In: *Frontiers in Self Psychology, Vol. 3,* ed. A. Goldberg. Hillsdale, NJ: The Analytic Press, pp. 3–25.

Beebe, B. & Stern, D. N. (1977), Engagement–disengagement and early object experiences. In: *Communicative Structures and Psychic Structures,* ed. N. Freedman & S. Grand. New York: Plenum, pp. 35–55.

Bergman, A. (1985), The mother's experience during the earliest phases of infant development. In: *Parental Influences in Health and Disease,* ed. E. J. Anthoney & G. H. Pollock. Boston: Little, Brown, pp. 165–181.

Bibring, E. (1937), On the theory of the therapeutic results of psychoanalysis. *Internat. J. Psycho-Anal.,* 18:170–189.

Bower, T. G. R. (1977), *A Primer of Infant Development.* San Francisco: Freeman.

Brazelton, T. B. (1983), Precursors for the development of emotions in early infancy. In: *Theory, Research, and Experience, Vol. 2,* ed. R. Pluchnik. New York: Academic Press, pp. 35–55.

Brazelton, T. B., Koslowski, B. & Main, M. (1974), The origins of reciprocity: The early mother–infant interaction. In: *The Effect of the Infant on Its Caregiver,* ed. M. Lewis & L. Rosenblum. New York: Wiley, pp. 49–76.

Buie, D. H., Jr. (1985), The therapeutically required but potentially hazardous therapist–patient relationship. Presented to Ontario Psychiatric Association, Toronto.

_____ & Adler, G. (1972), The uses of confrontation with borderline patients. *Internat. J. Psychoanal. Psychother.,* 1:90–108.

Censullo, M., Lester, B. & Hoffman, J. (1985), Rhythmic patterning in mother–infant interaction. *Nurs. Res.,* 34:342–346.

DeCasper, A. J. & Carstens, A. A. (1981), Contingencies of stimulation: Effects on learning and emotion in neonates. *Infant Beh. & Devel.,* 4:19–35.

Demos, V. (1983), Discussion of papers by Drs. Sander and Stern. In: *Reflections on Self Psychology,* ed. J. D. Lichtenberg & S. Kaplan. Hillsdale, NJ: The Analytic Press, pp. 105–112.

_____ (1987), *Susan Wise Symposium Number 2,* Boston Psychoanalytic Institute and Society.

_____ & Kaplan, S. (1986), Motivation and affect reconsidered: Affect biographies of two infants. *Psychoanal. Contemp. Thought,* 9:147–221.

Emde, R. N. (1983), The prerepresentational self and its affective core. *The Psychoanalytic Study of the Child,* 38:165–192. New Haven, CT: Yale University Press.

_____ (1988), Development terminable and interminable: Part 1. Innate and motivational factors from infancy. *Internat. J. Psycho-Anal.,* 69:23–42.

Epstein, S. (1987), Implications of cognitive self-theory for psychopathology and psychotherapy. In: *Self, Symptoms, and Psychotherapy.* ed. N. Cheshire & H. Thomae. New York: Wiley, pp. 43–58.

Feldstein, S. & Welkowitz, J. (1978), A chronography of conversation: In defense of an objective approach. In: *Nonverbal Behavior and Communication.* ed. A. W. Siegman & S. Feldstein. Hillsdale, NJ: Lawrence Erlbaum Associates, pp. 329–378.

Fifer, W. P. & Moon, C. (1988), Auditory experience in the fetus. In: *Behavior of the Fetus,* ed. W. P. Smotherman & S. R. Robinson. Caldwell, NJ: Telford Press, pp. 175–188.

Freud, A. (1965), *Normality and Pathology in Childhood.* New York: International Universities Press.

Freud, S. (1900), The interpretation of dreams. *Standard Edition,* 4 & 5. London: Hogarth Press, 1953.

_____ (1913), On beginning the treatment. *Standard Edition,* 12:121–144. London: Hogarth Press, 1958.

_____ (1920), Beyond the pleasure principle. *Standard Edition,* 18:7–64. London: Hogarth Press, 1955.

Gianino, A. & Tronick, E. Z. (1988), The mutual regulation model: The infant's self and interactive regulation and coping and defensive capacities. In: *Stress and Coping,* ed. T. Field, P. McCabe, & N. Schneiderman. Hillsdale, NJ: Lawrence Erlbaum Associates, pp. 47–68.

Graves, P. G. (1980), The functioning fetus. In: *The Course of Life.* ed. S. Greenspan & A. Lieberman. Washington, DC: Government Printing Office, pp. 235–256.

Greenspan, S. I. (1988), The development of the ego: Insights from clinical work with infants and young children. *J. Amer. Psychoanal. Assn.,* Suppl. 36, pp. 3–55.

Grotstein, J. (1980–1981), The significance of Kleinian contributions to psychoanalysis: 2. Freudian and Kleinian conceptions of early mental development. *Internat. J. Psychoanal. Psychother.,* 8:393–428.

Hadley, J. (1989), The neurobiology of motivational systems. In: *Psychoanalysis and Motivation,* ed. J. D. Lichtenberg. Hillsdale, NJ: Analytic Press, pp. 337–372.

Harrison, I. B. (1986), On "merging" and the fantasy of merging. *The Psychoanalytic Study of the Child,* 41:155–170. New Haven, CT: Yale University Press.

Hendrick, I. (1942), Instinct and the ego during infancy. *Psychoanal. Quart.,* 11:33–58.

Hofer, M. A. (1988), On the nature and function of prenatal behavior. In: *Behavior of the Fetus,* ed. W. P. Smotherman & S. R. Robinson. Caldwell, NJ: Telford Press, pp. 3–18.

Horner, T. (1985), The psychic life of the young infant. *Amer. J. Orthopsychiat.,* 55:324–344.

Hunt, J. McV. & Uzgiris, I. C. (1964), Cathexis from recognitive familiarity: An exploratory study. Presented at Convention of the American Psychological Association, Los Angeles.

Kaye, K. (1977), Toward the origin of dialogue. In: *Studies in Mother-Infant Interaction,* ed. H. R. Schaffer. London: Academic Press, pp. 89–117.

Kimberly, R. P. (1970), Rhythmic patterns in human interaction. *Nature,* 228:88–90.

Klein, G. (1976), *Psychoanalytic Theory: An Exploration of Essentials.* New York: International Universities Press.

Klein, M. (1981), On Mahler's autistic and symbiotic phases. *Psychoanal. Contemp. Thought,* 4:69–105.

Kohut, H. (1977), *The Restoration of the Self.* New York: International Universities Press.

_____ (1984), *How Does Analysis Cure?* ed. A. Goldberg & P. Stepansky. Chicago: University of Chicago Press.

Lichtenberg, J. D. (1989), *Psychoanalysis and Motivation.* Hillsdale, NJ: The Analytic Press.

Mahler, M. S., Pine, F. & Bergman, A. (1975), *The Psychological Birth of the Human Infant.* New York: Basic Books.

Meares, R. (1988), On boundary formation. In: *Frontiers in Self Psychology: Progress in Self Psychology, Vol. 3,* ed. A. Goldberg. Hillsdale, NJ: The Analytic Press, pp. 237–252.

Murphy, L. B. & Moriarty, A. E. (1976), *Vulnerability, Coping, and Growth.* New Haven, CT: Yale University Press.

Papoušek, H. & Papoušek, M. (1975), Cognitive aspects of preverbal social interaction between human infants and adults. In: *Parent-Infant Interaction,* Ciba Foundation Symposium 33. New York: Elsevier, pp. 241–260.

Peterfreund, E. (1978), Some critical comments on psychoanalytic conceptualizations of infancy. *Internat. J. Psycho-Anal.,* 59:427–441.

Pine, F. (1986), The "symbiotic phase" in light of current infancy research. *Bull. Menn. Clin.,* 50:594–569.

Reppert, S. M. & Weaver, D. R. (1988), Maternal transduction of light–dark information for the fetus. In: *Behavior of the Fetus,* ed. W. P. Smotherman & S. R. Robinson. Caldwell, NJ: Telford Press, pp. 119–139.

Sander, L. W. (1976), Issues in early mother–child interaction. In: *Infant Psychiatry.,* ed. E. N. Rexford, L. W. Sander, & T. Shapiro. New Haven, CT: Yale University Press, pp. 127–147.

_____ (1983), Polarity, paradox, and the organizing process in development. In: *Frontiers of Infant Psychiatry,* ed. J. D. Call, E. Galenson, & R. Tyson. New York: Basic Books, pp. 334–346.

_____ (1987), Awareness of inner experience: A systems perspective on self-regulatory process in early development. *Child Abuse Negl.,* 2:339–346.

Schneirla, T. C. (1965), Aspects of stimulation and organization in approach/withdrawal processes underlying vertebrate behavioral development. In: *Advances in the Study of Behavior, Vol. 1,* ed. E. Lehrman, R. Hinde, & E. Shaw. New York: Academic Press, pp. 1–74.

Silverman, L. H. Lachmann, F. M. & Milich, R. H. (1982), *The Search For Oneness.* New York: International Universities Press.

Smotherman, W. P. & Robinson, S. R. (1988), Dimensions of fetal investigation. In: *Behavior of the Fetus,* ed. W. P. Smotherman & S. R. Robinson. Caldwell, NJ: Telford Press, pp. 19–34.

Spitz, R. (1957), *No and Yes.* New York: International Universities Press.

Stechler, G. & Carpenter, G. (1967), A viewpoint on early affective development. In: *The Exceptional Infant, No. 1,* ed. J. Hellmath. Seattle: Special Child Publications, pp. 163–189.

Stechler, G. & Kaplan, S. (1980), The development of the self: A psychoanalytic perspective. *The Psychoanalytic Study of the Child,* 35:85–105. New Haven, CT: Yale University Press.

Stern, D. (1974), Mother and infant at play: The dyadic interaction involving facial, vocal, and gaze behaviors. In: *The Effect of the Infant on its Caregiver,* ed. M. Lewis & L. Rosenblum. New York: Wiley, pp. 187–213.

_____ (1977), *The First Relationship.* Cambridge, MA: Harvard University Press.

_____ (1985), *The Interpersonal World of the Infant.* New York: Basic Books.

_____ (1989), Developmental prerequisites for the sense of a narrated self. In: *Psychoanalysis: Toward the Second Century,* ed. A. Cooper, O. F. Kernberg, & E. Spector-Person. New Haven, CT: Yale University Press, pp. 168–178.

Storr, A. (1988), *Solitude.* New York: Ballantine.

Stroufe, L. A. (1989), Relationships, self, and individual adaptation. In: *Relationship Disturbances in Early Childhood,* ed. A. J. Sameroff & R. N. Emde. New York: Basic Books, pp. 70–94.

Trevarthen, C. (1977), Descriptive analyses of infant communicative behavior. In: *Studies in Mother–Infant Interaction,* ed. H. Schaffer. New York: Academic Press, pp. 227–270.

Tronick, E. Z., Als, H. & Adamson, L. (1979), Structure of early face-to-face communicative interactions. In: *Before Speech,* ed. M. Bullowa. Cambridge, UK: Cambridge University Press, pp. 349–372.

Tronick, E. Z., Als, H., Adamson, L., Wise, S. & Brazelton, T. B. (1978), The infant's response to entrapment between contradictory messages in face-to-face interaction. *J. Amer. Acad. Child Psychiat.,* 17:1–13.

Watson, J. S. (1972), Smiling, cooing and "the game." *Merrill-Palmer Quart.,* 18:323–339.

Watzlawick, P., Beavin H. J. & Jackson, D. (1967), *The Pragmatics of Human Communication.* New York: Norton.

White, R. W. (1959), Motivation reconsidered: The concept of competence. *Psychol. Rev.,* 66:297–333.

Winnicott, D. W. (1953), Transitional objects and transitional phenomena. In: *Collected Papers: Through Paediatrics to Psycho-Analysis.* London: Tavistock, 1958, pp. 229–242.

_____ (1956), Primary maternal preoccupation. In: *Collected Papers: Through Paediatrics to Psycho-Analysis.* London: Tavistock, 1958, pp. 300–305.

_____ (1958), The capacity to be alone. In: *The Maturational Process and the Facilitating Environment.* New York: International Universities Press, 1965, pp. 29–36.

_____ (1960), Ego distortion in terms of true and false self. In: *The Maturational Process and the Facilitating Environment*. New York: International Universities Press, 1965, pp. 140–152.

_____ (1963), Communicating and not communicating leading to a study of certain opposites. In: *The Maturational Process and the Facilitating Environment*. New York: International Universities Press, 1965, pp. 179–192.

_____ (1967), The mirror role of the mother and family in child development. In: *Playing and Reality*. New York: Basic Books, 1971, pp. 111–118.

A Chronology of Freud's Writing His Psychological Works

GEORGE F. MAHL

In a previous study I determined the frequency with which Freud used the terms *father* and *mother* in his psychological works written in the years 1886–1939 (Mahl, 1985). These years span the period from the date of his earliest writing in *The Standard Edition of the Complete Psychological Works of Sigmund Freud* (Strachey, 1953–1974) to his death. The achievement of those research goals concerning Freud's usage of *father* and *mother* required my assistant and me to determine the chronology of Freud's production of his works and the number of pages in each work. It was also necessary to determine the frequency of *father* and *mother* in each work. This we derived from the *father–mother* entries in the *Concordance to the Standard Edition of the Complete Psychological Works of Sigmund Freud* (Guttman, Jones, and Parrish, 1980). From these classes of basic data I was able to portray the density of usage of *father* and *mother* throughout Freud's scientific career as a psychologist (density = *n father (mother)/n* pages), and I was able to show the impact of his own father's death and his self-analysis in the late 1890s and of his mother's death in 1930 on those indices. As an ancillary finding I portrayed Freud's yearly creation of the pages of the *Standard Edition* (see Figure 1). I refer the reader to my report (Mahl, 1985) for relevant details and a discussion of them.

The purpose of this chapter is to present the chronology of Freud's works and the number of pages they contain, thus providing background information for the interested reader of my previous report. In addition, I make available bibliographic source material not presented elsewhere.

I am very grateful to Carmel Lepore for her amiable, dedicated assistance.

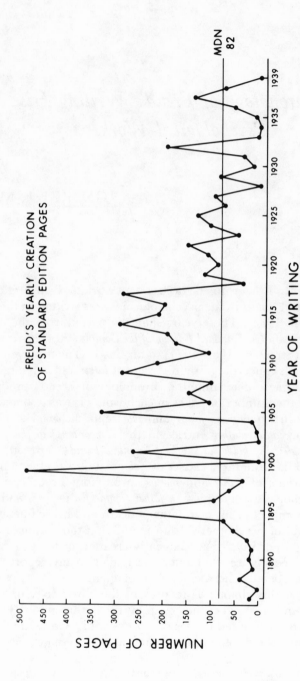

FIGURE 1. *Freud's yearly creation of Standard Edition* pages. Work is dated according to the year of actual writing or major completion, not the year of publication. Footnotes and other additions in later revisions are assigned to the years of their writing (from Mahl, 1985).

50

Joshua Hoffs

FIGURE 2. *Sigmund Freud, 1856–1939. Left to right. Top row: 8 (1864), 16, 20, 29 years old. Second row: 35 (1891), 39, 50, 50 years old. Third row: 53 (1909), 55, 60, 64 (1920) years old. Bottom row: 66 (1922), 73, 82, 82 (1938) years old (from Mahl, 1985).*

The chronology is based on the year of writing or of major completion, not the year of publication. When the year of writing differs from the date of publication, it is based on the historical information that Strachey included in his introductions to the various items in the *Standard Edition*. Usually, this dating was a clear-cut, straightforward matter. For example, the Schreber paper was published in 1911. Yet Strachey says that Freud composed it in the fall of 1910 and wrote both Abraham and Ferenczi, on December 16, 1910, that he had finished the paper (Freud,

1911, p. 3).[1] Thus, I dated the paper as written in 1910. As another example, the volume on anxiety was published in 1926. Yet Strachey cites Ernest Jones to the effect that Freud first wrote it in July of 1925 and revised it in December of 1925 (Freud, 1926, p. 78); thus, I dated it as written in 1925. "The Ego and the Id" was published in April, 1923, yet Freud was reported to have said in a paper he read in September 1922 at the Seventh International Psycho-Analytic Congress that he had written a book, "The Ego and the Id," that was to be published soon (Freud, 1923, pp. 3-4). Thus, I dated this item as written in 1922.

Sometimes the dating involved a judgment on my part. This was so, for example, when work on an item spanned several years. Freud worked on "Moses and Monotheism," for instance, from 1934 into 1938. Yet I judged from Strachey's introduction that the dates of major completion were 1936 for the first and second essays and 1937 for the third essay.

I know of two comparable chronologies in English of Freud's psychological works: They are subsumed in the complete bibliography of all his writings prepared by the editor of Volume 24 of the *Standard Edition* and the bibliography by Grinstein (1977). My chronology is unique in two important respects. First, I believe I have been the most consistent in making the distinction between the date of writing or major completion and the date of publication. Strachey attempted to specify the dates of writing and of publication, where they did not coincide. He did this in his introduction to each essay in those volumes of the *Standard Edition,* which he edited. He was not always consistent, however, in this practice. For example, he did not specify both dates for the Schreber paper or for the monograph on anxiety, among other works. Nor did Grinstein make the distinction consistently.

The bibliography of Volume 24 of the *Standard Edition* is also inconsistent in this regard. I discovered 25 instances in which that bibliography failed to date the year of writing or major completion where it differed from the *date of record* of publication. Twenty-one of these 25 failures were major in that they did not involve mere prefaces Freud wrote to his own works or introductions he wrote for works by colleagues or contemporaries. The most plausible explanation for these errors of the bibliogra-

---

[1]The dates given in this chapter and its bibliography for the Freud references are the dates of record of original publication, which sometimes differ from the actual dates of publication. For example, the original publication date of record for "The Interpretation of Dreams" is 1900, although it was actually published late in 1899. The date of writing, which often differs from the date of publication, is not given in the text or the bibliography in order to avoid unnecessary confusion. It is, of course, given in the chronology contained herein.

phy of Volume 24 is that Strachey did not supervise its compilation. He died in 1967, prior to the beginning of the work on Volume 24 and six years before its completion.

The second feature unique to my chronology is my specification of the dates and quantity of all material added to later editions of Freud's works.

These two features that I claim are unique to my chronology might make it useful to future historical researchers. Minimally, the chronology informs the reader of exactly what works and what number of pages were assigned to which years in conducting the previously mentioned study (Mahl, 1985). (Since the completion of the chronology I have discovered a small number of minor errors in it. The Postscript describes these.)

My chronology, however, in no way replaces the complete bibliographies of Volume 24 or of Grinstein. They are invaluable because they include Freud's nonpsychological writings and the dates of the German, as well as the English, publications.

In the following chronology all references are to *The Standard Edition of The Complete Psychological Works of Sigmund Freud* (Strachey, 1953-1974). For each item the volume number and the first page of the text proper, not that of Strachey's introductory material, are given. No page references are presented for the major works taking up a complete volume of the *Standard Edition*. Material added to a work in subsequent editions is indicated by "Additions" and is itemized under the year of the later editions.

The following criteria were used in determining the page counts presented in the chronology: They are counts of material written by Freud (e.g., that by Breuer in *Studies on Hysteria* was not counted). Except for both footnotes and text insertions added in subsequent editions the page count equals the number of numbered pages of text in the *Standard Edition*. (Thus, portions of pages were counted as whole pages.) In the case of footnotes and text insertions added in subsequent editions, the page count was based on estimates derived from the number of printed lines. (In such cases, appropriate subtractions were made from the number of numbered text pages in order to determine the page counts for the first editions.)

The Chronology

Year	Title and *Standard Edition* Reference	N text pages
1886	1. Report on my studies in Paris and Berlin. *1*, 5.	11
	2. Preface to the translation of Charcot's *Lectures on the diseases of the nervous system. 1*, 21.	2

Year	Title and *Standard Edition* Reference	*N* text pages
	3. Observation of a severe case of hemi-anaesthesia in a hysterical male. *1*, 25.	7
	Total =	20
1887	1. Review of Averbeck's *Die akute Neurasthenie*. *1*, 35.	1
	2. Review of Weir Mitchell's *Die Behandlung gewisser Formen von Neurasthenie und Hysterie*. *1*, 36.	1
	Total =	2
1888	1. Hysteria. *1*, 41.	17
	2. Hystero-epilepsy. *1*, 58.	2
	3. Preface to the translation of Bernheim's *Suggestion*. *1*, 75.	11
	4. Some points for a comparative study of organic and hysterical motor paralyses. *1*, 160 [Parts I, II, III].	10
	Total =	40
1889	1. Review of August Forel's *Hypnotism*. *1*, 91.	12
	Total =	12
1890	1. Psychical (or mental) treatment. *7*, 283 [see *1*, 63].	20
	Total =	20
1891	1. Hypnosis. *1*, 105.	10
	2. Words and things. *14*, 209.	7
	Total =	17
1892	1. A case of successful treatment by hypnotism. *1*, 117.	12
	2. Preface to the translation of Charcot's *Tuesday Lectures*. *1*, 133.	4
	3. Sketches for the 'Preliminary communication' of 1893. *1*, 147.	8
	4. Draft A, Fliess letters. *1*, 177.	2
	Total =	26
1893	1. Some points for a comparative study of organic and hysterical motor paralyses. *1*, 160 [Part IV].	4
	2. Draft B and Fliess letter 14. *1*, 179.	8
	3. On the psychical mechanism of hysterical phenomena: Preliminary communication. *2*, 3.	15
	4. Charcot. *3*, 11.	13
	5. On the psychical mechanism of hysterical phenomena: A lecture. *3*, 27.	13
	Total =	53

Year	Title and *Standard Edition* Reference	*N* text pages
1894	1. Extracts from Freud's footnotes to his translation of Charcot's *Tuesday Lectures. 1,* 137.	7
	2. Drafts and Fliess letters. *1,* 186.	14
	3. The neuro-psychoses of defence. *3,* 45.	17
	4. Obsessions and phobias: Their psychical mechanism and their aetiology. *3,* 74.	9
	5. On the grounds for detaching a particular syndrome from neurasthenia under the description 'Anxiety neurosis.' *3,* 90.	26
	Total =	73
1895	1. Drafts and Fliess letters. *1,* 200.	19
	2. Project for a scientific psychology. *1,* 295.	90
	3. Studies on hysteria. *2,* 48.	185
	4. A reply to criticisms of my paper on anxiety neurosis. *3,* 123.	17
	Total =	311
1896	1. Preface to the second German edition of the translation of Bernheim's *Suggestion. 1,* 86.	2
	2. Drafts and Fliess letters. *1,* 220.	20
	3. Fliess letter. *1,* 388.	4
	4. Heredity and the aetiology of the neuroses. *3,* 143.	14
	5. Further remarks on the neuro-psychoses of defence. *3,* 162.	23
	6. The aetiology of hysteria. *3,* 191.	31
	Total =	94
1897	1. Drafts and Fliess letters. *1,* 240.	34
	2. Abstracts of the scientific writings of Dr. Sigm. Freud. *3,* 227.	30
	Total =	64
1898	1. Fliess letters. *1,* 274.	3
	2. Sexuality in the aetiology of the neuroses. *3,* 263.	23
	3. The psychical mechanism of forgetfulness. *3,* 289.	9
	Total =	35
1899	1. Fliess letters. *1,* 276.	5
	2. Screen memories. *3,* 303.	20
	3. Autobiographical note. *3,* 325.	1
	4. The interpretation of dreams. *4* and *5.*	463
	Total =	489

Year	Title and *Standard Edition* Reference	*N* text pages
1900	(*N* Items = 0) Total =	0
1901	1. On dreams. *5*, 633.	50
	2. The psychopathology of everyday life. *6*.	111
	3. Fragment of an analysis of a case of hysteria. *7*, 7.	103
	Total =	264
1902	(*N* Items = 0) Total =	0
1903	1. Freud's psycho-analytic procedure. *7*, 249.	6
	2. Review of Georg Biedenkapp's *Im Kampfe gegen Hirnbacillen*. *9*, 253.	2
	Total =	8
1904	1. On psychotherapy. *7*, 257.	12
	2. Review of John Bigelow's *The Mystery of Sleep*. *9*, 254.	2
	3. Obituary of Professor S. Hammerschlag. *9*, 255.	2
	Total =	16
1905	1. Fragment of an analysis of a case of hysteria. *7*, 7, "Additions."	11
	2. Three essays on the theory of sexuality. *7*, 130.	83
	3. My views on the part played by sexuality in the aetiology of the neuroses. *7*, 271.	9
	4. Jokes and their relation to the unconscious. *8*.	226
	Total =	329
1906	1. Preface to Freud's collection of shorter writings on the theory of the neuroses from the years 1893–1906. *3*, 5.	2
	2. Psychopathic characters on the stage. *7*, 305.	6
	3. Delusions and dreams in Jensen's *Gradiva*. *9*, 7.	87
	4. Psycho-analysis and the establishment of the facts in legal proceedings. *9*, 103.	12
	Total =	107
1907	1. The psychopathology of everyday life. *6*, "Additions."	52
	2. Obsessive actions and religious practices. *9*, 117.	11
	3. The sexual enlightenment of children. *9*, 131.	9
	4. Creative writers and day-dreaming. *9*, 143.	11
	5. Contribution to a questionnaire on reading. *9*, 245.	3

Year	Title and *Standard Edition* Reference	*N* text pages
	6. Prospectus for *Schriften zur angewandten Seelenkunde. 9,* 248.	2
	7. Addendum [to *Notes upon a case of obsessional neurosis*]. Original record of the case. *10,* 254, 259.	61
	Total =	149
1908	1. Prefaces [to *Studies on hysteria*]. *2,* "Additions."	1
	2. The interpretation of dreams. *4* and *5,* "Additions."	30
	3. Hysterical phantasies and their relation to bisexuality. *9,* 159.	8
	4. Character and anal erotism. *9,* 169.	7
	5. 'Civilized' sexual morality and modern nervous illness. *9,* 181.	24
	6. On the sexual theories of children. *9,* 209.	18
	7. Some general remarks on hysterical attacks. *9,* 229.	6
	8. Family romances. *9,* 237.	5
	9. Preface to Wilhelm Stekel's *Nervous Anxiety-States and Their Treatment. 9,* 250.	2
	Total =	101
1909	1. Three essays on the theory of sexuality. *7,* 130, "Additions."	3
	2. Preface to Sandor Ferenczi's *Psycho-Analysis: Essays in the Field of Psycho-Analysis. 9,* 252.	1
	3. Analysis of a phobia in a five-year-old boy. *10,* 5.	141
	4. Notes upon a case of obsessional neurosis. *10,* 155.	95
	5. Five lectures on psychoanalysis. *11,* 9.	47
	Total =	287
1910	1. The psychopathology of everyday life. *6,* "Additions."	20
	2. Leonardo da Vinci and a memory of his childhood. *11,* 63.	71
	3. The future prospects of psycho-analytic therapy. *11,* 141.	11
	4. The antithetical meaning of primal words. *11,* 155.	7
	5. A special type of choice of object made by men (Contributions to the psychology of love I). *11,* 165.	11
	6. The psycho-analytic view of psychogenic disturbance of vision. *11,* 211.	8

Year	Title and *Standard Edition* Reference	*N* text pages
	7. 'Wild' psycho-analysis. *11*, 221.	7
	8. Contributions to a discussion on suicide. *11*, 231.	2
	9. Letter to Dr. Friedrich S. Krauss on *Anthropophyteia*. *11*, 233.	3
	10. Two instances of pathogenic phantasies revealed by the patients themselves. *11*, 236.	2
	11. Review of Wilhelm Neutra's *Letters to Neurotic Women*. *11*, 238.	1
	12. Psycho-analytic notes on an autobiographical account of a case of paranoia (dementia paranoides). *12*, 9.	71
	Total =	214
1911	1. The interpretation of dreams. *4* and *5*, "Additions."	36
	2. On dreams. *5, 633*, "Additions."	4
	3. Psycho-analytic notes on an autobiographical account of a case of paranoia (dementia paranoides). *12*, "Additions."	3
	4. The handling of dream-interpretation in psycho-analysis. *12*, 91.	6
	5. Dreams in folklore. *12*, 180.	24
	6. On psycho-analysis. *12*, 207.	5
	7. Formulations on the two principles of mental functioning. *12*, 218.	9
	8. The significance of sequences of vowels. *12*, 341.	1
	9. 'Great is Diana of the Ephesians.' *12*, 342.	3
	10. Totem and taboo. *13*, 1 [First essay].	17
	11. Footnote to Stekel's paper 'Zur Psychologie des Exhibitionismus.' *18*, 274, fn.	1
	Total =	109
1912	1. The psychopathology of everyday life. *6*, "Additions."	33
	2. Jokes and their relation to the unconscious. *8*, "Additions."	2
	3. Delusions and dreams in Jensen's *Gradiva*. *9*, 7, "Additions."	2
	4. On the universal tendency to debasement in the sphere of love (Contributions to the psychology of love II). *11*, 179.	12
	5. The dynamics of transference. *12*, 99.	10

Year	Title and *Standard Edition* Reference	*N* text pages
	6. Recommendations to physicians practising psycho-analysis. *12*, 111.	10
	7. Types of onset of neurosis. *12*, 231.	8
	8. Contributions to a discussion on masturbation. *12*, 243.	12
	9. A note on the unconscious in psycho-analysis. *12*, 260.	7
	10. Totem and taboo. *13*, 1 [second and third essays].	82
	Total =	178
1913	1. On beginning the treatment (Further recommendations on the technique of psycho-analysis I). *12*, 123.	22
	2. An evidential dream. *12*, 269.	9
	3. The occurrence in dreams of material from fairy tales. *12*, 281.	7
	4. The theme of the three caskets. *12*, 291.	11
	5. Two lies told by children. *12*, 305.	5
	6. The disposition to obsessional neurosis. *12*, 317.	10
	7. Introduction to Pfister's *The Psycho-Analytic Method*. *12*, 329.	3
	8. Preface to Bourke's *Scatalogic Rites of All Nations*. *12*, 335.	3
	9. Preface to Maxim Steiner's *The Psychical Disorders of Male Potency*. *12*, 345.	2
	10. Totem and taboo. *13*, 1 [fourth essay].	63
	11. The claims of psycho-analysis to scientific interest. *13*, 165.	26
	12. Observations and examples from analytic practice. *13*, 193.	6
	13. The Moses of Michelangelo. *13*, 211.	26
	Total =	193
1914	1. The interpretation of dreams. *4* and *5*, "Additions."	35
	2. Three essays on the theory of sexuality. *7*, 130, "Additions."	18
	3. Remembering, repeating and working-through (Further recommendations on the technique of psycho-analysis II). *12*, 147.	10

Year	Title and *Standard Edition* Reference	*N* text pages
	4. Observations on transference-love (Further recommendations on the technique of psycho-analysis III). *12*, 159.	13
	5. Fausse reconnaissance ('déjà raconté') in psycho-analytic treatment. *13*, 201.	7
	6. Some reflections on schoolboy psychology. *13*, 241.	4
	7. On the history of the psycho-analytic movement. *14*, 7.	58
	8. On narcissism: An introduction. *14*, 73.	30
	9. Letter to Frederik van Eeden. *14*, 301.	1
	10. From the history of an infantile neurosis. *17*, 7.	115
	Total =	291
1915	1. Instincts and their vicissitudes. *14*, 117.	24
	2. Repression. *14*, 146.	13
	3. The unconscious. *14*, 166.	39
	4. A metapsychological supplement to the theory of dreams. *14*, 222.	14
	5. Mourning and melancholia. *14*, 243.	16
	6. A case of paranoia running counter to the psycho-analytic theory of the disease. *14*, 263.	10
	7. Thoughts for the times on war and death. *14*, 275.	26
	8. On transience. *14*, 305.	3
	9. Letter to Dr. Hermine von Hug-Hellmuth. *14*, 341.	1
	10. Introductory lectures on psycho-analysis: Part I. Parapraxes. *15*, 15.	65
	Total =	211
1916	1. Footnote to Ernest Jones's 'Professor Janet über psychoanalyse.' *2*, xiii, fn.	1
	2. Some character-types met with in psycho-analytic work. *14*, 311.	23
	3. A mythological parallel to a visual obsession. *14*, 337.	2
	4. A connection between a symbol and a symptom. *14*, 339.	2
	5. Introductory lectures on psycho-analysis: Part II. Dreams. *15*, 83.	157
	6. On transformations of instinct as exemplified in anal erotism. *17*, 127.	7

Year	Title and *Standard Edition* Reference	*N* text pages
	7. A difficulty in the path of psycho-analysis. *17*, 137.	8
	Total =	200
1917	1. The psychopathology of everyday life. *6*, "Additions."	38
	2. The taboo of virginity (Contributions to the psychology of love III). *11*, 193.	16
	3. Introductory lectures on psycho-analysis. Part III. General theory of the neuroses. *16*.	224
	4. A childhood recollection from *Dichtung und Wahrheit*. *17*, 147.	10
	Total =	288
1918	1. The interpretation of dreams. *4* and *5*, "Additions."	25
	2. Lines of advance in psycho-analytic therapy. *17*, 159.	10
	3. On the teaching of psycho-analysis in universities. *17*, 171.	3
	Total =	38
1919	1. The psychopathology of everyday life. *6*, "Additions."	12
	2. Leonardo da Vinci and a memory of his childhood. *11*, 63, "Additions."	3
	3. 'A child is being beaten.' *17*, 179.	26
	4. Introduction to *Psycho-Analysis and the War Neuroses*. *17*, 207.	4
	5. The 'uncanny.' *17*, 219.	34
	6. E. T. A. Hoffmann on the function of consciousness. *17*, 234, fn.	1
	7. Preface to Reik's *Ritual: Psycho-Analytic Studies*. *17*, 259.	5
	8. A note on psycho-analytic publications and prizes. *17*, 267.	4
	9. James J. Putnam. *17*, 271.	1
	10. Victor Tausk. *17*, 273.	3
	11. The psychogenesis of a case of homosexuality in a woman. *18*, 147.	26
	Total =	119
1920	1. The psychopathology of everyday life. *6*, "Additions."	13

Year	Title and *Standard Edition* Reference	*N* text pages
	2. Three essays on the theory of sexuality. *7*, 130, "Additions."	8
	3. Memorandum on the electrical treatment of war neurotics. *17*, 211.	5
	4. Beyond the pleasure principle. *18*, 7.	57
	5. A note on the prehistory of the technique of analysis. *18*, 263.	3
	6. Associations of a four-year-old child. *18*, 266.	1
	7. Dr. Anton von Freund. *18*, 267.	2
	Total =	89
1921	1. The interpretation of dreams. *4* and *5*, "Additions."	1
	2. Fragment of a letter to Edouard Claparède. *11*, 214, fn.	1
	3. Award of prizes. *17*, 269.	1
	4. Beyond the pleasure principle. *18*, 7, "Additions."	1
	5. Group psychology and the analysis of the ego. *18*, 69.	75
	6. Psycho-analysis and telepathy. *18*, 177.	17
	7. Some neurotic mechanisms in jealousy, paranoia and homosexuality. *18*, 223.	10
	8. Preface to J. J. Putnam's *Addresses on Psycho-Analysis*. *18*, 269.	2
	9. Introduction to J. Varendonck's *The Psychology of Day-Dreams*. *18*, 271.	2
	Total =	110
1922	1. Analysis of a phobia in a five-year-old boy. *10*, 5, "Additions."	2
	2. Prize offer. *17*, 270.	1
	3. Dreams and telepathy. *18*, 197.	24
	4. Two encyclopaedia articles: (A) Psycho-analysis. *18*, 235.	20
	5. Two encyclopaedia articles: (B) The libido theory. *18*, 255.	5
	6. Medusa's head. *18*, 273.	2
	7. The ego and the id. *19*, 12.	48
	8. A seventeenth-century demonological neurosis. *19*, 72.	34
	9. Remarks on the theory and practice of dream-interpretation. *19*, 109.	13

Year	Title and *Standard Edition* Reference	*N* text pages
	10. Preface to Raymond de Saussure's *The Psycho-Analytic Method. 19*, 283.	2
	Total =	151
1923	1. Fragment of an analysis of a case of hysteria. *7, 7,* "Additions."	2
	2. Analysis of a phobia in a five-year-old boy. *10,* 5, "Additions."	2
	3. Leonardo da Vinci and a memory of his childhood. *11,* 63, "Additions."	1
	4. On the history of the psycho-analytic movement. *14,* 7, "Additions."	1
	5. From the history of an infantile neurosis. *17,* 7, "Additions."	1
	6. The infantile genital organization. *19,* 141.	5
	7. Neurosis and psychosis. *19,* 149.	5
	8. A short account of psycho-analysis. *19,* 191.	19
	9. Josef Popper-Lynkeus and the theory of dreams. *19,* 261.	3
	10. Dr. Sándor Ferenczi (on his 50th birthday). *19,* 267.	3
	11. Preface to Max Eitingon's *Report on the Berlin Psycho-Analytical Policlinic. 19,* 285.	1
	12. Letter to Fritz Wittels. *19,* 286.	3
	13. Letter to Señor Luis Lopez-Ballesteros y de Torres. *19,* 289.	1
	Total =	47
1924	1. Studies on hysteria. *2,* "Additions."	2
	2. The psychopathology of everyday life. *6,* "Additions."	6
	3. Three essays on the theory of sexuality. *7,* 130, "Additions."	1
	4. On the history of the psycho-analytic movement. *14,* 7, "Additions."	1
	5. The economic problem of masochism. *19,* 159.	12
	6. The dissolution of the Oedipus complex. *19,* 173.	7
	7. The loss of reality in neurosis and psychosis. *19,* 183.	5
	8. The resistances to psycho-analysis. *19,* 213.	10

Year	Title and *Standard Edition* Reference	*N* text pages
	9. A note upon the 'mystic writing-pad.' *19*, 227.	6
	10. Letter to *Le Disque Vert*. *19*, 290.	1
	11. Editorial changes in the *Zeitschrift*. *19*, 293.	1
	12. An autobiographical study. *20*, 7.	62
	Total =	114
1925	1. The interpretation of dreams. *4* and *5*, "Additions."	4
	2. Some additional notes on dream-interpretation as a whole. *19*, 127.	12
	3. Negation. *19*, 235.	5
	4. Some physical consequences of the anatomical distinction between the sexes. *19*, 248.	11
	5. Preface to Aichhorn's *Wayward Youth*. *19*, 273.	3
	6. Josef Breuer. *19*, 279.	2
	7. Letter to the editor of the *Jewish Press Centre in Zurich*. *19*, 291.	1
	8. On the occasion of the opening of the Hebrew University. *19*, 292.	1
	9. Inhibitions, symptoms and anxiety. *20*, 87.	86
	10. Psycho-analysis. *20*, 263.	8
	Total =	133
1926	1. The question of lay analysis. *20*, 183.	68
	2. Address to the society of B'nai B'rith. *20*, 273.	2
	3. Karl Abraham. *20*, 277.	2
	4. To Romain Rolland. *20*, 279.	1
	5. Prefatory note to a paper by E. Pickworth Farrow. *20*, 280.	1
	6. Dr. Reik and the problem of quackery: A letter to the *Neue Freie Presse*. *21*, 247.	2
	Total =	76
1927	1. The Moses of Michelangelo. *13*, 211, "Additions."	2
	2. The question of lay analysis. *20*, 183, "Additions."	8
	3. The future of an illusion. *21*, 5.	52
	4. Fetishism. *21*, 152.	6
	5. Humour. *21*, 161.	6
	6. A religious experience. *21*, 169.	4
	7. Dostoevsky and parricide. *21*, 177.	18
	Total =	96
1928	(*N* Items = 0) Total =	0

Year	Title and *Standard Edition* Reference	*N* text pages
1929	1. The interpretation of dreams. *4* and *5*, "Additions."	1
	2. Civilization and its discontents. *21*, 64.	82
	3. A letter from Freud to Theodor Reik. *21*, 195.	2
	4. Some dreams of Descartes. *21*, 203.	2
	5. Dr. Ernest Jones (on his 50th birthday). *21*, 249.	2
	Total =	89
1930	1. Totem and taboo. *13*, 1, "Additions."	1
	2. Introductory lectures on psychoanalysis. *15* and *16*, "Additions."	2
	3. Letter to Dr. Alfons Paquet. *21*, 207.	1
	4. Address delivered in the Goethe House at Frankfurt. *21*, 208.	5
	5. The expert opinion in the Halsmann case. *21*, 251.	3
	6. Introduction to the special psychopathology number of *The Medical Review of Reviews*. *21*, 254.	2
	7. Introduction to Edoardo Weiss's *Elements of Psycho-Analysis*. *21*, 256.	1
	8. Preface to *Ten Years of the Berlin Psycho-Analytic Institute*. *21*, 257.	1
	Total =	16
1931	1. Libidinal types. *21*, 217.	4
	2. Female sexuality. *21*, 225.	19
	3. Preface to Hermann Nunberg's *General Theory of the Neuroses on a Psycho-Analytic Basis*. *21*, 258.	1
	4. Letter to the Burgomaster of Příbor. *21*, 259.	1
	5. The acquisition and control of fire. *22*, 187.	7
	6. Letter to Georg Fuchs. *22*, 251.	2
	Total =	34
1932	1. New introductory lectures on psycho-analysis. *22*, 5.	178
	2. Why war? *22*, 203 [Einstein's letter, 199].	13
	3. My contact with Josef Popper-Lynkeus. *22*, 219.	6
	4. Preface to Richard Sterba's *Dictionary of Psycho-Analysis*. *22*, 253.	1
	Total =	198
1933	1. Sándor Ferenczi. *22*, 227.	3

Year	Title and *Standard Edition* Reference	N text pages
	2. Preface to Marie Bonaparte's *The Life and Works of Edgar Allen Poe: A Psycho-Analytic Interpretation. 22,* 254.	1
	Total =	4
1934	(*N* Items = 0) Total =	0
1935	1. An autobiographical study. *20,* 7, "Additions."	6
	2. The subtleties of a faulty action. *22,* 233.	3
	3. To Thomas Mann on his sixtieth birthday. *22,* 255.	1
	Total =	10
1936	1. A disturbance of memory on the Acropolis. *22,* 239.	10
	2. Moses and monotheism: Three essays. *23,* 7 [first and second essays].	47
	Total =	57
1937	1. Moses and monotheism: Three essays. *23,* 7 [third essay].	84
	2. Analysis terminable and interminable. *23,* 216.	38
	3. Constructions in analysis. *23,* 257.	13
	4. Splitting of the ego in the process of defense. *23,* 275.	4
	5. Lou Andreas-Salomé. *23,* 297.	2
	Total =	141
1938	1. An outline of psycho-analysis. *23,* 144.	64
	2. Some elementary lessons in psycho-analysis. *23,* 281.	6
	3. A comment on anti-Semitism. *23,* 291.	3
	4. Findings, ideas, problems. *23,* 299.	2
	5. Anti-Semitism in England. *23,* 301.	1
	Total =	76
1939	(*N* Items = 0) Total =	0

Postscript

Since completion of the chronology and publication of the study based in part upon it (Mahl, 1985), I have discovered seven small errors of omission and two of commission in it. The following changes in the chronology rectify those errors. (Some of the changes are compensatory.) This method of indicating the corrections, rather than directly changing the chronology, preserves the integrity of the original data base of the aforementioned study. None of these changes affects the results or conclusions of that study.

Year	Title and *Standard Edition* Reference	*N* text pages
Add to chronology:		
1891	1. Psycho-physical parallelism. *14*, 206.	3
1906	1. Contribution to a questionnaire on reading. *9*, 245. (See *24*, 57)	3
1910	1. Typical example of a disguised Oedipal dream. *5*, 398 fn.	1
1911	1. Footnote to translation of Putnam's paper. *17*, 271 fn.	1
	2. The psychopathology of everyday life. *6*, "Additions." (See *6*, 30 fn.)	2
1912	1. Open forum: request for examples of childhood dreams. *17*, 4.	1
1913	1. Children's dreams with a special significance. *17*, 4.	1
1926	1. Freud and Ewald Hering. *14*, 205.	1
1931	1. The interpretation of dreams. *4* and *5*, "Additions."	1
Subtract from chronology:		
1907	1. Contribution to a questionnaire on reading. *9*, 245.	3
1912	1. The psychopathology of everyday life. *6*, "Additions."	2

Summary

This chapter presents a chronology of Freud's creation of his psychological writings in the *Standard Edition*. The dates of the chronology are of the actual writing or major completion of the individual works, not the dates of publication. Since no other comparable chronology is known to exist, the present one may be of value to future historical researchers.

References

Freud, S. (1900), The interpretation of dreams. *Standard Edition,* 4 & 5. London: Hogarth Press, 1953.
_____ (1911), Psycho-analytic notes on an autobiographical account of a case of paranoia (dementia paranoides). *Standard Edition,* 12:9–82. London: Hogarth Press, 1958.
_____ (1923), The ego and the id. *Standard Edition,* 19:12–59. London: Hogarth Press, 1961.
_____ (1926), Inhibitions, symptoms and anxiety. *Standard Edition,* 20:87–172. London: Hogarth Press, 1959.

Grinstein, A. (1977), *Sigmund Freud's Writings.* New York: International Universities Press.

Guttman, S. A., Jones, R. L. & Parrish, S. M. (1980), *The Concordance to the Standard Edition of the Complete Psychological Works of Sigmund Freud.* Boston: G. K. Hall.

Mahl, G. F. (1985), Freud, *father,* and *mother:* Quantitative aspects. *Psychoanal. Psychol., 2,* 99–113.

Strachey, J., ed., (1953–1974), *The Standard Edition of the Complete Psychological Works of Sigmund Freud, Vols. 1–24.* London: Hogarth Press.

What an Affect Means:
A Quasi-Experiment About Disgust

ROBERT M. GALATZER-LEVY
MAYER GRUBER

Controversies about the interpretation of patients' associations, texts, and other materials are rarely amenable to experimental or empirical exploration. One may look to criteria beyond the given data in the attempt to validate interpretive strategies. For example, Freud (e.g., Freud, 1940) insisted that the interpretation of psychological events be consistent with biological "facts." Alternatively, interpretations may be judged by the extent to which they elaborate and enrich understanding (Ricoeur, 1970, 1977, 1986). Interpretations may be judged for their pragmatic efficacy in producing therapeutic change or providing a basis for decisions (e.g., in law). Generally, interpreters adopt a congenial and/or traditional point of view whose broad outlines they rarely question.

In the course of his clinical work as a psychoanalyst one of us (R. G-L.) has repeatedly found himself attracted to two mutually contradictory interpretive positions. One position is that all human interests are transformations of bodily experiences and concerns and can be usefully interpreted as such. The other sees apparent bodily interests as expressions of attempts to organize experience on various abstract planes. In an attempt to explore and compare the value of these two interpretive strategies, clinical material was reviewed for instances that make particularly clear distinctions between them.

Expressions of disgust were often found to be amenable to both interpretations. Disgust is a deeply visceral experience, usually closely linked to specific bodily sensations and images. At the same time, it is commonly aroused by experiences that are manifestly unrelated to the body. Interpretation in either direction is possible: disgusting experiences may be assumed to have latent associations to bodily matters, or they may arise as a means by which bodily metaphors concretely express the intense feelings associated with more abstract concerns. Clinical experience suggested that the latter occurrence was far more common. The recurrent finding that what had been disgusting no longer aroused this affect once a sense of order and meaning was introduced suggests that disgust is primarily rooted in concerns about order. Furthermore, an extensive interpretive literature is consistent with this understanding. On this basis the analyst author hypothesized that disgust is an affective response to the abstract sense of disorder when order is expected.

A way was sought to confirm this hypothesis through means other than repeated observations of the phenomena that led to the hypothesis. If it were possible to explore the meanings of disgust in a context other than the ones from which the hypothesis was derived, one could perform a quasi-experiment about the validity of these broad interpretative modes.

The hypothesis entails the prediction that in any substantial body of human productions that do not reflect the idiosyncrasies of one individual's psychology, it should be possible to demonstrate that disgust commonly arises as a response to failure to find organizing principles or contexts for an experience. We further predict from this hypothesis that disgust will be expressed in terms of the language of the body but that the experiences that generate disgust will often not be closely related to bodily experiences (assuming the text significantly addresses nonbodily concerns.) Hebrew Scripture (commonly called "the Old Testament") is a massive collection of well-studied writings in which it should be possible, if the hypothesis is correct, to demonstrate the common emergence of disgust in contexts distant from bodily concerns.[1]

In order to test this hypothesis one author (M.G.) systematically explored biblical references to concepts of disgust to see the extent to which they referred to abstract or concrete matters. He also characterized the matters to which they did refer. The search was designed to be inclusive so that all terms close to disgust were explored. His researches empirically disconfirmed the analyst's hypothesis. Each and every instance of terms related to disgust used in Hebrew Scripture refers to a specific concrete event of a particular bodily experience and refers almost exclusively to what passes through the mouth.

---

[1]For these purposes we might have chosen any sufficiently rich text that was somewhat distant from our own culture. Hebrew Scripture was chosen because of the availability of expertise about the text, the depth with which it has been studied, and the richness of available commentary on it.

We believe this work is important not only because of its intrinsic interest but because it demonstrates how a psychoanalytic hypothesis has been disconfirmed by specific data, in a quasi-experimental study. Before describing the results of the study of Hebrew Scripture in detail, we review the ideas that led to the question of the meaning of disgust and the two interpretive positions.

The Body in the Mind or the Mind in the Language of the Body

The major contemporary psychological theories of symbol formation are associated with distinctive ideas about the structures of meaning and concepts of motivation. How symbols, in the broad sense, are thought to develop is contingent on the major themes they are believed to represent. Throughout his career, Freud believed that bodily urges for sexual and aggressive activity were the major motives of mental life. For him, the content of mental activity primarily represented disguised and trans-formed representations of the body, its instincts (whose mental representation were equated with drives), and the aims and objects of these drives. Freud's early psychoanalytic contributions, and much of early psychoanalytic investigation in general, can be understood as a system-atic attempt to decode the representation of the body in the mind (e.g., Breuer and Freud, 1893–1895; Freud, 1900, 1901, 1905).

A distinctly different group of motives for mental activity is repre-sented in the work of a variety of structuralists (Piaget, 1970). Thinkers like Piaget and his followers in psychology and Lévi-Strauss and his followers in anthropology hold that psychological activity is primarily directed at ordering experience into cohesive wholes. The apparent concreteness and bodily orientation of thought represents, for them, a specific means by which individuals and societies attempt to work out abstract but urgent propositions (e.g., Lévi-Strauss, 1967). Psychological theories of motivation have included a variety of theories that posit relatively abstract (as opposed to biological) goals as the aim of behavior and mental activity. For example, White (1959) posited the concept of the need for effectance, a motive as abstract as those of the structuralist. With regard to symbolism in particular, Douglas (1966) derives a major portion of human symbolic activity from a wish to order experience and action. In psychoanalysis, self psychology is among the theories that asserts abstract overarching motives (i.e., the coherence of self and experience). Self psychologists regard the body as either largely periph-eral to central psychological motives (rather like the paper and binding in which a novel is physically located) or as a source for concrete symbols and representations in which to attempt to solve the problem of personal coherence and vigor (Kohut, 1976). Erotization as a means to solve problems of threatened incoherence or devitalization of the self involves using the body to solve fundamentally psychological, nonbodily problems (Kohut, 1971, 1976, 1984).

A third group of psychological thinkers, who probably come closer to the way clinicians ordinarily function, describe a wide set of primary motives that range from physiological homeostasis to some version of coherence and effectance (e.g., Lichtenberg, 1989). In Jung's work the issue of symbol and motive are closely joined; wishing to demonstrate that sexuality and aggression do not encompass all human motives, Jung and his followers ranged widely over the fields of human creativity and religious symbols, claiming to show that their primary meanings were not bodily desires. The theory that emerged, while multimotivational, posits a search for meaning and significance, in whatever form, as a primary psychological motive (Jung, 1956). In this view symbolism is one route to the creation of psychological meaning.

Psychoanalysts generally avow an ideal of an agnostic position about the underlying meanings and structures of patients' material and hope to discover such structures by way of careful inspection of the patients' associations. We attempt to correct our interpretations by examining the patient's response to them. In fact, we listen with a relatively elaborate and rich set of ideas regarding the likely meanings of what is said. Like any other interpreter of materials and texts, we require a context and framework of meaning to begin our exploration. However, once committed to such a context, it is extremely difficult to include alternative hypotheses about the basic structure of the patient's communications. In addressing such a broad issue as whether people's central concerns are derivatives of bodily experience or whether the body is used to symbolize concerns that can only be stated precisely using abstraction, it is virtually impossible to provide convincing data from psychoanalytic materials in one direction or another.

For example, attempts such as those of Kohut (1978) and Goldberg (1978) to provide sufficient analytic data to show that a self psychology point of view is preferable to one derived from the psychology of conflict in understanding a group of patients with "disorders of the self" by and large failed to change anyone's opinion about this matter. Those who believed the self psychology formulations found confirmatory evidence in the material while those who did not already find self psychology an attractive interpretive framework believed that conflict interpretations had not been adequately pursued. The criteria for the validity of the psychoanalytic interpretation, like those used to discuss the validity of interpretation in any discipline, remain controversial. Criteria include the sense that an interpretation simply "feels right," the specific notion that the interpretation that brings forth new material is correct, the congruity of the interpretation with existing or forthcoming analytic material, and the efficacy of the interpretation in the relief of symptoms. The consistency of analytic interpretations with data drawn from other disciplines has at various times been put forward as a sine qua non of their validity (Masling, 1983, 1986) or seen as not merely irrelevant to psychoanalytic inquiry but detrimental to it (Goldberg, 1989).

Part of the reason that these matters are so hotly debated is that it is rare for specific hypotheses about psychoanalytic controversies to lead to falsifiable predictions. The psychoanalytic data almost always allow multiple understandings so that data that seem to falsify a hypothesis may be legitimately reinterpreted to support the same hypothesis. As in other disciplines, the more broad and general a statement is, the more difficult it is to produce unambiguous data supporting or refuting the statement. This is particularly true in the study of humankind, where, unlike physics, we expect exceptions to general rules. Microscopic predictions about events within analytic sessions are far more subject to systematic empirical investigation than large-scale ideas. In fact, in psychoanalysis, just as in virtually every other discipline, the nature of a satisfactory explanation and the terms in which it is given are far more a function of the worldview of the individual theorist than of the features of an absolute external reality (Galatzer-Levy and Cohler, 1990).

Especially valuable, then, is the rare instance in which one can design something approximating a test of such a large-scale distinction as to whether a psychological function is entirely or largely derived from physiological urges or whether the body is used to symbolize less concrete concerns.

Disgust and Disorder

As a clinician observing the emergence of affect in patients' discourse, one of us (R. G-L.) observed on many occasions how the affect of disgust commonly emerged as patients described disordered, chaotic, or out-of-place situations. For example, a young man in analysis described walking through his neighborhood, a place for which he had the expectation of ordered safety. As he walked, he witnessed a group of young men harassing a couple on the street and attempting to take the woman's purse. His primary conscious affective experience was one of disgust and loathing. It was, he said, as though he had come across "a pile of shit in the middle of the street." He felt physically nauseated and spoke of a wish to "clean up the area." Further analytic work on his reaction to this scene led to a gradual understanding of his own hostile and aggressive impulses, which disturbed him not so much, it seemed, because of any specific guilt or anxiety they aroused but because of their incompatibility with his image of himself. Interpretations that focused on the meanings of his hostile aggressiveness in terms of various bodily impulses produced little that was convincing about specific anxieties. However, the interpretation that his coherent sense of himself was interrupted by the feeling of being hostilely aggressive led to elaboration of his thoughts and ideas.[2] The idea that disgust represented a sense of riddance and expulsion of unwanted inner contents similarly carried little weight in terms of an enriched understanding of the patient. Several episodes like this led both the patient and the analyst to understand his disgust as a primary response to disorder and chaos in the experience of the world and himself.

It is a common finding that disgust and fascination often occur together. When something that was disgusting and not understood or not placed within an existing order comes to be comprehensible and integrable within some existing order, the sense of disgust commonly disappears. For example, it would seem that the disappearance of disgust in medical students at the site of viscera reflects not primarily desensitization but, rather, the experience of being able to place what they see into some kind of order. With the emergence of order, disgust disappears. The fascination that so often accompanies disgust is ordinarily understood as a more direct expression, not the derivative of repudiated interest in looking at the forbidden. Disgust is the more direct expression of the repudiation of this wish to look. However, the combination of fascination and disgust could also be understood as reflecting different aspects of a normative response to disorder, fascination reflecting the spontaneous effort to

---

[2]For example, the interpretation that the actions of the young men on the street reminded the patient of his own wish to intrude on his mother and stepfather's relationship or of the wish to forcefully grab from the analyst the pleasures to which he felt entitled yielded agreement that these were plausible interpretations but no new or enriched material. In contrast, a later interpretation to the effect that the scene reminded the patient of how easily his seemingly orderly world and view of himself could be disrupted by the emergence of hostility resulted in a description of how distressing it was to have angry impulses toward the analyst that disrupted the feeling of calm order in the sessions and in the recollection of several childhood episodes in which his anger led to a "sickening" feeling of chaos. Obviously, it could be argued that the failure of the first group of interpretations to elicit richer material only demonstrates that they were poorly timed, inappropriately phrased, or otherwise technically defective. We are back to the difficulty that there is no adequate way to demonstrate the *incorrectness* of psychoanalytic interpretations.

bring order to the disorderly situation by close attention to it, disgust the displeasure at such disorder.

Disgust and disorder in the experience of the self have found literary representation in such works as Sartre's *Nausea,* in which a sense of meaninglessness and triviality about personal existence finds it major representation in an ever-growing sense of nauseated disgust (see Klass and Offenkrantz, 1976; Wolf, 1988).

Developmental studies also suggest that disgust is a primary response to disorder. The children age 18 months to 2 years express an emerging concern and distaste for items that are broken or not according to the correct form; they tend to regard such items as "yukky" and to display the facial expression of disgust (Kagan, 1981). Phenomenologically similar findings have been understood by psychoanalysts to reflect specific concerns about bodily transformations. For example, it is thought that a damaged physical object, or object that otherwise recalls excrement, elicits disgust.

Nonpsychoanalytic Interpretation of Disgust

According to Izard (1978), the affect of disgust is characterized by its distinctive motivational-experiential features. It is aroused by anything perceived as deteriorating or spoiled. When the affect of disgust occurs, one feels as though one has a bad taste in one's mouth, and in intense disgust there is a sense of being sick to one's stomach. There is a wish to be rid of the disgusting object or state. Disgust commonly combines with anger and leads to destructive behavior. As Izard notes, anger is characterized by a feeling of wanting to attack, disgust by a desire to be rid of something. This desire is directed against something that is perceived as deteriorated or spoiled, either organically or psychologically. Theorists have associated disgust with hunger, believing that its proto-type is the experience of having a bad taste in the mouth.

In disgust, the facial expression in full force is one of gagging or spitting something out; the upper lip is pulled up and the nose is wrinkled. Frequently, there is an appearance of squinting (Ekman, 1975). Having a bad taste in the mouth and wanting to get away from the object of disgust may also be associated with actual nausea. The feeling is not unlike to anger except that the level of interest in the object is higher in anger than in disgust, and the distress associated with anger tends to be somewhat lower. The object of anger captures the alert attention of the person more than does the object of disgust, an affect that motivates the person to turn his attention elsewhere.

Psychoanalytic Ideas About Disgust

Freud (1926) understood disgust as predominantly a reaction formation against interests and wishes toward the disgusting object. He characterized this reaction formation as one of the typical defenses against anal sexual interest. Such reaction formation in response to anal pleasures and interests may be seen as primarily motivated or as a result of regression from oedipal-level concerns (Nagera, 1966)

Disgust has been understood psychoanalytically primarily as a defense against positive interest in feces during the anal phase. It is sometimes manifest, for example, in a reaction toward younger children who lack bowel control or toward substances reminiscent of feces, such as messy foods or foods otherwise like feces, such as brown candy (Nagera, 1966). In early adolescence it is commonly a response to feared passivity and dependency and is often directed at those individuals who embody these traits, for example, male homosexuals. Disgust is employed as a defense against genital feelings at the resolution of the oedipal phase and in adolescence, where it may show up as puritanism. Disgust is commonly manifested in response to public nudity or open displays of affection. Disgust can be felt toward someone who fails morally, such as a corrupt politician. Jacobson (1964) asserted that disgust was never a simple repudiation but reflected an undercurrent of strong oral desires. Miller (1986), in her comprehensive review of psychoanalytic concepts of the affect of disgust, observed that to regard disgust simply as a defense was to miss the richness of the variety of feelings characterized as disgust and thus the multiple meanings of disgust. According to Miller, who explored disgust from a developmental point of view, disgust derives from responses to bad smells and taste. For example, disgust in response to disorganization is a very high order derivative and transformation of an innate response to bad smells and taste. Disgust begins as a primary affective state whose generalization accounts for a growing range of responses. However, it is an unwarranted assumption that because babies can manifest the appearance of disgust and do so in response to stimuli that can produce disgust in adults, their underlying feeling state is the same, though many believe disgust is one of the primary affects (Engel, 1963; Izard, 1971; DeRivera, 1977) as opposed to affective states that, through subtle gradations, color ongoing experience (Goldstein, 1951; Gendlin, 1962)

According to Miller's developmental theory, the infant's innate response to bad smell and taste generalizes to a wish for riddance; it becomes important to touch only good things.

The wish for riddance refers to the matters that most preoccupy the child, which depend on his libidinal developmental phase. Miller observes that disgust almost always arises in association with the idea of contact with the disturbing substance and that digestive images are almost always appropriate. Disgust includes the idea of something bad at some distance, tasting bad in the mouth, or feeling bad in the stomach. The affect of disgust is usually accompanied by an actual or anticipated unpleasant skin sensation, which is described as a response to something slimy, sticky, or mucky, and is more rarely associated simply with ideas or visual images. The mode of expression in disgust is always oral and extrusive, but this is not to say that its origin is an oral experience. The central feeling always seems to involve the stomach, though sometimes there is an image of pushing something away with the arms or hands. More often, the image is of spitting out or vomiting.

Miller describes several psychological functions of disgust: it separates the self and non-self, the inside and outside, and the good and the bad. By way of spitting out or vomiting, one can put the bad outside, thus producing a self that is purified and undisturbed. Contempt and anger may serve a similar function. Disgust can serve the purpose of reaction formation, as in opposing genital excitement; Miller's clinical experience is that this is the most common function of disgust—an observation not confirmed by the analyst author of this chapter. Disgust may also be used to repudiate oral wishes and to repudiate narcissistic injury at the hands of others, in combination with angry attack and blaming that is supported by projection. The global nature of the disgust response serves to diminish distinction so that the individual elements of an experience are lost either defensively or coincidentally.

Juni (1984) explored disgust using Rorschach methods. Using the hypothesis that disgust is a derivative of the anal stage of psychosexual development through the mechanism of reaction formation and is used to counter libidinal fixations, she posited that disgust would correlate with the intensity of specific libidinal fixation and that disgustedness, as a character trait, would correlate in general with anal compulsive character. Using 34 male and 23 female undergraduates, she employed a self-administered Rorschach that yielded fixation indices of orality, anality, and sadism. The same subjects rated the disgustingness of a variety of activities. The first hypothesis was found to be untestable because of the high intercorrelation of all disgust reactions, but the second hypothesis was supported.

Disgust and Disorganization

The stimuli that produce disgust, whether they are thought of as primary stimuli (disgusting tastes or excrement) or as secondary generalizations of those primary stimuli, share the feature of being disorganized. Could disorganization be their chief quality? Or is the distaste for what is disorganized virtually always based on the unconscious association between such things and the primary stimuli that produce disgust?

Clinical findings might distinguish between these two possibilities, for example, by demonstrating that disgust appears earlier than anal concerns or by examining associations to disgust-provoking stimuli to determine whether disorganized content or specifically anal matters appear in the associations. Disgust is a response not only to decaying or deteriorated materials but also to novelty that the individual cannot readily integrate. In this sense, it may be regarded as the opposite of a feeling of interest.[3] However, disgust is commonly associated with fascination. Horror movies, for example, clearly stimulate great interest in objects that elicit revulsion and disgust. The viewer experiences tension between his fascination in looking and a wish to turn away. Typically, what is horrible is slimy, moist, decaying, disordered, and disorganized. The disgusting object is often terrifying not so much because it represents mortal danger but because it threatens the person with the state of being dirtied, soiled, or contaminated. In the movie *Ghostbusters* the specific danger from most of the ghosts is of being "slimed." This highly undesirable state is not further characterized by any other specific harm or danger. The feature of the disgusting object that is evidenced by this humorous derivative is repeated in many horror movies, where something similar to being "slimed" is the primary danger. Furthermore, the interest in looking at what is disgusting, a motive accounting for the popularity of the horror film genre, suggests a need to become acclimated to that which is disgusting. When people become acclimated to what is disgusting, it is often by virtue of putting the object of disgust into some reasonable order or context, an act that, once done, eliminates the sense of disgust.

The idea that disgust is principally a signal of disorganization can be supported by many aspects of the phenomenology of disgust. In children, disgust at food does not refer to the anticipation that the food will taste bad or to the judgment that it is spoiled but to the perception that it is in

---

[3]We can observe disgusted responses to novelty in high-level intellectual life (often combined with contempt), although these responses are invariably explained on the basis of the qualities of the object of disgust. Much of the negative response to deconstructionism involves strong elements of disgust that arise in the context of feeling seduced into interest in material that appears brilliant but then seems, to the dissatisfied reader, both empty and chaotic (Lehman, 1991). Similarly, the biochemist Chargaff (1978) describes a disgusted response he experienced to developments in molecular biology that he perceived as spoiling the beauty of his own quantitative biochemical investigations.

some sense disorganized, chaotic, or messy. Though this reaction could be seen as a generalization of anal concerns, it can also be understood as a regulator of early behavior.

The phenomenology of disgust is indeed characterized by images of oral expulsion. Repugnant ideas or abstract entities commonly bring forth metaphors of making people vomit or wish to spit them out. The expelled thing is then the object of loathing and hatred. There is often anger that what was expelled was once part of the individual. Sometimes the disgusting thing, once "ingested," cannot be spat out or removed, in which case self-disgust is not uncommon. Tactile disgust seems to differ phenomenologically from oral disgust. It is commonly elicited by body substances or, more rarely, body parts that are no longer part of the body. In the movie *Blue Velvet,* for example, the image of a detached ear with ants crawling on it is intended to be vividly disgusting; more typically, feces, urine, blood, dribble, nasal mucus, and semen are regarded as disgusting. According to Miller (1986), "one must vigorously say, 'This is not me,'" (p. 305) that is, "This is disgusting," in order to exclude the nonfunctional and damaged thing or substance from the concept of the self.

Disgust in Hebrew Scripture

Hebrew Scripture seems to offer significant support for the view that disgust is a primary emotional response to potential ingestion of spoiled or bad-tasting substances but does not seem to offer support for the view that disgust is a typical reaction against the wish to be involved with excrement. In stark contrast to the scores of references to disgust as a primary emotional response to potential ingestion of spoiled or bad-tasting substances, the entire 24 books of Hebrew Scripture offer only three references to feces as an object provoking disgust, each in an unusual context. While Hebrew Scripture suggests that semen, menstrual blood, and abnormal (disease-related) discharge from the male or female genitals are disgusting, it never suggests that normal vaginal mucus is disgusting. Hebrew Scripture forbids human consumption of blood, but it is understandable that it does not label blood (other than menstrual blood) by any of the terms that seem to refer to disgust: after all, blood of sacrificial animals was fed, as it were, to God on the altar of Israel's ancient sanctuaries.

Terms for disgust are also used in Hebrew Scripture to refer to matters not directly related to ingestion. These uses often refer to a wish to be rid of situations, actions, or things, but chaos or disorganization are not

particularly prominent features of the objects of disgust. Let us look at
references to disgust in detail.

VERBS AND VERBAL IDIOMS WHOSE SEMANTIC DEVELOPMENTS PARALLEL
THE ONTOGENY OF DISGUST

The term for disgust in Hebrew from the first centuries of the Christian
era until now is the participle *mi'us*.[4] This participle is derived from the
verb *ma'as*, "to reject," which is employed in Isa. 7 with reference to a
newly weaned child's rejection of bad-tasting food. The infant's rejection
of bad-tasting food, it should be recalled, is associated with the characteristic facial expression of disgust (Rozin and Fallon, 1987). The famous
passage in Isaiah (8th century B.C.E.) reads as follows:

> Therefore the LORD Himself will give you a sign. Look, the young
> woman is pregnant, and she is about to give birth to a son. She will
> name him Immanuel. He will eat yogurt and date honey when he has
> learned to reject sour [food] and choose sweet [food]. Indeed, before
> the lad will learn to reject sour and choose sweet the land whose two
> kings you dread *[qaṣ]* will have been abandoned [Isa. 7:14–16].

It is quite possible that the use of the verb *qaṣ*, whose primary meaning
is "to be disgusted (with food)," may represent a deliberate play on words.
In any case, the verb is one of a group of verbs employed in Biblical
Hebrew whose primary meaning is "to be disgusted (with spoiled food)"
and whose extended meanings are (1) "to be disgusted with/reject
(persons, objects, behavior)" and (2) "to dread." It should be noted that
this semantic development corresponds to three phases in the ontogeny of
the emotion of disgust.

The primary meaning of the verb *qas* is illustrated in Num. 25:5,
wenaphshenu qaṣah ballehem haqqeloqel, "our throat is disgusted by this very
spoiled food." In the following six cases the verb *qaṣ* appears to refer to
secondary disgust for objects other than food:

> I am disgusted with my life because of the Hittite women. If Jacob
> marries a Hittite woman like these, from among the native women,
> what good will life be to me? [Gen. 27:46]

> They were disgusted with the Israelites [Exod. 1:12; cf. the classic
> commentary of Rashi, 1040–1105].

---

[4]Transliteration of Semitic Languages: ` = aleph; ' = ayin; ṣ = ṣade; ṭ = ṭet; sh =
shin; ḥ = ḥet.

It is because they did all these things [forbidden forms of sexuality, which, according to Lev. 20:22, make the very land of Israel vomit] that I was disgusted with them [Lev. 20:23].

He [Rezon] was disgusted with [Aram's being subject to the hegemony of] Israel, and he became king of Aram [1 Kings 11:25].

Do not reject [tim'as; a form of the verb ma'as, discussed earlier] the discipline of the LORD; do not be disgusted by His rebuke [Prov. 3:11].

In addition to Isa. 7:14–16, one other verse, Num. 22:3, seems to attest to the use of the verb qaṣ in the tertiary meaning, "to dread": there we read, "Moab dreaded the Israelites."

The secondary meaning, "to be disgusted (with persons)" is assigned to the cognate qaṭ, which probably entered Hebrew from Aramaic in the 6th century B.C.E. or later, in the following five texts:

They shall be disgusted with themselves because of all the evil they did with respect to all their abominations [Ezek. 6:9].

You will be disgusted with yourselves because of all your evils which you have done [Ezek. 20:43].

You will be disgusted with yourselves because of all your iniquities and your abominations [Ezek. 36:31].

Forty years I was disgusted [ʾaquṭ] with that generation [Ps. 95:10].

My throat [naphshi] is disgusted with my life [Job 10:1].

The same semantic development that we observed with respect to the Biblical Hebrew verb qaṣ, "to be disgusted" seems to be shown even more clearly with respect to the anatomical expression ga'alah nephesh. This expression, it should be noted, has long been treated as the semantic equivalent of qaṭ (Mandelkern, 1896, p. 1018). The primary meaning of the verb ga'al is "to abandon, spill, drop." This meaning is reflected in 2 Sam. 1:21b, which is universally recognized as one of the oldest lines in Hebrew Scripture, dating from c. 1000 B.C.E. It is as an extension of the primary sense of "to abandon, spill, drop" that the verb is employed in the causative form yag'il in Job 21:10: "His bull impregnates, and he [the bull] does not let it [his semen] spill out; his cow calves, and she does not miscarry."

In five of its remaining nine occurrences the verb ga'al, "to abandon, spill, drop," is the predicate of the noun nephesh, whose primary meaning is "throat, gullet" (Dürr). In each of these five cases the literal meaning of ga'alah nephesh is "gullet expels, discharges; vomit," and it refers metaphorically either to God's rejection or (with the negative particle) nonrejection of Israel (Lev. 26:11, 30; Jer. 14:19) or to Israel's rejection of God's laws (Lev. 26:15, 43). In four out of five of these instances (the exception is Lev. 26:30) the expression *ga'alah nephesh* (literally, "the throat expels") appears as the poetic synonym of the verb *ma'as*, "reject," which, as we have seen, is employed in Isa. 7:15 to refer to the newly weaned child's spitting out of sour food.

In only one place in the Hebrew Bible (Ezek. 16:5) is there the nominal expression *go'al naphshek*, "your disgusting state" *(Tanakh),*[5] literally, "vomit of the gullet." The latter expression is used in Ezek. 16 to refer to the image of an abandoned newborn girl "kicking helpless in her own blood" (cf. New English Bible, 1970).

An extension of the primary sense of the expression *ga'alah nephesh*, "vomit, reject," and *go'al nephesh*, "disgusting state," is the use of the verb *ga'al*, appearing once in Lev. 26:44 and twice in Ezek. 16:45. As we have seen in 2 Sam. 1:21b and in Job 21:10, the verb *ga'al* is employed in its original and neutral sense, "abandon, spill, drop." In other instances examined earlier the verbal root is used with the noun *nephesh*, "throat, gullet," to refer to vomiting either as a primary response to the sight of an unwashed newborn wallowing in her own blood (Ezek. 16:5) or meta-phorically to refer to rejection of God's laws by Israel or of God's consequent rejection of Israel. A clear extension of the metaphoric usage is the use of the verb *ga'al* without the noun *nephesh* to mean 'reject' in Lev. 26:44 and in Ezek. 16:45 (twice). Even in these passages, however, the verb is not far removed from its primary, concrete sense. In Lev. 26:44 it is employed in juxtaposition with *ma'as*, "reject, spit out" while in Ezek. 16 it is juxtaposed with *go'al naphshek*, "your disgusting (vomitous) state."

It is universally agreed that the verb *ga'al* II (to be distinguished from *ga'al* I, which means "redeem"), which appears primarily in late Biblical texts composed after the destruction of Solomon's Temple in 586 B.C.E., is a late development from the previously discussed verb *ga'al* (see Brown, Driver, and Briggs, 1952, p. 146a). The verb *ga'al* II is found in the Hebrew Bible twelve times (not counting the problematic Job 3:1, about which see the various commentaries). The primary meaning of *ga'al* II is "to be disgusting," and it refers to spoiled food unfit for sacrifice (see Mal. 1:7, 12). Secondarily, a participial form *nig'alah*, "sullied," is applied to disobedient Jerusalem in Zeph. 1:8. According to Dan. 1:8, nonkosher food is to be avoided lest it result in contamination; the latter idea is expressed by the reflexive form of the verb *ga'al* II. By extension, the verb *ga'al* II is employed in a special conjugation in Isa.

---

[5]For another interpretation of the expression, see Greenberg, 1987, p. 275.

59:3 and Lam. 4:14 (see Gesenius, 1910, #51h) and in the causative conjugation in Isa. 63:3 to mean "to be soiled, stained" (with blood; i.e., the guilt of homicide).

Just as ga'al, which is most frequently employed in expressions referring to disgust, is also employed to mean simply "reject," so too is ga'al II so employed in very late texts (Ezra 2:62; Neh. 7:64; 13:26). Ezra 2:62 is typical: "These people searched for their genealogical records, but they could not be found, and so they were rejected from the priesthood."

The Verb and Noun "Vomit" and the Ontogeny of Disgust

The verb qa'ah, "vomit," is found nine times in the Hebrew Bible. In one instance the verb refers to vomiting as a consequence of drunkenness (Jer. 25:27), as do three (Isa. 19:14, 28:8; Jer. 48:26) out of the four occurrences of the noun qi', "vomit." (The fourth, Prov. 26:11, is a simile referring to the observed fact that dogs may eat their own vomit.) In two cases (Prov. 26:16; Job 20:15) the verb refers to vomiting as a consequence of overeating. The great fish is said to have vomited up Jonah at the end of three days in response to a divine command. (Jon. 2:11). In one case (Prov. 23:8) vomiting, an expression of physical disgust, is said to be the proper treatment of food served by the stingy. Although a common cause of nausea and vomiting among humans is morning sickness in pregnancy, reference to this phenomenon is conspicuously absent from Hebrew Scripture.

The remaining four instances of the verb qa'ah, "vomit," all seem to refer to disgust as a reaction against wishes (a) to engage in forbidden forms of sexuality (bestiality, homosexuality, incest, sexual relations during menses) or (b) not to be bound by the Mosaic Law. The disgust in question is attributed to the land of Israel, which is said to have vomited out the aboriginal Canaanites who preceded the arrival of the Israelites in the late 13th century B.C.E. under the leadership of Joshua. Moreover, the Israelites are warned that should they, like the Canaanites, engage in the aforementioned forbidden forms of sexuality, they too will be vomited out by the land. The three instances are as follows:

> Thus [i.e., by the inhabitants engaging in forbidden forms of sexuality] the land became defiled; and I called it to account for its iniquity, and the land *vomited* out its inhabitants [Lev. 18:25].

> So let the land not *vomit* you out for defiling it as it *vomited* out the nation that came before you [Lev. 18:28].

> You shall faithfully observe all My laws and all My regulations, lest the land to which I bring you to settle in *vomit* you out [Lev. 20:22].

The Root ṭ (To Be Unclean) as an Expression
Referring to Disgust

Virtually all the occurrences of the verbal root *ṭmʾ*, "to be (ritually) defiled, unclean" are found in Lev. 11–15; and Num. 19. In those two contexts the verbal root in question and its nominal and adjectival derivatives refer to flesh of animals, the ingestion of which is forbidden (Lev. 11), human corpses (Num. 19), semen (Lev. 15:16–18), menstrual blood (Lev. 15:19–24), abnormal discharges from the penis or vagina (Lev. 15:2–15, 25–30), and conditions of the skin, garments, and dwellings, which Lev. 13–14 designate collectively as *ṣaraʿat*, which is traditionally translated "leprosy."[6] Numerous other passages in Hebrew Scripture refer to these primary sources of *ṭumʿah*, which, probably not coincidentally, are universally disgust objects (on these, see Rozin and Fallon, 1987, pp. 27–29). In addition, Lev. 18:20, 23, 25, 27 refer to forbidden forms of sexuality (which are also labeled as causing the land to vomit in Lev. 18) as sources of *ṭumʿah*, "disgust." This latter usage is reflected also in Num. 5:13, 14, 20, 27, 28, 29, where "to defile herself" means "to commit adultery," and in Ezek. 18:6, 11, 15; 33:26, where "defile (someone)" means "commit adultery (with someone)," and in Ezek. 22:11, where "defile his daughter-in-law" means "commit incest with his daughter-in-law." This same usage is reflected also in Hos. 5:3 and Hos. 6:10, where the verb *niṭmaʿ* "he (the people of the Kingdom of Israel collectively) defiled himself" is employed as a poetic synonym for *zanah*, "fornicate." The use of the verbal root *ṭmʾ*, whose primary signification seems to be "to be disgusting," to refer to forbidden sexual relations seems to exemplify disgust as a reaction against various forms of forbidden sexuality. Two further extensions of this latter phenomenon exemplified in the Hebrew Bible are (1) the designation of forbidden forms of religion as sources of contamination *(ṭumʿah)* in Lev. 19:31; 20:3 and in Ezek. 22:3–4 and (2) the use of the intensive form of the verb *ṭmʾ* in the sense "to make (her) disgusting by means of forbidden sex" as a metaphor for idolatry (disloyalty to God) in Ezek. 23:13, 17 (3 times), 18. (It should be noted that in the second context, which extends to the end

---

[6]Hulse (1975) has argued that the skin disease designated in Hebrew Scripture by the term *ṣaraʿat* is psoriasis, which provokes disgust because the victim of this noncontagious disease tends to bleed on everything in sight. Like the Hebrew *ṣaraʿat*, the Akkadian term *saharshubbu* has traditionally been rendered "leprosy." Recently, however, Adamson (1988), independently of Hulse, suggested that the Akkadian term also should be rendered "psoriasis." Meier (1989) points out that while Biblical Hebrew uses the single term *ṣaraʿat* to designate psoriasis and fungal infections of houses and clothing, Akkadian uses distinct terms: *saharshubbu* to refer to the skin condition, *katarru* and *kamūnu* to refer to the infections on the wall or door of a house.

of Ezek. 23 and therefore includes Ezek. 23:28, there are found all five of the instances of the expression *naqa'ah nephesh,* which corresponds semantically to *ga'alah nephesh* and means "gullet rejects.")

A further extension of the idea that forbidden sex, forbidden religion, and forbidden behavior in general (Ps. 106:39) is disgusting and therefore contaminating is the use of the intensive form of the verb *ṭm'* to refer to (1) Israel's contaminating God's sanctuary by virtue of its misbehavior (Jer 7:30, 32:34; Ezek. 5:11; 2 Chron. 36:14) and, by extension, to (2) the desanctification of illicit sanctuaries (2 Kings 23:8, 10, 13, 16, twice) and of illicit objects of worship (Isa. 30:22):

> You will treat as disgusting *[we ṭimme'tem]* the silver overlay of your images and the golden plating of your idols. You will keep them away like a menstruous woman. 'Out!' you will call to them. [Isa. 30:22]

Interestingly, here the extended use of the verb *ṭm'* to denote "to desecrate" is juxtaposed with a simile "like a menstruous woman," which is clearly meant to evoke the primary sense of disgust.

Piggul

The noun *piggul,* "an offensive thing," is found four times in the Hebrew Bible. In Lev. 7:18 and Lev. 19:7 it appears to have its primary meaning of "meat that is disgusting because it has begun to decay," (see Greenberg, 1987, p. 107); and it designates as forbidden "the flesh of a peace offering eaten on the third day [after slaughter]." In Isa. 65:4b there is condemnation of "those who eat the flesh of swine//with broth of unclean things *[piggulim]* in their bowels." The fourth occurrence of the noun *piggul* is in Ezek. 4:14, where the prophet Ezekiel protests against the divine command that he eat bread which has been roasted over human dung. It is generally acknowledged that the substitution of human feces for animal dung, which was commonly used as fuel, is meant to provoke disgust (see commentaries of Wevers (1969) and Zimmerli, 1979). It is explained in Ezek. 4:13, that this is meant to serve as an analogy of the experience of *ṭum'ah* 'uncleanness', which is the state in which all food is consumed outside of the Holy Land (for the idea that all lands outside of Israel are 'unclean' see also Hos. 9:3; Am. 7:17).

The several usages of the rare noun *piggul* all point to the equation of the unclean by divine prohibition with that which is disgusting because it is "spoiled animal matter" (see Rozin and Fallon, 1987, p. 28).

Sheqeṣ

Another term for disgust, whose primary meaning is "distasteful object," is *sheqeṣ.*

The Hebrew noun *sheqeṣ* is found ten times in the Hebrew Bible. Lev. 7:21, Isa. 66:17, and Ezek. 8:10 support the view that *sheqes* designates a bird or aquatic creature, which it is forbidden to eat (see Paran, 1987, p. 47); hence, the term "unclean *sheqeṣ* " is juxtaposed with "unclean animal" in Lev. 7:21 while it is juxtaposed with pig and mouse in Isa. 66:17. Likewise, in Lev. 11 the same term is applied repeatedly to forbidden aquatic creatures (vv. 10–12), forbidden birds (13), and to most other swarming creatures and land animals (vv. 41–42). The use of a single term, *sheqeṣ,* "abomination" (so *Tanakh* at Lev. 11:40–41), to refer to the flesh of most fauna supports the view that "all animals or animal products are potentially disgusting" and that "nondisgusting animals and animal products in any culture" are "exceptions to the rule" (Rozin and Fallon, 1987, p. 28).

The development from the noun *sheqeṣ* of a denominative verb *shiqqeṣ* , "to abominate" (Lev. 11:11, 13, 43; 20:25; Deut. 7:26; Ps. 22:25) and of the derived participle *shiqquṣ* "abomination' to refer both to forbidden objects of worship (1 Kgs. 11:5, 7; 2 Kgs. 23:24; etc.) and to abominable behavior in general (Ezek. 5:11, 11:18; etc.) lends credence to the contention that the verbal root *ṭmʿ* semantically developed from a verbal root designating distasteful comestibles to a verb meaning 'abominate, desanctify, desecrate.'

References to Feces in Hebrew Scripture

Hebrew Scripture employs three terms that may designate feces. These are *ṣeʾah ṣoʾah* and *haraʿ.* The first of these terms is found only twice — once in Ezek. 4:12, to the context of which reference has been made previously in our discussion of *piggul* above — and a second time in Deut. 23:14–15. The second of these terms is found three times — in Isa. 4:14 and 28:8; and Prov. 30:12. In the first and last of these occurrences the term *ṣoʾah,* which replaced *ṣeʾah* and *haraʿ* as the common term for excrement in post-Biblical Hebrew, clearly denotes metaphoric "filth," that is, "guilt," just as Akkadian *qātu* often designates the metaphoric hand as opposed to the anatomical hand, which is called *rettu,* and just as Biblical Hebrew *shod* designates the metaphoric breast as opposed to the anatomical breast, which is called *shad* (see Gruber, 1989). Hence, in Isa. 28:8, it has been pointed out (Luzzatto, pp. 319, 409), *qi ʾṣoʾah* means "filthy vomit" and not "vomit (and) excrement."

The only attestation of *ṣoʾah* in the sense 'excrement' in Hebrew Scripture is in the marginal reading *(qere)* at 2 Kgs. 18:18 = Isa. 36:12. In this text a high official of the Assyrian King Sennacherib urges the people of Jerusalem to capitulate at once lest during the protracted siege of the city they be reduced to eating excrement and drinking urine. The consonantal text employs the terms *shenehem* and *harehem* which are otherwise unattested in Biblical Hebrew, to designate respectively 'their urine' and 'their excrement.' It should be pointed out that this verse points not to a fascination with excrement on the part of the Assyrian official or his Israelite audience but to the realities of life in a city under military siege (see also Montgomery, 1951, pp. 489, 385). It has been noted that the marginal euphemistic reading *(qere)* substitutes not for the normal late Hebrew *me rasleyhem*, "their urine," but for the anomalous *meymey rasleyhem*, literally, "the drinking water of their legs" (Luzzatto, 1867, p. 409). In light of this observation, it is reasonable to suggest that the marginal euphemistic reading *ṣo'atam* was deliberately chosen because in Biblical Hebrew it can only mean "filth" (usually metaphoric) while *ṣe'atam* can only mean "their excrement."

Thus we see that there is not a shred of evidence in the Hebrew Bible that disgust is a reaction formation against the wish to be involved with excrement whereas there is abundant evidence in Hebrew Scripture for the thesis that disgust may represent a reaction formation against both a wish to eat what is forbidden and a wish to engage in various forms of forbidden sexuality.

Since it has been abundantly demonstrated that ancient Israel was primarily a rural society, (see, e.g., Shiloh, 1980 p. 30) it is reasonable to suggest that the limited references to feces in general as an object of disgust may derive from the fact that in rural life feces of domesticated animals are a part of everyday life and disposal of human feces is not especially problematic. In urban society, on the other hand, the feces of domesticated animals are much less taken for granted and the disposal of human feces is a major endeavor. The disposal of human feces in the military camp is likewise a major problem; this is addressed in Deut. 23:14–15.

DISGUST AS A REACTION FORMATION AGAINST THE DESIRE TO ENGAGE IN FORBIDDEN FORMS OF SEXUALITY

Aside from the designation of forbidden comestibles and forbidden sexual relations as sources of *ṭum'ah*, "defilement," Hebrew Scripture uses three terms whose primary meaning seems to be "disgust" in the etymological sense of "bad taste," almost exclusively to refer to forbidden forms of sexuality. These terms are *tebel*, "perversion"; *ḥesed* II, "disgrace"; and *zimmah*, "depravity, wantonness."

The noun *tebel*, a word of uncertain etymology, is used only twice in the entire Hebrew Bible, in Lev. 18:23 and 20:12, which read as follows, respectively:

You [masculine singular] should not have intercourse with any beast so as not to become disgusting *[leṭame'ah]* through it; and let no woman allow a beast to mate with her; it is *tebel*.

If a man has intercourse with his daughter-in-law, they shall both be put to death; they have done *tebel;* their blood is upon them.

To many persons in both modern times and antiquity the activities here designated by the term *tebel,* clearly a term of opprobrium, constitute matters of lifestyle rather than crimes. The use of a special term of opprobrium in Lev. 18:23 and 20:12 for both bestiality and sexual relations between father-in-law and daughter-in-law suggests a reaction on the part of the Torah against a widespread desire to engage in those forms of sexuality.

Another rare term for disgust is *ḥesed,* "disgrace," which is found in Hebrew Scripture only in Lev. 20:17 and Job 6:14[7] and which is a homonym of the frequent noun *ḥesed* meaning "loyalty, kindness." The label *ḥesed,* "disgrace," in Lev. 20:17, like the label *tebel* in Lev. 18:23 and 20:12, suggests that here again we have an example of disgust as a reaction formation against a widespread desire to engage in incest. Lev. 20:17 reads as follows:

If a man marries his sister, the daughter of either his father or his mother so that they have sex with each other, it is *ḥesed;* they shall be publicly banished; he had sex with his sister; he shall bear his guilt.

Found nine times in Hebrew Scripture—three times in Leviticus (Lev. 18:17, 19:29, 20:14), four times in Ezekiel (Ezek. 16:27; 22:9, 23:48, 24:13); and once in Judges (Judg. 20:6)—the Hebrew noun *zimmah,* "depravity, wantonness," like the less frequently attested *tebel,* is a term of opprobrium applied to forbidden forms of sexuality, namely, incest (Lev. 18:17, 20:14; Ezek. 22:9, 11), gang rape (Judg. 20:6), and prostitution (Lev. 19:29), as well as adultery, which is employed as a metaphor for idolatry (the people of Israel are conceived of as the collective wife of God whose disloyalty is compared by the Prophets Hosea, Jeremiah, and Ezekiel to a married woman's cheating on her husband [Ezek. 16:17, 23:48, 24:13]). The noun *zimmah,* like the noun *tebel,* seems to refer to disgust as a reaction against a widespread desire to engage in forbidden forms of sexuality.

---

[7]The cognate verb meaning "to treat with contempt" is attested in Prov. 25:10, while the same noun is frequently attested in the sense "disgrace, abomination" in Aramaic, which is a Semitic language closely related to Hebrew.

TO'EBAH 'ABOMINATION'

In recent years a number of scholars have pointed out that the Hebrew *to'ebah,* "abomination," refers primarily to "disgust" in the latter's etymological meaning "distaste" and that Hebrew *to'ebah* 'abomination' corresponds semantically to the Akkadian[8] *ikkibu* (Hallo, 1985; Toorn, 1985, p. 43; Klein and Sephati, 1988). The latter form of *to'ebah,* it has been pointed out, is employed most frequently as the object of either the verb *epēshu,* "to do," or the verb *akālu,* "to eat" (Toorn, 1985, p. 43). That is to say, the semantic development of the Hebrew term *to'ebah,* "abomination," and of its semantic equivalent in Akkadian also points to the development in human culture of disgust as a reaction formation to forbidden food, forbidden sex, forbidden social behavior, and forbidden religion out of a primary response of the infant to bad-tasting food.

Conclusion

The comparison of grand interpretive strategies is always difficult, and choosing between them on a basis of anything beyond personal preference is almost impossible. The questions of whether abstract configuration observable in texts and patient's associations is best reduced to biologically based concerns or best understood as a manifestation of primary abstract mental configurations and whether concrete thought is best understood as an instantiation of abstract configuration seem to remain unanswered on more solid grounds. Both produce interesting and enriching interpretations that are sometimes moving and sometimes therapeutic.

In the course of studying a particular psychological phenomenon, disgust, it became apparent that interpretive approaches from either side had much to recommend them. On the basis of clinical investigation the approach that favored an abstract mental configuration seemed more convincing, and a hypothesis was framed that disgust would be found in other contexts to be an expression of this abstract configuration. The hypothesis was tested on the Hebrew Scripture and found to be wrong. Not only that, the use of terms for disgust were consistently found to refer directly to oral distaste or to be clearly and closely connected etymologically with such terms. Even the generalization that associates disgust with excrement was weak.

Obviously, this quasi-experiment does not definitively answer the broad question of interpretative strategy. The quasi-experiment itself has

---

[8]The major Semitic language of ancient Iraq, which was recorded on clay tablets from the middle of the 3d millennium B.C.E. until the beginning of the Christian era.

difficulties because of the general concreteness of the text studied. However, there are innumerable places in the Hebrew Scripture where opportunities to describe abstract ideas in terms of disgust are available. This never happens. Thus, the data strongly disconfirm the hypothesis of disgust as a general response to chaos and disorder, and support the hypothesis that disgust is a specific, but generalizable, response to spoiled and bad-tasting food. They are consistent with the concept of the reduction of abstract responses to concrete bodily experience and inconsistent with the idea of abstraction as primary.

References

Adamson, P. B. (1968), Infective and allergic conditions in Ancient mesopotamia. *Revue d'assyriologie et d'archéologie orientale,* 82:163–171.

Breuer, J. & Freud, S. (1893–1895), *Studies on Hysteria. Standard Edition.* London: Hogarth Press, 1955.

Brown, F., Driver, S. & Briggs, C. (1952), *A Hebrew and English Lexicon of the Old Testament* (corrected impression). Oxford: Clarendon Press.

Chargaff, E. (1978), *Heraclitean Fire.* New York: Rockefeller University.

DeRivera, J. (1977), *A Structural Theory of Emotions.* New York: International Universities Press.

Douglas, M. (1966), *Purity and Danger.* London: Routledge & Kegan Paul.

Dürr, L. (1925), Hebr. nephesh = akk. napishtu = Gurgel, Kehle. *Zeitschrift für die altestamentliche Wissenschaft,* 43:163–171.

Ekman, P. (1975), *Unmasking the Face.* Englewood Cliffs, NJ: Prentice-Hall.

Engel, G. (1963), Toward a classification of affects. In: *Expression of the Emotions in Man,* ed. P. Knopp. New York: International Universities Press, pp. 195–229.

Freud, S. (1900/1901), The interpretation of dreams. *Standard Edition,* 4 & 5. London: Hogarth Press, 1953.

_____ (1901), The psychopathology of everyday life. *Standard Edition,* 6. London: Hogarth Press, 1960.

_____ (1905), Three essays on the theory of sexuality. *Standard Edition,* 7:135–243. London: Hogarth Press, 1953.

_____ (1926), The question of lay analysis. *Standard Edition,* 20:183–250. London: Hogarth Press, 1959.

_____ (1940), An outline of psychoanalysis. *Standard Edition,* 23:144–208. London: Hogarth Press, 1964.

Galatzer-Levy, R. & Cohler, B. (1990), The developmental psychology of the self: A new worldview in psychoanalysis. *The Annual of Psychoanalysis,* 18:1–43. Hillsdale, NJ: The Analytic Press.

Gendlin, E. (1962), *Experiencing the Creation of Memory.* New York: Free Press of Glencoe.

Gesenius, W. (1910), *Hebrew Grammar* (ed. & enlarged by E. Kautzsch; 2nd Eng. ed. revised by A. E. Cowley). Oxford: Clarendon Press.

Goldberg, A. (1978), *The Psychology of the Self.* New York: International Universities Press.

_____ (1989), A shared view of the world. *Internat. J. Psycho-Anal,* 70:16–20.

Goldstein, K. (1951), On emotion: Considerations from the organismic point of view. *J. Psychol.,* 31:37–49.

Greenberg, M. (1987), *Anchor Bible, Ezekiel 1-20: (Vol. 22)*. Garden City, NY: Doubleday.

Gruber, M. (1990), Breast-feeding practices in biblical Israel and in Old Babylonian Mesopotamia. *Ancient Near Eastern Society,* 19:61-83.

Hallo, W. (1985), Biblical abominations and Sumerian taboos. *Jewish Quarterly Review,* 76:21-40.

Hulse, E. V. (1975), The nature of biblical "Leprosy" and the use of alternative terms in modern translations of the Bible. *Palestine Exploration Quarterly, 107:* 87-105.

Izard, C. (1971), *The Face of Emotion.* New York: Appleton Century Crofts.

_____ (1978), Emotion as motivations: An evolutionary developmental perspective. *1978 Nebraska Symposium on Motivation,* ed. R. Dienstbier. Lincoln/London: University of Nebraska Press, pp. 163-200.

Jacobson, E. (1964), *The Self and the Object World.* New York: International Universities Press.

Jung, C. (1956), *Symbols and Transformation.* Princeton: Princeton University Press.

Juni, S. (1984), The psychodynamics of disgust. *J. Genetic Psychol.,* 144:203-208.

Kagan, J. (1981), *The Second Year.* Cambridge, MA: Harvard University Press.

Klass, D. & Offenkrantz, W. (1976), Sartre's contribution to the understanding of narcissism. *Internat. J. Psychoanal. Psychother.,* 5:547-565.

Klein, J. & Sephati, Y. (1988), The concept of abomination in the Bible. *Beer Sheva,* 3:131-146 (in Hebrew).

Kohut, H. (1971), *The Analysis of the Self.* New York: International Universities Press.

_____ (1976), Creativeness, charisma and group psychology. In: *The Search for the Self, Vol. 2.* New York: International Universities Press.

_____ (1978), *The Search for the Self,* ed. P. Ornstein. New York: International Universities Press.

_____ (1984), *How Does Analysis Cure?* ed. A. Goldberg & P. E. Stepansky. Chicago, IL: University of Chicago Press.

Lehman, D. (1991), *Signs of the Times.* New York: Poseidon.

Lévi-Strauss, C. (1963), *Structural Anthropology.* New York: Basic Books.

Lichtenberg, J. D. (1989), *Psychoanalysis and Motivation.* Hillsdale, NJ: The Analytic Press.

Luzzatto, S. (1867), *Il Profeta Isaia.* Padua: Bianchi.

Mandelkern, S. (1896), *Veteris Testamenti Confordantiae.* Leipzig: Veit et Comp.

Masling, J. (1983), *Empirical Studies of Psychoanalytic Theories, Vol. 1.* Hillsdale, NJ: The Analytic Press.

_____ (1986), *Empirical Studies of Psychoanalytic Theories, Vol. 2.* Hillsdale, NJ: The Analytic Press.

Meier, S. (1989), House fungus: Mesopotamia and Israel (Lev. 14:33-53). *Revue Biblique,* 96:184-192.

Miller, S. B. (1986), Disgust: conceptualization, development and dynamics. *Internat. Rev. Psycho-Anal.,* 13:295-307.

Montgomery, J. A. (1951), *A Critical and Exegetical Commentary on the Books of Kings,* ed. Henry Snyder Gehman. Edinburgh: T. & T. Clark.

Nagera, H. E. (1966), *Early Childhood Disturbances, the Infantile Neurosis and the Adult Disturbances.* New York: International Universities Press.

Paran, M. (1987), Comment on Lev. 7:21. In: *Encyclopedia Olam Ha-Tanakh: Leviticus* (p. 47), ed. Baruch A. Levine. Ramat-Gan, Israel: Revivim (in Hebrew).

Piaget, J. (1970), *Structuralism.* New York: Basic Books.

Rashi (R. Solomon Isaaki) (1040-1105 C. E.), *Commentary on the Pentateuch,* and Silberman, A. M. (1929-1934). *Pentateuch with Targum Onkelos, Haphtaroth and Rashi's*

Commentary Translated into English and Annotated., ed. M. Rosenbaum & A. M. Silberman. London: Shapiro, Vallentine.

Ricoeur, P. (1970), *Freud and Philosophy.* New Haven, CT: Yale University Press.

_____ (1977), The question of proof in Freud's psychoanalytic writings. *J. Am. Acad. Psychoanal.*, 25:835–871.

_____ (1986), La psychanalyse confrontée à l'epistemologie [Psychoanalysis vis-à-vis epistemology]. *Psychiatrie Française,* 17 (Special issue 11–23).

Rozin, P. & Fallon, A. (1987), A perspective on disgust. *Psychoanal. Rev.,* 9:21–43.

Sartre, J. (1938), *Nausea* (trans. L. Alexander). New York: New Directions, 1964.

Shiloh, V. (1980), The population of Iron Age Palestine in the light of a sample analysis of urban plans, areas, and population density. *Bull. Amer. Schools Oriental Res.,* No. 239, pp. 25–35.

Tanakh: A New Translation of the Holy Scriptures According to the Traditional Hebrew Text. (1985), Philadelphia: Jewish Publication Society.

The New English Bible: The Old Testament (1970), Oxford University Press & Cambridge University Press.

Toorn, K. van der (1985), Sin and sanction in Israel and Mesopotamia: A comparative study. *Studia Semitica Neerlandica.* Assen/Maastricht: Van Gorcum.

Wevers, J. (1969), *Century Bible, New Series: Ezekiel.* London: Nelson.

White, R. (1959), Motivation reconsidered: The concept of competence. *Psychol. Rev.* 66:297–333.

Wolf, E. (1988), *Treating the Self.* New York: Guilford Press.

Zimmerli, W. (1979), *Ezekiel I* (trans. R. Clements). Philadelphia: Fortress.

II

CLINICAL STUDIES

Screen Language and Developmental Metaphor

HENRY F. SMITH

When Freud (1899) concluded in his paper "Screen Memories," "It may indeed be questioned whether we have any memories at all *from* our childhood: memories *relating to* our childhood may be all that we possess" (p. 322, emphasis Freud's), he challenged us to consider the ubiquity of screening phenomena; for if childhood memories do not replicate the original event, in an objective sense, can it be said that any memories do? In this early topographical notion of "screening," Freud anticipated later explorations into the subjectivity of memory by Kris (1956a) and Arlow (1969b) and, more recently, Schafer (1983), Schwaber (1983b), Spence (1982), and Gray (1973), among others (see also Smith, 1988.)

Viewed topographically, all memories can be seen to possess this "screening" characteristic, whereby other memories, fantasies, and conflicts lie behind and are expressed through the manifest content of the memory in question. And if this is so, what limits the term *screening* to the specific function of memory? In 1908 Freud, in fact, spoke of "screen phantasy" (p. 171, n. 2). Fenichel (1927, 1945), Glover (1929), Deutsch (1930), Greenacre (1949), Lewin (1950), Reider (1953), Kris (1956b), and Greenson (1958), among others, have all either added to the list of specific screen phenomena or discussed aspects of the screening process in general, thus broadening the concept. Even if we consider a screen memory to be a unique phenomenon in our work, with a characteristic "ultra clear" quality observed by Freud, and even if screen memory may occupy a "special place in reconstructive work" (Mahon and Battin-Mahon, 1983, p. 476), as Greenacre has suggested, may we not also be talking of some manner in which the mind, at least as seen through the lens of the analytic process, organizes all experience, including fantasy, language, and perception itself?

The theory of screening can be used to describe a general process by which mental content is organized as well as to denote a specific phenomenon, such as a screen memory, much as other psychoanalytic concepts may describe both a process and an entity. We commonly speak of the general process of reconstruction, for example, and also use the term when referring to a specific reconstruction. Similarly, we use the overarching concept of compromise formation as well as focus on specific compromise formations, as Brenner (1982) does in *The Mind in Conflict,* where he describes compromise formation, in effect, as the molecular unit of the mind or psyche; it is the fundamental concept in his general theory of mind.

As topographical theory is the ancestor of structural theory, so screening can be seen as the ancestor of compromise formation. Viewed structurally, a screen memory or other screen phenomenon *is* a compromise formation. Both screening and compromise formation describe the organization of mental content at different levels of abstraction, inference, and complexity. Screening remains closer to the descriptive surface of the observational field of analysis, the surface of the patient's mind, and conveys the unfolding process of analysis: what was once concealed is now revealed. It is, as we shall observe, a characteristic of development that while one phenomenon or one explanatory concept evolves into another, both may still retain their integrity.

When Freud (1899) said he hoped to have "clarified the concept of 'screen memory' as one which owes its value as a memory not to its own content but to the relation existing between that content and some other" (p. 320), he pointed toward a topography of the mind as a series of screens behind which, or in front of which, other screens, representing other pieces of experience, lay hidden. This was his current general theory of mind. But Freud (1901) also used the term *screen memory* to designate certain specific entities noted for their "indifferent and unimportant" (p. 43) appearance, behind which lurked deeper conflictual matters.

From the analysis of one of my patients I would like to describe a particular phenomenon. It is, I believe, specific enough as an entity and yet so illustrative of the general principles just outlined as to be considered an example of "screening" by either criterion. As it involves the use of a particular phrase, and as I have not seen it described before, I propose to call it "screen language." After describing the phenomenon, I shall use it to illustrate certain aspects of the architecture of development.

Screen Language

It began in the fifth month. My patient, a nurse in her early thirties, was describing the anxiety and excitement she felt for a new man in her life. I referred to the image from a recent dream: "You're afraid you'll go hurtling down the mountain without any skis on and it will be very frightening, and no one will be in control." She completed my statement: "And I'll get hurt. Goddam. If I have all these feelings what does it mean to be out of control? Ay-yi-yi [pronounced as in "eye-eye-eye," spoken quickly]."

"Ay-yi-yi" was the phrase in question, an exclamation that appeared so often during the early part of our work it became a kind of cliché, "indifferent and unimportant" in itself, as Freud had indicated, though not, as we were to learn, in what it concealed and revealed, for, like all pieces of mental content, it both concealed and revealed other content. Almost unnoticed at first by both of us, "ay-yi-yi" appeared, like an overused exclamation point in a child's text, to mark moments of transferential intensity, moments when repression was lifting to reveal yet another screen behind the manifest content, moments that punctuated the emergence of a different developmental level of the transference. In this particular instance my patient was beginning anxiously to glimpse her erotic excitement for her friend and for me. Her fall down the mountain seemed to reflect her descent into the erotic transference. "Ay-yi-yi" had an almost orgasmic cadence.

In the eighth month she became more explicit about the transference: "I don't want to get close to you because it might hurt. I have to be perfect so I won't get hurt." Her words were vague; she sensed their inadequacy: "No, that's not it; it's something else — ay-yi-yi." That was the close of the hour. The "something else" was not yet clarified.

But earlier in the same hour she had spoken of details from a period in her life that, in retrospect, was hovering behind the "ay-yi-yi," details that included a remembrance of her sister, B., and signaled the presence of transferences screened behind the erotic: "We used to do all these things together. She was almost a twin. You know that's weird; you're sort of like B. She and I shared a room the whole time growing up." She wished for somebody "all-knowing, all-caring," the way it had been "before my sister was born." Her sister had been born when she was 18 months old. She remembered wanting to be diapered again at the time, and she remembered her rage and anguish: "I wanted to kill her. I almost killed myself. It was okay before she was born." While her mother was in the hospital giving birth, the patient had been sent to a neighbor's house, where she had climbed defiantly onto the railing of a third-floor balcony, so terrifying the neighbor that she had refused ever to baby-sit again. "I wanted to hide my sister's toys . . . I wanted to kill my sister, but back then I didn't have any words . . ." The phrase "I didn't have any words" hung in the air.

For the better part of a year the analysis returned time and again to the concealment and disclosure of childhood sexual fantasy. The patient was driven by curiosity, past and present. Oedipal and preoedipal matters lurked one behind the other, each screening the horrors of the other, both with a life of their own. In the eleventh month the patient concluded an hour with an especially long "ay-yi-yi-yi-yi," adding that she was scared of being hurt but wouldn't say why. Five days later she revealed with embarrassment that she had once thought that the only way to be close to her father was to "make love" to him but that "it would hurt and was wrong." She pictured herself as five years old at the time.

In the fifteenth month she began again, "Ay-yi-yi — I can't do this," and then remembered that when her mother was away giving birth to another sibling, she and her sister B. used to "suck on each other's breasts." Now the birth of another sibling at age five was linked to that of the first at 18 months, with the patient and her sister B., like twins in their mother's absence, each playing mother to the other, and both the first birth and the second were linked associatively in some way to "ay-yi-yi."

Behind her intense erotic fear and excitement for me and for her father, the patient expressed curiosity, longing, and a deep ambivalence toward the mother whose absence she felt so keenly. The agony of these explorations was palpable: "I still love my mother. It's easier to hate her than to love her. . . . Every time I talk about this I feel I'm going to start screaming. I feel like I'm getting burned." And the cry to accompany the flames was, appropriately, "ay-yi-yi." Several weeks later she felt she was being "strangled, choked to death." Suddenly she exclaimed, "I didn't think you could remember something like that" and explained she had just pictured herself as a hungry infant, nursing at the breast and choking, "My mother would push me away. I was overeating — ay-yi-yi — Whenever I wanted anything, I got pushed away." And she remembered at age five or six taking "forever to eat," choking on her food as she tried to swallow it. Again the juxtaposition of the infantile and the oedipal periods, each screened by the other, linked perhaps by the breast-feeding she had witnessed at 18 months and at age five, as well as by her own experiences of hunger and of feeding.

In the 27th month of the analysis and on the day before Thanksgiving, the topic again was food, but the patient's thoughts were erotic. She pictured an earlier Thanksgiving, herself a young child. She wasn't hungry. Instead, she found herself underneath the table, "because it's more fun under the table . . . I can't talk about it." And then, "All this sexual activity under the table — ay-yi-yi." This time I asked her, "Where does 'ay-yi-yi' come from?" She seemed surprised and a bit annoyed by my question: "I used to say that all the time when I was a kid. Haven't you heard that before?" I had, of course, heard it many times from *her* and might, in retrospect, have asked about her irritation at my apparent "stupidity." But for the moment she seemed to say that it was just an "indifferent and unimportant" expression, as Freud had predicted she might. "My sister B. and I used to say it all the time," she continued. And so I asked, "What did it mean?" She answered, "It was an exclamation. We would say it when we were surprised or shocked or excited. So, it was an explanation — ah — an exclamation. It would come up when we were having fun."

I puzzled, silently, over her slip. What sort of "explanation" lay behind this "exclamation"? Something to do with her sister, born when she was 18 months? She spoke next with excitement of her approaching vacation and then of her yearning to settle in one place. She spoke of leaving and then feared I would leave her. Was this movement away and back an echo of that time at 18 months, or earlier perhaps, when she "didn't have words"?

The approaching December holidays, when there would, in fact, be two interruptions — for her vacation and for mine — filled her with dread: "It's scary to be by myself . . . I'd like to see you Saturdays and Sundays . . . I picture a little kid there screaming and crying and covered with shit . . . well, I was four for a while, I might as well be two now." As she talked further she felt "buried beneath shit" and finally declared, "I *was* the shit I produced; going to the bathroom felt good at the same time as it felt shitty — that's why I'm stuck."

Elizabeth Geleerd (1969) reminds us that the "anal-sadistic phase of libidinal development coincides with the subphases of 'practising' and 'rapprochement.' " In the following weeks my patient wrestled with her wish to escape the "death grip" of her mother and her wish to stay "possessed by someone." Interlaced with her terror of being alone was her fury at being held, "stuck in shit," with its explicitly anal imagery of pleasure and anger. Her mood oscillated rapidly between the elation and discouragement that Mahler has so evocatively described in toddlers (Mahler, Pine, and Bergman, 1975).

As the maternal transference deepened, the hours were peppered with intervals of silence. One such day I commented, "You seem to be having more trouble than usual talking today," and she answered, "I don't want to get any closer to you." But she desperately wanted me to say *something:*

"Because I still want to know you're there." The following day she arrived and announced, "I don't want to be here. I want to be able to do what I want to do . . . I'm so mad I'm afraid I'm going to kill somebody." She wrestled with her murderous impulses for about 15 minutes and then she left.

It felt like a toddler's inevitable "darting away" but more desperate, a rapprochement crisis with its anal-period fury and struggle for independent survival. The patient seemed terrified of her sadism and of her regressive longing for maternal union. When she returned the following day, she was more reflective: "You want me to be exactly like you, and I can't stand it." She found me intrusive, she said, "just like my mother. I know half of it isn't real, but I can't stand it." She explained my half of it: "You said I have a lot of trouble talking. I wasn't having trouble. I didn't *want* to talk . . . I want to kill you when you hit that nerve . . . I want to cut you up in little pieces. You really have become like this hostile side of my mother." Thinking back she said, "When I walked out of here I was so mad I didn't have any other way of controlling how mad I was."

When she returned from vacation she was "still mad" and felt "like killing everybody." She was furious at a male friend's withdrawal into depression. She said, "You told me around leavings I get upset . . . I don't know why I feel it so much around leavings." Thinking of her friend, of her mother, and of me, I said, "Leavings, depressions, withdrawals . . ." She asked plaintively, "How are you supposed to tolerate these things? They happen all the time. I get so mad." Picturing her again with her new sister at 18 months, I said, "So mad you could hide her toys, walk off a balcony." She stopped, "Wait a minute. Is that when you're saying it started? I can't deal with that. That's terrible. I can't deal with how angry I am. I'm so angry that if I remember how angry I was I'll be angry forever. I'll just sit and scream and scream and scream." I said, "Little children do that. They sit and scream and scream and scream. Sometimes it seems they could scream forever." And she: "I wanted her to be dead . . . I wanted to kill everything, including I wanted to hurt my mother. And it's so painful, like having a temper tantrum. I feel like I want to go up and kick her crib." She paused and then said quietly, "This is creepy . . . it's like it cuts to the core. So all I'm left with is going to sleep . . . Nobody was around. There wasn't anybody." In the silence of that aloneness I spoke next, "Nothing to do but scream and sleep." And she: "It wouldn't have been so bad if there was somebody there. I didn't have any words." Here again the echo of a time before words. But then: "I wanted to kill her, but they would have killed me for saying that. So not only did I not have any words, but I didn't *want* to have any words."

The echo then was not only to a time before words but also to a wish for a regression in language, to a time before the time when words, like weapons, could kill. Janet believed the earliest words were derived from the cries of animals and savages to attack (Piaget, 1930). I think of the child's catchphrase that articulates the differentiation of word from weapon and the hope of mastering that developmental conflict: "Sticks and stones can break my bones but words can never hurt me."

And then, in that very hour, the regression in language that she had wished for, a regression that was simultaneously an advance, took place. She had performed it many times before, but this time she made it articulate, observed it, and interpreted it: "I just had this picture going ay-yi-yi. It's the same thing I was doing before except it was I—capital I—capital I, and when you do it really fast it comes out ay-yi-yi. So bizarre . . . It gives me the creeps." The hour ended.

Was this then the "explanation" for the "exclamation?" Was this the "language" behind the "screen language"? We seemed together to have reconstructed a moment when, as she perceived it now, she had felt abandoned by her mother at 18 months, and that experience itself seemed to be a screen for the sense of maternal absence she had perceived over many years. The erotic, excited "ay-yi-yi," which she had shared with her sister throughout their latency and shared also with me, who reminded her of that sister, now fell away to reveal a desperate, defiant attempt to assert the presence of an "I-I-I." Since it came in the depths of a transference regression in which she longed for the maternal union she thought she had experienced before her sister was born, "I-I-I" also accompanied her impulsive "darting away," her assertion of independence and motility. Our previous reconstructions of oedipal and latency anxiety, curiosity, and exposure, with their accompanying "ay-yi-yi's," now fell away like "screen" reconstructions, "screen" developmental moments, to reveal this earlier reconstruction and its "I-I-I," an earlier reconstruction with a more sophisticated use of language.

In describing the development of what he calls a "verbal self," Stern (1985) designates the 18th month as the point at which children can begin to "objectify" themselves (p. 165). As an indication of this new cognitive leap, it is also the moment at which children first begin to use the personal pronoun "I" to refer to themselves. The psychologist W. Stern described a similar moment, in terms suggestive of Mahler's exuberant toddlers, when he said, "The child 'makes the greatest discovery of his life,' that 'each thing has its name' " (Vygotsky, 1934). And so it is with this sense of discovery that my patient returned to a moment at 18 months to say to her mother, to her sister, to me, and to the world, "I-I-I." Her "ay-yi-yi" had been a shared language with her "almost-twin" sister B. Her "I-I-I" was an individual statement in an interpersonal context, an assertion that took her back to a sense of abandonment at her sister's birth; it now heralded the reassertion of her own autonomy, which was the major work of the final year and a half of her analysis. Termination seemed truly to begin at the moment she could articulate the language behind the screen, her reconstruction of an "I-I-I."

In the analysis of a screen memory, once the compromise formation has been examined and the content behind the "indifferent" appearance of the screen revealed, the screen memory itself tends to drop from view, no longer appearing as frequently in the hours at hand. Mahon and Battin-Mahon (1983) regard this phenomenon, the "decathexis" (p. 459) of the screen memory, as a measure of the working through process and a criterion for termination (see also Mahon and Battin, 1981). So it was with my patient's screen language. Her "ay-yi-yi," which had been sounding a repeated and insistent note in the months leading up to her "I-I-I" reconstruction, reappeared only once again in its original form, a brief reassertion in the following week, before disappearing altogether.

Developmental Origins and Transformations

To this point I have been describing in its simplest form the entity my patient discovered, which I have called screen language. But is it too much to speculate that "ay-yi-yi" might have had its roots in even earlier moments of infantile cries, echolalia, and babble — sounds that may have accompanied earlier experiences of aloneness and excitement? My patient had many times referred to an earlier "time before words." She had, in fact, announced in the first weeks of her analysis:

> When you're hunting you take along a gun. When you're swimming you have a bathing suit. You know what to do. I don't know what to do when I get hurt or angry. You have nothing to take along with you. You've got to use words, and I never had any words. Now I have words, and I don't know what to say.

Although she might as well have been referring to the origins of language itself, she was describing in phallic imagery her analytic dilemma: being unprotected, with no words yet to express inarticulate feelings. And she may also have been referring to experiences that were never — or not yet — represented in language. In the hour of her "I-I-I" reconstruction she had returned to a time of "first language," in Brown's (1973) phrase. But there was continually the echo of an actual "time before words," when she could, as she said, only "scream and sleep."

As the termination period progressed, my patient deepened her experience of these earliest moments. Two days before my final summer vacation she dreamed of an "emaciated kid, four or five months old, lying there with its mouth open." She wondered in the dream, "Why does this baby look so emaciated when all the food is gone? It must be Failure to Thrive." Suddenly she thought, "Maybe the mother was eating its food." And then she wanted to go to sleep. She felt lethargic. There was an eerie, I should say anaclitic, silence in the room. The following day she said, "I really fell asleep yesterday . . . It's okay for *me* to leave. It's hard when *you* do. I feel deprived, depressed, like I can't move. I just lie there, stare at the wall." I said, "Like a depressed baby." And she: "I must have gotten depressed when my mother was like that." She was referring to her mother's depression when she was 3½ years old.

Several weeks later and feeling my absence *after* my return, the patient was left alone by her roommate when a hurricane struck nearby. How often do transference reenactments of earliest times take advantage of such adventitious events? She felt "so abandoned." She sobbed all evening, "shaking . . . I felt I could cry forever." This time she thought of herself again at 18 months: "I think when all that happened I felt like I lost everything. I felt like I couldn't exist unless my mother was there. I felt like myself went away. It was like losing myself. There must be some way of knowing no matter what, even though everything's gone, I'll still be okay." She remembered that she had once been unable to finish a research paper "for the longest time." The subject: how a two-year-old feels when her parents return from an absence. "I had to figure out how to end this thing. I didn't know my mother was going to come back." She literally had had "no words" to end her paper.

This patient's termination was a most poignant working through of this recreated sense of separation and abandonment before the full benefit of object constancy. It was an attempt to find words for the inexpressible. Thus, she hoped whimsically that I would leave her appointment times open forever: "It's the only way you will remember me." I commented, "You're not sure I'll remember you, that something of you will stay here as well as go." Now words failed her. She sobbed deeply and repeatedly. I was struck that each sob trailed off in a long, mournful "ai-yi-yi-eeee." It was the sound of an infant wailing plaintively in the night, her keens adopting or recreating the vocalization so familiar by now from other contexts.

Language theorists have debated for years whether the path from earliest cries and babble to the beginnings of language is continuous or discontinuous, whether the sounds of infancy are the precursors of language. In 1941 Jakobson suggested that children must relearn linguistic sounds when language appears (cited in Bloom and Lahey, 1978). Recently, H. Gardner (1983), on the other hand, has written, "The roots of spoken language can be found in the child's babbling during the opening months of life." The debate is pertinent to our interest in the recoverability of early affect states and experience. I do not propose to settle the issue, but our data suggest certain continuities.

Stern (1985) argues that the development of language simultaneously provides access to and obscures preverbal experience. So it is with all developmental advance, all screens, all mental content; they all obscure and simultaneously provide access; they are all both continuous and discontinuous. Valenstein (1973) spoke to this point in his paper "On Attachment to Painful Feelings and the Negative Therapeutic Reaction." In summarizing he wrote, "On this fundamentally pregenital base may be grafted more sophisticated object-oriented experience deriving from beyond the oral level." Could "ay-yi-yi" provide a clue as to the nature of the graft?

If the development of language reflects the introduction or activation of new neurological structure and hence a discontinuity on the cognitive level, "ay-yi-yi" seemed to accompany my patient back in time to her earliest moments and hence to suggest a continuity with what may be the affective and conative origins of language. Spitz (1965) too explored these origins. Interested in the infant's "dialogue" with both animate and inanimate objects, he wrote, "There cannot be any doubt that the precursors of the dialogue originate in the nursing situation" (p. 188).

More recent infant observers have elaborated the interpersonal context of the dialogue (Sander, 1983; Stern, 1985). The earliest forms of gesture, affect, and verbalization seem to begin in an interpersonal context and supply an ever-expanding meaningful vocabulary to the communication between adult and infant. Even if words arrive as new structures, they must enter an already existing dictionary with its own language of gesture, sound, and affective attunement.

Thus, if "ay-yi-yi" began as infantile cries and babble, as part of an echolalic antiphony between mother and child, it evolved into a shared latency language between two sisters, each nursing at the other's breast, a latency reenactment of an infantile dialogue in the face of maternal deprivation. In either period of development "ay-yi-yi"—or its 18-month version, "I–I–I"—is both a personal statement with intrapsychic meaning and an interpersonal communication to mother, sister, me, and the world at large. The context is continuous, each moment screened by the other.[1]

I do not mean to imply that "ay-yi-yi" has all the formal syntactical characteristics of a true "language" when I use the term *language* to describe it any more than I believe that an "infantile dialogue" necessarily involves words. Rather, I want to suggest the continuity of one communicative moment with another and thus to emphasize the screening function inherent in the development of language and manifest in all elements of communication including affect, gesture, words, and sounds of all sorts.

Stern's underlying concept of development asserts such continuity, as developmental issues, in his view, remain open for the lifespan, not buried in past phases. Stern gives a developmental conceptualization to the continuities of Freud's topographical notion of screening, wherein the content screened might derive from later as well as earlier experience. The screen that faces forward can be illustrated too with "ay-yi-yi," as the next few paragraphs demonstrate.

In the termination phase of her analysis my patient's conflicting wishes to join with me and also to achieve a separate sense of herself could be seen as a simultaneous reflection of both toddlerhood and adolescence, a kind of developmental overdetermination or double exposure, in which the two images overlapped but still could be observed discretely. In fact, one epoch was so closely intertwined with the other as to make them inseparable, yet each retained its own integrity.

Listen to how the terminology of the earlier developmental period reappeared instantaneously in the later. One week after the reconstruction of her "I–I–I" experience at 18 months, the patient spoke about a new man in her life: "I can't believe I moved so quickly from one boyfriend to the other," she said. "Ay-yi-yi, I feel like I'm eighteen. All I do is run around and do things . . . I stopped talking to my parents when I was a

---

[1]It has been suggested that this shared dialogue between the patient and her "almost-twin" sister is reminiscent of the secret or private language of twins, as in Sacks's (1985) twin "idiots savants." After searching the literature, Gifford and Murawski (1980) concluded that, in the absence of mental defect or childhood autism, the private language of twins is an exceedingly rare occurrence. How then do we explain its more common acceptance? Perhaps the phenomenon, which sounds so plausible, is itself a shorthand or screen for the interpersonal dialogue outlined here, the language of babble, gesture, and affect shared between mother and child, a dialogue that almost certainly must be shared in some form as well between twins. Screened also is that secret world with its secret languages that we impute to all children (as well as, on occasion, to animals, fantasy creatures, etc.); our fantasy has many developmental roots, including the fascination that latency children themselves commonly have for secret languages and codes.

teenager, and I don't want to talk to you." Eighteen months for eighteen years, "I-I-I" for "ay-yi-yi"; how suddenly the inarticulateness and motility of the toddler gave way to the defiance and action language of the adolescent. This was the last appearance of "ay-yi-yi" in its original form. Now screens were lifting not regressively but progressively, as Freud had said they might.

And in the week preceding her cry from the cradle, "ay-yi-yi-eeee," the patient had spoken of the future: "If we don't get married, who knows if I'll be able to have kids?" Her intended husband was her new "boyfriend", but she added "I can count on you to be here. There's no guarantee of that anywhere else." And then she interrupted her words with a long wistful, "Ay-yi-yi-yi-do-do-do." Was it infantile babble? Or an acceptance of marriage ("I do")? Either way, the screen now seemed to depict a developmental step she hoped she might take on her own.

Thus her "screen language" adapts itself to each developmental period and to time past, present, and future. Earlier, I commented (Smith, 1988, p. 78) that past, present, and future repeatedly mix themselves together in our work: "It is that way in the unconscious, 'timeless,' as Freud (1915, p. 187) called it, and in dreams. It is that way in psychosis and in such altered states as déjà vu (Arlow, 1984; Hartocollis, 1983). It is that way, as Freud pointed out, in the work of creative writers, in daydreams, in memory, and in the transference," where past experience, present perception, and future wish come together in one analytic moment. So it is with "screen language." "Ay-yi-yi" defines a latency dialogue with the vocabulary of infancy in the cadence of adult erotic excitement, simultaneously condensing all these developmental moments and more into one multiply determined expression, which at the same time continues to define each moment discretely. And this curious semantic trick by which multiple entities can be linked and yet remain discrete, which is the essence of metaphor, appears to accompany the patient in the ongoing developmental journey of her life. As the patient develops, she apparently uses and reuses this linguistic element of her experience to orchestrate each present moment. At least this is the view she gives us through the perceptual lens of her analysis.

The adaptability of the mental and emotional content of developmental experience is not limited to elements of language. Another patient of mine punctuated his hours with silence, not words. The silences, we learned, were moments of expectancy; he was waiting for a cue from me. Cuing or the silent wish for cues seemed to have accompanied him all his life, from earliest moments of aloneness and expectancy to later experiences with a mother he perceived as intrusively attentive to his every cue and a father he wished had been more so. The search for cues had led him through countless developmental doors into the bathroom and the parental bedroom, for example, developing, in fact, into a lifelong characterological search for cues of all sorts. In short, the search for cues was a multiply determined compromise formation that surfaced, as did "ay-yi-yi," at each developmental shift of the transference; and at each such surfacing one could hear the accretion of multiple developmental moments simultaneously fused and expressed in his watchful silence.[2]

We can speak of "ay-yi-yi," of cues and silence, or of an infinite number of other pieces of experience that lend themselves to repeated use in development. Perhaps all experience, once crystallized as mental content, can be used and reused, like images in a dream or metaphors in a poem, by the creative imagination of the developing individual. It speaks to the promiscuous nature of development itself that the imagination will of necessity use whatever pieces of mental and emotional content are available, bending them to the purposes of each succeeding developmental phase. Thus, "ay-yi-yi" travels from the cradle to the marriage ceremony, and the cues of infancy become the cues of the primal scene, which evolve into a lifelong search for cues as a particular postoedipal character trait. Thus are an infinite number of moments telescoped through the metaphors of development so that each cue, each "ay-yi-yi," contains past, present, and future, as seen through the eye of the present moment.

That the imagination, even at its most creative, is limited by the footprints of its own history can be verified by a close look at the life work of any writer. While Shakespeare's plays undergo radical change from comedy through history to tragedy and finally romance, the details of language, character, and action repeat and extend themselves in a slow evolutionary process, not unlike the manner in which a parent extends a

---

[2]I have described this analysis at greater length elsewhere (Smith, 1990) in considering the phenomenon of cuing and the importance of attending to the patient's perception of the analyst's participation. In the analysis considered here, such attention might have added a further dimension to our understanding of the transferential and historical evolution of my patient's "screen language," including her experience of what was separate and what was shared, which seemed fundamental to every aspect of her analysis. As I noted earlier, such a moment was her apparent irritation at my question "Where does 'ay-yi-yi' come from?" Had I inquired further into her reaction, we might have discovered that my question had disrupted her sense of a "shared language" with me, since for 22 months I, like her sister, had simply accepted her "ay-yi-yi's" without "challenging" their origin. It might similarly have been useful to inquire into her experience of our collaborative reconstructing, to learn the meaning to her of this shared analytic language and activity (e.g., see Friedman, 1988, pp. 464–471). In any case, the cues and "ay-yi-yi's" from these two rather different analyses suggests that developmental metaphor may appear in a form consistent with the vocabulary of every analysis and may be manifest in elements of process as well as in content.

child's "zone of proximal development," (p. 193) as Stern (1985) puts it, or an analyst works within the patient's and the analyst's "edge-of-awareness," in M. R. Gardner's (1983) phrase. The retrospective exhibition of a painter fascinates us for similar reasons. We see variations on a theme of form, color, and composition. The new transforms the old; the old explains the new. Both retain their own value and integrity. Thus in *The Seagull* Chekhov (1896) mocks the idealistic young playwright, Trepleff, who rants, "We must have new forms," as if they did not have to evolve from an already existing context.

Whether we view the context as a limitation or as a stimulus to invention, it is, necessarily, both stimulating and limiting *and* a necessary component of any creative process — even, as Freud (1915a) pointed out, in the gathering of scientific data. In the brilliant opening paragraph of "Instincts and their Vicissitudes," he wrote:

> Even at the stage of description it is not possible to avoid applying certain abstract ideas to the material at hand, ideas derived from somewhere or other but certainly not from the new observations alone. . . . [We] come to an understanding of [the] meaning [of these ideas] by making repeated references to the material of observation from which they appear to have been derived, but upon which, in fact, they have been imposed [p. 117].

This view of development, in which past and present have a hand in creating each other, is an extension of Kris's (1956) observations on the transformations of memory and of Arlow's (1961) model of superimposed photographic transparencies, by which he explained the hierarchical organization of unconscious fantasy in the psychic life of the individual. Arlow's model is fundamentally a topographical one. If the view I am describing takes us back to such early topographical notions as screening, it is because those first enunciations of analytically derived and seemingly nondevelopmental conceptions of the mind described aspects of the evolution of mental content that are only now, I believe, being rediscovered and redefined in the hypotheses derived from infant observation.

It seems to me we are looking not just at the conflictual organization of fantasy and memory but at something that pertains to the ongoing organization of all mental or psychic life. I do not mean by this to minimize the importance of unconscious fantasy in the metaphorical organization of experience, which Arlow (1979) has so eloquently detailed. Nor do I dispute his view that "metaphor is an inherent quality of language in general and of how the human mind integrates the experiences of the individual" (1979, p. 373). Rather, I want to suggest that we may be looking at a phenomenon that predates the time we customarily assign to the emergence of symbolic thinking and the organizing influence of unconscious fantasy, hence, a phenomenon that may be related to the preconflictual origins of compromise formation. Furthermore, if the "metaphors" we have been describing begin in the first moments of life, then—as with Stern's (1985) view of the organization of "lived episodes" (p. 95)—we may be observing some complex interaction between perception and experience that influences the ongoing and continuous organization and development of the individual from the beginning. Thus, the metaphorical internalization of experience might determine in part the direction of development, not merely its integration. (See also Smith, 1990.)

To return to Valenstein's notion of the "grafting" of later experience onto a "pregenital"—or, I would say, preconflictual—base: if indeed there is such a graft, it is a far from simple notion, for the cues and screen language we have been observing, like other such metaphors of development, are infinitely adaptable yet remain discrete entities. Each stage of development transforms and is transformed by all preceding ones, and yet each is potentially observable as seen through the experience of the present moment. If we could construct a model to describe the results of such a graft, a plant that assumes infinite shapes and yet retains the outline of each previous configuration, the protean structures thus produced would be as kinetic and complex as the ten-dimensional images that Sashin (1985; Callahan and Sashin, 1987) described in his work on affect and catastrophe theory.

How then are we to understand these creative transformations, shapes that evolve and yet remain the same? In an earlier paper (Smith, 1988), I discussed Arlow's (1969a, 1969b) model of psychic reality in which the images of two movie projectors are superimposed on a screen, one projector deriving images from unconscious fantasy, the other from the perception of external reality. I wondered what his model might tell us about the link between perception and creativity and whether one could apply some version of the model to early infancy in order to explore when infants might begin to create their own experience. In response, Arlow (personal communication, 1985) suggested that each moment of perception can be viewed as a creative moment in the life of the individual. But the question remained, When does this creative process begin?

A final look at infant observation may help us begin to locate the origins of Arlow's model. On a microstructural level, Stern and others have concluded that the infant is capable, through some as yet unknown mechanism, to translate the data from one perceptual modality into another. Stern (1985) writes, "Infants appear to experience a world of perceptual unity, in which they can perceive amodal qualities in any modality from any form of human expressive behavior, represent those qualities abstractly, and then transpose them to other modalities" (p. 51). Infants thereby can recognize visually the shape of an object they have only heretofore touched, not seen. Stern imagines that the infant's experience in so doing may be a primitive form of déjà vu. Thus, touch may be transformed into shape, sound into vision.

The hypothesis of cross-modal perception in fact establishes a link between creativity and perception at its most fundamental level, the beginning of life. Not only does this concept fix the origins of cross-modal artistic creativity, a common feature of poetic metaphor, as Stern (1985, p. 155) points out, but it suggests a prototype for the developmental metaphors we have been observing whereby one piece of mental content may be transformed into another and yet remain distinct.

If these are the origins of perceptual transformations on a microstructural level, Stern and others hypothesize, on a somewhat larger interactive scale, that infants have an ability to generalize their ongoing interpersonal experience, utilizing what amount to presymbolic representations. Stern (1985) writes, "Lived episodes immediately become the specific episodes for memory, and with repetition they become generalized episodes . . . of interactive experience that are mentally represented," adding, "these memories are retrievable whenever one of the attributes of the [representation] is present" (p. 110).

If the hypothesis of presymbolic representation is correct, it would extend to earliest times the notion that all perception, all memory, all mental life is a subjective phenomenon, idiosyncratic to the individual, and it would suggest that in those earliest representations of interpersonal experience lie the origins of the individual's capacity to create experience and the infantile origins thereby of such phenomena as transference, screening, and psychic reality. It would, furthermore, lend additional developmental credence to Schwaber's (1983a, 1983b) position that the examination of the patient's perceptual experience of the analytic context may provide access to preverbal anlage.

*   *   *

One week before termination my patient spoke of a "huge void" in her life. On the manifest level she was referring to her lack of female friends. Ever since she had begun spending so much time with a man, her female friends no longer called her. And then she returned for one last look at the reconstruction that had been so important in her analysis: "I wanted to kill my sister. I was enraged at my mother. The only thing I wanted then was missing too." I asked her what that was, and she replied, "I wanted a female friend." And then she gasped and with a note of astonishment, in which she might have been speaking of the creative process of her analysis and of her development, as we had been examining it, and of the origins of psychic experience itself, she added, "I've recreated the whole thing. I didn't have my mother. I don't have a female friend. It's like déjà vu. That's why this is so intense. I created the whole thing."

Summary

Freud's concept of screening describes specific entities, such as screen memories, and also reflects a general theory of mental organization. An example is given of "screen language," in which a patient's use of a particular phrase screens an earlier version of the same phrase and an early reconstruction. "Screen language" illustrates the manner in which phenomena from any given period may reappear in different forms throughout development. When viewed in analysis, these pieces of development function metaphorically to link and express discretely multiple developmental moments. Drawing on the findings of infant research, an infantile origin is suggested for Arlow's two-projector model of psychic reality and thus for such phenomena as transference, screening, and the individual's capacity to create experience.

References

Arlow, J. A. (1961), Ego psychology and the study of mythology. *J. Amer. Psychoanal. Assn.*, 9:371–393.

———— (1969a), Unconscious fantasy and disturbances of conscious experience. *Psychoanal. Q.*, 38:1–27.

———— (1969b), Fantasy, memory, and reality testing. *Psychoanal. Q.*, 38:28–51.

———— (1979), Metaphor and the psychoanalytic situation. *Psychoanal. Q.*, 48:363–385.

———— (1984), Disturbances of the sense of time, with special reference to the experience of timelessness. *Psychoanal. Q.*, 53:13–37.

Bloom, L. & Lahey, M. (1978), *Language Development and Language Disorders.* New York: Wiley.

Brenner, C. (1982), *The Mind in Conflict.* New York: Int. Univ. Press.

Brown, R. (1973), *A First Language: The Early Stages.* Cambridge, MA: Harvard University Press.

Callahan, J. & Sashin, J. I. (1987), Models of affect-response and anorexia nervosa. *Proc. N. Y. Acad. Sci.*, 504:241–259.

Chekhov, A. (1896), *The Seagull.* In: *Best Plays by Chekhov,* tr. S. Young. New York: Modern Library, 1956, pp. 1–70.

Deutsch, H. (1930), Hysterical conversion symptoms: Fits, trance states. In: *Neuroses and Character Types.* New York: Int. Univ. Press, 1965, pp. 57–73.

Fenichel, O. (1927), The economic function of screen memories. *Collected Papers, Vol. 1.* New York: Norton.

———— (1945). *The Psychoanalytic Theory of Neurosis.* New York: Norton.

Freud, S. (1899), Screen memories. *Standard Edition,* 3:303–322. London: Hogarth Press, 1962.

―――― (1901), The psychopathology of everyday life. *Standard Edition,* 6. London: Hogarth Press, 1960.

―――― (1908), Character and anal erotism. *Standard Edition,* 9:167–175. London: Hogarth Press, 1959.

―――― (1915a), Instincts and their vicissitudes. *Standard Edition,* 14:117–140. London: Hogarth Press, 1957.

―――― (1915b), The unconscious. *Standard Edition,* 14:166–204. London: Hogarth Press, 1957.

Friedman, L. (1988), *The Anatomy of Psychotherapy.* Hillsdale, NJ: The Analytic Press.

Gardner, H. (1983), *Frames of Mind.* New York: Basic Books, 1985.

Gardner, M. R. (1983), *Self Inquiry.* Hillsdale, NJ: The Analytic Press, 1988.

Geleerd, E. R. (1969), Introduction to panel on child psychoanalysis. *Internat. J. Psycho-Anal.,* 50:91–94.

Gifford, S. & Murawski, B. J. (1980), Learning and language-development in twins. Unpublished manuscript.

Glover, E. (1929), The screening function of traumatic memories. *Internat. J. Psycho-Anal.,* 10:90–93.

Gray, P. (1973), Psychoanalytic technique and the ego's capacity for viewing intrapsychic activity. *J. Amer. Acad. Psychoanal.,* 21:474–494.

Greenacre, P. (1949), A contribution to the study of screen memories. *The Psychoanalytic Study of the Child,* 3/4:73–84. New York: International Universities Press.

Greenson, R. R. (1958), On screen defenses, screen hunger, and screen identity. In: *Explorations in Psychoanalysis.* New York: International Universities Press, 1978, pp. 111–132.

Hartocollis, P. (1983), *Time and Timelessness.* New York: International Universities Press.

Kris, E. (1956a), The recovery of childhood memories in psychoanalysis. *The Psychoanalytic Study of the Child,* 11:54–88. New York: International Universities Press.

―――― (1956b). The personal myth. *J. Amer. Psychoanal. Assn.,* 11:54–88.

Lewin, B. D. (1950), *The Psychoanalysis of Elation.* New York: Norton.

Mahler, M. S., Pine, F. & Bergman, A. (1975), *The Psychological Birth of the Human Infant.* New York: Basic Books.

Mahon, E. & Battin, D. (1981), Screen memories and termination. *J. Amer. Psychoanal. Assn.,* 29:939–942.

Mahon, E. & Battin-Mahon, D. (1983), The fate of screen memories in psychoanalysis. *The Psychoanalytic Study of the Child,* 38:459–479. New Haven, CT: Yale University Press.

Piaget, J. (1930), *The Language and Thought of the Child.* New York: New American Library, 1959.

Reider, N. (1953), Reconstruction and screen function. *J. Amer. Psychoanal. Assn.,* 1:389–405.

Sacks, O. (1985), The twins. *New York Review of Books,* Feb. 28, pp. 16–20.

Sander, L. S. (1983), To begin with: Reflections on ontogeny. In: *Reflections on Self Psychology,* ed. J. D. Lichtenberg & S. Kaplan. Hillsdale, NJ: The Analytic Press, pp. 85–104.

Sashin, J. I. (1985), Affect tolerance: A model of affect-response using catastrophe theory. *J. Social Biol. Struc.,* 8:175–202.

Schafer, R. (1983), *The Analytic Attitude.* New York: Basic Books.

Schwaber, E. (1983a), A particular perspective on analytic listening. *The Psychoanalytic Study of the Child,* 38:519–546. New Haven, CT: Yale University Press.

_____ (1983b), Construction, reconstruction, and the mode of clinical attunement. In: *The Future of Psychoanalysis,* ed. A. Goldberg. New York: International Universities Press, pp. 273–291.

Smith, H. F. (1988), Time, reconstruction and psychic reality. *J. Amer. Acad. Psychoanal.,* 16:71–81.

_____ (1990), Cues: The perceptual edge of the transference. *Internat. J. Psycho-Anal.,* 71:219–228.

Spence, D. P. (1982), *Narrative Truth and Historical Truth.* New York: Norton.

Spitz, R. A. (1965), Evolution of dialogue. In: *Dialogues from Infancy,* ed. R. N. Emde. New York: International Universities Press, 1983, pp. 179–195.

Stern, D. N. (1985), *The Interpersonal World of the Infant.* New York: Basic Books.

Valenstein, A. F. (1973), On attachment to painful feelings and the negative therapeutic reaction. *The Psychoanalytic Study of the Child,* 28:365–392. New Haven, CT: Yale University Press.

Vygotsky, L. (1934), *Thought and Language,* trans. A. Kozulin. Cambridge, MA: MIT Press, 1986.

On Being a Scientist or a Healer: Reflections on Abstinence, Neutrality, and Gratification

ERNEST S. WOLF

It is a generally accepted truism that psychoanalytic theory guides the methods of psychoanalytic technique and, vice versa, that clinical experiences with psychoanalytic methods influence the development and modifications in psychoanalytic theory. Little attention has been paid to a number of other factors that have been consequential for the specific forms of the theories and practices that have found ready acceptance among psychoanalysts. From their early beginnings some of the tensions and controversies that accompanied the growth of psychoanalytic theories seem to have been reflected in the development of therapeutic technique in psychoanalysis. When Freud first gave up hypnosis as a method for influencing patients, he substituted other methods of suggestion. For example, he would forcefully tell a patient to remember certain traumas and accompany the suggestion by pressing down on the patient's forehead. Naturally, many patients complied by dutifully remembering. Eventually, of course, he abandoned overt suggestion and adopted the method that Breuer's patient Anna O. had invented—she called it "chimney sweeping"—that is, the method of free association. In his discussion of the treatment of hysteria Freud (1895) summarized his therapeutic attitude:

> One works to the best of one's power, as an elucidator (where ignorance has given rise to fear), as a teacher, as the representative of a freer or superior view of the world, as a father confessor who gives absolution, as it were, by a continuance of his sympathy and respect after the confession has been made. One tries to give the patient human assistance, as far as this is allowed by the capacity of one's own

115

personality and by the amount of sympathy that one can feel for the particular case [pp. 282–283].

In these words Freud emerges as a kind but firm father/teacher/confessor who can listen sympathetically and give absolution and who, within the limits of his own personality, can be compassionate and render assistance. He seems far from the austere creator of the abstinent ambience that he advocated in his 1912 technique papers. However, Freud (1895) still carried with him some of the authoritarianism that is an integral part of hypnotic practice: "It is of course of great importance for the progress of the analysis that one should always turn out to be in the right *vis-a-vis* the patient, otherwise one would always be dependent on what he chose to tell one" (p. 281). In the end he reaches the point that would become the major determinant in his analytic technique: he makes the patient into a collaborating investigator like himself. "By explaining things to him, by giving him information about the marvelous world of psychical processes . . . we make him himself into a collaborator, induce him to regard himself with the objective interest of an investigator" (1895, p. 282).

In this chapter I intend to demonstrate that Freud's passionate commitment to the truth, as exemplified in the methods of scientific research, became the decisively determining influence on his analytic technique. Doing psychoanalytic psychotherapy must have been Freud's ambivalent resolution of the age-old conflict of medical professionals who are caught in the opposing motivations of the pursuit of truth and the pursuit of healing. However, the therapeutic results of psychoanalytic treatment did not live up to either Freud's or his patient's expectations. In contrast to Freud, some of his colleagues were less interested in the aim of scientific investigation and more concerned with achieving therapeutic successes. The resulting tensions between Freud and some of his contemporaries were the forerunner of analogous controversies throughout the development of psychoanalysis. I shall attempt to illustrate some of these struggles within the psychoanalytic movement. It would lead beyond the confines of this chapter to discuss in detail some of the motivations that lie behind an individual analyst's choice of adhering to Freud's standard analytic technique versus accepting modifications that make the therapeutic process more amenably acceptable for patients. Nevertheless, I at least mention certain aspects of the analyst's value system that appear to have a decisive influence on the approval or disapproval with which developments in psychoanalysis are greeted. In turn, such a basic orientation toward life, whether it be labeled philosophic or religious, depends to a large extent on the individual's self-image. That is to say, past experiences that have shaped personality and character also find expression in the choices made when faced with competing personal or professional ideals. Persons dedicated to the care of others are subject to an internal conflict of clashing tendencies: the aim to understand and learn more (i.e., to study scientifically) and the aim to provide as much succor and healing as fast as possible. How an individual analyst responds to such a conflict may well be the decisive factor in the choices that are made.

Freud

Almost since its beginning at the bedside of Breuer's and Freud's patients, psychoanalysis has been riven by the tension between the research aspirations of the analyst as scientist and the humanistic goals of the analyst as healer. Medical professionals will recognize immediately that this conflict is not peculiar to psychoanalysis but pervades all of medical practice. Does the doctor order all these esoteric (and expensive) laboratory procedures because they are relevant to his management of this particular patient, or is he ambitious to expand scientific knowledge? Usually, both motives are operative, but often the doctor must admit to himself that his scientific curiosity got the better of him. Both Breuer and Freud were heirs to the scientific tradition in physiology and medicine, of which the venerated Helmholtz was the patron saint. Though Breuer was the first ever to sit with a psychiatric patient hour after hour, day after day, month after month (to let Anna O. tell him her story), in medical circles he is still best known today for his respiratory and vestibular system researches. Freud had a successful career as a researcher in a neuropathology laboratory before he was forced into medical practice by the economic necessity of supporting a growing family. Both men became skilled scientists and competent physicians, yet I think I can detect subtle differences in their attitudes. Breuer practiced medicine with enthusiasm, and one can sense that his researches were motivated primarily by his wish to become a better medical practitioner. He abandoned psychotherapeutic practice when its emotional demands on him became an interference and frightened him. Freud disliked medical practice; his ambitions were guided by his idealization of scientific knowledge. He made one aspect of psychoanalysis, the search for knowledge about the inner life of humanity, the foremost goal of his life's work. However, though the advancement of psychoanalytic knowledge and the search for truth clearly dominated his approach to clinical as well as theoretical problems, Freud never lost sight of the fundamental reason patients come to see physicians: for help, comfort, and, if possible, cure. Nor did Freud ever forget that the source of all knowledge was the work with patients. In his *"New Introductory Lectures"* he wrote:

> As you know, psychoanalysis originated as a method of treatment; it has far outgrown this, but it has not abandoned its home-ground and it is still linked to its contact with patients for increasing its depth and for its further development. The accumulated impressions from which we derive our theories could be arrived at in no other way. . . . You are perhaps aware that I have never been a therapeutic enthusiast [1933, p. 151].

Freud's passion was to be the *conquistador,* to discover unknown territories of the mind. He set out to explore the unconscious, that vast empire beneath the surface consciousness, to become the first depth psychologist. Like an explorer discovering a new continent, Freud mapped out the psyche into the realms of id, ego, and superego. As Bacal (1990) has pointed out, Freud's theoretical formulations "constituted a one-body model" (p. 3), and therefore his theories focused on intrapsychic dynamics. Freud's emphasis on the structure of the psyche shaped his conceptualizations. He developed a system of dynamic concepts distant from the clinical experience: it is to those constructs in the space beyond the immediacy of the psychoanalytic situation that the term *metapsychology* applies.

In Freud's first systematic formulation, the topographical model, everything is arranged according to an analogy with the layers described in archaeological excavations (Wolf and Nebel, 1978). In the second, the tripartite model, the psyche is depicted as structured into three parts — id, ego, and superego. However, though Freud talked much about transference and countertransference, the focus on the intrapsychic dynamics of the analysand had the unintended effect of neglecting the dynamic relations between analyst and analysand. A consideration of these relations was relegated to the rather slighted area of psychoanalytic technique. Freud wrote a number of papers making recommendations for the technique of psychoanalytic treatment. These are remarkable for describing what analyst and analysand should or should not do — without, however, extensively discussing the metapsychology of the therapeutic relationship. Freud's interest in psychoanalytic technique apparently did not extend to a theory of technique. His interest had become focused on the structure of the psyche (i.e., psychoanalytic metapsychology). Haynal comments that "Freud was passionately engaged in theoretical explorations but technique, practice and its unique relationship were not in the center of his concerns" (Haynal, 1989, p. 13, my translation).

Ferenczi

Most of the gradually emerging psychoanalytic community followed Freud down this road (Bacal, 1990) of metapsychological speculation without too much focus on therapeutic technique, with the exception of Sándor Ferenczi, whose interests turned to the analytic situation as a two-body situation that called for a two-body model of theorizing. As we shall see presently, Ferenczi soon found himself in conflict with his good friend Freud.

Ferenczi was one of Freud's closest collaborators and friends. He remained always respectful of Freud and his concepts, though he seems to have been intimidated by his idealization of the great man. However, Ferenczi soon began to notice shortcomings in his therapeutic results, which led him into experimenting with modifications of psychoanalytic technique. Without being critical of Freud's technical recommendations, Ferenczi introduced a number of innovative suggestions in his 1919 paper on technique. For example, he recommended, "active therapy" to help patients over dead points in the analysis (p. 196). Later, he noted the detrimental effects of too strict an adherence to the principle of frustration: "I feel impelled to propound another principle, not hitherto formulated, even if tacitly accepted. I mean the *principle of indulgence,* which must often be allowed to operate side by side with that of frustration" (1929, p. 115).

In a letter to Freud in 1930 Ferenczi (1988, p. xiii) states his concern for therapeutic technique:

> I do not share, for instance, your view that the therapeutic process is negligible or unimportant, and that simply because it appears less interesting to us we should ignore it. I, too, have often felt "fed up" [this phrase is in English in the original] in this respect, but overcame this tendency, and I am glad to inform you that precisely in this area a whole series of questions have now come into a new, a sharper focus, perhaps even the problem of repression [letter to Freud of 17 January 1930].

Ferenczi (1928) also explicitly put empathy in the center of his therapeutic approach: "I have come to the conclusion that it is above all a question of psychological tact whether one or when one should tell the patient some particular thing. . . . But what is 'tact'? The answer is not very difficult. It is the capacity for empathy." (p. 89).

Ferenczi made a start on a new metapsychological conceptualization of the therapeutic process. He suggested that a dissolution of the superego can bring about a radical cure and that a sufficiently deep character analysis must get rid of any kind of superego, although he clarified this idea as follows:

> An over-logical mind might interpret this as implying that my technique aimed at robbing people of all their ideals. In reality my objective was to destroy only that part of the super-ego which had become unconscious and was therefore beyond the range of influence. I have no sort of objection to the retention of a number of positive and negative models in the pre-conscious of the ordinary individual [pp. 100–101].

Furthermore — and this was radically innovative — he called attention to "a problem that has not been considered, [namely,] that of the metapsychology of the analyst's mental processes during analysis. His cathexes oscillate between identification (analytic object-love) on the one hand and self-control or intellectual activity on the other" (p. 98).

In the face of criticism by Freud that his researches did not "appear capable of leading toward any desirable goal" Ferenczi responded as follows:

> I do not at all wish to deny that with me subjective factors influence, often substantially, the means and content of production. But I believe I finally was able to recognize where and how I went too far. . . . I am, above all, an empiricist. . . . Ideas are always closely linked with the vicissitudes in the treatment of patients, and by these are either repudiated or confirmed [10 October 1931] [p. xv].

Next to Freud himself it is Ferenczi who has had the greatest long-term influence on the development of psychoanalysis as a method of treatment. According to Haynal (1989), the question, Is an analytic psychotherapy possible, and if so, under what conditions? intrigued not only Ferenczi but also his fellow Hungarians Alexander and Balint (p. 113). The former brought his research on this question to Chicago, the latter to London. In Chicago, Alexander worked out a clinical approach, that alienated him from the strictly ego-psychological wing of the American psychoanalytic movement. In London the dynamics of psychotherapeutic relationships became a primary interest for the Independent group at the British Psychoanalytic Society, though I cannot be sure of the influence of Ferenczi via Balint on these therapeutic concerns.

Alexander

Franz Alexander founded the Chicago Institute for Psychoanalysis in the middle thirties. Here he attracted a group of analysts, most prominently Karen Horney and Therese Benedek, whose courage in advancing the young science matched his own determination. Like Ferenczi, Alexander was dissatisfied with the therapeutic results of psychoanalysis. Alexander's modification of the standard classical technique came to be known as the "corrective emotional experience."

What is the corrective emotional experience? Through the courtesy of Mrs. Kiki Levine, Franz Alexander's daughter, we can get a glimpse of the clinical event that precipitated Alexander's thinking. Apparently, Alexander had been analyzing a young man who attempted to defend himself by hiding his fearful anxieties behind an adolescent type of arrogant bravado. Analytic progress was slow; perhaps a threatened stalemate had already caused Alexander's patience to wear thin. Then on one of those not infrequent cold, wet, and windy Chicago days the patient came in for his session and plunked himself onto the couch; but instead of placing his muddy shoes on the piece of plastic that Alexander had thoughtfully provided to protect the fabric, the young man dirtied the couch with the mud from his shoes. This was too much for Alexander, and firmly, perhaps even somewhat sharply, he asked his patient to get his dirty shoes off the couch. The incident proved to be a turning point in the treatment, which henceforth progressed speedily. Alexander, who was always on the lookout for better ways to manage the clinical therapeutic process, finally came to the conclusion that his annoyed intervention had a surprising beneficial effect. He knew from the young man's developmental history that he had been indulged by an overly permissive father. Out of this empirical observation, together with historical reconstructions, Alexander then began the process of conceptualization that eventually led to the hypothesis of the corrective emotional experience. This hypothesis says, in essence, that the curative moment in an analysis arises when the patient experiences the analyst in a way that is intense and radically different from the way the parent was experienced in an analogous situation during childhood. Thus, by being significantly different the new emotional experience with the analyst becomes corrective. Alexander (1946) put it very clearly in the following passage:

> The intellectual reconstruction of the past is more important for the therapist than for the patient for whom it has only an accessory therapeutic significance. The emphasis upon the corrective emotional experience as the essence of dynamic psychotherapy brings the emotional aspects of the treatment into the foreground and the intellectual reconstruction of the past becomes subordinated to this fundamental therapeutic factor. . . . All etiologically oriented, pro-longed forms of psychotherapy . . . consist essentially in an emotional training by giving the Ego opportunity to face again and again, in

smaller or larger doses, formerly unbearable emotional situations and to deal with them in a different manner than in the past.

However, this can only be learned by actual experience. Intellectual insight alone is not sufficient. This corrective emotional experience is the common basis of all etiologically orientated psychotherapy. The re-experiencing of the unsettled old conflict but now with a new ending is the secret of every penetrating therapeutic result. Only the actual experiencing of a new solution in the transference or in life situations gives the patient the conviction that a new solution *is* possible and induces him to give up the old neurotic pattern [pp. 110–115].

Alexander was an impatient man and careless about hiding his enthusiasms. He seemed to advocate that the analyst playact the role of being different from the patient's parents, and this earned him the strong disapproval of the analytic community. *Corrective emotional experience* undeservedly became a synonym for superficial psychotherapy that was not acceptable to serious psychoanalysts. In addition, Alexander's attempts to shorten psychoanalytic treatment and to focus the transference on separation problems by planned interruptions were condemned as manipulative. Nevertheless, we must now recognize that Alexander, like Ferenczi before him, was serious about psychoanalysis as not just a theory but as a treatment and that he forcefully brought to our attention the centrality of the curative experience as the criterion for judging the analyst's interventions.

Balint

Michael Balint was particularly interested in understanding the vicissitudes of object relationships, especially in their early, or primitive, forms, and in applying this understanding to improve the therapeutic effectiveness of psychoanalysis and psychotherapy (Bacal, 1990, p. 121). He never lost sight of the fact that the analytic situation consisted of two persons and that the analyst's contribution was as important as the patient's. Balint believed that the analyst must create the conditions, the climate, in which the patient can experience the analyst as a primary object in relation to whom archaic needs can become evident.

While these developments in analytic technique were taking hold in postwar Europe, especially in Britain, the mainstream of psychoanalysis in the United States remained identified with Freudian ego psychology, which in its technical application was framed by Eissler's (1953) parameters. A mild dissent was registered by Stone (1961), who gave voice to the "special considerations derived from the dynamic situation itself" and took "cognizance of the important intellectual ferment of recent years in the discussions of transference and countertransference" (pp. 10–11).

Kohut

All the post-Freudian analysts mentioned so far, as well as many others, of whom Melanie Klein, Donald Winnicott, and Margaret Mahler are the most prominent, had in common that their modifications in psycho-analytic theory and in psychoanalytic technique did not question the basic structural model of id, ego, and superego or the basic assumptions of the motivational centrality of the infantile instinctual drives. Indeed, when Heinz Kohut (1966) began to express his clinical dissatisfaction by proposing some modifications of the concept of narcissism, he remained, at least on the surface, within the classical frame. The decisive step in the evolution of self psychology came with the realization that the neuroses are a special case of a wider spectrum of psychological disturbances that can be characterized as disorders of the self.

Classical Freudian psychoanalytic theory was and is a most elegant and illuminating way to think about the human psyche as it reveals itself in the neuroses. As we have seen, from the very beginning, however, there was dissatisfaction with the curative power of the obtained psychoanalytic insights. Freud was able to dismiss these inconvenient results because of his immense achievements in gaining access to a hitherto unknown region of knowledge. Others felt enormously challenged to translate these insights into palpable therapeutic results even with the more intractable patients, those whom Freud had dismissed as unanalyzable because of the narcissistic structure of their psyches.

As we have seen, experiments with modifications of the technique of psychoanalysis led to related modifications in theory without touching on the basic structural libidinal model. It had long been generally accepted that narcissistic patients were fundamentally different from the usual neurotic. They were thought to be unanalyzable without the introduction of parameters that made the treatment something other than psychoanal-ysis. In contrast to the neuroses, which could be understood as miscarried resolutions of the Oedipus complex, these narcissistic disorders were understood by conceptualizing a preoedipal origin of their psychopathol-ogy. Thus, it became increasingly important to explore the early histories and the development of object relations, explorations that, in turn, produced data that became the cornerstones of the theoretical structures built by Melanie Klein, Winnicott, and Mahler.

Kohut went a step further by moving the concerns of the narcissistic patients into the center of his interest. Instead of confining himself to the experience-distant inferences obtained by the application of classical theory, Kohut took the more difficult experience-near route to obtaining data by prolonged empathic immersion in the inner experience of his analysands. While this may seem to us today as the most natural way for obtaining psychological data, we must remember that until recently empathy was regarded as unscientific and empathic data as unreliable. To be sure, Ferenczi (1928) had stressed the importance of empathy — or, as he often called it, tact — in doing psychoanalytic treatment. He thought that tact was a force of analytic encouragement that was essential in establishing the psychological atmosphere that would make it possible for patients to open themselves to the analysis: "With our help the analysand is able to face, to bear, even to react to, situations which formerly were too much for him in his state of isolation and helplessness to which he had to surrender unconditionally, even surrender with pleasure" (Ferenczi, 1930, p. 226).

It is this psychoanalytic encouragement that I have come to call the "therapeutic ambience" (Wolf, 1976). Such an ambience depends on the analyst's empathic attunement to the analysand. But beyond this precondition for therapeutic progress, Kohut (1984) specifically saw empathy as a method for obtaining data. However, "the capacity to employ empathy in a way that facilitates the collection of undistorted data, particularly in the area of scientific depth psychology, will vary greatly depending on many factors. These factors, which include both biological equipment and, especially, childhood experience, deserve much careful investigation" (p. 83).

The proper therapeutic ambience, therefore, became for Kohut and other self psychologists an essential *sine qua non* for therapeutic success. Specifically, self psychology results in an attitude and an atmosphere that differ from those that tend to prevail when the analyst sees narcissistic demands as defenses and drive manifestations (especially the patient's rage) as primary rather than reactive phenomena (p. 90). Similar considerations pertain to manifestations of aggression and sexuality. If the analyst sees these phenomena as primary expressions of the patient's personality, he will have a different attitude toward the patient than if he sees such phenomena as secondary and symptomatic reactions to traumatic experiences or the fear of them. These different attitudes, in turn, will have significantly different influences on the therapeutic process: "However softened by the compassion and tact of the analyst, interpretations of infantile seductive and aggressive behavior . . . will be experienced by the patients as subtly censorious and disapproving" (p. 90–91). On the other hand, interpretations by the self-psychologically informed analyst of the disruption of the selfobject transference, for which the analyst will take some responsibility, are likely to be experienced without shame and as enhancing self-understanding.

However, there is even more involved than mere theoretical conviction. Haynal (1989, p. 125) asks whether there are two kinds of analysis: one more fatherly, rational, and based on remembering and on insight, the other more motherly, regressive, and based on interactive experiences and preverbal communications at a deeper level. Are there, as Gilligan (1982) has suggested, two kinds of thinking, feeling, and reasoning — a male type and a female type? Kohut was once asked whether female therapists were naturally more empathic than male therapists because in their roles as mothers of babies they have more opportunity than males ever have to become skillful in the exercise of their empathic capacities. Kohut thought briefly and then allowed that, indeed, women had this natural advantage over men. But, he went on to say with a smile, men realize this advantage of women and with their natural competitiveness they try harder and become equally or more empathic!

Reflections on Abstinence, Neutrality and Gratification

I have chosen, therefore, to generalize from my personal experiences as analysand and as analyst and to state my preferences based on this experience. I have been asked, for example, whether I as a self psychologist do better psychotherapy than a more classically oriented therapist, and I must answer that negatively. I cannot make such comparisons since I do not know what goes on in other therapists' consulting rooms. But I do know something about my therapeutic practice now as compared to 20 years ago, and I know I am more empathic and more effective in what I am doing. And yet, maybe that's only because I am older, calmer, and more experienced. I still believe, as I did in 1976 when I published "Ambience and Abstinence," that the therapeutic ambience is one of the most important factors in predicting a therapeutic outcome. An optimal ambience can be described with reference to abstinence, neutrality, and gratification as subheadings for variable conditions that affect the therapeutic process.

ABSTINENCE

I still believe that all therapists, psychoanalytic or otherwise, should be totally abstinent from giving or receiving any kind of erotic gratification within the therapeutic situation. I say this not just on moral grounds but also from my perception of the point of view of self psychology, being fully aware that my perception is not necessarily shared by other self psychologists. Sexual arousal or drivenness within the psychoanalytic situation, whether of therapist or of patient, is always a sign of some fragmentation of the self. In a cohesive and well-functioning self, sensuality and sexuality are integrated into a coherent and harmonious matrix that allows sexual excitement and arousal by *psychological* stimuli only under circumstances that are learned and culturally sanctioned. (Arousal can occur anywhere, of course, as a result of nonpsychological physical-mechanical stimuli such as touching.) The therapeutic situation is not one of these circumstances in which sexual excitement in the healthily functioning analyst can be expected to occur even though the analyst may be quite aware of the attractiveness of the patient. When excitement and arousal occur, they should be treated like any other symptomatic manifestation of self-disintegration, that is, with understanding and explaining but not acting out.

GRATIFICATION

Does that mean that no gratification is legitimate in the therapeutic situation? Freud's advocacy of abstinence was not as rigid as his writing indicated and was probably limited to abstinence from sexual gratification. Freud fed the Ratman when he was hungry; he also sent him postcards and lent him a book. Freud did not hesitate to take his patients into rooms other than his consulting room in order to show them his collection of antiquities. This was reported by at least two of his patients (H. D. and Money-Kyrle). At times, Freud did not hide his own feelings: for example, as H. D. reports, he hit the couch angrily and called Alix Strachey greedy when she wanted to tell him the rest of a dream after he had given her a partial interpretation.

Total abstinence from all gratification is a myth. Moreover, if it were possible to deprive patients of all gratification, the result would clearly be antitherapeutic. The least that any patient can expect is that the therapist customarily be present, be reasonably attentive, and sincerely try to be understanding: all of these are gratifying in varying degrees, depending on the particular state of the patient's self. It is the patient's need for affirmation, a variety of mirroring, that would be gratifyingly responded to by the therapist's caring interest and attention. Similarly, the therapist's professional reputation, his dignified demeanor, the appearance of his office, and the intelligence, even wisdom, of his words all tend to create for the patient an ambience in which the patient may well experience the therapist as an idealized selfobject, thus gratifying a selfobject need to be able to look up to and feel accepted by someone whom one respects greatly. I would agree with Terman (1988) and Bacal (1985) that Kohut's concept of "optimal frustration" be replaced with "optimal responsiveness." The difference here may be subtle and, perhaps, unimportant to many patients, but I think it will often make a significant difference to the progress of the therapeutic enterprise.

NEUTRALITY

Finally, some comments on the issue of the therapist's neutrality: Initially, this meant that the analyst remain neutral vis-à-vis id, ego and superego and also with respect to conflicts between the patient and his family or other parts of the environment. I think such neutrality may well interfere with the progress of the analysis because it interferes with the establishment of a good working analyst–analysand relationship. Most people go into treatment because they want to be helped to feel better, rather than to advance psychoanalytic science. Most people, therefore, want the therapist not only to be understanding but willing to help with his knowledge. Patients sense and perceive much about the therapist's agenda and commitments. In the painful and expensive struggle of the patient with the forces that threaten the cohesion and vitality of the self, the therapist is expected to be on the patient's side.

It is the analyst's personality-determined philosophical orientation and value system that is reflected in the choice of his theoretical commitments. Thus, I believe that a certain vulnerability of the self to its own excitements leads to a self-protective posture of the analyst that favors structure, distance, laws, certainty, and scientific reasoning, for example, Freud's emphasis on intrapsychic dynamics and the associated emphasis on abstinence, neutrality, and denial of gratification in treatment. On the other hand, I think that a stronger self, one less vulnerable to its affects, can afford a posture of flexibility, emotional closeness, tolerance for uncertainty, spontaneity, and empathic responsiveness without endangering its structural integrity. Kohut's reliance on empathic immersion and elucidation of subjective experiences resulted in greatly diminished emphasis on abstinence, in the abandonment of neutrality in favor of establishing an identification with the interests of the analysand, and, finally, among contemporary self psychologists, in allowing optimal responsiveness to replace abstinence. The great emphasis on rigidly prescribing abstinence, neutrality, and absence of gratification for psychoanalytic technique is an archaic residue from the early days of psychoanalysis. In those days of a Victorian type of superficial Puritan morality in a society that was characterized by almost universal acting out, especially sexually, Freud was forced to be extremely scrupulous about the ethical behavior of his followers. They were often neurotic and artistic in temperament, and many were Jewish intellectuals who were socially peripheral to the mainstream of the ruling classes. Thus, Freud had to lean over backwards and ordain rules of conduct for therapists that were not always needed or always in the best interests of the therapeutic process. He certainly did not consider himself bound by those rules, as many of his patients have testified. Nor would I think that many of his early Viennese followers were too scrupulous in obeying these rules. However, when transported to the United States in the thirties by refugee analysts, the rules of abstinence, neutrality, and absence of gratification became the dominant guides to conducting psychoanalytic treatment. These rules make the difficult task of treatment even more formidable. Except for a tiny minority of patients, the deprivations imposed by these rules are fragmenting rather than therapeutic. By contrast, optimal responsiveness, as defined and elaborated by Terman and Bacal, results in an ambience and therapeutic process that are much more conducive to getting positive therapeutic outcomes. We need not look far for the reasons for this. It is the need of every human being, patient or analyst, to be surrounded by a responsive selfobject matrix. That means, in essence, to be understood both cognitively and empathically. Nothing in this, however, condones the acting out of sexual or aggressive urges, by either patient or analyst. In fact, such acting out usually is most destructive to any therapeutic endeavor. So I would modify these rules as follows: (1) Do not abstain from gratifying the patient with friendly responsiveness and understanding. (2) Do not be neutral vis-à-vis the patient's struggles in life, but be firmly on the patient's side, including stopping the patient from doing things that will be harmful. (3) Let yourself be guided by the patient's interests and welfare, not by advancing science or your own education.

References

Alexander, F. (1946), Individual psychotherapy. *Psychosom. Med.,* Vol. 8, No. 2, March-April, pp. 110–115.

Bacal, H. (1985), Optimal responsiveness and the therapeutic process. In: *Progress in Self Psychology, Vol. 1,* ed. A. Goldberg. New York: Guilford Press, pp. 202–226.

_____ (1990), Introduction and overview. In: *Theories of Object Relations,* ed. H. Bacal & K. Newman. New York: Columbia University Press, pp. 1–14.

Eissler, K. R. (1953), The effect of the structure of the ego on psychoanalytic technique. *J. Amer. Psychoanal. Assn.,* 1:104–143.

Ferenczi, S. (1919), On the technique of psychoanalysis. In: *Further Contributions to the Theory and Technique of Psycho-Analysis, Vol. 2.,* New York: Brunner/Mazel, pp. 177–189, 1926.

_____ (1928), The elasticity of psychoanalytic technique. In: *Final Contributions to the Problems and Methods of Psycho-Analysis, Vol. 3.* New York: Brunner/Mazel, pp. 87–101, 1955.

_____ (1929), The principle of relaxation and neocatharsis. In: *Final Contributions to the Problems and Methods of Psycho-Analysis, Vol. 3.* ed. New York: Brunner/Mazel, pp. 108–125, 1955.

_____ (1930), Thoughts on pleasure in passivity. In: *Final Contributions to the Problems and Methods of Psycho-Analysis, Vol. 2.* New York: Brunner/Mazel, p. 226, 1955.

────── (1988), *The Clinical Diary of Sándor Ferenczi,* ed. J. Dupont. Cambridge, MA: Harvard University Press, 1988, p. xiii.

Freud, S. (1895), The psychotherapy of hysteria. *Standard Edition,* 2:281–283. London: Hogarth Press, 1955.

────── (1933), New introductory lectures. *Standard Edition,* 22:151. London, Hogarth Press, 1964.

Gilligan, C (1982), *In a Different Voice: Psychological Theory and Women's Development.* Cambridge, MA: Harvard University Press.

Haynal, A. (1989), *Die Technik-Debatte in der Psychoanalyse.* Frankfurt: Fischer Taschenbuch Verlag.

Kohut, H. (1966), Forms and transformation of narcissism. In: *The Search for the Self, Vol. 1,* ed. P. Ornstein. New York: International Universities Press, 1978, pp. 427–460.

────── (1984), *How Does Analysis Cure?* Chicago: University of Chicago Press.

Stone, L. (1961), *The Psychoanalytic Situation.* New York: International Universities Press.

Terman, D. (1988), Optimum frustration: Structuralization and the therapeutic process. In: *Learning From Kohut: Progress in Self Psychology, Vol. 4,* ed. A. Goldberg. Hillsdale, NJ: The Analytic Press, pp. 113–125.

Wolf, E. (1976), Ambience and abstinence. *The Annual of Psychoanalysis,* 4:101–115. Hillsdale, NJ: The Analytic Press.

────── & Nebel, S. (1978), Psychoanalytic excavations: The structure of Freud's cosmography. *American Imago,* 35:178–202.

Abstinence, Neutrality, Gratification:
New Trends, New Climates, New Implications

The Thesis

Most of our patients live in an internal atmosphere chronically peopled
by malignant introjects or selfobjects. The environmental failures that
contribute to the creation of these internal figures compose a twofold
trauma. First is the inadequate parental response to primary needs,
which leaves the self in a state of vulnerability with varying degrees of
deficiency in self-regulation and with a pervasive sense of frustration.
The second, equally important, problem is a failure on the part of the
early caregivers to help the child sufficiently in the management of
intense affect states consequent to the failure to gratify primary needs for
mirroring and tension regulation. Often, the critical step producing
pathological character formation and constricted or "frozen" object
relations is this secondary failure in the holding environment. The
resultant crippling character defenses can be considered to be the product
of heroic but distorted efforts to quiet the dangerously seething internal
environment. This pathologic environment contains the presence of the
caretaker who failed or was in some way unreliable as a good-enough
object, that is, who was in some way unable to enhance the self of the
child or to help it contain its painful affects.

If we are to alter this pathologic atmosphere, I believe the most vital
issue to be the provision or creation of a "usable" object capable of
modifying the nature of this pathologic state. This can best occur through
the experience of an analytic relationship that differs in significant ways
from one based on more traditional thinking. In the next section of this
chapter I review, briefly, contributions by Winnicott, Kohut, and others,
which highlight crucial ideas and background components for my thesis.

Background Concepts: A Brief Literature Review

Before work on deeper conflicts can be confronted safely and new structures developed, the patient must achieve a connection to the therapist, whom the patient experiences as "usable." This term, first referred to by Winnicott (1971), implies an object whom the patient views as separate and as a source of emotional sustenance for the matrix of the self. The patient must be able to experience this new object (relationship) as relatively free of the compromise solutions characterized by the pathological bonds (false self) established as a reaction to the original environmental failure. How patient and analyst establish a usable connection to create something mutative and new can only be learned by trial and error over time and often only after stalemates, countertransference lapses, and empathic breaks. The concept of "optimal responsiveness" (Bacal, 1985) is especially helpful in thinking about the quality that helps establish such a relationship. As Bacal and others (e.g., Terman, 1988; Tolpin, 1988) attempted to counter old ideas about the benefits of abstinence, they naturally had to clarify the meaning of gratification as it relates to optimal responsiveness.

The troublesome issue of gratification in clinical theory can be introduced by starting with Winnicott's (1958) observations on those factors that lead to growth, enhancement, and strengthening of the self-matrix. He emphasized that the capacity to recognize an external object and place it outside of oneself comes in the context of gratifying experiences with an available mother who can adapt herself to the primary needs of the infant. Frequently using almost poetic or vague terms, Winnicott underscored the importance of the availability and presence of the maternal object, thus challenging existing tenets regarding the beneficial effects on development of optimal frustration. Application of this developmental view to the clinical situation involves the therapist's providing an environment of "usability" to facilitate the forging of a new object experience. Winnicott recognized that often the patient's resistance to accepting this provision was manifest in the rigidity of the false-self character; considerable creativity was often required on the part of the therapist to offer a mutative new object experience. In keeping with this developmental view, Winnicott (1958) advocated the selective provision of components of need satisfactions. The various ways in which he imagined the therapist might accommodate the patient were not always clear, but he did speak to a major controversial issue when he stated that "many patients . . . cannot dare to express their hurts or their needs until some part of these needs are in some symbolic or even tangible way met" (p. xxiii). This is clearly a marked departure from the classical view that frustration promotes the verbal expression of wishes, fantasies, and needs. Terman (1988) offers compelling evidence from infant research that it is the presence of a gratifying object that leads to new structures in the growing infant. In the clinical situation it is the analyst's understanding attunement and responsiveness to the patient's needs that strengthens and enhances the self, thus making it possible for new pathways to grow and old ones to be explored. In Terman's (1988) view (and my own), frustration is seen as playing a secondary role in the building of structure or the acquiring of patterns. In his paper Terman acknowledges Kohut as the source for the concept that positive connectedness is a necessary precondition for the patient's use of the analyst for constructive self-cohesion as well as conflict resolution.

Kohut's influence on our current thinking on the needs of the self and how it develops must be underscored. In positioning the developing and vulnerable self as the core of much of pathology, Kohut (1984) explicitly sanctions the therapist's role as transforming selfobject. By stressing the importance of permitting the self–selfobject relationship to be established as the foundation of the clinical encounter and by decentralizing the role of drives to a secondary consideration, Kohut (1977) moved closer to a nonadversarial position with respect to his patients.

The shift in clinical theory of psychoanalysis to a less adversarial, less drive-oriented relationship was further elaborated by the concept of intersubjectivity, that is, transference as a two-party system. Hoffman (1983) addresses the importance of the patient as interpreter of experience—both his own and the analyst's. This requires a revision of the classical tenets that considered the therapist merely as a receptacle for distortions and as the interpreter, as well as arbiter, of reality. The recognition that the therapist plays a crucial role in effecting the patient's immediate experience and, in turn, is himself influenced emotionally by the patient's conscious and unconscious productions changes our understanding of the overall clinical environment, largely by shifting the site and focus of therapeutic action.

These newer concepts regarding the role of the analyst are reflected in a reconsideration of the issue of management of affects and of the role of the early parent's "container" function. I refer especially to Winnicott's work on the "holding environment" and his concept of survival of destruction. Like many later clinicians (e.g., Krystal, 1975; Basch, 1984; Stolorow and Socarides, 1985; Newman, 1988). Winnicott was interested in the management of affect states, especially those activated by frustration or injury. He saw the role of the early caretakers as involving tolerance for the intensity of the infant's feelings while still remaining available and psychologically alive for the infant. This holding function could then provide the containment and integration necessary for even painful feelings to be embraced within the matrix of the infant's subjective self. I believe that faulty responses by objects to the infant's negative, rageful feelings are a critical, developmentally ominous aspect of selfobject failure. These authors have made more or less explicit the watershed effect whereby pathological defenses become instituted when the object's failure renders the fear of affects a threat to *both* the subject's psyche and his tie to the object. In many ways this reasoning parallels Winnicott's motivational explanation for false-self development.

Clinical Example I

A few years ago I held to a technical approach that often ignored the crucial significance of the atmosphere necessary for a patient to safely relive intense feelings. Let me offer an example. A patient quickly permitted herself a therapeutic regression that opened up early developmental failures and needs. When I returned from a vacation, she requested more frequent appointments and often some extra phone contact. I was hesitant to fulfill these requests and chose instead to interpret them as an attempt to have us collude to cover over the depth of her hurt, loneliness, and accompanying rage. These interventions were always met with varying degrees of despair and protest, but fortunately the patient retained enough positive alliance to indicate to me in compelling terms the ways in which I was misguided. The gist of the matter was that while she recognized that rage was embedded in her overall reactions, she in no way could safely face these intense feeling states until I first made the steps necessary to gather our relationship back in. It was only from a position of feeling reconnected (a self–selfobject union) that she could feel more secure in expressing her rage.

The issues may be illuminated by a comparison: How do our own children behave after a separation from us, and how do we relate to them? When we return from a vacation most of our children express the need for more immediate and prolonged contact, and trouble really begins if we treat this as spiteful, manipulative, or otherwise "illegitimate." But, actually, we would consider it ludicrous were we to say to a four-year-old left for one or two weeks, "Come on now, don't be so clinging or insist on spending more time with me; you know it's only a reaction formation against your rage." It is becoming more apparent that if we really want to help our patients integrate intense affects, we will do so best by first providing the frame to allow them to regain a sense of union both with us and within themselves. This is the security position from which they can begin to express their hurt, their loss, and their anger, both currently and as these feelings connect to the past.

In recent years the notion that we need to provide an atmosphere for safety prior to the exploration and interpretation of deeper conflicts pivoted around the concept of the therapeutic alliance. Early diatrophic (parental) components of development that contribute to the formation of the self and the maturation of the ego serve as the foundation for therapeutic and analytic work. Support for or responsiveness to these issues was seen as a necessary prerequisite for later interpretive work.

Self psychology has extended the idea of the therapeutic alliance with the addition of the idea that the vulnerable self needs a more complex connection to a selfobject in order to feel safe enough to access its deeper, more threatening reaches. Furthermore, this connection is not only a prerequisite but constitutes the beginning of the emergence of a core transference in itself.

It is the acceptance of the need for this vital transference connection that leads to the stability as well as the expansion of the self. The yield to the patient of this self–selfobject connection is the improved capacity to gain an understanding of his inner world and the acceptance of needs and hope for a new response. This then permits deeper regressions to unfold, setting the stage for more work on conflicts and primitive affect-laden material.

Clinical Example II

Another clinical vignette offers an opportunity to contrast a more traditional therapist's approach with some of the modern views just outlined.

The patient, a divorced woman in her thirties, came for analysis because of recurrent depressions and a history of misadventures with a series of uncaring men. She had been seeing her male analyst for several weeks when she reported the following dream: the patient was to meet her analyst after regular hours on the balcony located just outside the latter's office and felt an anticipatory pleasure at the thought of the meeting.

In her associations the patient thought of her compulsive mother, who brought her up by the rules. She remembered a specific incident that occurred when she was four years old: she had been put outside and was not allowed to come in until a prescribed time had passed despite the fact that it was winter and extremely cold that day.

The analyst's interpretation was that the patient wanted him to meet her in a special place and time as a way of breaking the rules; that is, the patient wanted to feel special in order to avoid the rage she had at her mother. Several months later, the patient requested that the therapist change a particular hour in order to accommodate a new job schedule. The therapist remained silent at first and finally, again, interpreted the patient's wish to break the rules. In both instances the patient responded with a period of silent withdrawal followed by a determined feeling that the analyst was withholding and was, in fact, as bound by rules as her mother had been.

The technique the therapist used to address this material may seem caricatured to some of you, but it does represent the essence of a sanctioned and familiar traditional approach. The therapist's interpretation was designed to undermine what he saw as the emergence of a transference defense designed to block access to the underlying hostile maternal transference. Although it was quite early in the treatment and little work had been done on establishing a working alliance, let alone the establishment of a self–selfobject transference, the therapist's assumption was that the patient's ego would be able to manage a direct confrontation with her anger without the assurance of a solid connection with the therapist. Many analysts (Kernberg, for example) could argue convincingly that an authentic alliance can only be established after the negative transference has been made conscious and then interpreted. While conflict over hostility is surely prominent in this woman's dynamics, I believe that care should have been given to the establishment of a more solid therapeutic relationship before expecting such affects to be usefully integrated.

Whether we refer to it as attending to the therapeutic alliance or following self psychology's model (that the patient needs a reliable self–selfobject relationship as a precondition for more regressive work), a different approach might have characterized the response of many clinicians to this dream. I would rather consider the patient's communication as a desire for a new experience (unlike that with her mother), one that transcended the therapist's agendas based on arbitrary evaluations of what was good for the patient. I would have spoken to the nature of her inner world and to her chronically feared and hated relationship with her mother. By responding at this level, I think I would convey my understanding both of what she hopes for in the treatment and of what she fears being repeated. If through my grasp of the patient's inner experience I hope to "seed" the possibility of a different relationship with me, I must first convey to her some evidence of my reliable understanding of her aims. By accepting and even verbalizing what the patient is trying to attain, rather than focusing on what is being covered over, I avoid the danger of automatically being experienced as the attacking mother. To focus at this time on what is being avoided can only be experienced as criticism. Incidentally, we might reflect (at least silently) on the creativity of the patient's constructing a dream that described a new space (open but dangerous?) in which to frame a new experience.

Countertransference: The Therapist's Dilemmas

Having established the importance of the newer attitudes, which may best be condensed in the term *optimal responsiveness,* we need to consider the therapeutic complexities that refine the concept.

Many of our patients, having suffered the twofold selfobject failures described earlier, have had to organize protective character armor that makes our recognizing and providing optimal and emotionally gratifying responses often difficult, if not tumultuous. Our patients naturally have erected defenses and other protective barriers that, for at least a time, make direct access to their core needs impossible. Not only do they suffer from unfulfilled needs, but they have the memory traces of needs that in their original form were thwarted; hence, the promise of reawakening hopes for fulfillment is also a threat. Why? Because it reawakens the stored-up frustration/rage/helplessness of previous encounters. The initial presenting character patterns of such patients may prevent them from making significant use of us; nor can simple empathy or logic alone help. We may be forced to stumble through a long period of trial and error before we can learn what they really need from us—and under what circumstances they will accept it. What is common to all these revisions in theoretical understanding is a recognition that however troublesome the impact on us, at root the patient is not an implacable or hostile adversary but is acting with the hope of fulfilling legitimate needs and claims. The patient should be trusted to have an ultimately reliable prescription for new constructive experience. It nearly always takes considerable time and creative effort on the part of the therapist to learn how best to provide the framework and nidus for new responsiveness.

On the way to this goal the pathological character of the patient's old solutions and restitutive (defensive) object relations will create massive obstacles that may temporarily ensnare the therapist. But out of this seemingly difficult morass of conflicts and affective storms the therapist may learn with increasingly fine sensitivity just how to be truly helpful. At a tactical level, just how does this occur?

Sampson and Weiss (1986) have referred to the unconscious plan of the patient to achieve a "non-confirmation of toxic introjects." The authors describe how the patient's character pathology confronts the therapist with a stiff test, yet the patient's ultimate hope is that the therapist will find his way out of the neurotic enmeshment and be able to offer a new, positive experience. This is a thesis that acknowledges in the patient an unconscious ally whose needs for a new constructive object — while often encoded in complex, if not contradictory, messages — can be viewed as a legitimate plea for optimal responsiveness. Like Racker (1968), these authors also see the stages of our colluding with the patient's old objects as forms of countertransference reaction. These reactions are potentially the most affectively immediate ways of tasting the patient's failed and frozen internal world. If we are willing to learn from our inevitable failures based on the interaction of the patient's character with our humanness, then the troublesome "way in" may often turn out to be the most therapeutically useful "way out."

Let's look at a spectrum of clinical examples that illustrate the obstacles created by our patients' character and the challenges they raise as we attempt to recognize what therapeutic conditions are needed to achieve optimal growth.

The more benign-appearing presentations, where we see the patient's compliant, false, or performing self (the "good" patient), can prove very gratifying to the therapist in the initial stages. If we are tuned into ourselves, disquieting noises will eventually signal us to be alert to messages from the patient's unconscious. When properly deciphered, these communications, often encoded in extratransference allusions, dreams, or even symptomatic acts, convey the patients' fear that they have been or will be seduced into a compromise bond. The critical issue here is not a matter of whether we have in reality accepted this role and hence are identified with aspects of the faulty introjects but how gracefully we accept our patients' view of the situation. When we become aware that we have been unconsciously replicating these identifications and enjoying too gladly our patients' intuiting our agendas, we then have a chance to provide a constructively new experience. We first have to listen for our patients' protests, and we must validate as correct in some way their perceptions about our participating unwittingly in a collusive bond similar to that of their childhood relationships. When we allow the patient to be the interpreter of our countertransference reaction (Hoffman, 1983), we set in motion a number of new and vital psychic events. By accepting our role in the current transaction, we are offering a new paradigm of "comfortable acceptance" for affect management. If we can absorb and contain without retaliation in any form the negative feelings that accompany the patient's disappointment, we can provide a holding environment that can help an internalizing process to begin.

Because this leads to a deepening of the transference, in certain patients it will result in the emergence of new demands and other "regressive" manifestations. As a major player in this occurrence, we need to be prepared to consider the multilayered management issues with which this "progress" confronts us, issues that are illustrated in the following scenario.

The patient, in the context of unfolding transference needs or rising tension, may request or insist upon some extra contact with the analyst. This has been described as an "archaic transference crisis" (Gunther, 1984). Most often the patient seeks some symbolically special experience with the analyst, such as a phone call (and may even require a protracted period before he can hang up). The patient usually expresses conflict over this "intrusion," which he fears burdens the therapist. While endeavoring to handle the situation with grace, at some point or on some occasion the therapist will feel oppressed but remain silent. It is here that the first serious empathic break may occur. The patient may quickly sense the therapist's reaction. Several outcomes are now possible. The patient may simply withdraw and become emotionally detached. Or, out of anxiety, he may become more intensely demanding and plead for reassurance. If the therapist already feels put upon, he may now become openly angry or withdraw. In spite of this deteriorating situation, I believe we can use this as an opportunity to both identify with the patient's malignant introjects and work our way out to a constructive therapeutic position based upon a careful understanding of the patient's world.

How to do this can be illustrated by looking at the transaction from the patient's vantage point. If the therapist is prepared to provide an atmosphere suitable to meeting regressive needs, then shouldn't he be welcoming these heretofore walled-off strivings? If we believe that significant therapeutic regressions bring forth these demands, then shouldn't we understand that we may have to not only accept being used as a new target of old object needs but also accept (willingly) for a time our own feelings of being so burdened? When we become overwhelmed and irritated by our patients and can taste the wish to criticize or even rid ourselves of them, we are getting a firsthand sample, albeit unwelcome, of their internal objects with whom we have unconsciously identified. We might silently think, "Now I know the kind of inner world you live in and why you dread showing needs and fear being rejected for being a burden, because for the moment I felt you were a burden and wished to be rid of you, too. But does this period of enactment, which I find so burdensome, even qualify as therapy?" This interaction also represents a potential new beginning and a chance to neutralize the toxic introjects. For once we can gain some separation from this temporary, if not inevitable, countertransference reaction, we may reclaim our positive tie to this patient, this "temporary child" of ours!

However, we must learn to discriminate between these regressive events — involving newly awakened, albeit intensely expressed, needs — and the repetition of old solutions that have no potential as "new beginnings." By the latter, I mean those addictive-like and exploitive behaviors (often described as "manipulative") organized early in life in collusion with parents who were unable to meet the child's original needs in an optimal manner, that is, behaviors that represent a kind of maladaptive expedient that made psychic survival possible for the child. Such discriminations are often difficult to make.

Bearing the sometimes burdensome aspects of adapting to the needs of those patients who are reliving newly awakened needs enables us to provide a new experience that can provide new patterns and structures for affect management. Part of the new experience is the therapist's availability for tension regulation. He adapts to the patient's prescription, which sometimes includes the need for almost immediate responsivity at times that may be quite inconvenient. By so adapting, I believe we are laying the groundwork for important structural accretion. How? The patients who require and even allow themselves this form of regression also need our inherent trust that they will not misuse this auxiliary maternal function we offer. The beneficial yield in these admittedly unique cases is that the patient's psyche does use our presence, as well as our capacity to bear the painful affects and storms, to gain strength and learn new pathways for tension discharge. In time, we begin to work on certain core conflicts. In the context of repeated experiences of having been understood, there are now periods where the patient permits delay and thereby makes it possible for us to explore and discriminate between the current reality and his conviction of having been abandoned or otherwise misused in the past. As we become more selective in our availability and responsiveness, we can introduce interpretations that take up the old issues of burden and rejection, as well as the repetitive use of maladaptive solutions in a vain attempt to heal old injuries.

The following case illustrates an especially common dilemma into which well-intended, empathically attuned therapists will occasionally fall. Our usual method of providing a therapeutic atmosphere sufficient to create a new experience rests upon a presumption of our available empathy, utilized to understand the inner world of our patients. However, the nature of patients' resistances makes this technique eminently more complex. Sheldon Meyers (1988), in writing about a supervised case with Kohut, presents a patient who reacted with extreme irritable sensitivity and bristling rage to many of his early interventions. The patient was especially enraged at those interpretations that, from the therapist's point of view, were attempts to explain his current "resistances" in terms of his chronic frustration with disappointing past objects. These interpretations were viewed by the patient as attempts by the therapist to force him prematurely into a "transference" relationship motivated primarily by the therapist's own needs. By having his constant negativism labeled as resistance, the patient felt not only rebuked but openly justified in his criticism of the therapist. He believed his therapist to be vulnerable to reality-based attacks both for misunderstanding him and for using genetic interpretations to distance himself from the validity of his attacks.

A rapidly evolving stalemate was recognized and reversed, with some collaborative help from Kohut, so that a therapeutic process could develop. To place the problem conceptually, this patient needed to have his current experience validated even though it was in large part transference-based. He needed a "holding experience" that could tolerate his criticism of the therapist, who did not sufficiently understand this patient's intense need for a totally empathic selfobject. Yet while doing this, the therapist had to restrain himself from identifying this transference. Furthermore, the patient required that the therapist refrain from labeling the "resistance" elements behind his need to negate his attachment to the therapy, and his beginning recognition of the many meanings of the treatment. In essence, the therapist had to contain and absorb the angry affect, validate the patient's feelings of being misunderstood, and refrain from pushing the patient to acknowledge his need for the therapeutic relationship.

The early stalemate occurred because the therapist had unwittingly duplicated the role of the toxic parental introjects. Specifically, the patient was experiencing the therapist as the parents who didn't understand sufficiently his hurt feelings and who wanted to focus his hostility and negative perceptions away from themselves and onto someone or something else. When the therapist attempted to recast the persistent hostility as some form of resistance or negative therapeutic reaction, the patient experienced this as parallel to the self-centeredness of his parents. For him, the demand that he drop his suspicion and see the therapist as meaningful and important only reproduced for him the sense he had that his parents needed him to focus on them.

This patient represents a number of patients who have reorganized their vulnerable selves around a specific kind of protective character armor. They have retreated from directly engaging their deeper emotions in meaningful contact with others. Their acute sensitivity to slight and misunderstanding is both a transference and a defense. What they require most of the therapist is that he see their world, and accept it, as emotionally valid. They especially need to have the therapist understand and tolerate (1) their massive needs for empathy, (2) their need to not have the therapist insist on the patients' acknowledgment of their multilayered transference needs prematurely, and (3) their need to have the therapist renounce his usual urge or zeal to interpret their denials as transference or resistance to insight.

For the therapist to adapt to and gratify this form of need requires considerable awareness and acceptance of the inevitable counter-transference, which universally accompanies the deprivation and its defensive adaptations, especially the narcissistic insult of not being considered important. But if one can transcend these countertransference affects and view the patient as frozen in a state of self-protection unconsciously awaiting the finding of a new object, one who can manage not being needed, then paradoxically, in time an interpretable transference and an analytic alliance can emerge.

Philip Bromberg (1983) extends the conceptualization of the therapist's problem in accepting the patient's inability to consider him in any way other than as an extension of his own defensive grandiosity. In contrast to Kohut's view of the "understanding" phase, Bromberg feels that explanations about the motive for the patient's resistance can be tactfully offered. But the overall atmosphere in which the therapy is conducted is one in which the therapist gratifies the patient's need not to have to be forced to recognize the transference. Requiring such a premature recognition by the patient would reduplicate his feelings regarding his early caretakers' narcissistic needs for centrality in the relationship. Bromberg stresses that these patients have a brittle tension-regulating system dependent on their own omnipotent control. By denying the separate existence of the other, they view the other as existing simply to confirm their ability to control input. Early active or "noisy" attention to the patient's need may seduce him into a relationship of vulnerable dependence, which may activate a regression for which the patient's deficit structure is unprepared. Allowing the patient to set the agenda is also a crucial form of holding, Bromberg suggests. It offers an object, the therapist, who will be attentive and affectively available for new pathways for structural growth while preserving the patient's illusion of self-sufficiency until the capacity for genuine dependency can be better tolerated.

Equally important is our recognizing that the patient's unconscious prescription for treatment is not violating some theoretical precept of what is therapeutic. Despite some room for controversy, I hold that it is crucial to recognize that certain patients need us not to be a significant object. If, in addition, we provide the proper setting of a usable object, the matrix of the self may silently begin to expand and acquire new pathways for affect integration and a gradual ability to accept and see us as separate and eventually valuable.

Summary

I have described in some of these more difficult character presentations an amplification of Winnicott's concept of the "usable" object, one that permits the patient to alter his chronically frozen, static hostile internal environment. There are many patients who have had to wall off their deeper attachments and affects for others because of their chronic distrust. It often requires time, creativity, and an adaptive holding environment before patients' trust in the object can render it constructively usable. Only then can their needs be met and their injured feelings managed. Part of our test as potentially new objects has to do with how well we can prove able to survive psychic destruction. This parallels the ability of the caregivers to help their infants not only contain but embrace intense affect states. We begin to offer this possibility to our patients when, in fact, we can (1) accept not being seen or valued as a transference object; (2) accept our patients' criticisms, particularly those that refer to the times when we have lapsed into a countertransference reaction; and (3) begin to understand the *communicative* as well as the defensive function of their attacks and their outrage. If we can immerse ourselves in these feelings to sample what is being communicated, we necessarily will sense the distrust and hatred behind the patient's need to distance, devalue, or ignore us. This is how we are permitted entry into the internal world of our patients to truly know with what kind of objects they have lived. From this powerful experience we may learn to avoid automatic temporary identifications with these old introjects. Rather than defend ourselves, or blame or cajole our patients, we can begin to offer something new. Often, we will find ourselves in the position of the parent from whom a child has, from necessity, distanced himself by hostility and skepticism. The patient needs us to accept both his withdrawal and the explicit criticism of our failures. When we are able to accept the "holding" functions implicitly required in this transaction, we can begin to provide a better paradigm for affect management, for self-esteem, and for new relationships in life.

References

Bacal, H. (1985), Optimal responsiveness and the therapeutic process. In: *Progress in Self Psychology*, Vol. 1, ed. A. Goldberg. New York: Guilford Press, pp. 202–226.

Basch, M. (1984), Self objects and self object transferences: Theoretical implications. In: *Kohut's Legacy: Contributions to Self Psychology.* ed. A. Goldberg & P. Stepansky. Hillsdale, NJ: The Analytic Press, pp. 21–420.

Bromberg, P. (1983), The mirror and the mask: On narcissism and psychoanalytic growth. *Contemp. Psychoanal.,* 19:359–387.

Gunther, M. S. (1984), The prototypical archaic transference crisis. In: *Psychoanalysis: The Vital Issues.* ed. G. H. Pollock & J. E. Gedo. New York: International Universities Press, pp. 69–95.

Hoffman, I. (1983), The patient as interpreter of the analyst's experience. *Contemp. Psychoanal.,* 19:387–422.

Kohut, H. (1977), *The Restoration of the Self.* New York: International Universities Press.
———— (1984), *How Does Analysis Cure?* ed. A. Goldberg & P. Stepansky. Chicago, IL: University of Chicago Press.

Krystal, H. (1975), Affect tolerance. *The Annual of Psychoanalysis,* 3:179–218. New York: International Universities Press.

Meyers, S. J. (1988), On supervision with Heinz Kohut. In: *Learning from Kohut: Progress in Self Psychology, Vol. 4,* ed. A. Goldberg. Hillsdale, NJ: The Analytic Press, pp. 43–60.

Newman, K. M. (1988), Countertransference: Its role in facilitating the use of the object. *The Annual of Psychoanalysis,* 16:251–275. New York: International Universities Press.

Racker, H. (1968), *Transference and Countertransference.* New York: International Universities Press.

Sampson, H. & Weiss, J. (1986), *The Psychoanalytic Process.* New York: Guilford Press.

Stolorow, R. & Socarides, D. (1985), Affects and self objects: *The Annual of Psychoanalysis,* 12/13:105–119. New York: International Universities Press.

Terman, D. (1988), Optimum frustration: Structuralization and the therapeutic process. In: *Learning from Kohut: Progress in Self Psychology, Vol. 4,* ed. A. Goldberg. Hillsdale, NJ: The Analytic Press, pp. 113–125.

Tolpin, P. (1988), Optimal affective engagement: The analyst's role in therapy. In: *Learning from Kohut: Progress in Self Psychology, Vol. 4,* ed. A. Goldberg. Hillsdale, NJ: The Analytic Press, pp. 160–168.

Winnicott, D. W. (1958), Masud Khan's introduction to *Through Paediatrics to Psychoanalysis.* New York: Basic Books.
———— (1971), The use of an object and relating through identification. In: *Play and Reality.* London: Tavistock, pp. 109–111.

III

APPLIED
PSYCHOANALYSIS

The Childhood of an Artist

W. W. MEISSNER

The figure of Vincent van Gogh stands out in the history of art and human experience as one of the most enigmatic cases in which severe psychopathology and a powerful creative genius were conjoined. He has taken his place as one of the towering figures in the world of art, one of the greatest painters of the 19th century (whose works, along with his 20th-century successor, Picasso, command the highest prices paid by collectors). Yet van Gogh's life, which ended in suicide, was an almost uninterrupted saga of hurt, abandonment, isolation, depression, desperation, hopelessness, and frustration.

Van Gogh's life experience draws the interest of the psychoanalytic investigator. The recently passed centennial of his death — he killed himself on July 29, 1890 — has been the occasion of renewed interest in his tragic life, resulting in a torrent of studies of many aspects of his life and career. The psychoanalytic observer can say little about the genius that shaped the splotches of paint that flowed from his brushes to the canvas to become works of great beauty and expression, but there is much to be thought and said about the driving forces behind his creative work, about the motivations, the wishes and ambitions, the complex and multiple determinants that led him along his abysmal path and were distilled into his art. We are curious to seek out the factors that came into play to make his life such an unutterable disaster at the same time as they made his artistic endeavors so profoundly and meaningfully creative and expressive.

We know that the rudiments of this story were laid down in childhood and that any sense we might make of Vincent's story must take its origins in his earliest years. Brought into play from the very beginning of his life experience were crucial determinants that cast a long shadow over the ensuing years and played their role in determining his life's course and dismal outcome. I will try to piece together the fragments of that early history, as far as we know them, to see how far we can go in reconstructing the determining influences in the early life of one of our greatest and most creative talents.

The Beginning

Vincent was born on March 30, 1853, the second child born to Theodorus and Anna van Gogh. Tragedy pervaded his life from its beginning to its end. It is fair to say that his tragedy began before his birth, even before his conception. Even before he saw the light of day the events had already occurred that were to cast a long and tragic shadow over the course of his life.

The story begins on March 30, 1852, when another Vincent was born — exactly one year to the very day before the birth of our Vincent. The first Vincent was given the Christian name Vincent Willem van Gogh; he was stillborn. On the very same day one year later, the second Vincent was born and was given the very same name. Not only was there an identity in time and name, but in the birth register of the parish church Vincent's name was recorded under the same number as his dead brother from the previous year (Nagera, 1967).

This simple fact of Vincent's birth has given rise to endless speculation and theorizing about the effect on a child when he is fated to replace a dead sibling.[1] The loss of a child has profound effects on the parents and can exercise a powerful influence on the child who becomes the substitute. The parents are drawn to make restitution for their loss and feel compelled to prove to themselves and the rest of the world that they are capable of bringing a child into the world and keeping it alive (Agger, 1988). Often the dead child comes to represent the idealized fantasies and hopes of the parents, and these expectations are subsequently imposed on the replacement. Agger (1988) has recently observed: "When the sibling death occurs before the birth of the subject, the conscious expectation of the family that the subject will be a replacement for the lost child preempts the significance of unconscious fantasy as a formative factor. In these instances, the parent has denied the loss of the child and often consciously resurrects it through conceiving another one" (p. 24). There

---

[1]The phenomenon of sibling loss has played a part in the life and work of other artists: Mary Cassatt, for example, suffered the loss of several siblings at critical phases of her own development, traumas that left her with an intense degree of survival guilt and may have influenced her to recreate these lost siblings on canvas (see Zerbe, 1987).

is a considerable literature on the replacement-child syndrome. The scenario was described by Cain and Cain (1964), who emphasized the psychological damage to the surviving child. Poznanski (1972) described the idealization of the dead child, Pollock (1972, 1989) stressed the unresolved mourning and idealization of the dead child by the parents, and Volkan (1981) discussed the role of the surviving child as a linking object.[2]

In Vincent's case the unconscious element in the replacement syndrome is reflected in the arranging of the circumstances of Vincent's birth to exactly correspond to those of the dead Vincent — exactly the same date of birth to the day — and even perhaps in the misplacing of the name in the parish birth register — one would expect that the pastor, Vincent's father, was the responsible agent. More conscious components of the replacement syndrome may have expressed themselves in the application of the same name.

But a replacement child can never live up to the idealized image of the dead sibling and thus becomes an inevitable disappointment to the parents (Kernberg and Richards, 1988). The parents, especially the mothers, are often tormented by anxious fantasies of the death of the substitute child as well, who may become an object of such solicitous anxiety and concern that a pervasive sense of vulnerability and inadequacy is implanted in him (Cain and Cain, 1964; Nagera, 1967). As Mahler (Mahler, Pine, and Bergman, 1975) observed, "It is the specific unconscious need of the mother that activates, out of the infant's infinite potentialities, those in particular that create for each mother 'the child' who reflects her own unique and individual needs" (p. 60).

And the child is compelled by these unconscious demands to develop in such a way as to fulfill these imposed characteristics.[3] The phenomenon

---

[2]Additional studies have focused on the effects of the replacement syndrome in the lives of such famous persons as Schliemann (Niederland, 1965), Ataturk (Volkan and Itzkowitz, 1984), and Stendhal (Wilson, 1988).

[3]The emphasis on the death of the other Vincent and the dynamics of the replacement-child syndrome are psychoanalytic and are generally given little play in the efforts to understand Vincent and his works by art historians. Hulsker (1990), for example, discounts the idea of the replacement-child syndrome since he traces it to a presumably inaccurate comment made by Vincent's nephew. Since the apparent source of the information is lacking, he argues, the conclusion is inapplicable. This highlights the differences in method and conceptualization between the psychoanalytic and the historical, even art historical, approaches. These issues are explored by Spector (1988) and are well displayed in the acerbic dialogue (debate?) between the psychoanalyst Gedo (1987a, b) and the art historian Reff (1987a, b) over the role of homosexuality in the personality of Cézanne. The evidence for the replacement syndrome in Vincent's case has been sufficient to persuade psychoanalytic writers (Nagera, 1967; Lubin, 1972) of the plausibility of the hypothesis.

of sibling loss and its effects on the remaining children in a family has been explored by Pollock (1961, 1962, 1972, 1989), who writes: "We know that children who are dead may remain powerfully in the mother's mind and so can become even more important rivals for the surviving sibling, who has no ability or opportunity for reality confrontation and correction of the image of the idealized dead child" (1972, p. 478). The effects on the surviving child can be various. He can become a victim of a survivor syndrome that involves both a sense of special privilege in being the one chosen to survive and an abiding sense of guilt for the death of the lost sib. There is often an unconscious fantasy that the dead sibling was destroyed by one's own destructive wishes, resulting in an unconscious need for punishment. The presence in the replacement-child syndrome of a variety of fears, pathological superego formations, and an internal sense of evilness and worthlessness are well known to child psychiatrists (Kernberg and Richards, 1988).

The sense of rivalry cannot be avoided, and the attendant sense of satisfaction at the elimination of the rival plays its part. But dead siblings can be more powerful rivals than live ones: the narcissistic injury from the chronic failure to measure up to parental expectations and match the idealized standard of the image of the dead child makes its inevitable mark. No effort is adequate, no achievement sufficient, no striving is enough to dent the parental sense of loss and depression. The burden is often significant and imprints a permanent stamp on the core sense of self of the surviving child (Balsam, 1988). There is little doubt that the dead Vincent cast a long shadow over the life of the living Vincent.[4]

His Mother

If we reconstruct the events, Vincent must have been conceived only three months after the death of his brother. At the time, his mother would still have been deep in mourning for the loss of her firstborn. Her niece, the wife of Vincent's nephew, has suggested that this grief persisted for several years afterward and may well have been transformed into a chronic melancholic state. Her hopes and wishes had been shattered, and a part of her may have felt that this new child was a usurper, destined to take the place of his brother, assume his place in her heart, assume the burden of her expectations and hopes. In some sense, acceptance of this

---

[4]Vincent's case provides another striking example of what Shengold (1975, 1979, 1988) describes as "soul murder," a vicissitude that plays a particular role in the life histories of a number of creative individuals. Shengold has written specifically about Kipling (1975) and Dickens (1988).

new child was a betrayal and abandonment of the old. But he was also a replacement, a substitute who would become a repository for all the hopes and expectations that had been generated around the first Vincent, now distilled and magnified by the process of loss and restitution (Rochlin, 1965). The frustrated and denied hopes were passed through a prism of pain and disappointment only to be revived anew and even more laden with narcissistic expectations.

We can only speculate on the degree to which these circumstances of Vincent's birth came to exercise a profound influence on his development and subsequent history. To what extent might his mother's depression have continued to exercise an influence on the course of events? Was she still significantly depressed by the time of Vincent's birth? Might this residual depression and the ambivalence connected with Vincent's position as the substitute have played a role in the bond between mother and child? Was the mother capable of being a warm, loving, and responsive maternal object? Or might she have become emotionally unavailable and unresponsive to her infant? Did the fact that this replacement could never salve the pain or satisfy the dreams associated with the first Vincent influence her relationship with him? Or might he have become the repository for her pain, her disappointment, her rage at fate and God for depriving and denying her wishes and hopes?

There seems little doubt that this melancholic theme pervaded Vincent's mother's consciousness as well as the atmosphere of the parsonage. The little grave of his brother was close at hand, and Vincent would have passed it whenever the family went to church or whenever he visited home. The inscription in Dutch read:

VINCENT VAN GOGH

1852

Suffer the little children

to come unto me

and forbid them not for such is

the KINGDOM

of GOD

We might imagine that this legend might have been as indelibly carved into Vincent's mind as into the unyielding stone of the grave (Figure 1).

FIGURE 1.   *The gravestone of the first Vincent (from Tralbaut, 1969).*

Vincent's nephew, his brother Theo's son, would later write that Vincent was "conceived and carried by a mother who was in deep mourning, was able to see the tomb of the one he was to replace every day from the time he was old enough to perceive." The disappointment in the death of her firstborn may have been all the more poignant for Anna since she was then 33, older than her husband by three years, and time was running out. According to the custom of the time, his parents would still have been in the mourning period when Vincent was born. The message, however unconscious and denied, was clear enough — to be dead was to be loved and cherished, to be alive meant rejection and hostility. Erikson (1956) might well have had Vincent in mind when he wrote: "For example, a mother whose firstborn son dies and who (because of complicated guilt feelings) has never been able to attach to her later surviving children the same amount of religious devotion that she bestows on the memory of her dead child, may well arouse in one of her sons that conviction that to be sick or to be dead is a better assurance of being 'recognized' than to be healthy and about" (p. 87).

This theme sounds a refrain that echoes through Vincent's subsequent life history. Needless to say, its psychological ramifications are many. Lubin (1972) summarizes this aspect of Vincent's fateful identity:

He was the unhappy outsider, ignored and rejected by a grieving mother whose affection lay with the dead brother who was buried in the earth but had ascended into heaven. In defense, the second Vincent developed an envious identification with the first, made almost inevitable by the mysterious coincidence of name and birthdate. In the fantasy of his artistic life, he alternated between depicting the depressed, unloved outsider, living in darkness, whose salvation lay in death, and the adored child, reborn on the earth or ascended into the light of heaven [pp. 86–87].

The van Gogh family was in many ways a close-knit one. Uncle Vincent and Vincent's father were separated by only one year in age; moreover, their wives were sisters. Uncle Vincent had no children, and there seems to have been some expectation that his namesake nephew might follow in his footsteps, possibly succeeding his uncle in the Goupil firm of art dealers. It was Uncle Vincent who later placed the lad in Goupil's house in the Hague. These generous plans for Vincent's future were eventually to come to naught.

Vincent's father, Theodorus, was pastor in the small Dutch Reform church in Groot Zundert; he was a handsome and pleasant man, well liked by his parishioners, but without any great gifts that would have led to ecclesiastical preferment. His career led him from one obscure village church to another. His mother, Anna, was a mild, loving, pedestrian woman who aspired to little more in life than a happy and comfortable home and family. Both parents were decent, God-fearing people, bourgeois in their views, middle-class in their values, concerned with proprieties, outward appearances, and the opinions of their neighbors (Wallace, 1969). The family included two brothers and three sisters.

His mother's attitude toward Vincent and his work in later years was ambivalent: she had little understanding of his painting and showed little interest in it — despite the fact that she had some talent and interest in art herself. There are occasional mildly positive comments in her letters to Theo, but little else. After her husband's death, in the course of breaking up the family home at Nuenen, she had Vincent's canvases packed away and left them with the local carpenter. He later sold them to a junk dealer for a pittance. Vincent was always a disappointment and torment for his mother (Nagera, 1967). He was difficult as a child — troublesome, self-willed, and subject to temper tantrums. Anna seemed to be unable to deal with his storms of temper and self-willed rebelliousness. On one occasion, his grandmother van Gogh came to visit and was treated to one of Vincent's tantrums. Having been battle-hardened by her experience raising her own dozen children, she took the renegade by the arm, boxed him on the ears, and put him out of the room. This was apparently terribly upsetting to Vincent's mother, who was offended by her mother-in-law's action and refused to speak to her for the rest of the day (van Gogh-Bonger, 1959).

We cannot put great trust in such a piece of family mythology, but it may tell us something about the relationship between mother and son. Was Vincent's mother so unable to provide him ordinary parental discipline, and if so why? Was the reason for her failure to discipline him her view of him as special, privileged? Was it her guilt and remorse for the dead Vincent he was to replace? Was it an effort on her part to deny and counter her rage at him for displacing her firstborn, for being such a difficult and disappointing child? Was it her own conflicts over aggression and her need to play out the victim role with her aggression-torn son, who may, if that were the case, have played out his mother's displaced and denied aggression (perhaps against her mother-in-law?)? At any rate, Vincent was to a remarkable degree denied the training, molding, and discipline that would have helped him to take a more adaptive and human place in the company of his fellow men. From another perspective, however, for the child of creative genius an average mother may turn out to be equivalent to a misattuned, narcissistic, and perhaps even unempathic, mother (Miller, 1981).

A governess later recalled Vincent's unusual behavior and his unpleasant and eccentric manners, for which he was constantly being punished. He was regarded as strange by his mother and sisters; for the whole family he was difficult and isolated. He had a knack for imaginative play that endeared him to his siblings, but he was also stubborn, hot-tempered, and often given to strange behavior. He was often unpleasant, had peculiar manners, impressed people with his eccentricity, and was frequently withdrawn and solitary.

We can add to this the somewhat stern, disapproving, and distant image of Vincent's father — the rather remote and moralistic Calvinist minister, preoccupied with his ministry and little involved in family affairs, especially in raising the children. He was apparently a pleasant and reasonable man, no hellfire and brimstone fanatic, but remote, bookish, and disapproving nonetheless (Sweetman, 1990). Vincent was left with a frustrated yearning for acceptance and approval from this olympian father, a yearning that was never satisfied and that left him with a sense of bitterness, disillusionment, and failure.

Nature

In his latency years Vincent developed a love of nature and collected natural specimens as a hobby. His sister Elizabeth later recounted:

> Their brother walked past the children without a word; out of the garden gate, through the fields, and along the path that leads to the meadows. He was going to the brook; the children saw this by the flask and the fishing net that he carried with him, but none of them would have called after him: "Can I go along, brother?" And yet, they knew only too well how clever he was at catching water insects. This he showed them when he came back with different types of beetles with shiny, dark-brown shells, great round eyes, and crooked legs that nervously pulled up as soon as they were brought from the water onto dry land.
>
> All the beetles, even those with enormously long antennae, had names, difficult to remember, but their brother already knew all the names by heart. After he had prepared them in camphor he pinned them in small cardboard boxes lined with white paper, labelling each with a little strip of paper above each animal on which its name was written — and that was in Latin! . . . With a thousand voices Nature spoke to him, and his soul listened. . . . As of yet he was only able to listen [Elizabeth du Quesne-Van Gogh, cited in Stein, 1986, p. 32].

Vincent's early immersion and fascination with nature was reflected in some of his early artistic efforts. We do not know the age of these early efforts, but they come from somewhere in his childhood and demonstrate his extraordinary talent and his sensitivity to the complexity and beauty of nature. His absorption in nature would become one of the hallmarks of his mature art.

The story is told that he showed early talent at drawing and watercoloring. His sister Elizabeth recalled:

> While still a small boy he modeled — with the greatest curiosity — a little elephant from clay given to him by a sculptor's assistant. At eight years of age, he surprised his mother with a drawing of a cat flying in a mad rage up a bare apple tree in the winter garden. These spontaneous expressions of artistic feeling were surprising, especially since they occurred so rarely — too rarely to be mentioned; so that only much later were they remembered by his parents [van Gogh-Bonger, 1959, p. 32].

His sister Johanna added a footnote to the story: when the family tried to praise the little elephant, Vincent became enraged and destroyed it (van Gogh-Bonger, 1959).

The Foreigner

Vincent's play with other children presented a problem since he was frequently excessively rough. Dissatisfied with the local school and perhaps feeling that his associations with the peasant lads of Groot Zundert was having a bad influence on Vincent's development, his father tried to educate him at home for two years. But apparently out of a sense of frustration and not knowing how to handle him, as well as from Vincent's need for more regular schooling, his father sent him to a boarding school in a neighboring town. Undoubtedly, the problem was due more to Vincent's eccentric and rebellious ways than to his association with the peasant lads. In any case, at age 11, he was exiled to the boarding school at Zevenbergen. And he did experience it as an exile. Years later, he recalled to Theo his feelings as his parents drove away; with tears in his eyes he stood and watched the little yellow carriage as it faded into the distance. All the pain of separation, abandonment, and rejection came to rest on his troubled head. Vincent remained in this exile for the next two years, until 1866, when he was deemed ready to advance to a private secondary school in Tilburg, the State Secondary School King Willem II. The school was admirable, noted for good teaching and its progressive ideas. Vincent learned much and did well and might have had the opportunity for a university scholarship. But for reasons not known, this venture came to an end in March 1868, in midterm, when Vincent returned home, where he remained for nearly 15 months (Hulsker, 1990). The separation had lasted for four years but, despite Vincent's evident success in his studies, must have had its painful effects. It can only have reinforced his sense of not being an accepted part of the family.

Indeed, Vincent was hardly the easiest person to live with. His father and sister commented that he lived in the family "as if a foreigner." There is little doubt that he was not understood by his family. He was awkward, sensitive to a fault, highly intelligent, gifted, and precocious. In a family and society that was preoccupied with convention and religious and social conformity, Vincent did not find an easy place. He was physically clumsy, and his behavior was so uninhibited and solitary that it was a constant embarrassment for the family. His siblings were afraid to walk with him in public. His slow and conventional father could only regard

Vincent's independent and peculiar ways with disapproval. His sister Elizabeth described him in her memoir at about age 15:

> Rather broad-shouldered than tall, his back slightly bent by his bad habit of keeping his head down, the short-cut reddish-blond hair under a straw hat, shading a strange face; certainly not a boy's face! The forehead already wrinkled, the eyebrows pulled together in deep thoughts above a pair of eyes, small and deep-set, now of blue, now of greenish color according to the impression things around him made. Not handsome, ungraceful, he was remarkable at such an early age because of the profoundness that was expressed in his whole being. His brothers and sisters were strangers to him; he was a stranger to himself; he was a stranger to his own youth [cited in Hulsker, 1990, p. 10].

There was not much common ground between Vincent and his family. They could not understand him, could not accept his strange behavior, could establish no bonds of deep affection or intimacy, and generally regarded him as an outsider, an intruder on the seamless web of family conventionality. His abrupt manners, his uncompromising candor, and his unexpected mood changes were disconcerting. Clearly, there was no one in this early environment who was capable of appreciating, understanding, and supporting his talent and rough-hewn virtues.

If there was anyone in this family matrix with whom Vincent could connect it was his brother Theo, born four years after him. They became playmates, boyhood comrades, and fast friends — almost like twins. Their relationship would remain constant and mutually sustaining throughout their lives — but that is another story.

Vincent blamed himself for his poor relations with his family, and his internalized humiliation pointed him toward a path of lifelong resentment, bitterness, and sense of alienation and estrangement from his fellow men. The lack of appreciation and valuation, of appropriate narcissistic mirroring (Kohut, 1971, 1977), in any child, even a child of genius, can have lifelong devastating effects. Vincent seems to have been doomed to live out over and over the pattern of these childhood humiliations (Gedo, 1983).

The Search for Meaning

All of van Gogh's lifelong searching for a meaningful vehicle for his existence was in the service ultimately of finding himself and bringing a meaning into his life that would satisfy needs that had their roots embedded deeply in the soil of his early life experience. The understanding that comes closest to van Gogh's situation and offers some partial glimpses into this obscure developmental anlage is in the analysis of the role of the family romance in the development of the artist. The motif and the peculiar role of the family romance in the early lives of great artists has been described by Greenacre (1958). While the family romance is a general developmental phenomenon, it seems to play a particularly significant role in the lives of creative artists. Greenacre describes the phenomenon in these terms: "The germ of the family romance is ubiquitous in the hankering of growing children for a return to the real or fancied conditions at or before the dawn of conscious memory when adults were Olympians and the child shared their special privileges and unconditional love without special efforts being demanded" (p. 10). Such well-organized fantasies emerge most clearly in the early latency period and reflect a strong degree of unresolved ambivalence toward the parents, usually corresponding to unresolved oedipal conflicts. The ambivalence is usually reinforced by the residues of unresolved ambivalence from the anal period, in which aspects of good and bad take extreme black-and-white forms as applied both to the child's sense of self and to the parents.

If it is true that the potential artist brings to this development a special endowment of heightened perceptiveness and sensitivity, then the basic experiences out of which he fashions his emerging sense of himself and of his parents will have somewhat different characteristics. If one of the parents can provide a model for identification that can sustain the burden of idealization and the marks of greatness and can maintain a satisfactory affective relation to the child—or even without the stamp of greatness, if one of the parents can sustain a belief in the child's potential for greatness—the chances for the child to fulfill his creative destiny are enhanced (Greenacre, 1958). For Vincent, these optimal conditions were entirely lacking. Yet even in the face of his harsh devaluation from his father and the failure of maternal empathy, Vincent managed to create an idealized image of his father and sought desperately to gain approval and acceptance from this olympian subdeity. Yet, as Greenacre observes: "Yet the developing gifted child, even in very untoward circumstances, will sometimes be able to find a temporary personal adult substitute or even to extract from a cosmic conception some useful personalized god conception on which to project his necessary ideal for his father and himself to enable him to develop further" (p. 11). This seems closer to Vincent's pattern.

For the potential artist, the inborn qualities of greater sensory responsiveness and sensitivity carry with them effects of heightened intensity in interpersonal relations and a more imaginative and animated connection with inanimate objects. Greenacre (1958) refers to these as the "field of collective alternates." The psychological effects can be seen in precocious development, greater diffusion of boundaries between libidinal phases, greater intensity and prematurity of oedipal development, greater difficulty in relinquishing oedipal strivings, and, possibly, disturbances in the perception of the external world and in emotional involvements with other human beings. All of these implications would seem to have their place in Vincent's story.

The dynamics of the family romance carry an added burden in the child's sense of difference from his social group. As Greenacre (1958) comments: "Whether unusual precocity has developed or the reverse picture of blocking and pseudostupidity is uppermost, in either case the child of great potential creativeness often feels different and strange among his colleagues, and at a time when, as in adolescence, there is a strong wish to conform, the family romance furnishes a further rationalization for this sense of difference and is reinforced by it" (pp. 32–33).

Inevitably, the child of genius is a lonely child. His sense of difference makes him feel isolated and often, as a result, inferior. When the artist finally finds the medium of creative expression and is able to immerse himself in it, only then does the sense of loneliness find relief. As Greenacre puts it: "I believe that this realization of ability is often of great relief to extremely talented people, not so much because of the narcissistic gratification of recognition and not because of realization of balance and harmony, but because of the temporary interruption of essential loneliness" (p. 35). These findings could hardly find more poignant application than to Vincent, and will have important implications for understanding the role of his art in his psychic life (Bak, 1958). Vincent's love for and immersion in nature became one the collective alternates that played a significant role in his artistic life.

The Suffering Son

These dynamic elements came to play a vital role in van Gogh's artistic life, found their poignant expression in his paintings, and finally drew him down the fateful path to his suicide. One component found expression in his immersion in nature, a fascination that issued in an outpouring of masterful landscapes, brilliant visions of the powerful sun, wheatfields and gardens, still lifes and flowers. But I wish to focus here on another powerful motif that found its way from the traumata of his childhood to his canvases, the motif of what I will call "the suffering son."

Vincent had never gained the sense of loving approval and acceptance that he had so desperately sought. He could not find it in any of his relationships, even from those who brought him into this world. His father, the Calvinist minister, was distant, unapproving, and disappointed and frustrated with his oldest son; he was contemptuous of Vincent's stumbling failures, his obstinacy and eccentricity, and withheld any sense of approval and acceptance. But perhaps even more significant was the attitude of his mother, the object of yearning for an affection and comfort that was constantly denied and withheld.

Warmth, understanding, and any sense of affectionate acceptance was never forthcoming. The distance and disappointment persisted even into Vincent's adult years; during one trying period he wrote to Theo:

> I should like it very much if you could persuade Father and Mother to be less pessimistic and to more good courage and humanity. . . . But I would rather they could understand more of my thoughts and opinions on many things. . . . One word from Mother this summer would have given me the opportunity of saying many things to her which could not be said in public. But Mother very decidedly refused to say that word; on the contrary, she cut off every opportunity for me [Letter 155, Etten, Nov. 1881] (van Gogh-Bonger and van Gogh, 1959).

And in another letter: "There really are no more unbelieving and hard-hearted and worldly people than clergymen and especially clergymen's wives" [Letter 161, Etten, November 23, 1881] (van Gogh-Bonger and van Gogh, 1959).

Van Gogh has left us only one portrait of his mother (Fig. 2). He received a photograph of her in Arles and this prompted him to paint two pictures: one of the parsonage in Etten and the other of his mother. The portrait of his mother was painted in "ashen gray," a deadly and depressive shade. He associated it to a poem:

> Who is the maid my spirits seek
> Through cold reproof and slanders blight?
> . . . wan and sunken with midnight prayer
> Are the pale looks of her I love . . . [Letter W18, St. Remy, January 1890] (van Gogh-Bonger and van Gogh, 1959)

These words do not speak of warm and loving attachment but of rejection, coldness, distance, and almost complete failure of maternal empathy.

We also have another less direct representation of Vincent's mental imagery regarding his mother. His painting of two women walking through a garden (Fig. 3) was not intended to immediately represent his

FIGURE 2. *Drawing of Vincent's mother, 1881. Courtesy of Fullerton Museum Center, Fullerton, CA.*

mother and sister, but there is no doubt that he had them in mind. He wrote about it to his sister Willy:

> I have just finished painting, to put in my bedroom, a memory of the garden at Etten; here is a scratch [sketch] of it. It is rather a large canvas. . . . The old lady has a violet shawl, nearly black. But a bunch of dahlias, some of them citron yellow, the others pink and white mixed, are like an explosion of color on the somber figure. . . . Here you are. I know this is hardly what one might call a likeness, but for me it renders the poetic character and the style of the garden as I feel it. All the same, let us suppose that the two ladies out for a walk are you and our mother; let us even suppose that there is not the least, absolutely not the least vulgar and fatuous resemblance—yet the deliberate choice of the color, the somber violet with the blotch of violent citron yellow of the dahlias, suggests Mother's personality to me. . . . I don't know whether you can understand that one may make a poem only by arranging colors, in the same way that one can say comforting things in music. In a similar manner the bizarre lines, purposely selected and multiplied, meandering all through the picture,

may fail to give the garden a vulgar resemblance, but may present it to our minds as seen in a dream, depicting its character, and at the same time stranger than it is in reality [Letter W9, — Arles, second half of November 1888].

The figure of the old woman — Vincent's mother — was cast not only in somber colors, flavored with a pinch of violence, but her bent figure and tragic face speak of despair, pain, bereavement, and a deep and lasting mourning, if not depression. She is absorbed in her grief, solitary, withdrawn, despite the companion at her side, to whom she does not speak and whose features are not etched in pain and sorrow. The image of this sad, withdrawn, and sorrowing woman came out of the depths of Vincent's unsatisfied yearning and frustrated desire for love from a mother whose love and affect lay elsewhere.

Mater Dolorosa

In some of van Gogh's paintings two powerful unconscious fantasies come into conjunction. One is the fantasied reunion with the wished-for mother who would receive him in her arms and lovingly embrace him. The other was a powerful but unconscious identification with Christ.

FIGURE 3. *Detail of Promenade in the Garden, 1888. Courtesy of the Hermitage Museum, St. Petersburg.*

There is conjecture that in his painting *Pietà* (Fig. 4) he painted his own features on the face of Christ. The grieving mother stretches her arms out to embrace her dead son; he is loved because he has suffered and died. The message is clear: it is better to be dead than alive, for only in death does the good mother love her suffering child.

Vincent's identification with Christ provides a deeply unconscious and far-reaching motif in his life. He identified particularly with the suffering Christ who was crucified, resurrected, and raised to heavenly sublimity. There is some suggestion of this motif in his painting *The Raising of Lazarus* (Fig. 5), where, again, the face of Lazarus with its red beard may be that of Vincent himself. Lazarus is awakening from the dead and is received into the outstretched arms of a woman in a green dress. Vincent's comments about the painting to Theo establish the connection between the woman in this painting and the figure of "La Berceuse": the woman who had stood for Vincent's mother in this painting assumes the

FIGURE 4. *Pietà (after Delacroix), 1889. Courtesy of the Rijksmuseum Vincent van Gogh, Amsterdam.*

FIGURE 5.   *The Raising of Lazarus (after Rembrandt), 1890. Courtesy of
the Rijksmuseum Vincent van Gogh, Amsterdam.*

character of an angelic figure welcoming Lazarus from the grave and
back to life. It was only through the Christlike torments of suffering and
death that one could achieve the blessings of resurrection and loving
acceptance from one's mother, what van Gogh had endlessly sought and
always been denied.

The identification lay at a deeply unconscious level but was accompanied by a more conscious wish to imitate the Savior. Under the print on
his wall at Dordrecht, van Gogh wrote: "Take my yoke upon you, and
learn of me; for I am meek and lowly of heart. . . . if any man will come
after me, let him deny himself and take up my cross and follow me — in
the kingdom of Heaven they neither marry, nor are given in marriage."
The Christ Vincent envisioned in himself was "the Great Man of Sorrows
Who knows our ills." Vincent's identification with the suffering Christ
served its unconscious purposes only to the extent that it won for him a
measure of love and admiration — especially from his mother. In his
Christlike role he could maintain his aloofness but continue to win the
love and admiration of his fellowmen and thus avoid the taint of
loneliness and rejection. Suffering and death were the heralds of a
glorious resurrection — as well as the tearful embrace of the mater
dolorosa. Vincent had a devotion to the "Mater dolorosa" that he had

acquired from his father; the picture of the "Mater dolorosa" that had hung in his father's study at Zundert found a place in Vincent's own room. The "Mater dolorosa" was his own mother caught in her unending grief over the death of her firstborn.

Van Gogh's identification with Christ thus served many functions. It justified his chronic depression and need to seek self-punishment. Masochism was elevated to martyrdom, and self-denial and asceticism were ennobled to new levels of narcissistic gratification. Failures in sexuality were transformed into virtues of Christlike abstinence. As Lubin (1972) observes:

> The figure of Christ was a ready-made mask of goodness behind which he could hide the badness he felt inside, thereby appeasing a conscience steeped in the ways of Calvinistic orthodoxy. As Christ, Vincent not only could compete with his dead brother; he could outdo him. When he became disillusioned with his father, he could consider his father a Pharisee and surpass him as a man of God. The figure of Christ both helped to shape his symptoms and became a blueprint for shaping his life's work [p. 107].

La Berceuse

Heiman (1976) relates Vincent's last ominous painting, *The Crows over a Wheatfield,* to another, painted some 18 months earlier of Madame Roulin and called *La Berceuse,* "the lullaby" (Fig. 6). Madame Roulin, the postman's wife, is a stand-in for Vincent's mother; Roulin had been transferred to Marseilles and had taken leave from his family, just as Vincent's father had taken leave in death[5] and left his mother behind. These circumstances had stirred some residues of Vincent's sympathy for his mother and, along with them, renewed wishes for some semblance of love and affection from her. At the time, Vincent's own losses were mounting: Gauguin had abandoned him and had left his dream of the Midi Studio in ruins; he was caught in a life-and-death struggle with the intermittent psychosis that had caused him to be hospitalized and was slowly destroying him; he was being put out of his yellow house; and, to top it all off, Theo was engaged to be married. Madame Roulin was a representation of his mother, who was so affectively distant and, in so many ways, unempathic.

Vincent painted *La Berceuse* no fewer than five times, from January to March 1889. He told Theo: "I am working on the portrait of Roulin's wife, which I was working on before I was ill" (Letter 573, Arles, January 23, 1889). And if there is any doubt that in Vincent's mind Roulin and his wife represented his own father and mother and that Madame Roulin

---

[5]Vincent's father died on March 26, 1885.

FIGURE 6.   *La Berceuse, Arles, 1888. Courtesy of the Art Institute of Chicago.*

bore the psychic marks of his own mother, Vincent went on to say in the same letter:

And I shall never forget Mother at Father's death, when she said only one little word: it made me begin to love dear old Mother more than before. In fact, as a married couple our parents were exemplary, like Roulin and his wife, to cite another instance.

Well, take that same road. During my illness I saw again every room in the house at Zundert, every path, every plant in the garden, the views of the fields outside, the neighbors, the graveyard, the church, our kitchen garden at the back—down to a magpie's nest in a tall acacia in the graveyard.

It's because I still have earlier recollections of those first days than any of the rest of you. There is no one left who remembers all this but Mother and me [Letter 573—Arles, January 23, 1889] (van Gogh-Bonger and van Gogh, 1959).

We are not surprised at the recurring references to the graveyard—the same graveyard in which the first Vincent had been laid to rest and through which Vincent passed every day of his young life. As Heiman (1976) comments:

> The painting of *La Berceuse* may be seen as a—desperate—attempt to regain his lost security through regression. In the context of what preceded the *La Berceuse* painting and what will follow, the attempt was not successful. He is still unable to master the raging instinctual forces of aggression within himself. He cannot look at the reality of his life— he is as uncompromising as ever before. . . .
> But the round, soft, big bosom of *La Berceuse* should not deceive us— neither should the inviting lullaby. When we meet them again, later, during July 1890 in Auvers, the haven for the abandoned and lonely will have changed into a threatening and terrifying image, and the lullaby into a siren-call to death [p. 73].

The feelings of neglect and abandonment were displaced onto van Gogh's paintings. When they were treated with neglect or indifference, van Gogh would erupt in a spasm of rage. The visit to the yellow house, where he found his paintings poorly taken care of and damaged by dampness, left him feeling depressed and suicidal. He returned to the hospital only to plunge into one of the worst of his psychotic episodes. When he discovered a number of canvases, both his own and other artists', lying around unframed in Gachet's house, he could not contain his wrath. The care of these paintings was a matter of life and death for Vincent: they were his children, his life's work, his claim on a degree of wholeness and self-esteem. We know the neglectful fate of the paintings Vincent had left with his mother, who seemingly valued them not at all.

This reaction to his neglected paintings reflected Vincent's sense of his own inner self and his sense of impoverished self-esteem as the rejected, abandoned, and unwanted son, based on a fantasy that provided an inner core of self-perception. This reaction also reflects the underlying function of a persistent and resistant introject derived from the internalization of the punitive and hostilely aggressive parent—in van Gogh's case, rejecting, unloving, and devaluing parents. This internalization gives the child a sense of inner evil, destructiveness, and worthlessness and subsumes the instinctually derived impulses of hateful destructiveness and infantile wishes to hurt and damage. This internalized destructiveness builds a negative sense of self that permeates the rest of the individual's life, experience, and activity. It colors all the rest and remains stubbornly resistant to any alteration by the influence of reality factors. The inner sense of evil means that the individual cannot perform good acts, cannot set useful goals, feels he has no right to hope or strive, and fears that what he produces must bear the stamp of its origin: worthlessness and evil. This pattern of self-devaluation and degradation was repeated with stunning consistency in van Gogh's life story and found its way onto his canvases. His childhood indeed cast a long shadow over his life and the works of art that came from his hands — even to the end of his life.

Summary

Certain aspects of the artistic experience of any great artist derive from the residues of infantile and developmental experience. The circumstances of the birth, early life, and family relations of Vincent van Gogh are discussed and related to his role in the family as the replacement child, the family scapegoat, and the stranger in the family. These elements are associated with the role of the family romance in the development of the artist (Greenacre, 1958). The influence of these aspects of Vincent's developmental experience on his subsequent artistic productions are traced, particularly in terms of the motifs of the depressive, grieving maternal figure and the suffering son.

References

Agger, E. M. (1988), Psychoanalytic perspectives on sibling relationships. *Psychoanal. Inq.,* 8:3–30.

Bak, R. C. (1958), Discussion. *The Psychoanalytic Study of the Child,* 13:42–43. New York: International Universities Press.

Balsam, R. H. (1988), On being good: The internalized sibling with examples from late adolescent analyses. *Psychoanal. Inq.,* 8:66–87.

Cain, A. C. & Cain, B. S. (1964), On replacing a child. *J. Amer. Acad. Child Psychiat.,* 3:443–456.

Erikson, E. H. (1956), The problem of ego identity. *J. Amer. Psychoanal. Assn.,* 4:56–121.

Gedo, J. E. (1983), *Portraits of the Artist: Psychoanalysis of Creativity and Its Vicissitudes.* New York: Guilford Press.

Gedo, J. E. (1987a), Interdisciplinary dialogue as a *lutte d'amour.* In: *Psychoanalytic Perspectives on Art, Vol. 2,* ed. M. M. Gedo. Hillsdale, NJ: The Analytic Press, pp. 223–235.

Gedo, J. E. (1987b), Paul Cezanne: Symbiosis, masochism, and the struggle for perception. In: *Psychoanalytic Perspectives on Art, Vol. 2,* ed. M. M. Gedo. Hillsdale, NJ: The Analytic Press, pp. 187–201.

Greenacre, P. (1958), The family romance of the artist. *The Psychoanalytic Study of the Child,* 13:9–36. New York: International Universities Press.

Heiman, M. (1976), Psychoanalytic observations on the last painting and suicide of Vincent van Gogh. *Internat. J. Psycho-Anal.,* 57:71–79.

Hulsker, J. (1990), *Vincent and Theo: A Dual Biography.* Ann Arbor, MI: Fuller.

Kernberg, P. F. & Richards, A. K. (1988), Siblings of preadolescents: Their role in development. *Psychoanal. Inq.,* 8:51–65.

Kohut, H. (1971), *The Analysis of the Self.* New York: International Universities Press.

―――― (1977), *The Restoration of the Self.* New York: International Universities Press.

Lubin, A. J. (1972), *Stranger on the Earth.* New York: Holt, Rinehart & Winston.

Mahler, M., Pine, F. & Bergman, A. (1975), *The Psychological Birth of the Human Infant.* New York: Basic Books.

Miller, A. (1981), *Prisoners of Childhood.* New York: Basic Books.

Nagera, H. (1967), *Vincent van Gogh: A Psychological Study.* London: George Allen & Unwin.

Niederland, W. G. (1965), An analytic inquiry into the life and work of Heinrich Schliemann. In: *Drives, Affects, Behavior,* ed. M. Schur. New York: International Universities Press, pp. 369–396.

Pollock, G. H. (1961), Mourning and adaptation. *Internat. J. Psychoanal.,* 42:341–361.

―――― (1962), Childhood parent and sibling loss in adult patients. *Arch. Gen. Psychiat.,* 7:295–305.

―――― (1972), Bertha Pappenheim's pathological mourning: Possible effects of childhood sibling loss. *J. Amer. Psychoanal. Assn.,* 20:476–493.

―――― (1989), *The Mourning–Liberation Process* (2 vols.). Madison, CT: International Universities Press.

Poznanski, E. O. (1972), The "replacement child": A saga of unresolved parental grief. *J. Pediatr.,* 81:1190–1193.

Reff, T. (1987a), The author, the authority, the authoritarian. In: *Psychoanalytic Perspectives on Art, Vol. 2,* ed. M. M. Gedo. Hillsdale, NJ: The Analytic Press, pp. 237–243.

―――― (1987b), John Gedo and the struggle for perception. In: *Psychoanalytic Perspectives on art, Vol. 2,* ed. M. M. Gedo. Hillsdale, NJ: The Analytic Press, pp. 203–221.

Rochlin, G. (1965), *Griefs and Discontents: The Forces of Change.* Boston: Little, Brown.

Shengold, L. (1975), An attempt at soul murder: Rudyard Kipling's early life and work. *The Psychoanalytic Study of the Child,* 30:683–724. New Haven, CT: Yale University Press.

―――― (1979), Child abuse and deprivation: Soul murder. *J. Amer. Psychoanal. Assn.,* 27:533–559.

―――― (1988), Dickens, Little Dorrit, and soul murder. *Psychoanal. Quart.,* 57:390–421.

Spector, J. (1988), The state of psychoanalytic research in art history. *Art Bulletin,* 70:49–76.

Stein, S. A., ed. (1986), *Van Gogh: A Retrospective.* New York: Park Lane.

Sweetman, D. (1990), *Van Gogh: His Life and His Art.* New York: Crown.

van Gogh-Bonger, J. (1959), Memoir of Vincent van Gogh. In: *The Complete Letters of Vincent van Gogh* (3 vols.), ed. J. van Gogh-Bonger & W. van Gogh. Greenwich, CT: New York Graphic Society.

―――― & van Gogh, W., ed. (1959), *The Complete Letters of Vincent van Gogh* (3 vols.), Greenwich, CT: New York Graphic Society.

Volkan, V. (1981), *Linking Objects and Linking Phenomena.* New York: International Universities Press.

Volkan, V. & Itzkowitz, N. (1984), *The Immortal Ataturk.* Chicago: University of Chicago Press.

Wallace, R. (1969), *The World of Van Gogh: 1853–1890.* New York: Time-Life Books.

Wilson, E. (1988), Stendhal as a replacement child: The theme of the dead child in Stendhal's writings. *Psychoanal. Inq.,* 8:108–133.

Zerbe, K. J. (1987), Mother and child: A psychobiographical portrait of Mary Cassatt. *Psychoanal. Rev.,* 74:45–61.

Silas Marner:
Psychological Change in Fiction

RICHARD ALMOND

Parallels between literature and therapy are useful for the study of psychological change. The literary text, unlike the psychoanalytic one, is definable, accessible, and static. The reader is not a party to its creation, as is the patient in the clinical situation, and thus is not subject to the biases consequent to being a participant in the events being described, although any particular reading of a text will have its share of "reader's transference." We can examine fictional characters and relationships with a view to improving our understanding of mutative processes, allowing authors to be our observers of human psychology and interaction (B. Almond, 1990a, 1990b; R. Almond, 1989, 1991). This examination allows for new perspectives on processes of change in psychotherapy and psychoanalysis, as well as fresh understanding of the literary works themselves.

In *Silas Marner* a man in mid-life recovers from chronic depression and social withdrawal. My goal is to show that elements of the novelist's depiction of psychological healing parallel psychoanalytic or psychotherapeutic processes and that *Silas Marner* can be read as a commentary on current controversies in the conceptualization of psychological change. I believe *Silas Marner*—along with many other novels of the 19th and 20th centuries—can be viewed as a novel about cure. George

*An earlier draft of this paper was presented at a Colloquium of the San Francisco Psychoanalytic Institute on Literary Process and Psychoanalytic Process, March 1, 1990.

The author would like to thank Drs. Barbara Almond, Katherine MacVicar, and Jerome Oremland and Professors Carolyn Williams (Rutgers University) and Dianne Middlebrook (Stanford University) for their many helpful comments and suggestions.

Eliot (1861) has embedded in the plot, characterizations, and descriptions of her novel a discussion of psychological change. Eliot, of course, does not consider change in terms of psychotherapy or psychoanalysis, but we can recognize in the fictional context many elements of clinical therapeutic process.

I pursue this discussion of *Silas Marner* at two levels, akin to the exploration of a dream. First, I examine the story of Silas — his traumatic rupture from the community of his youth, his subsequent retreat to the rural village of Raveloe, and his eventual healing after he adopts the little girl, Eppie. Second, I examine the novel as a whole, concentrating particularly on the two other major characters, Dunstan and Godfrey Cass, and the interrelations between Silas, Dunstan, and Godfrey. This analysis is akin to the discovery of the latent dream and enables a deeper interpretation of George Eliot's understanding of personality and change. I argue that the latent meaning of *Silas Marner* involves a richer, more complex understanding of intrapsychic change than the more apparent version we experience in concentrating on Silas alone. Eliot has elaborated different aspects of the change process in a way that can be used to understand and integrate different psychoanalytic theories of change. Specifically, I suggest that *Silas Marner* integrates elements of what is in clinical thinking conceptualized as libido theory, ego psychology, or self psychology.

Silas Marner reads like a morality tale, a story of faith lost and regained, but a strong case can be made that its central theme is therapeutic change, that the reader is interested in the story because it concerns psychological recovery. What today we would call a psychotherapeutic approach to mental illness was, in fact, known as "moral treatment" in the 19th century (see, for example, Almond, 1974). Silas's initial disillusioned retreat is discussed in the narrative as a loss of faith. In psychoanalytic language it is the loss of confidence in object relations, the loss of confidence that one can be effective and trusting toward the other and that the other will behave predictably and sympathetically. *Silas Marner* is the story of the loss of this confidence, of Silas's substitutive activities undertaken to survive psychologically, and of his slow restoration of trust through caring for a child. In a wider view, this novel can be interpreted as a commentary, through several characters, on the multiple strands of the process of psychological recovery.

The Novel

At the outset of the story Silas Marner is already an isolated, miserly man, living on the outskirts of the village Raveloe. We learn how he came there. As a young man he had been a member of a religious community in an unnamed city. Silas's close friend of ten years, William, betrayed him by stealing the chapel funds, discovering the "proof" that Silas is guilty by finding the money bag in Silas's room, and then denouncing him to the community. In biblical fashion lots were drawn to determine whether Silas was indeed responsible; they declared his guilt. He was threatened with termination of his membership in the community unless he confessed. Silas responded angrily by accusing William and denouncing "a God of lies, that bears witness against the innocent" (p. 15).

For the reader, it is unclear why Silas has been singled out in this way. The elements of a triangle are present — Silas had just become engaged — but Silas appears to be largely a victim of his friend's ambition and his own over-trusting nature. Only later in the novel do we learn of an early trauma — the loss of his mother and sister during his childhood — that may have sensitized Silas to the impact of this adult betrayal. Eliot has chosen to make none of this clear. The true problem — its origin and nature — remains obscure, hidden like the crucial wounds of childhood behind a protective amnesia.

After the betrayal, Silas turns to his loom for solace. His fiancée sends a message rejecting him and within a month marries William. Silas leaves the town and wanders through the country disoriented, adrift both personally and spiritually. What is unmistakable is the presence of the unresolved mourning and depression that follow his betrayal:

> Minds that have been unhinged from their old faith and love have perhaps sought this Lethean influence of exile in which the past becomes dreamy because its symbols have all vanished, and the present too is dreamy because it is linked with no memories [p. 16].

Silas settles in the village of Raveloe, where his skill at weaving is useful to the local women, who need their spun flax woven into linen. He works for long hours to lose himself in repetitive activity: "Every man's work, pursued steadily, tends in this way to become an end in itself, and so to bridge over the loveless chasms of his life" (p. 18).

For his first work Silas is paid five guineas. Eliot makes it clear that the monetary value of the gold is of no great significance to him:

> But what were the guineas to him who saw no vista beyond countless days of weaving? It was needless for him to ask that, for it was pleasant to him to feel them in his palm, and look at their bright faces, which were all his own: it was another element of life, like the weaving and the satisfaction of hunger, subsisting quite aloof from the life of belief and love from which he had been cut off [p. 18].

Silas becomes obsessed not so much with the gold itself but with its characteristic feel, shine, and capacity to grow in amount. At night, when he is done weaving, he takes out the gold and plays with it as though it were animate: "he would on no account have exchanged those coins, which had become his familiars, for other coins with unknown faces" (p. 21).

Eliot inserts here a psychologically telling incident: Silas trips and breaks a brown earthenware pot he has used for 12 years to carry water. Like the gold, the pot has obtained semi-animate status. It was "his companion . . . its form had an expression of willing helpfulness" (p. 22). When the pot breaks, Silas props the three pieces together "for a memorial." He has withdrawn from man and God, but the ability to appreciate, to care, and to feel loss remains. He has not lost the capacity for attachment; he has only turned away from human objects and from God, the symbol of trustfulness itself. At the same time, Silas does not want to risk the complete sense of isolation that he fears would follow new trust and new disappointment.

Paradoxically, it is a second traumatic loss that begins the process of psychological recovery. Marner's gold hoard is stolen, and he turns to the villagers—not for solace but for restoration of the gold:

> This strangely novel situation of opening his trouble to his Raveloe neighbors, of sitting in the warmth of a hearth not his own, and feeling the presence of faces and voices which were his nearest promise of help, had doubtless its influence on Marner, in spite of his passionate preoccupation with his loss. *Our consciousness rarely registers the beginning of a growth within us* any more than without us: there have been many circulations of the sap before we detect the smallest sign of the bud [p. 59, emphasis mine].

The theft alters Silas in two respects: To the villagers he is humanized; they now can feel sorry for him and see him as weak and needy, not someone to fear. It also represents a potential opportunity for alteration in the depression that has kept Silas isolated. He has scorned human society, in effect damning his Raveloe neighbors along with his friend William and his congregation family. Eliot tells us that this disillusionment is not final, that hope has not been given up:

> To anyone who had observed him before he lost his gold, it might have seemed that so withered and shrunken a life as his could hardly be susceptible of a bruise, could hardly endure any subtraction but such as would put an end to it altogether. But in reality *it had been an eager life,* filled with immediate purpose, which fenced him in from the wide cheerless unknown. *It had been a clinging life;* and though the object

round which its fibres had clung was a dead, disrupted thing, it satisfied the need for clinging [p. 78, italics added].

Marner is thrown once again into acute grief by the loss of his gold. He returns to his loom. "As he sat weaving, he every now and then moaned low, like one in pain" (p. 79). His prior mode of dealing with loss, through withdrawal and substitutive lovemaking to his loom and its golden yield, no longer is effective. Now Silas grieves. Sympathetic visitors come. The pastor urges him to attend church. Silas listens, though with little clear effect. Dolly Winthrop, a good-hearted neighbor, comes with her youngest son, Aaron, bringing Silas cookies. Silas accepts them and, in turn, offers one to the shy boy, who has sung him a carol. Their exchange foreshadows the means of Marner's recovery: caring and being cared about. The coin-shaped cookie is exchanged rather than hoarded.

Running parallel to the story of Marner and his gold is another story, involving the two oldest sons of Squire Cass, the leading landowner in the village. Godfrey Cass, the oldest son, is being manipulated and blackmailed by his profligate younger brother, Dunstan. Godfrey has married, out of lust, a poor woman in another village; he has kept the marriage a secret from his family and his neighbors. His wife has borne him a daughter, now two years old. Dunstan uses his knowledge of the marriage to extort money and favors from Godfrey, who fears being disinherited and therefore holds back from confessing his dilemma to Squire Cass.

It is, in fact, Dunstan who has stolen Silas's gold: after a series of misadventures brings him nearby, he finds the door open and Silas away. Dunstan has heard of Silas's hoard. He locates the gold in its simple hiding place, takes it, but falls into the quarry pit in the fog.

A few weeks after the theft of Silas's gold, on New Year's Eve, Godfrey's wife, who is now an opium addict, sets out with her two-year-old daughter to embarrass Godfrey by appearing at Squire Cass's annual celebration. On the way she collapses from the effect of the drug just outside Marner's cottage and dies of the cold. The child, who has been asleep in her mother's arms, awakens and toddles toward the light of Silas's hearth. Silas, hearing the New Year's revels, has opened his door and has fallen into a fit (by Eliot's description, probably petit mal epilepsy), leaving the door open. This allows the child time to enter his hut. When he recovers consciousness and sees her, Silas (being nearsighted) initially mistakes her golden hair for his lost coins. Then, recognizing this is a child, Silas makes an immediate connection to a younger sister he helped care for, a sister who died in childhood. He feeds the little girl.

When Silas discovers the body of the child's mother outside his hut, he goes for help to Squire Cass's house. Godfrey returns with the rescue party but neither acknowledges his wife's body nor claims the child. Silas wants the little girl, though his interest in her has a quality of ownership, reminiscent of his relation to the inanimate gold: "No—no—I can't part with it, I can't let it go," said Silas, abruptly. "It's come to me—*I've a right to keep it*" (p. 119, emphasis mine). Silas has transferred his wish to possess from the gold to the child, even referring to her as "it." Dolly Winthrop observes the child's attachment to Silas and supports his plan to care for her with practical advice and hand-me-down clothes. Silas insists on managing the child's care himself, possessively fending off any suggestions of outside aid.

"Eppie"—Silas names the child for his mother and sister—becomes the link to Silas's renewed psychological development and to social reconnection. The gap is bridged through the renewal of relatedness,- both with Eppie and with the community that parenthood opens to Marner.

> As the child's mind was growing into knowledge, his mind was growing into memory: as her life unfolded, his soul, long stupefied in a cold, narrow prison, was unfolding too, and trembling gradually into full consciousness [p. 131].

As Eppie grows older, Eliot makes this causal sequence even clearer. By "seeking what was needful for Eppie," Marner embraces the customs of local life, and this in turn reawakens faith and trust. He now wants to understand, to connect his past and present. He talks to Dolly, who after much mulling tells him that his error was the abandonment of faith in God, the abandonment of trust. This conclusion, the only explicit "moral" Eliot gives us, feels incomplete to the reader. It is a harsh moral, requiring faith and trust when events and people go terribly awry, requiring faith in the God of Job. When Silas takes Eppie to see the places and people of his youth, he finds them gone with no trace; his past exists now only in memory, and in the characterological developments time has engendered.

This idea is reiterated when, years later, the nearby quarry pit is drained, exposing the skeleton of Dunstan Cass with Silas's gold. In spite of his vindication and financial recovery, Silas says of the gold, "It takes no hold of me now" (p. 169). What *is* satisfying is realization of his love for Eppie and the value the gold will have to help her.

A third iteration of this idea that altruistic love replaces possessive attachment in recovery is expressed through Godfrey Cass. Moved by the uncovering of Dunstan's crime and punishment, he confesses to his wife that he had been previously married to Eppie's mother. His wife forgives him, and in their reconciliation he (still selfishly) acknowledges the teenage Eppie and offers her the benefits of his status and wealth. Silas naturally is horrified at the prospect of losing Eppie but puts the choice in her hands. She decides without hesitation to remain with Silas. The Casses are hurt, angry, and disappointed but recognize the fairness of her decision. Godfrey continues his support of Silas and Eppie. He thus pays the price of fearing to lose his position as first son and of wishing to marry well. Like Marner's, Godfrey Cass's life is resolved but only partially fulfilled. Marner has had no wife; Cass has had no child.

Discussion

In my analysis of *Silas Marner* I proceed in two steps. First, I examine the more obvious process of change: Silas's recovery through his rearing of Eppie. Second, I suggest that a full appreciation of how this novel addresses the question of change involves looking at the three major male characters—Silas, Godfrey, and Dunstan—and their interplay in the plot. I take each character as a psychological principle, an aspect of the personality that comes into play during the psychological development necessary for change. This view of the novel, of course, ignores more familiar meanings and literary critical approaches to the text. It borrows the text of *Silas Marner,* as Freud did the Oedipus myth, to highlight certain psychological issues, in this case issues that relate to clinical process. My purpose in using a novel in this way is to suggest that while its material is from a different realm than the clinical, we may be able to discover some unifying ideas about change exactly because Eliot does not have our preconceptions. In other words, I am attempting to answer the following questions: How does a sensitive novelist depict a transformative process, and how can we read between the lines to understand this depiction in terms that relate to and may enhance understanding of the clinical situation?

At first consideration, the argument that examining a novel can help clarify the complexity of clinical change may seem unlikely. I believe that the logic of this approach will become more persuasive if we consider briefly current discussions of psychic structure and psychoanalytic process. Each of these topics has been the focus of an entire issue of a major psychoanalytic journal in recent years (the *Psychoanalytic Quarterly,* Vol. 59, 1990, and the *Journal of the American Psychoanalytic Association,* Vol. 36, 1988). While the papers in these journals contain a richness of thinking and specific elaboration of what various authors mean by "structure" or "intrapsychic change," there is little consensus amidst this richness. For example, in the issue of the *Psychoanalytic Quarterly* devoted to psychoanalytic process, several contributors acknowledge the difficulty of achieving consensus even among participants in a special Committee on Psychoanalytic Education study group (Boesky, 1990), mainstream American ego psychology–oriented analysts. Some of the difficulty has to do with definitions; for example, is "process" what the analyst strives for, the ideal first defined by Freud as the interpretation of transference and resistance? Even among those who hold this view, there can be differences in emphasis between a focus on transference, which tends to focus on impulse and conflict, and a focus on resistance, which tends to focus on defensive activity. Or does "process" refer to what actually happens in analysis? In the latter case, does process refer to the evolving intrapsychic state of the patient or to the interaction of patient and analyst, including the analyst's psychology?

Similarly, papers in the issue of the *Journal of the American Psychoanalytic Association* devoted to the concept of structure do not present a consensus on structural change but, rather, different points of view on how to frame the issue. Weinshel (1988), for example, maintaining a link with Freud's original definition of psychoanalysis, proposes that structure changes through the progressive, incremental understanding and interpretation of resistances. This view emphasizes the patient's internal life, with the analyst's role one of interpretation. Goldberg (1988) proposes that each patient requires the analyst to develop a particular model for understanding. This is consistent with his self-psychological point of view, which he elaborates in proposing that the process of structural change occurs through a gradual passing-the-baton of understanding from the analyst to the patient. Wallerstein (1988) points out that not only are the formulations of clinical process different but the degree of structural change does not conform to expectations: the long-term follow-ups of patients from the 1950s Menninger study reveal that "structural change" may occur as the result of both ego-supportive psychotherapy and nontherapeutic relationships, as well as where expected — psychoanalysis. Wallerstein acknowledges both the difficulties in understanding how change takes place and the problems of defining that change in terms of differing "languages." He advocates research on structural change using measures of function that are as atheoretical and inclusive as possible.

As Wallerstein's approach suggests, much of the difficulty in these discussions stems from the important role of theory in analytic listening. To make sense of the rich, complex data of the analytic hour, to render understanding into interpretation to the patient, and to communicate such experiences to professional colleagues, the analyst needs a model of personality. Almost inevitably, this model becomes part of the "data report." That is, what an analyst "discovers" in analytic work includes theory—probably as soon as he conceptualizes, most likely when he formulates an interpretation to the patient, and certainly when he makes a professional report. The ego psychologist will think in terms of conflict and defenses, the self psychologist will envision a deficit and the search for a selfobject, and the object relations psychologist will describe pathological interaction patterns.

While the novel cannot solve all these semantic and conceptual problems, it offers some advantages for the study of change. The novelist, especially a pre-Freudian like George Eliot, is free of preconceptions—or, at least, free of *our* current preconceptions. In devising the plot and characters of *Silas Marner,* Eliot gives us not only an accessible "manifest" story about change in Silas but a latent story woven among several characters. The latter story contains what we might term a speculation about how change occurs, a latent level of interpretation. Interestingly, we can find in each of the major characters of *Silas Marner* a recognizable psychoanalytic point of view. That is, each character exemplifies some aspect of mind that has become important in psychoanalytic discourse. Since Eliot brought these themes together in a plot, we can look for the respective roles of each and thus identify her theory of change.

It can be argued that the requirements of plot are different from those of personality function and change in real-life situations, let alone in psychoanalysis. I agree, and suggest that this interpretation of a novel presents a *possible* integration of the elements of the process of change. In favor of this approach, though, I would suggest that the enduring popularity of certain novels is an indication that they speak successfully to core psychological themes. This was, of course, why Freud appealed to literature so often for support of his ideas.

EPPIE: THE THERAPEUTIC EFFECT OF AN IDEALIZED CHILD

My first level of interpretation concerns Silas's recovery from a depressive state after he adopts the child. Eppie functions in *Silas Marner* as a human deus ex machina. The child of Godfrey's lust, she becomes Silas's healer. Whether we take her literally, as a child whom Marner must feed, protect, and nurture, or symbolically, as the child in himself with whom he reconnects, Eppie is the central figure in Silas's process of internal alteration.

Like Silas, Eppie reacts to her experience unselfconsciously; she also acts, like any child, with spontaneity. Eppie has little complexity but embodies an idealized developmental process. In this process Silas relives development from the parental position; he is able to provide Eppie the loving, empathic conditions needed to undo the traumatic experiences of his own past.

First Silas must learn to feed and clothe the child. His initial wish to possess her leads, through the gratification of relatedness, to a wish for what is best for her, which in turn means involvement in the social life of Raveloe. For example, his possessive, protective stance leads Silas to agree to Eppie's christening and to take her with him on his rounds, providing him and his neighbors with a focus of sociability.

Later, Silas must deal with Eppie's innocent mischievousness as she wanders away from the cottage and almost falls in the quarry pit. Dolly Winthrop tells him he must correct Eppie's behavior with physical punishment or rejection, but these are too disturbing to Silas. Instead, punishment is replaced with solicitous close observation.

The bond of attunement, loyalty, and gentle concern between Eppie and Silas is also idealized. As she matures, Eppie is as much a mother as a daughter and takes care of Silas; later, she approaches marriage in a way that reassures Marner that she will never abandon him. While this bond seems too good to be true, it is intuitively convincing in describing the degree of conflict-free relationship Silas needs in order to recover from the wounds of his youth.

Eppie also represents the hope a child often signifies for a parent: the chance to "start over." We find this idea in various forms in clinical theory. For example, Loewald (1960) has suggested that from the outset the analytic relationship involves a resumption of incomplete development through a new object relationship. Settlage (1985), in a similar vein, has argued that many treatments recapitulate development, particularly in the separation–individuation phase. Weiss and Sampson (1986) have demonstrated that therapy taps into an unconscious "plan" of the patient's ego for testing pathogenic beliefs, a finding that suggests that change is the consequence of resumed development and that the patient is the active, directing party. Each of these formulations of process involves the idea that the treatment situation offers the opportunity to "start over." Outside the therapeutic context, parenthood itself can stimulate psychological development by evoking earlier developmental phases through identification with the child, with the possibility of both positive and negative consequences (Benedek, 1959). In *Silas Marner* the child represents the birth of new possibilities in a depressed man. Starting over taps into his vulnerability by discovering hidden hope.

Unlikely as it seems on first consideration, I believe Eppie has important qualities in common with the therapist. Eppie is functionally similar to an important aspect of the analytic attitude (Schafer, 1983). In recommending listening with "evenly suspended attention," neutrality, and abstinence, Freud (1912) described role qualities much like Eppie's traits (she is loyal, loving, and uncritical). Eppie makes few demands for herself beyond the expectable needs and foibles of childhood. The idealized, harmonious quality of the relationship between Silas and Eppie allows him to rebuild a feeling of trust. It is this aspect of the psychoanalytic relationship that enables the patient, in the throes of the transference neurosis, to tolerate the intense affects and distortions of the analytic experience. Eppie, then, represents an aspect of the analytic function, enabling what Greenacre (1954) referred to as the "basic transference," an aspect Kohut has underscored with his emphasis on empathy (1977). However, *Silas Marner* is a more complex novel; the lives of the Cass brothers are inextricably woven into the plot. Dunstan and Godfrey can be seen as representative of other major psychological themes, themes that play significant roles in change.

THREE CHARACTERS, THREE ASPECTS OF CHANGE

Silas

Marner *experiences,* and he reacts to his experience in a reflexive, automatic fashion. In a reaction to trauma he turns away from social attachment, rather than give up all hope of goodness in life. His unconscious goal is equilibrium, the maintenance of psychological balance or wholeness in the face of massive disappointment. Since social ties have been the source of this disillusionment, Marner withdraws from them. He cannot give up hope for connection and love but his caring is now directed toward his gold and the round of his daily activity.

Like many defensive compromises, Silas's is severely limiting. Whatever the psychological nature and meaning of his original injury (e.g., whether we interpret it as early loss, oedipal defeat, or traumatic betrayal), Silas must have felt enraged, powerless, and rejected by his religious community. In turning to his work he "pulls in" his world. Dangerous archaic, aggressive impulses are controlled by a withdrawal of involvement, a sphincteric containment that Shengold describes as "anal defensiveness and anal narcissism" (1985). The world is killed off and protected at the same time by withdrawing oneself behind a safe barrier of isolation. Within his limited domain Silas can retain the purity of his "eager" and "clinging" life by limiting his emotional involvement to the gold, which, like fecal products, he experiences as completely in his control. The trauma has been too great for Silas to mourn; he has transferred the object ties his loss has left behind to the simple activities and objects of his solitary existence.

This depiction is a psychologically accurate account of a narcissistically dominated adaptation after traumatic experience. But somehow *Silas Marner* does not make sense as a novel solely about recovery from trauma and withdrawal. Why the other characters and plot elements? It is through Godfrey and Dunstan that we learn about sin, anxiety, guilt, and impulsive action. I believe *Silas Marner* is phenomenologically accurate in this sense: we do not feel guilt from impulses or sin directly; what we feel is disapproval and rejection by internalized objects. Silas's "unjust" condemnation by his congregation (and God) is felt subjectively as overwhelming repudiation by his object world, as abandonment and loss. Although Eliot assigns Silas no responsibility for his initial betrayal by his friend, the novel contains in other characters issues of sin and morality. We shall see through analysis of these other characters that a person can bring such punishment on himself and that impulse may be the means of cure as well as a component of conflict.

Godfrey

Like Silas, Godfrey Cass also wishes for love and connection. Unlike Silas, he has *the capacity for self-observation,* for feeling accountable for his actions. From Eliot's information we might reconstruct that the death of Godfrey's mother during his childhood left behind unresolved mourning, yearning, rage, and guilt. By marrying the attractive, alcoholic, and lower-class Molly Farren, Godfrey enacts all of these feelings: the yearning is gratified by sex, the rage by binding himself to a woman unacceptable to his father, and the guilt by depriving himself of marriage to his social equal, Nancy Lammeter. But this is speculation; it is more important that Eliot has portrayed Godfrey — unlike Marner — as a man aware of his actions and of his responsibility for them. Hamlet-like, Godfrey is unable to act when opportunities arise for facing consequences. His dilemma is that he wants to serve both desire and conscience; he balances guilt and wish in a way that prevents action and resolution. Godfrey's problem is self-doubt and the desire to have his patrimony while misbehaving behind his father's back. He wants status without the risk of coming to terms with guilt and responsibility. When, years later, the truth emerges, he is a sadder, wiser man, more aware of the consequences of sin and his hesitation to confess. He recognizes the consequent limitations on happiness. But throughout the novel Godfrey's self-awareness does not bring about action in a new direction.

In psychoanalytic terms we may analogize Godfrey to the ego, a

significant character in the psychic drama but one required to serve
several masters. We know how in analysis the multiple tasks of the ego
may sometimes result in endless loops of resistance, how entrenched
patterns may be repeated without significant structural alteration, reflecting the stability of compromises arrived at early in life. Godfrey
represents such a tendency; multiple, contending internal pressures lead
to inaction.

Dunstan

Dunstan Cass is a significant linking figure in understanding the
change process in Silas Marner. He is all *impulse and ruthlessness,* a
depiction of drivenness, of the pleasure principle; he is focused on
immediate gratification or relief of tension. Dunstan knows about right
and wrong but does not care. He is a character with energy. In contrast,
neither Silas nor Godfrey have motivational energy available for change
once they take their equilibrium-seeking or defense-driven positions.
Dunstan does not have purpose in the sense of life goals—his direction is
formed out of wishes or exigencies of the moment—but he acts continuously and almost always destructively. Yet his destructiveness also
propels the novel, creating the turn in Silas's affairs that leads him back
to society. He is ultimately behind Godfrey's sin and repentance and is
the agent that brings Eppie to Silas.

How is it that what seems like a purely evil, impulsive, destructive
figure is the catalyst of positive change? I suggest that this can be
understood if put psychologically. Dunstan, representing impulse
unrestrained, is dangerous, a source of guilt and anxiety for Godfrey and
the cause of Silas's second traumatization. But he also represents, id-like,
the source of motivation and action. Without his presence there would be
no movement in the plot of *Silas Marner.* In psychoanalysis a crucial
aspect of movement in the therapeutic process comes from the impulses
that the analytic situation stimulates. (This is a significant part of what
we mean by "regression.") Impulses are disturbing to patients and the
basis of extensive resistive activity. But impulses are also what moves the
process along, creating the intensity that is part of transference and the
transference neurosis.

In *Silas Marner* Dunstan's role in the story is brief: he blackmails
Godfrey with his knowledge of Godfrey's secret marriage into covering a
debt he himself has incurred. Then, to pay the debt, Dunstan suggests
that he sell Godfrey's valuable horse at the hunt. Godfrey agrees. During
the hunt Dunstan impales the horse taking a fence, killing it. Walking
home, passing Silas's cottage, he thinks of the weaver's gold as a solution

to the loss of the horse; when he finds that Silas is not at home, he impulsively steals the hoard. Then he disappears.

The loss of his gold jolts Silas out of his deeply embedded, depressive, anal narcissistic retreat, an internal equilibrium only a significant disruption could imbalance. Dunstan's impulsive, selfish act has the explosive energy to do this. Dunstan's theft triggers Silas into a grief that reopens his need and makes him receptive to Eppie. Dunstan's disappearance with the gold is then necessary in the plot to provide Silas with opportunity, motivation, and time to change.

Again, we can analogize to psychoanalytic process. Regression releases old desires into the therapeutic relationship. Like the nearsighted Silas groping about his cottage, confusing Eppie's golden hair for his coins, patients seize on the analyst as the object from whom they hope to obtain what they feel was denied them in the past. Like Silas, their motivations are initially narcissistically determined. They wish to possess and control the analyst completely; they want to "start over" with life on their terms. Yet, as with Silas and Eppie, there is in the new object relationship of analysis a potential for concern for the analyst, for guilt about harm and exploitation. This capacity stems from the nature of the new object: the analyst, like Eppie, is empathic, noncritical, and appropriately caring. Identificatory processes are inevitable in the closeness of analysis, and these traits begin to become internalized by the patient. These traits then, it is hoped, are turned to the advantage of recognizing prior maladaptive compromises and substitutions. This self-knowledge in turn, frees up the capacity for action in the service of better adaptation.

Dunstan's drowning can be read psychologically in relation to both Silas and Godfrey and what they represent. For Godfrey, Dunstan's disappearance is repression of an impulse–guilt constellation. Freed from the threat that Dunstan might reveal his prior marriage, Godfrey can marry the woman he wishes. The barrenness of their union seems a representation of punishment for his sins of the past. And while Dunstan has disappeared, there is always the threat that he could return. When Dunstan's body is revealed 15 years later, when the quarry pit is drained, Godfrey is finally motivated to confess to Nancy his earlier marriage. Though he fails to obtain Eppie as a child at this late date, his conscience is now clear and there is no longer a guilty secret separating him from his wife.

The sequence of internal events that the characters in *Silas Marner* experience resembles one that might occur in the course of psychological arrest and subsequent therapeutic change. Traumatic early experience and conflict are followed by a pathological, narcissistically dominated compromise. Infantile wishes are not given up but, rather, are redirected from relationships and the hope of good experiences with others to controllable physical objects and soothing rhythmic bodily activity in work ("an eager life . . . a clinging life").

It is the forced breakdown of Silas's defensive position that allows change. When Dunstan steals the hoard, Silas is truly grief-stricken. He reaches out to the villagers in a desperate attempt to retrieve his gold. In their way, the villagers now reach out to him; Marner is engaged once again in the social matrix. This sets the stage for the correction of his universal protective mistrust.

Eliot presents Silas's motivation in keeping Eppie as selfish; he wants to possess the child as he did the gold. Only with time does he come to value the human bond above the material; by the time the gold is finally found, it no longer has its earlier, vital, substitutive meaning for him.

COMPARISON WITH THERAPEUTIC PROCESS

I believe George Eliot's depiction of the process of change, illustrated through the three major figures in *Silas Marner,* illuminates therapeutic process. It does so by teasing out different strands of experience that are ordinarily so densely interwoven that they are difficult to recognize:

1. Every patient experiences events, whether intrapsychic or impinging from without, as happening to the self; at any given moment life is experienced, not observed. Eliot represents Silas in this way. Awareness of experience tends to focus on affect states, especially signal affects, cues that operate to stimulate equilibrium seeking. Each of Silas's actions is taken in this manner, even his attempts to take control or to understand. While he is alone, Silas's actions are only marginally successful in creating a satisfactory equilibrium. Once Eppie is in his life, Silas is able to achieve a far more stable and internally rich state.

2. Like Godfrey, patients become *more aware* of their motives and conflicts over the course of treatment as they become less paralyzed by ambivalence and avoidance. Godfrey, too, begins frozen by his conflict. Time and events guide him toward confession, atonement, and awareness. These relieve his guilt and allow him to enjoy the satisfactions that are really available to him.

3. Finally, for therapy to progress and carry over into outside life there must be the element of *action,* represented by Dunstan Cass. During a successful treatment, action comes under greater ego control. Taking Dunstan, the theft, and the quarry pit as metaphor, action begins as ruthless and destructive but is repressed until it can reemerge in sublimated form, its old quality now just a skeleton. Action becomes less impulsive and, at the same time, freer.

A correspondence to psychoanalytic clinical theory can now be drawn: Dunstan, embodying impulsive activity, is like a libido theory viewpoint on the process of change. Dunstan "drives" the plot—as the exemplar of impulse, of the self out of control, as the source of Godfrey's guilt; and, finally, as the vehicle of Silas's rehabilitation. In the early years of psychoanalysis the emphasis was on drive and the unconscious. Reactivated in the transference neurosis, early wishes were interpreted to the patient, compared to the external reality of the patient–analyst relationship, and brought into a new resolution by the working of the conscious mind. While analytic theories of technique have moved on, the idea of gaining greater control over impulse, through uncovering and consciousness, remains part of clinical theory. In *Silas Marner,* Dunstan is literally uncovered, an uncovering that leads to the revelation of sexual and aggressive secrets—and to their resolution.

Godfrey, whom I have designated as representing self-awareness, can be analogized to an ego psychological therapeutic orientation: After the publication of "The Ego and the Id" (Freud, 1923), psychoanalysis added to the clinical paradigm a concern with activities of the ego and superego—defenses, guilt, manifestations of character resistance. The analyst, no longer simply the instrument for bringing the unconscious into awareness, now was interested in interpreting conscious experience and ego and superego activities in order to widen the patient's awareness of conflict. During the middle part of *Silas Marner,* while Silas is rearing Eppie, Godfrey, in the background, plays a supportive role, helping Silas with furnishings and enlargements of the cottage. Here is ego activity, quietly operating to "build structure" in a new way. During the same time that the reparative process has had its time to work in Silas, Godfrey becomes able to recognize his own prior weakness and reconcile himself to confession and disappointment.

Silas himself, as I have pointed out, is unreflective. Yet the novel's greatest emotional appeal is his recovery, passively experienced though it is. We can identify with Silas in his disorientation, in his reactiveness to the emotional experience of the moment, and, most of all, in his delight as he returns to relatedness. This resembles psychological experience as elucidated by Heinz Kohut (1977): in therapy, and in life in general, Kohut argues, one searches for "selfobjects" necessary to psychological equilibrium. When there have been early traumatic experiences, whether sudden or chronic, the damage may become overwhelming, leading to regression to "archaic" psychological states. The need for the selfobject may be so urgent yet so guarded that its outcome is restricting. Silas's loss of friend, fiancée, and community would have been sufficient to dislocate a strong personality; his earlier loss of mother and sister may have made this adult experience all the more unmanageable. He turns away from people to routine labor and then to the gold, a physical selfobject.

In Kohut's terms, Eppie provides the necessary therapeutic figure by meeting Silas's need for admiration, to restore his self-esteem and sense of power, and his need for an idealized figure who will help him restore his capacity for human attachment and love. Kohut (1984) suggests that the key to change in treatment centers on disruptions of the fragile connectedness of patient to analyst. In the exploration of such "empathic failures" the patient internalizes the capacity to identify the source of these disruptions. Many of the events in Eppie's childhood can be viewed in these terms, that is, as disruptions and restorations of empathic connectedness, occurring now for Silas in manageable increments.

Whether an analysis is conducted with a formal self-psychological framework or not, it is inevitable that the daily fare of the psychoanalytic dyad will consist of many moments of distress and disruption, optimally followed by understanding through interpretation. During these moments it is common for the patient (and often the analyst) to have little sense of what is happening. Silas-like, the experience of analysis is one of momentary affects, thoughts, reactions, and pieces of comprehension.

As a thorough psychologist, Eliot moves us back and forth between these views, just as I believe skillful analysts and psychotherapists move between empathic understanding and interpretation of impulse derivatives, affects, and defenses. In the plot of *Silas Marner*, Dunstan and Godfrey go offstage during the period of Eppie's childhood, that is, during Silas's recovery. Only near the close, when Silas is again a part of the community, fully reengaged with people and loving relationships, do Dunstan and Godfrey reappear. Dunstan is now known to be dead; that is, the threat he represents to psychic equilibrium is now past. Godfrey reappears to confess his past sin, resolving the unstable neurotic compromise of concealment; he also now represents the capacity for understanding. He recognizes finally the justice of his punishment of childlessness — one cannot have it all.

In long-term psychoanalytic treatments the course is so often the same: for most of the treatment we are caught up with the patient's sensitivities, struggles for control, and need for us to listen — or even to care more actively. "Starting over" in treatment means forming a new object relation and then struggling through a whole series of developmental issues in that relation (Loewald, 1960; Settlage, 1985), just as Silas and Eppie do in the novel. Only after much of this reworking, frequently near or even after the completion of treatment, does the patient become capable of being self-aware, able to think and act comfortably, and more content with his lot in reality.

Silas, Godfrey, and Dunstan do not come from different species of humankind; their qualities have to do with different, but not irreconcilable, aspects of human experience. It is interesting that sophisticated descriptions of analytic process by representatives of self psychology (Kohut, 1984) and of ego psychology (Calev, 1987) include both empathy with and interpretation of experience: Kohut, for all his emphasis on empathy, considers the conveying of understanding by the analyst to be a critical stabilizing component of cure. For lasting analytic change, Kohut feels, the patient needs to learn from the analyst the origin for his vulnerability. Then he will be able to internalize an ideational content he can use in the future when there is narcissistic injury or disequilibrium.

Calev (1987), from an ego psychological point of view, describes the analytic process as involving extensive interpretation of resistances, especially narcissistic and superego resistances, during the greatest part of an analysis. It is, he believes, only after much work on these resistances that it will be possible to uncover repression resistances that guard the most pathogenic unconscious conflicts. In the end, both Kohut and Calev seem to be describing the same elephant, though with different language. The common elements in their conceptions of clinical process are quite similar to those we have delineated in our study of *Silas Marner*. To change, we need to be comforted and confronted, cared about and encouraged out of withdrawal, in a process that is both new and a reworking of the past. To complete change, and to retain it, we need to understand ourselves and gain a greater capacity for self-awareness. *Silas Marner* enables us to see that there may be a core psychoanalytic process that transcends theoretical differences in conceptualizing the mind.

To summarize the picture of psychoanalytic therapeutic process that is suggested by this study of *Silas Marner*: A psychological sufferer, such as the depressed weaver, enters a state of narcissistic withdrawal, reflected in symptomatic behavior and social isolation. Crucial human needs are met in safe, controllable ways. Subjectively, the patient experiences a limited, unhappy life—but one in a sort of equilibrium. Even when treatment is voluntarily sought, the sufferer is not truly ready to relinquish this safety. Instead, he must be helped, as Silas is by Eppie's golden locks, into forming a new attachment. Once the new relationship takes hold, it is the arena for a developmental process, a process not identical to original development but one taking a course necessary for the sequential mastery of prior problem points. Motivating all this is drive, the wish for erotic and aggressive satisfaction, as well as a more neutralized urge for mastery. The process is kept on course by the equilibrium-maintaining tendency that is associated with self states. Ultimately, if a new equilibrium is reached, it can be stabilized by the self-awareness we signify as insight.

I believe this abbreviated description, drawn from the novel *Silas Marner*, suggests the need for integration of present models of therapeutic process. As clinical study and research move toward that goal, we may find that authors of classic novels have been able to tap into the phenomena of human function and change and to render highly accurate accounts of how change occurs.

Summary

I have examined George Eliot's *Silas Marner* as a novel about cure, that is, as a story in which the central character recovers from psychological damage, with the central plot action involving this recovery. This view permits a comparison with change brought about in psychoanalytic treatments. At one level the novel depicts cure as the result of Marner's taking on the care of the orphaned child, Eppie. At another, more complex level *Silas Marner* deals with personality, psychological conflict, and recovery. To this end, George Eliot has constructed a plot, with other significant characters and their actions, that makes us aware of the complexity of personality and change.

In comparing change in *Silas Marner* with psychoanalytic process I have highlighted three aspects of personality, each of which plays a different part in change. Each is represented in the novel by a different character. I interpret these as three aspects of how someone changes: experiencing, self-reflecting, and acting. This comparative approach brings out the relevance of fictionally represented "treatment" to clinical psychoanalytic work. In particular, I show that Eliot's characters and story contain an understanding of how change comes about that reconciles different clinical theories—libido theory, ego psychology, and self psychology.

References

Almond, B. (1990a), A healing relationship in Margaret Drabble's novel *The Needle's Eye*. The *Annual of Psychoanalysis*, 19:91–106. Hillsdale, NJ: The Analytic Press.
_____ (1990b), "The Secret Garden": A therapeutic metaphor. *The Psychoanalytic Study of the Child*, 45:477–494. New Haven, CT: Yale University Press.
Almond, R. (1974), *The Healing Community*. New York: Aronson.
_____ (1989), Psychological change in Jane Austen's *Pride and Prejudice*. *The Psychoanalytic Study of the Child*, 44:307–324. New Haven, CT: Yale University Press.

_____ (1991), *Jane Eyre:* A novel of Psychological Development and Change, in *Psychoanalysis and Culture* ed. R. Ginsburg. Stanford: Stanford University Press (in prepration).

Benedek, T. (1959), Parenthood as a developmental phase. *J. Amer. Psychoanal. Assn.,* 78:389-417.

Boesky, D. (1990), The psychoanalytic process and its components. *Psychoanal. Quart.,* 59:550-584.

Calev, V. (1987), The process in psychoanalysis. *Dialogue,* 7:13-21.

Eliot, G. (1861), *Silas Marner.* New York: Signet Classics, 1981.

Freud, S. (1912), Recommendations to physicians practising psychoanalysis. *Standard Edition,* 12:109-120. London: Hogarth Press, 1958.

_____ (1923), The ego and the id. *Standard Edition,* 19:12-59. London: Hogarth Press, 1961.

Goldberg, A. (1988), Changing psychic structure through treatment: From empathy to self-reflection. *J. Amer. Psychoanal. Assn.,* 36:211-224.

Greenacre, P. (1954), The role of transference. *J. Amer. Psychoanal. Assn.,* 2:671-684.

Kohut, H (1977), *The Restoration of the Self.* New York: International Universities Press.

_____ (1984), *How Does Analysis Cure?* ed. A. Goldberg and P. Stepansky. Chicago: University of Chicago Press.

Loewald, H. (1960), On the therapeutic action of psychoanalysis. *Internat. J. Psycho-Anal.,* 41:16-33.

Schafer, Roy (1983), *The Analytic Attitude.* New York: Basic Books.

Settlage, C. (1985), Adult development and therapeutic process. Presented at the Edward G. Billings' Lectureship on Clinical Implications of Adult Development, Denver.

Shengold, L. (1985), Defensive anality and anal narcissism. *Internat. J. Psycho-Anal.,* 66:47-73.

Wallerstein, R. (1988), Assessment of structural change in psychoanalytic therapy and research. *J. Amer. Psychoanal. Assn.,* 36:241-262.

Weinshel, E. (1988), Structural change in psychoanalysis. *J. Amer. Psychoanal. Assn.,* 36:263-282.

Weiss, J. & Sampson, H. (1986), *The Psychoanalytic Process.* New York: Guilford Press.

Blutbrüderschaft and Self Psychology in D. H. Lawrence's Women in Love

JAMES C. COWAN

> The primordial discovery of the novel is that of self—and *primordial* is intended here in a privileged way: the primordial as preeminent, as the prior, the first validating condition for intelligibility.
>
> —Edward Said (1975, p. 141)

One of the means by which D. H. Lawrence sought to reconcile spiritual and sensual components of the self and to establish a "nourishing creative flow" between the self and the other was the concept of Blutbrüderschaft. Long before he introduced the term in *Women in Love,* Lawrence had tentatively explored the theme in *The White Peacock* and *Sons and Lovers.* But the reconciliation of spiritual and sensual modes of consciousness through male bonding was to become a dominant theme in *Women in Love, Aaron's Rod, Kangaroo,* and *The Plumed Serpent.* Sacramental though the action may be in Cyril and George's bathing scene in *The White Peacock,* the ritual is that of pastoral romance, not the open invitation to vows of blood brotherhood that Rupert Birkin offers to Gerald Crich in *Women in Love.*[1]

Women in Love contrasts the developing relationship of Ursula Brangwen and Rupert Birkin with that of Ursula's sister Gudrun and Gerald Crich and parallels these relationships with that of the two men to each other. Ursula is a teacher and Gudrun an artist, while Birkin is a school inspector and Crich the well-to-do son of a mine owner and,

---

I would like to thank Laurence Pollinger Ltd. and the Estate of Frieda Lawrence Ravagli for their generous permission to quote from the letters and works of D. H. Lawrence and Frieda Lawrence.

[1]All references to *Women in Love* are to the Cambridge University Press edition (1987).

ultimately, a captain of industry who adopts ruthless management policies. Birkin, who emerges as the focal character for most of the novel, is in the process of extricating himself from an unsatisfying love relationship with the socially prominent Hermione Roddice, a relationship he has come to feel as artificial, destructive, and spiritually devouring. He wants to establish his new relationship with Ursula on a structured basis of equal balance and individual autonomy. But he is equally concerned with establishing a complementary, irrevocably bonded, male–male relationship with Crich to counterbalance his male–female relationship with Ursula. Tracing the development of both types of relationship in the interactions among the four young adults, the novel explores psychological themes of merger, separation–individuation, marriage, homoeroticism, idealization, sadomasochism, creativity, dissolution, and death. Largely for the artistic maturity of its presentation of the complex interrelationships of characters, imagery, themes, and structure in an apocalyptic anatomy of modern society, *Women in Love* is generally recognized as one of Lawrence's two or three greatest novels.

What Rupert Birkin proposes to Gerald Crich is the kind of "Blutbrüderschaft" the "old German knights" had sworn by making "a little wound in their arms" and rubbing "each other's blood into the cut," swearing "to be true to each other, of one blood, all their lives. — That is what we ought to do," Birkin says. "No wounds, that is obsolete. — But we ought to swear to love each other, you and I, implicitly and perfectly, finally, without any possibility of going back on it" (pp. 206–207).

Presented with a proposal that would convert the strong bond between the men into something like male marriage, Gerald Crich is understandably bewildered. Confused, ambivalent, pleased but wary of what may seem, on one level, Birkin's sexual advances in a calculated seduction, Gerald demurs: "We'll leave it till I understand it better" (p. 207). Literary critics, not surprisingly, have been equally confused, expressing widely divergent views on the meaning of a proposal that sounds like a homosexual pledge but is not acted out sexually beyond an erotically tinged nude wrestling scene.[2]

As I try to show, Birkin's wish for blood brotherhood is not disguised

---

[2]Opposing viewpoints on this critical issue are presented by Squires (1990) and Donaldson (1986; see note 10). Squires places Birkin in a novelistic tradition of seducers and suggests that in earlier works his dalliance would have been with a woman (p. 54). Opposing views on the place and significance of the canceled "Prologue" are presented by Meyers (1977) and Ross (1980). For Meyers, the "Prologue" clarifies such aspects of the novel as Birkin's destructive relationship with Hermione, his intimacy with Crich, and his repressed homosexual desires (p. 143). For Ross, a study of the manuscripts clarifies Lawrence's artistic intentions in canceling the "Prologue" and leaving the Blutbrüderschaft theme submerged until chapter 16, "Man to Man" (p. 181).

homoeroticism; indeed, Birkin's homoerotic fantasies are not disguised at all in the canceled "Prologue" and scarcely so in the novel. Rather, Birkin's concept of Blutbrüderschaft as an irrevocable male bond tantamount to marriage in sacramental commitment is a form for experiencing emotional closeness that includes sensual, physical awareness in which sexual feeling is elevated to noble ideals of male devotion and loyalty rather than expressed directly in sexual behavior. The concept enables Birkin to press into the service of ego defense those feelings that, on an immediate level, are experienced as sexual but that in reality mask a defense against the same psychic danger as his fear of being swallowed up by women, namely, "the threatened dissolution of the self" (Kohut, 1971, p. 131).

To what extent Birkin's meanings are Lawrence's is, of course, a critical question. It would be simplistic to identify the authorial voice exclusively with Birkin's point of view, since Lawrence's literary meaning emerges fully only in the narrator's presentation of the interaction of all the characters. While Birkin is more fully objectified than such autobiographical characters as Paul Morel in *Sons and Lovers*,[3] most readers have intuitively felt a psychic affinity between the novelist and this protagonist. Sigmund Freud (1908) comments in "Creative Writers and Day-Dreaming" that in such psychological novels "[o]nly one person — once again the hero — is described from within. The author sits inside his mind, as it were, and looks at the other characters from outside" (p. 150). As Paul Delany (1978) observes, "One source of freedom, certainly, was the creation of Birkin as hero: through him Lawrence could both express his own impulses directly and open them to countervailing pressures from other characters" (p. 227). Rather than look for autobiographical equivalence in the narrative action of *Women in Love,* I suggest that Birkin is the carrier of Lawrence's major psychic issues, revived by his stressful situation at the time but actually deriving from his relationships with his earliest selfobjects. Specifically, these issues included, from his close symbiotic merger with his mother, both grandiose merger needs and fears of engulfment, expressed in his ambivalence toward women, and, from his traumatic disappointment in his father, both the need for stable ideals and the longing for paternal nurturance, expressed in various idealizing male friendships and sometimes in homoerotic yearnings.[4]

---

[3]*Sons and Lovers,* though autobiographical in fictional terms, cannot be taken literally at face value. Paul is more independent, less intellectual and educated, and more conventional and "ordinary" than Lawrence (Worthen, 1991, pp. 52, 181, 317–318).

[4]Lawrence's merger with his mother and hatred of his father are described with remarkable lucidity in his letter to Rachel Annand Taylor of 3 December 1910 (Lawrence, D. H., 1979, pp. 190–191).

The interpretation that the homosexual strivings encoded in the idealization of male bonding in his fiction indicate a primary homosexual motive on Lawrence's part persists in the minds of some readers.[5] The unstated assumption of such criticism is that an object-instinctive drive has been uncovered as the underlying motive and that nothing further lies behind it. Lawrence's homoerotic impulses notwithstanding, his basic sexual identity, I believe, was heterosexual. While one may find additional evidence in his fiction of homoerotic feeling between men, this feeling, expressed variously as admiration or close male bonding, is not acted out by his protagonists in overt homosexual behavior. On the contrary, homosexuality in Lawrence's work is usually presented critically in a defensive maneuver that leaves little doubt about the impulses that Lawrence feared in himself enough to defend against them. Male homosexuals are often treated with satiric amusement, as in the association of homosexuality with charming surface wit rather than depth of intellect and feeling in the dialogue of James Argyle and Algy Constable in *Aaron's Rod* (chap. 16, "Florence"), but they are sometimes judged more harshly, as in the characterization of Loerke in *Women in Love* or the captain in "The Prussian Officer," as exploiters of other people for mechanistic sensation. Female homosexuals are usually presented negatively as anti-life, as in the portraits of Winifred Inger in *The Rainbow* (chap. 12, "Shame") and Jill Banford in *The Fox* or in Mellors's railing against "Lesbians" in *Lady Chatterley's Lover* (chap. 14).

Sexuality for Lawrence was sacred, and sexual expression a sacrament. Thus, "sex in the head" or sexual activity merely for sensation was a blasphemy against life. As Lawrence (1981) writes to the poet Henry Savage (15 November 1915): "Sex is the fountain head, where life bubbles up into the person from the unknown — you conduct life further and further from sex — it becomes movement — expression — logic. The nihilists . . . never tried to love —" (p. 102). Since he associates homo-

---

[5]See, for example, Meyers (1977, pp. 130–161) and a contrasting view by Delany (1978, pp. 222–226, 309–315). Worthen (1991), in a nonpsychoanalytic discussion of Lawrence's homoeroticism, comes to some of the same views as mine in this paper, an earlier, shorter version of which was presented in a scholarly forum in which both he and I participated (D. H. Lawrence Society program, Modern Language Association Convention, December, 1989). I have no argument with Worthen's common-sense statement that Lawrence's experiencing homoerotic feelings and expressing them in his work is not the same as being a homosexual. But I think that a clearer understanding of the psychological issues involved leads to a conclusion of greater complexity than the notion that Lawrence's occasional physical closeness with men was "uncomplicatedly happy" and his attractions to their beauty unthreatening (p. 158). The text of the "Prologue" provides compelling evidence of the "despair," "deep misery," and "suffering" these homoerotic feelings evoked and the "long torture of struggle" against them (pp. 502–505).

sexuality with nihilism, Lawrence (1981), in another letter to Savage (2 December 1913), is puzzled by the homosexual motive of most great men, an assumption that remains unproven. In an apparent attempt to resolve the ambivalence of his sexual identification, Lawrence sets forth there a theory of human sexuality, drawing a facile, if familiar, distinction between the narcissistic object relationships of homosexuality and instinctual heterosexual object love:

> I should like to know why nearly every man that approaches greatness tends to homosexuality, whether he admits it or not: so that he loves the *body* of a man better than the body of a woman — as I believe the Greeks did, sculptors and all, by far. I believe a man projects his own image on another man, like on a mirror. But from a woman he wants himself re-born, reconstructed. So he can always get satisfaction from a man, but it is the hardest thing in life to get ones [*sic*] soul and body satisfied from a woman, so that one is free from oneself. And one is kept by all tradition and instinct from loving men, or a man — for it means just extinction of all the purposive influences [p. 115].

Lawrence's intellectual theories of this sort were generated in part in an effort to control internal objects and conflicts such as the soul–body dichotomy in this letter. After he was introduced to an intellectual coterie of Bloomsbury homosexuals, including John Maynard Keynes, Francis Birrill, and Duncan Grant, Lawrence was so distressed by their mode of living that he said they made him dream of black beetles. The depth of Lawrence's disturbance is revealed in his letter to David Garnett (19 April 1915), in which furious negative feelings about what he saw as their upper-class intellectual nihilism, frivolous lifestyle, lack of reverence for life, and homosexuality are amalgamated in an angry homophobic reaction formation that, in Lawrence's own word, approaches madness (1981, pp. 320–321).

Despite his fears and defenses, homosexuality was not the dominant sexual preference in Lawrence's life. For the record, the biographical evidence of overt homosexuality is scant and contradictory, consisting of two possible homosexual relationships, neither of which has been established authoritatively. Writing over 40 years after the fact, Compton Mackenzie (1966) remembers Lawrence's once telling him, "I believe that the nearest I've ever come to perfect love was with a young coal-miner when I was about sixteen" (p. 168). Delany (1978) thinks Lawrence was alluding to a young farmer, Alan Chambers (p. 314). But Derek Britton (1988) cites an unsubstantiated account by a "brutish" miner called Tom of an incident in his adolescence when after his bath his mother "came home early to find the young Lawrence kneeling on the floor, biting her son's buttocks" (p. 52). Sexual exploration among boys in adolescence is normative, and experimentation involving polymorphously perverse component instincts is not indicative of the dominant sexual organization that will ultimately emerge. But speculation has also centered on Lawrence's close relationship in his early thirties with the young Cornish farmer William Henry Hocking. Members of the Hocking family were reticent about a subject they had obviously discussed in private. According to Arthur Eddy, an in-law, William Henry had once confided to him that Lawrence was homosexual: "He said Lawrence used to come down to the farm and talk to him about it a lot." But Hocking's younger brother, Stanley, asked if Lawrence was homosexual, replied, "Certainly not! Not to my knowledge. He may have been a bit effeminate. But I refuse to believe that Lawrence was homosexual. He already had a woman to dapple with" (Stevens, 1988, pp. 32–33).

Lawrence's extensive heterosexual experience and lifelong heterosexual commitment indicate a clear sexual preference and primary sexual identity. The evidence for homosexual experience, based almost entirely on hearsay given at third hand, suggests that if Lawrence acted out the homoerotic impulses that he became aware of in adolescence, he did so very briefly in a period of crisis in his young adult life following the suppression of *The Rainbow*. At work on revisions of the manuscript that became *Women in Love*, Lawrence was struggling with multiple personal difficulties, four examples of which may be cited: First, his ill health following his double pneumonia and long convalescence, accompanied by depression in the year after his mother's death (9 December 1910), continued in his subsequent pulmonary problems, which Ernest Jones, M.D., apparently told him stemmed from his having had tuberculosis (Lawrence, D. H., 1981, p. 623). Second, there was the continuous battle of his marriage to Frieda von Richthofen Weekley, a sexually amoral German aristocrat who had left her English husband, a respected Nottingham professor, and three small children to elope with Lawrence after previous extramarital affairs in Germany with an early member of Freud's circle, Otto Gross,[6] and with the painter Ernst Frick, and whose various infidelities continued during her marriage to Lawrence (Meyers, 1990, p. 91, enumerates six such love affairs). Third, the threat of

---

[6]For Gross's early associations with psychoanalysis, see Freud's and Jung's correspondence about the brilliant but erratic young physician whom Freud referred to Jung for treatment and whose illness Jung ultimately diagnosed as dementia praecox (Freud and Jung, 1974, pp. 141, 151, 152, 155–157). A special issue of the *D. H. Lawrence Review*, 22, no. 2 (1990) is devoted to "The Otto Gross–Frieda Weekley Correspondence. transcribed, translated, and annotated," by John Turner, with Cornelia Rumpf-Worthen and Ruth Jenkins, pp. 137–227.

wartime conscription elicited Lawrence's enraged response to a mass preinduction physical examination by medical authorities, which he felt to be willfully intrusive and humiliating (Lawrence, D. H., 1984, pp. 287–288; also described graphically in *Kangaroo,* chap. 12, "The Nightmare"); and repeated official harassment in Cornwall on the unfounded suspicion that the Lawrences were spying for the enemy led to their expulsion from Cornwall on 15 October 1917 (Stevens, 1988, pp. 99–113). Fourth, though he could still publish poetry and periodical fiction and essays, Lawrence found it difficult to earn a living in the face of censorship of his work, the notoriety of *The Rainbow* suppression (5 November 1915) delaying trade publication of *Women in Love* for seven years.

The homoerotic feelings that Lawrence experienced in this period of crisis emerged, I believe, in response to what he felt as multiple assaults on the self. These feelings, expressed in the passionate attachment to William Henry Hocking and described explicitly in the canceled "Prologue" to *Women in Love* (composed 1916), were also channeled into the bond of blood brotherhood that he sought desperately to establish with John Middleton Murry, the emotional model for Gerald Crich. Murry's self-serving account cannot be taken at face value: "He wanted me to swear to be his 'blood-brother,' and there was to be some sort of sacrament between us." Ordinary friendship was "not enough: there ought to be some mingling of our blood, so that neither of us *could* go back on it." When Murry, "half-frightened, half-repelled," shrank from any such ritual enactment, Lawrence responded with vindictive narcissistic rage: " 'I hate your love, I *hate it.* You're an obscene bug, sucking my life away' " (Murry, 1933, p. 79). Murry's (1931) assumption, vaguely formulated on drive theory, was that Blutbrüderschaft did not represent a relationship "additional to marriage," as Birkin claims, but a substitution for it, Lawrence's "escape to a man from the misery of his own failure with a woman" (p. 119). Without understanding the deficit Lawrence was seeking to heal, Murry describes his repetition compulsion: "But always it was brief and fugitive. Lawrence was always, and inevitably, disappointed" (Murry, 1931, p. 119). The intensity and urgency of Lawrence's longing for Murry suggest that archaic selfobject needs were being remobilized in an effort to establish a selfobject matrix to preserve self-cohesion in the face of threatened annihilation of the self. The relationship this maneuver required was, however, finally unworkable. "Lawrence's hunger for a man could never have been satisfied," Murry says (1931, pp. 120–121), with little insight on the nature of that hunger.

This interpretation is confirmed by two of Frieda Lawrence's letters. To Lawrence's friend and biographer Richard Aldington (5 April 1949), she writes: "Yes, those war years were terrible for Lawrence, he was not quite sane at times, as you say. . . . You also know (between you and me) in his bewilderment he had a passionate attachment for a cornish farmer, but of course it was a failure" (Lawrence, F., 1981, p. 93). In a subsequent letter (6 August 1953) to Murry about his and Lawrence's failed friendship, she writes:

> There was a real bond between you and L. If he had lived longer and had been older, you would have been real friends, he wanted so desperately for you to understand him. I think the homosexuality in him was a short phase out of misery—I fought him and won—and that he wanted a deeper thing from you [Lawrence, F., 1964, p. 360].

The stress of the crisis situation reactivated, in Kohutian terms, conflicts that Lawrence felt as sexual but that actually derived from earlier disturbances in the formation of his nuclear self in relation to both parental imagos.[7] What was being activated on an experiential level was a need for affirmation in relation to the idealized paternal imago. It is clear that Lawrence's own father met few, if any, of his needs for nurturance, although Lawrence's boyhood friend G. H. Neville (1981) gives a moving account of Arthur Lawrence's coming to the door of the sickroom, filled with awkward, unspoken tenderness and concern for his son when Lawrence was ill (p. 63). Lawrence's need for male nurturance in his adult life, emerging in times of crisis or transition, was revived in the service of stabilizing a fragile self and would spontaneously disappear, like Birkin's homoerotic attractions (p. 505), whenever a sense of balance could be restored. Lawrence's homoerotic feelings were not a primary psychological configuration but "disintegration products," as the unmet developmental need to merge with the greatness of an idealized omnipotent paternal selfobject was replaced by "the sexualized replica of the original healthy configuration" in the form of preoccupation with the penis as an isolated symbol of adult male power (Kohut, 1977, pp. 172-173). These homoerotic feelings were expressed primarily by means of fantasy and in a series of idealizing relationships with men, through which he repeatedly sought to heal the split between sensual and spiritual being and, in the absence of a viable paternal imago, to fill the deficit left

---

[7]Birkin's judgmental view of himself, "It is the ultimate mark of my own deficiency, that I feel like this" (p. 505), is analogous to the analytic interpretation that such feelings are an attempt to fill a structural deficit. Lawrence's early childhood developmental context is well known. The emotional situation is set forth clearly in Lawrence's letter to Rachel Annand Taylor (Lawrence, D. H., 1979, see note 4). See also Neville (1981, pp. 35-70) and memoirs collected in Nehls (1957, Vol. 1, pp. 5-41). For biographical accounts with varying emphases, see those in Moore (1974, pp. 7-31), Delavenay (1972, pp. 3-14), and Worthen (1991, pp. 57-79).

by his severe disappointment in his father.[8] Lawrence's pattern of idealization, attempted merger, and disappointment in regard to significant male figures like John Middleton Murry compulsively repeated the original traumatic disappointment without healing the injury. Specifically, Lawrence's object hunger, idealizing merger needs, and longing for quasi-religious sacramental union with another man were fixations on archaic forms deriving from deficits in his frustrating relationship with a father unavailable for idealization.

Lawrence's homoerotic impulses were also, I believe, a screen for more deep-seated and fearful conflicts involving survival and dependency needs in relation to the mirroring maternal imago. While the attraction to men was evoked by deficits in relation to the idealized paternal imago, the intensity of the feelings involved suggests that they originated from a more primitive source less accessible to consciousness than disappointment in the father, that is, from the intensity of the grandiose merger he had had and lost rather than from the idealizing merger he had never had. In *Sons and Lovers* Lawrence consciously aggrandizes the mother and depreciates the father. The role model his own father provided for masculine identification was systematically devalued by the mother. Lawrence's early feelings of weakness, inferiority, sickliness, effeminacy, and shame were dysphoric effects of the gratifying merger with his mother and were reinforced by his father's abdication. The first cost of the merger was Lawrence's participation in rejection of the father and in elaboration of grandiose fantasies of sharing his life with his mother. The lasting cost was his unresolved dependency needs, which were clearly centered in preserving the supportive, if crippling, relationship with his mother since his depreciated father was in no position to provide the alternative idealizing relationship. As Heinz Kohut (1971) interprets this kind of emotional situation, the son senses "the mother's fear of the strong male figure with the adult penis and realizes (unconsciously) that her exaltation of him, the son, is maintained only so long as he does not develop into an independent male" (p. 147). Specifically, Lawrence's adult dependency needs and his correlative fear of engulfment in merger, his need for mirroring by an ever-changing roster of disciples, the overt grandiosity of his "leadership" novels, and his sudden eruptions of narcissistic rage were fixations on archaic forms deriving from deficits in his symbiotic relationship with the mother, who provided excessive

---

[8]Delany (1978) observes that "Lawrence's homoerotic fantasies often seem to involve his being held and soothed by a stronger, usually older man, a desire that might have more to do with his need for security and affection than with any active homosexuality" (p. 314).

mirroring at times and used him for her own selfobject needs but who was unable to respond appropriately to his actual needs for separation–individuation and autonomy. It is in this early developmental context in relation to both parental imagos that the homoerotic feelings that emerged from time to time are to be understood.

Women in Love does encode such feelings, but the seduction theory — explicitly rejected by Donaldson (1986, pp. 60–61) and effectively argued by Squires (1990, pp. 55–57), both on the evidence of persuasive textual analysis — does not, at least for me, fully account for the unconscious motivation behind Birkin's homoerotic impulses or for his overt sexual behavior. Birkin has sexual intercourse with Ursula and other women and experiments with Ursula in sensual touching and manual stimulation (and, possibly, anal penetration) but has none of these with Crich or any other man.[9] What Birkin is offering to Crich is not the acting out of intimacy in overt homosexuality but the sublimation of homoerotic desire into blood brotherhood through sacramental ritual.

The argument that Birkin is a "latent homosexual" (Ober, 1979, p. 109) — that is, by definition, "one in whom the homosexual impulse [is] either conscious or unconscious, but not overtly acted out" (Ovesey, 1969, p. 31) — is misleading. Strictly speaking, I believe, Birkin's conflict, under the cover of homosexual striving, derives from motives that are not aimed primarily at sexual gratification but at preservation of the self. In this interpretation, I am extending the distinction that Lionel Ovesey makes between true homosexual identity and "pseudohomosexuality," although this term has not gained wide usage in clinical or theoretical discussions and is not essential to my meaning. Whereas an actual homosexual motive has as its aim the orgastic satisfaction of an instinctive drive, "pseudohomosexual" conflict, according to Ovesey, involves dependency and power strivings that are not sexual in origin, though they may employ sexual feelings and genital apparatus in their expression (Ovesey, 1969, p. 31). I would argue that one of the major conflicts that such preoccupations are employed by Birkin to defend against is the fear that the self may be annihilated. My concern, however, is not to deny the homoerotic feelings that Birkin obviously experiences but to maintain a distinction between a feeling and the acting out of that feeling in overt behavior, between a feeling and its root motive, and between a particular erotic impulse and the basic sexual identity of the individual. The erotic

---

[9]Meyers (1977) reads Birkin's homoerotic attractions in the "Prologue" as overt "homosexual affairs with working men" (p. 143) and thinks that "the homosexuality in 'Gladiatorial' *is* overt" (p. 148). The "Prologue," however, states clearly that Birkin's "reserve, which was as strong as a chain of iron in him, kept him from any demonstration" (p. 502). "For he could never acquiesce to his own feelings, to his own passion" (p. 504).

component in Birkin's attraction to Gerald Crich, which in view of Lawrence's canceled "Prologue" cannot even be described as unconscious, is not in question.[10] The real issues are *what it means, where it comes from, and what he does with it.*

What Birkin's homoerotic feeling means in terms of psychoanalytic self psychology is not a drive toward object-instinctive gratification but a search for a magical solution to conflicts that Heinz Kohut describes as a "primary narcissistic disturbance," that is, a disturbance in the structure of the nuclear self, which has been sexualized in the present but which is correlated with "an early ego defect" (Kohut, 1971, p. 69). Birkin himself sees his conflict as deriving from self-division: "He knew he obtained no real fulfillment in sensuality, he became disgusted and despised the whole process as if it were dirty. And he knew that he had no real fulfillment in his spiritual and aesthetic intercourse with Hermione. That process he also despised, with considerable cynicism." Yet he cannot "unite the two halves of himself" by an act of will (p. 500).

In the "Prologue" Birkin, struggling with the same self-division that had tormented Paul Morel in *Sons and Lovers,* can find no fulfillment in either half: "He would not sacrifice the sensual to the spiritual half of himself, and he could not sacrifice the spiritual to the sensual half" (p. 500). Birkin has been unable to reconcile the two sides of his nature in relation to women, apparently because he finds women too powerful to approach as whole objects and projects his own dichotomy by relating to them only as part objects: "To be spiritual, he must have a Hermione, completely without desire: to be sensual, he must have a slightly bestial woman, the very scent of whose skin soon disgusted him, whose manners nauseated him beyond bearing" (p. 500).

From the perspective of Freudian drive theory, Birkin's splitting would seem clearly to illustrate the theory of psychic impotence in response to the incest taboo, as set forth in Freud's essay "On the Universal Tendency to Debasement in the Sphere of Love":

> The whole sphere of love in such people remains divided in the two directions personified in art as sacred and profane (or animal) love. Where they love they cannot desire and where they desire they cannot love. They seek objects which they do not need to love, in order to keep their sensuality away from the objects they love . . . [Freud, 1910b, p. 183].

A further condition for sexual pleasure for men "in whom there has not been a proper confluence of the affectionate and the sensual currents" is

---

[10]Donaldson (1986) does question this idea and denies that "information provided by the 'Prologue' . . . can be applied directly to *Women in Love*" (p. 60).

that "they have retained perverse sexual aims whose non-fulfillment is felt as a serious loss of pleasure, and whose fulfillment on the other hand seems possible only with a debased and despised sexual object" (Freud, 1910b, p. 183).

Lawrence, however, does not present Birkin's splitting in the oedipal terms in which, in his letter to Edward Garnett (14 November 1912), he describes Paul Morel's inability to love (1979, pp. 476–477) but in terms of depressive feelings of emptiness in the self: "[H]e became more hollow and deathly, more like a spectre with hollow bones. He knew that he was not very far from dissolution" (p. 501). In Kohutian terms, what the developmentally impaired individual is defending against is not castration anxiety and inhibition of desire in relation to love objects associated unconsciously with the mother but the even more devastating threat of loss of the self. According to Kohut (1984), "disintegration anxiety" is "the deepest anxiety man can experience"; it is the fear of "loss of humanness: psychological death" and "the ascendancy of a nonhuman environment." It is "the threatened loss of the self-cohesion–maintaining responses of the empathic selfobject" (pp. 16–19), a loss to which the vulnerable self may react with "fragmentation, serious enfeeblement, or uncontrollable rage" (Kohut, 1977, p. 138).

To protect himself from this threatened dissolution of the self, Birkin turns to the magical solution of passionate "friendships with men of no great intelligence, but of pleasant appearance: ruddy, well-nourished fellows, good-natured and easy, who protected him in his delicate health more gently than a woman would protect him" (p. 502). In this situation he also finds himself attracted to men in the street—a policeman, a soldier, a young man in flannels. As he grows older, at 28 and 29, Birkin feels hopeless of ever escaping the "bondage" of this attraction, yet he will not acquiesce in it. Unable to tolerate a view of himself as a homosexual, he cannot accept in himself "this keen desire to have and to possess the bodies of such men" (p. 504). In Kohutian terms, the nucleus of Birkin's anxiety is "related to the fact that his self is undergoing an ominous change—and the intensity of the drive is not the cause of the central pathology (precariousness of self-cohesion), but its result. The core of disintegration anxiety is the anticipation of the breakup of the self, not the fear of the drive" (Kohut, 1977, p. 104).

One of Heinz Kohut's (1971) case histories, of a heterosexual man with a similar disturbance in nuclear self-structure, strikingly parallels Birkin's situation in several respects:

> Mr. A.'s homosexual tendencies had not exerted a widespread second-ary effect on the ego or led to diffuse drive regression. . . . He had

never engaged in homosexual activities and — apart from some sexually tinged, playful wrestling in adolescence and the buying of "physical culture" magazines which contained photographs of athletic men — his homosexual preoccupations were consummated only in fantasy, with or without masturbation. The objects of his homosexual fantasies were always men of great bodily strength and of perfect physique. His own fantasied activity consisted in maintaining a quasi-sadistic, absolute control over these men. In his fantasies he manipulated the situations in such a way that, even though he was weak, he was able to enslave the strong man and to make him helpless [pp. 69–70].

In *Women in Love,* when the two men join in naked wrestling in "Gladiatorial" (chap. 20), Birkin, though slighter, weaker, and of frailer health than Gerald, has skills that enable him to dominate the heavier, stronger man. Their bodies are described in phallic terms as "very dissimilar": "Birkin was tall and narrow, his bones were very thin and fine. Gerald was much heavier and more plastic. His bones were strong and round, his limbs were rounded, all his contours were beautifully and fully moulded" (p. 269). Birkin, who cannot accept his desire for sexual contact with another man, substitutes the close body contact of a nude wrestling match in which his dominance of the other man is conceptualized metaphorically as penetration: "It was as if Birkin's whole physical intelligence interpenetrated into Gerald's body, as if his fine, sublimated energy entered into the flesh of the fuller man, like some potency, . . . through the muscles into the very depths of Gerald's physical being" (p. 270). Lawrence's description does make the union sound something like Iago's "beast with two backs" in *Othello* (1.1.118): "the swift, tight limbs, the solid white backs, the physical junction of two bodies clinched into a oneness" (p. 270). The psychological sensation of an altered state of consciousness is marked by "the strange tilting and sliding of the world" into darkness (p. 271). The language is certainly sexual but, as the word *sublimated* suggests, the "energy" that is being "interpenetrated into Gerald's body" also empowers Birkin's "physical being" with the "potency" not of literal penile penetration but of metaphorically phallic incorporation, as homoerotic feeling is transformed into blood brotherhood to defend against the threatened dissolution of the self, in particular, against the threat of absorption by women. Birkin's attachment to Gerald is the expression not of an object-instinctive drive but of the longing for merger in an idealized selfobject relationship. Psychologically, the presence of Gerald's penis may provide reassuring evidence that Birkin can wrestle with him without being devoured by the vagina dentata that another of Lawrence's male protagonists, Oliver Mellors, fears ("the old rampers have beaks between their legs, and they tear at you with it till you're sick"

[Lawrence, D. H., 1928, p. 242]). Birkin, who has already sought healing contact with nature by rolling naked among primroses and hyacinths and stinging his skin with thistles and fir needles (pp. 106–107) to free himself from corruptive contact with Hermione after she clouts him murderously on the head with a lapis lazuli paperweight, now seeks the refuge of male bonding as protection against the disintegrative and devouring relationship with a woman. What Birkin seeks to incorporate, however, is not Gerald's actual penis but, through that powerful symbol, the strength that Gerald's athleticism, masculinity, and authority represent in Birkin's idealizing gaze (p. 490). The unconscious motive behind this wish is not sexual per se but a mechanism of psychic defense against the threat of dissolution of the self.

In this light, Birkin's homoerotic attractions in the "Prologue" may be seen as unsuccessful attempts at magical reparation of the injury to his self, for he inevitably perpetuates the split by relating to men too only in halfness:

> They divided themselves, roughly, into two classes: these white-skinned, keen-limbed men with eyes like blue-flashing ice and hair like crystals of winter sunshine, the northmen, inhuman as sharp-crying gulls, distinct like splinters of ice, like crystals, isolated, individual; and then the men with dark eyes that one can enter and plunge into, bathe in, as in a liquid darkness, dark-skinned, supple, night-smelling men, who are the living substance of the viscous, universal, heavy darkness [pp. 503–504].

The rituals of Blutbrüderschaft are a further conscious attempt to heal the split and achieve self-cohesion by establishing a balance between spiritual and physical being. After the nude wrestling match, Birkin says to Gerald: "We are mentally, spiritually intimate, therefore we should be more or less physically intimate too—it is more whole" (p. 272). Although Birkin sees in the other man parts and qualities that he himself needs, the narrator presents Gerald as one of the isolate, icy northmen, and Birkin has about as much chance of establishing a relationship of mutual affirmation and wholeness with this half being as he does with Hermione.

Where the conflict comes from is not an easy question to answer, since *Women in Love* offers little information about Birkin's early background. His view of Hermione, however, as a possessive female vulture who threatens to devour him psychologically, provides at least a clue. Judith Ruderman (1984), who identifies the twin poles of "[t]he longing for merger and the fear of merger" in Lawrence, observes that "this psychic conflict is rooted in the author's earliest experiences with his caretaker mother. The blood brotherhood . . . a relation of men—allows Lawrence the security of merger without the threat of annihilation that he associates with women" (p. 148).

It will be helpful at this point to survey briefly and sequentially the interpretations of this psychological situation from the perspectives of classical drive theory and of object relations theory in order to point up the unique contribution of self psychology to understanding the issues involved.

A classical psychoanalytic interpretation would attribute Birkin's psychic impotence in spiritual relationships with women unconsciously associated with the mother to intrapsychic conflicts rooted in unresolved oedipal problems (Freud, 1910b, p. 182). In Freud's developmental theory, the boy's oedipal guilt feelings and castration anxiety are partially resolved by his identification with the father, as idealization of the father leads to the emergence of the ego ideal and the repression of the Oedipus complex (Freud, 1923, pp. 31, 34–37). On the theory that "a human being has originally two sexual objects — himself and the woman who nurses him," Freud postulates "a primary narcissism in everyone," which in homosexuals may reemerge as a narcissistic attachment to self. "[P]eople whose libidinal development has suffered some disturbance, such as perverts and homosexuals, . . . in their later choice of love-objects . . . have taken as a model not their mother but their own selves. They are plainly seeking *themselves* as a love-object, and are exhibiting a type of object-choice which must be termed 'narcissistic' " (Freud, 1914, p. 88). The individual most vulnerable to this narcissistic regression has had, "during the first period of childhood," "a very intense erotic attachment" to the mother, which "was evoked or encouraged by too much tenderness on the part of the mother herself, and further reinforced by the small part played by the father" in the boy's early development (Freud, 1910a, p. 99). In Freudian terms, the son in Lawrence's work, unable to make the identification with the father necessary for full maturation, is caught between two unsatisfactory object choices, each of which presents a dilemma. If he makes a heterosexual object choice, he must choose between a spiritual woman who is a forbidden oedipal object and a degraded woman who is for this very reason an unsatisfactory substitute. If he makes a homosexual object choice, it is inevitably narcissistic, as Lawrence (1981) himself indicates in his letter to Savage of 2 December 1913 (p. 115).

Object relations theory would see Birkin as driven by the failure of his emotional relationships with external objects to seek the compensatory satisfactions of oral and anal erotic forms of infantile sexuality in an attempt to salvage natural relationships with internal objects that have broken down (Fairbairn, 1954, p. 40). Birkin's homoerotic attractions and his longing for Blutbrüderschaft would be interpreted in the context of an object relational situation in which the unavailability of the father for idealization as a whole object means that the son cannot be conclusively assured that he is genuinely loved by the father or that his love for the father is genuinely accepted. Hence, he resorts to the homoerotic search for his father's penis as a part object that can substitute for the father himself. As Fairbairn (1941) explains the mechanism, this substitution involves a regression that also revives the original oral relationship with the original part object, the breast (p. 262). The son's "search for his father's penis thus resolves itself, so to speak, into a search for his father's breast" (Fairbairn, 1954, p. 41). In object relational terms, the son in Lawrence's work is playing out in the external world a drama of objects in the internal world, seeking in their external representatives the protection of the internalized paternal imago against the threat of devourment and absorption by the internalized maternal imago.

Finally, in Kohut's nonpejorative theory of narcissism, self psychology proposes a line of development for the self distinct from that of drive-oriented object love. A self-psychological interpretation goes beyond earlier psychoanalytic models in attributing the deficits in the child's nuclear self structure to flaws in the responses of his earliest selfobjects. Thus, in Birkin, both the split between spiritual and sensual love, with the concomitant fear of devourment by women, and the search for protective nurturance in an idealizing merger with another man are displacements of the son's needs, derived both from reactivated archaic selfobject needs and from phase-appropriate needs in the present, for a responsive selfobject matrix (Wolf, 1988, p. 186). The "traumatic disruption" of this selfobject relationship "accounts for the intensity and urgency of the attempts to set up and maintain merger relationships . . . with other selfobjects in a desperate (and often unworkable) effort to resurrect the harmonious selfobject relatedness that obtained prior to its disruption or to install this relatedness as a fresh experience" (Bacal and Newman, 1990, p. 249). In Lawrence's case, the self-psychological interpretation of his symbiotic merger with the mother from early childhood until her death and his severe disappointment in the need for idealizing merger with the father explains, more persuasively than either classical drive theory or object relations theory, both his dependency needs and the deficits in his archaic nuclear self structure that he sought repeatedly and urgently to heal.

Kohut's (1977) description of Mr. A correlates in part with what we know of Lawrence's own early psychic experience. Not having received what he needed from either parent, Mr. A had "experienced his body-self as fragmented and powerless (as a consequence of the absence of adequate joyful responses from the maternal self-object)," and the "barely established structure of his guiding ideals had been severely weakened (in consequence of the traumatic destruction of the paternal omnipotent self-object)" (p. 126).

The consequent later idealization is attributable as much to conflicts in the relation to the mother as to deficiencies in the relation to the father. Kohut (1971) observes that "behind the imagery concerning the relationship of a boy's grandiose self with a depreciated father . . . lies regularly the deeper imago of the dangerous, powerful rival-parent" (p. 146). As a specific example, "[T]he intensity of Mr. A's idealization of his father (and thus the traumatic intensity of his disappointment in him) was due to the earlier disappointment in the mirroring self-object" (Kohut, 1977, p. 11 n. 2). In Lawrence's case, maternal mirroring served not only his need for support but also his mother's need to tie him dependently to her in symbiotic merger—to feed on his life, as it were, and live through him—and she actively participated in the destruction of the paternal selfobject, leaving the son with a lifelong search, intensely pressing at times, for an idealizable male, instinctual and earthy like his father but, unlike him, a figure of physical power and psychic strength.

The nature of the problem, as Ruderman has shown, indicates that it derives from the preoedipal (i.e., prephallic) period, in which divisions in the bipolar self, such as Birkin's split between spiritual and sensual being, originate. According to Kohut (1971), "the basic neutralizing structures of the psyche are acquired during the preoedipal period." In Mr. A's case, "a moderate weakness in his basic psychic structure" resulted in "an impairment of its neutralizing capacity" and led to the sexualization of his "narcissistically invested objects" in three areas relating to the two parent imagos and the self: Mr. A had sexualized and remained fixated on his "idealized father imago," which he needed because he had not internalized a firmly established ego ideal; he had sexualized and remained fixated on the "mirror image" of his "grandiose self," Kohut's term for the ambitious, aspiring, exhibitionistic sector of the self as mirrored by the joyful admiration and encouragement of the maternal selfobject, which he needed because he had not internalized a secure "(pre)conscious image of the self"; and he had sexualized both "his *need* for idealized values and reliable self-esteem" and the "psychological *processes*" of internalization "by which ideals and self-esteem are acquired." Kohut (1971) observes, "The patient's homosexual fantasies can thus be understood as sexualized statements about his narcissistic disturbance, analogous to the theoretical formulations of the analyst. The fantasies stood, of course, in opposition to meaningful insight and progress since they were in the service of pleasure gain and provided an escape route from narcissistic tensions" (pp. 70–71).

What Birkin does with his homoerotic preoccupations and with his fear of the devouring female that correlates with them is to encode them in theoretical systems that safely structure his concerns about both male–female and male–male relationships. Birkin's elaborate theories of both "star polarity" with a woman and "Blutbrüderschaft" with a man are designed to make intimacy possible by establishing codes of balance and psychic distance that will protect him against the threat of merger and dissolution of the self in the process. Birkin's concept of marriage as "star polarity," in which, as in the solar system, a magnetic force holds the partners in balance like planets and prevents one from plunging into and being absorbed by the other, becomes a male metaphor for the ideal heterosexual relationship, which, by preserving the separate integrity of each partner, provides a psychic defense against the danger that he will fall into or be devoured by the woman.

In the canceled "Prologue," Birkin's homoerotic impulses emerge in the context of his frustrating attempt to force sexual satisfaction out of the spiritual relationship with Hermione (p. 497). As an effect of the split between spiritual and sensual love with women, Birkin turns toward men with "the hot, flushing, roused attraction which a man is supposed to feel for the other sex" (p. 501). Not surprisingly for a man who fears being devoured, his own fantasies center on oral incorporation. Seeing "a strange Cornish type of man" in a restaurant, "Birkin would feel the desire spring up in him, the desire to know this man, to have him, as it were to eat him, to take the very substance of him" (p. 505). As Ovesey (1969) explains the principle, the "dependent pseudohomosexual male," seeking the "protection of an omnipotent father-substitute via the equation, *penis* = *breast*," "aspires to repair his castration through a magical reparative fantasy of oral or anal incorporation of the stronger man's penis, thus making the donor's strength available to him. This maneuver is doomed not only because it is magical and hence cannot succeed in any case, but also because the fantasied act of incorporation is misinterpreted as truly homosexual in its motivation" and thus serves only to intensify the "pseudohomosexual anxiety" (p. 58).

Birkin's reparative fantasies, in Kohutian terms, express the need for self structure. In this kind of "preconscious fellatio fantasy," according to Kohut (1971), "swallowing the magical semen stands for the unachieved internalization and structure formation" of the self (p. 72). In Kohut's (1977) account of the analysis, Mr. A was able to discern a motivational connection between his feelings of emptiness and "certain intensely sexualized fantasies to which he turned when he felt depressed, in which he imagined himself subduing a powerful male figure with his 'brains,' chaining him through the employment of some clever ruse in order to imbibe, via a preconscious fellatio fantasy, the giant's strength" (p. 126). The "nonsexual significance of the perverse sexual fantasy that accompanied his masturbatory activities" was "the attempt to use the last remnant of his grandiose self (omnipotent thought: the ruse) in order to regain possession of the idealized omnipotent self-object (to exert absolute control over it — to chain it) and then to internalize it via fellatio" (p. 126). In the novel Birkin, who is arguably Lawrence's most intellectual character, does not attempt to actualize his fantasies in overt homosexual activity but to transform them into the highly intellectualized theory of Blutbrüderschaft. He turns again, in other words, to what has proven to be the most powerful and reliable part of his grandiose self, the mind.

Neither Birkin's attraction to men in the "Prologue" nor the homoerotic feeling evident in Blutbrüderschaft derives from an object-instinctive drive toward orgastic satisfaction in a basically homosexual identity. The homosexual yearnings evident in Birkin's fantasies represent an attempt on his part to repair a defect in his nuclear self by magically incorporating the other man's strength. In this light, Birkin's fantasies may be seen, as Kohut (1971) sees Mr. A's homosexual preoccupations, "as sexualized statements concerning the nature of his psychological defect and of the psychological functions which had to be acquired." In "the absence of a stable system of firmly idealized values" as a source "of the internal regulation of self-esteem," Mr. A "had in his sexual fantasies replaced the inner ideal with its sexualized external precursor, an athletic powerful man"; and in place of the self-esteem derived from living up to one's standards, he had substituted "the sexualized feeling of triumph" derived from robbing "the external ideal of its power and perfection," thus in fantasy acquiring these qualities for himself and achieving "a temporary feeling of narcissistic balance" (p. 72). There is an obvious parallel in Birkin's temporary feeling of wholeness in physical and spiritual intimacy after robbing Gerald of his power and perfection, triumphing over him by the cunning use of jiujitsu in the wrestling match. In Blutbrüderschaft, Birkin takes the process one step further in the attempt to transmute the need for an idealizable omnipotent paternal selfobject underlying his fantasies into a viable ego ideal that he can live by: a standard of commitment and loyalty in male bonding that does not include the exploitation of grossly sensational, overtly sexual acting out.

Birkin's homoerotic feeling is a psychic mechanism thrown up recurrently by the ego during a disturbing transitional period of his life as a defense against dissolution in the service of preservation of the self. But as the narrator comments, "The wrestling had some deep meaning to them — an unfinished meaning" (p. 272). In his homoerotic fantasies in the "Prologue," Birkin, as Kohut (1971) says of Mr. A, has sexualized both "his *need* for idealized values and reliable self-esteem" and the *process* of internalization by which these qualities are acquired (pp. 70–71). In the theory of Blutbrüderschaft, a relationship comparable to marriage in commitment, there is still a prominent element of magical thinking aimed at pleasure gain rather than realistic insight. For this reason, Birkin's attempt to transmute the need for an idealizable omnipotent paternal selfobject into the ego ideal by way of male rituals that dramatize such a relationship cannot be entirely successful.

Where his object relationships with women are concerned, Birkin tries to make his way out of the impasse through a series of exercises that adapt his anal eroticism to the task of psychological desensitization. First, he channels his forbidden sexual inclinations into aesthetic appreciation of a statuette of a standing female:

> . . . a tall, slim, elegant figure from West Africa, in dark wood, glossy and suave. It was a woman, with hair dressed high, like a melon-shaped dome. He remembered her vividly; she was one of his soul's intimates. Her body was long and elegant, her face was crushed tiny like a beetle's, she had rows of round heavy collars, like a column of quoits, on her neck. He remembered her: her astonishing cultured elegance, her diminished, beetle face, the astounding long elegant body, on short, ugly legs, with such protuberant buttocks, so weighty and unexpected below her slim long loins [p. 253].

The grace and beauty of the figure's formal aesthetic lines are correlated with her abstracted beetle face, recalling Lawrence's dream of black beetles in response to the Cambridge homosexuals, and the arousing grossness of her protuberant buttocks, encoding Birkin's homoerotic desire.

Later, in "Excurse" (chap. 23), though Birkin initially feels "tight and unfree," he submits to Ursula's initiative as, "overwhelmed with a sense of a heavenful of riches," she stimulates him manually by tracing "with her hands the line of his loins and thighs, at the back." This sensual experimentation establishes "a new current of passional electric energy, between the two of them, released from the darkest poles of the body," and leads to "a perfect passing away for both of them, and at the same time the most intolerable accession into being, the marvellous fullness of immediate gratification, overwhelming, outflooding from the Source of the deepest life-force, the darkest, deepest, strangest life-source of the human body, at the back and base of the loins" (pp. 313–314). While Lawrence evokes the prostatic and sacral chakras of kundalini yoga in his reference to the "mystically-physically satisfying" "strange fountains of his body," he alludes, on a more mundane level, to erotic satisfaction at the anal erogenous zone: "And now, behold, from the smitten rock of the man's body, from the strange marvellous flanks and thighs, deeper, further in mystery than the phallic source, came the floods of ineffable darkness and ineffable riches" (p. 314). Birkin, by means of this unconventional sexual experience with a woman he can both love and desire, begins the healing process that can restore his self-division.

Finally, Birkin channels these impulses into a conscious process of debasement from the spiritual to the profane in love. Like the West African statuette, he seems to Ursula both fascinating and repellant at once: "His licentiousness was repulsively attractive. But he was self-responsible . . ." (pp. 412–413). The result is uninhibited sex with Ursula, and her developing response conveys the liberating effect of the experience for both partners:

> They might do as they liked—this she realised as she went to sleep. How could anything that gave one satisfaction be excluded? What was degrading?—Who cared? Degrading things were real, with a different reality. And he was so unabashed and unrestrained. Wasn't it rather horrible, a man who could be so soulful and spiritual, now to be so— she balked at her own thoughts and memories: then she added—so bestial? So bestial, they two!—so degraded! She winced.—But after all, why not? She exulted as well. Why not be bestial, and go the whole round of experience? She exulted in it. She was bestial. How good it was to be really shameful! There would be no shameful thing she had not experienced.—Yet she was unabashed, she was herself. Why not?—She was free, when she knew everything, and no dark shameful things were denied her [p. 413].

Their precise sexual practices, veiled in shadowy, suggestive, but generic language, are not specified, but the emphasis upon anality in the protruding buttocks of the West African statuette, in the anal eroticism of the sexual experimentation in "Excurse," and in the sense of liberation through "degrading," "shameful," and "bestial" sexuality suggests that their activities included anal intercourse. What is involved is not the simple substitution of the female body for the preferred male body of Birkin's fantasies in the "Prologue." Rather, a familiar pattern of arousal has been adapted in a process of de-idealization that makes possible a relationship with a woman on a basis other than either spiritual elevation or sexual disgust.

Birkin has achieved in some measure the restructuring that Lawrence sees as an aim of heterosexual relationships. The need for affirmation of the self by means of an irrevocable bonding with a stronger male remains. In their poignant dialogue after Gerald's death at the end of *Women in Love,* Birkin's longing and Ursula's insistent reality are both reasserted. Birkin's compromise has been to accept the "sheer intimacy" of heterosexual marriage as sufficient for overt sexuality, provided he could also have the emotionally satisfying bond of "eternal union with a man too: another kind of love." In Ursula's view, "It's an obstinacy, a theory, a perversity." "You can't have two kinds of love," she declares. "It seems as if I can't," Birkin admits. "Yet I wanted it" (p. 481). Ursula's final comment, "You can't have it, because it's false, impossible," suggests her insight on why he is prevented from having what he wants: because he will not, or cannot, accept the realistic limits of such a relationship. His intransigent reply, "I don't believe that" (p. 481), is more ambiguous. He has not given up his longing for merger with an idealizable male, but his tone is wistful and sad and the intensity of his need seems somewhat diminished in strength. The dialogue has shown that Blutbrüderschaft, as a practical means of gratifying Birkin's longing, is doomed to tragic failure and disappointment. But as a psychological maneuver, the concept has enabled him to incorporate this longing and to preserve the self-cohesion needed to function creatively.

For Lawrence, as for Birkin, the subject was not closed. Variations on the theme continued in his subsequent "leadership" novels, in which the Blutbrüder figure comes more and more to resemble the idealized nurturing father:[11] Rawdon Lilly restoring the ill and depressed Aaron Sisson to health by sensual massage in *Aaron's Rod* (chap. 9, "Low-water Mark"), Ramón Carrasco ordaining Cipriano Viedma into masculine godhead by religious ritual involving quasi-hypnotic touch in *The Plumed Serpent* (chap. 22, "The Living Huitzilopochtli"). Lawrence (1923) even returns to the issue in two essays in *Studies in Classic American Literature,* in which Herman Melville becomes the proxy through whom he criticizes his own hopeless quest for blood brotherhood: "Yet to the end he pined for this: a perfect relationship; perfect mating; perfect mutual understanding. A perfect friend" (p. 142). The lost merger was not to be restored: "Right to the end he could never accept the fact that *perfect* relationships cannot be" (p. 142). As hard as it was for Lawrence to hear

---

[11]Ruderman (1984) suggests that the real function of the leader in Lawrence's leadership novels is not to lead the masses but to provide the male nurturance that will prevent the man's being devoured by woman in her Magna Mater role (pp. 174–175).

it above the insistent demands of his own needs and wishes, that was the voice of the reality principle.

References

Bacal, H. A. & Newman, K. M. (1990), *Theories of Object Relations: Bridges to Self Psychology.* New York: Columbia University Press.

Britton, D. (1988), *Lady Chatterley: The Making of the Novel.* London: Unwin Hyman.

Delany, P. (1978), *D. H. Lawrence's Nightmare: The Writer and His Circle in the Years of the Great War.* New York: Basic Books.

Delavenay, E. (1972), *D. H. Lawrence: The Man and His Work,* trans. K. M. Delavenay. Carbondale: Southern Illinois University Press.

Donaldson, G. (1986), "Men in Love"? D. H. Lawrence, Rupert Birkin and Gerald Crich. In: *D. H. Lawrence: Centenary Essays,* ed. M. Kalnins. Bristol, UK: Bristol Classical Press, pp. 41–67.

Fairbairn, W. R. D. (1941), A revised psychopathology of the psychoses and psychoneuroses. *Internat. J. Psycho-Anal.,* 22(Parts 3–4):250–279.

_____ (1954), *An Object-Relations Theory of the Personality.* New York: Basic Books.

Freud, S. (1908), Creative writers and day-dreaming. *Standard Edition,* 9:141–153. London: Hogarth Press, 1957.

_____ (1910a), Leonardo da Vinci and a memory of his childhood. *Standard Edition,* 11:63–137. London: Hogarth Press, 1957.

_____ (1910b), On the universal tendency to debasement in the sphere of love. *Standard Edition,* 11:179–190. London: Hogarth Press, 1957.

_____ (1914), On narcissism: An introduction. *Standard Edition,* 14:73–102. London: Hogarth Press, 1957.

_____ (1923), The ego and the id. *Standard Edition,* 19:12–59. London: Hogarth Press, 1961.

_____ & Jung, C. G. (1974), *The Freud/Jung Letters: The Correspondence Between Sigmund Freud and C. G. Jung,* ed. W. McGuire, trans. R. Manheim & R. F. C. Hull. Princeton, NJ: Princeton University Press.

Kohut, H. (1971), *The Analysis of the Self.* New York: International Universities Press.

_____ (1977), *The Restoration of the Self.* New York: International Universities Press.

_____ (1984), *How Does Analysis Cure?,* ed. A. Goldberg and P. Stepansky. Chicago: University of Chicago Press.

Lawrence, D. H. (1920), *Women in Love,* ed. D. Farmer, L. Vasey & J. Worthen. Cambridge: Cambridge University Press, 1987.

_____ (1923), *Studies in Classic American Literature.* New York: Viking Press, 1961.

_____ (1928), *Lady Chatterley's Lover.* New York: Grove Press, 1959.

_____ (1979), *The Letters of D. H. Lawrence, Vol. 1,* ed. J. T. Boulton. Cambridge: Cambridge University Press.

_____ (1981), *The Letters of D. H. Lawrence, Vol. 2,* ed. G. J. Zytaruk & J. T. Boulton. Cambridge: Cambridge University Press.

_____ (1984), *The Letters of D. H. Lawrence, Vol. 3,* ed. J. T. Boulton & A. Robertson. Cambridge: Cambridge University Press.

Lawrence, F. (1964), *Frieda Lawrence: The Memoirs and Correspondence,* ed. E. W. Tedlock, Jr. New York: Knopf.

_____ (1981), *Frieda Lawrence and Her Circle,* ed. H. T. Moore & D. B. Montague. Hamden, CT: Archon Books.

Mackenzie, C. (1966), *My Life and Times: Octave 5.* London: Chatto & Windus.

Meyers, J. (1977), *Homosexuality and Literature: 1890–1930.* Montreal: McGill-Queen's University Press.

_____ (1990), *D. H. Lawrence.* New York: Knopf.

Moore, H. T. (1974), *The Priest of Love.* New York: Farrar, Straus & Giroux.

Murry, J. M. (1931), *Son of Woman.* London: Jonathan Cape.

_____ (1933), *Reminiscences of D. H. Lawrence.* London: Jonathan Cape.

Nehls, E., ed. (1957), *D. H. Lawrence.* Madison: University of Wisconsin Press.

Neville, G. H. (1981), *A Memoir of D. H. Lawrence (The Betrayal),* ed. C. Baron. Cambridge: Cambridge University Press.

Ober, W. B. (1979), Lady Chatterley's what? In: *Boswell's Clap and Other Essays.* Carbondale: Southern Illinois University Press, pp. 89–117.

Ovesey, L. (1969), *Homosexuality and Pseudohomosexuality.* New York: Science House.

Ross, C. L. (1980), Homoerotic feeling in *Women in Love:* Lawrence's "struggle for verbal consciousness" in the manuscripts. In: *D. H. Lawrence,* ed. R. B. Partlow, Jr., & H. T. Moore. Carbondale: Southern Illinois University Press, pp. 168–182.

Ruderman, J. (1984), *D. H. Lawrence and the Devouring Mother.* Durham, NC: Duke University Press.

Said, E. (1975), *Beginnings, Intention and Method.* New York: Basic Books.

Squires, M. (1990), Dickens, Lawrence, and the English novel. In: *The Challenge of D. H. Lawrence,* ed. M. Squires & K. Cushman. Madison: University of Wisconsin Press, pp. 42–59.

Stevens, C. J. (1988), *Lawrence at Tregerthen.* Troy, NY: Whitston.

Wolf, E. (1988), *Treating the Self.* New York: Guilford Press.

Worthen, J. (1991), *D. H. Lawrence: The Early Years, 1885–1912.* Cambridge, UK: Cambridge University Press.

Ramakrishna and the Mystical Experience

SUDHIR KAKAR

The psychoanalytic understanding of any phenomenon begins with the narrative, with the echoes and reverberations of individual history. The individual I have selected for my own explorations in mysticism is the 19th-century Indian saint Sri Ramakrishna. He is a particularly apt choice for a psychoanalytic study of ecstatic mysticism since Freud's observations on the mystical experience, on what he called the "oceanic feeling," an omnibus label for all forms of extreme mystical experience, were indirectly occasioned by Ramakrishna's ecstasies.

It was the biography of Ramakrishna that Romain Rolland was working on when he wrote to Freud in 1927 to tell him that though he found his analysis of religion (in "The Future of an Illusion") "*justé*," he would ideally have liked Freud to "make an analysis of spontaneous religious feelings, or more exactly, religious sensations which are entirely different from religion proper and much more enduring" (Harrison, 1979, p. 409) Rolland went on to call this sensation "oceanic," without perceptible limits, and mentioned two Indians who had such feelings and "who have manifested a genius for thought and action powerfully regenerative for their country and for the world." Rolland added that he himself had all his life found the oceanic feeling to be a source of vital revival. Freud's response to Rolland, his analysis of the "oceanic feeling," was then spelled out in "Civilization and its Discontents" (1930). It is highly probable that the term *oceanic feeling* itself is taken from Ramakrishna's imagery to describe the ineffable. For instance, one of

An expanded version of this chapter appeared as Chapter 1 of *The Analyst and the Mystic,* Chicago: University of Chicago Press, 1992. With the permission of the University of Chicago Press.

Ramakrishna's oft-repeated metaphors is of the salt doll that went to measure the depth of the ocean: "As it entered the ocean it melted. Then who is there to come back and say how deep is the ocean?" Of course, the use of the ocean as a symbol for boundless oneness and unity in which multiplicities dissolve and opposites fuse not only goes back to the Upanishads in the Hindu tradition but is one of the preferred metaphors of devotional mystics for the melting of ego boundaries in the Buddhist, Christian, and Muslim traditions as well. Christian mystics, for instance, have been very fond of the metaphor: "I live in the ocean of God as a fish in the sea."

Freud's response to Ramakrishna, as generally to "Mother India," was one of unease. Although of some professional interest, Ramakrishna's florid ecstasies were as distant, if not distasteful, to Freud's sensibility as the jumbled vision of flesh—the labyrinth flux of the animal, human, and divine—in Indian art. In his acknowledgment of Rolland's book on Ramakrishna, Freud (1930b) writes, "I shall now try with your guidance to penetrate into the Indian jungle from which until now an uncertain blending of Hellenic love of proportion, Jewish sobriety, and philistine timidity have kept me away. I really ought to have tackled it earlier, for the plants of this soil shouldn't be alien to me; I have dug to certain depths for their roots. But it isn't easy to pass beyond the limits of one's nature" (p. 392).

We are, of course, fortunate that the last four years of Ramakrishna's life, from 1882 to 1886, were recorded with minute fidelity by a disciple, Māhendranath Gupta (1897) or M. as he called himself with modest self-effacement. Let me then begin with the outer scaffolding of the story, a brief narration of events of Ramakrishna's early life.

Ramakrishna was born in 1836 into a Brahmin family in the village of Kamarpukur in Bengal. His parents were pious and very poor, but what I find exceptional about them in the context of 19th-century village life in India is their ages at the time of Ramakrishna's birth. At a time when the average longevity was less than 30 years, when maternal death during childbirth was fairly common, and when the sexually reproductive years of the woman were over by her early thirties, Ramakrishna's father was 61 and his mother 45 years old when he was born. In the family there was a 31-year-old brother, a 27-year-old sister, and an 11-year-old brother. Yet another sister was born when Gadhadhar (Ramakrishna's given name) was 4 years old.

Ramakrishna later remembered his mother, Chandra, as a simple soul without a trace of worldliness who could not even count money. She said whatever came to her mind, without obfuscation or concealment, and people even called her a "simpleton." Devoted to her youngest son, the fruit of old loins, she was nevertheless, as elderly parents often tend to be, inordinately anxious about any harm befalling him when he was not within view. A curious and lively child, intent on exploring the world, Ramakrishna did not exactly help in allaying his mother's anxieties. She sought to master these by daily prayers to the family deity, whom she begged for the continued welfare of her little boy. Perhaps Ramakrishna's later anxiety whenever he was physically incapacitated, his almost hypochondriacal concerns at such times, can be directly traced to the elderly mother's concerns about her youngest son.

The incident given as an example of the boy's willfulness, which sometimes ignored the conventional rules of conduct, concerns his hiding behind a tree and peeping out at women while they washed clothes and bathed at the village tank. One of the women complained to Chandra, who then admonished the boy that all women were the same as his mother: shaming them was shaming her, insulting their honor was insulting hers. We are told that the mortified boy never again repeated his behavior. To us post-Freudians, the incident involves a child's natural sexual curiosity, which the mother dampened by associating it with incestuous anxiety. Interestingly, in later life, Ramakrishna would use the following mythological version of this personal experience, wherein the incestuous urgings and fears are much more explicit, to explain a part of his attitude toward women: One day, during his childhood, the god Ganesha saw a cat, which, as some boys are apt to do, he proceeded to torture in various ways till the cat finally made its escape. When Ganesha came back home, he saw to his surprise the bruises and marks of torture on the body of his mother, the goddess Parvati. The mother revealed to her son that all living beings in female form were part of her and that whatever he did to any female he did unto his mother. On reaching marriageable age, Ganesha, lest he marry his mother, decided to remain celibate forever. "My attitude to women is the same," was Ramakrishna's final comment (Saradananda, 1983, pp. 276–277).

Khudiram, Ramakrishna's father, was a gentle man who is reported to have never scolded his son. He took a quiet pride in the boy's evident intelligence and phenomenal memory, which were further displayed to advantage when he started attending the village school at the age of five. However, though he was good at school (but bad at arithmetic), what the boy most enjoyed was painting pictures and spending time with the village potters learning how to make clay images of gods and goddesses. The artistic streak in Ramakrishna was strongly developed, and it seems appropriate that his first ecstasy was evoked by the welling up of aesthetic emotion; an episode of "nature mysticism," it was the consequence of an aesthetically transcendent feeling:

I was following a narrow path between the rice fields. I raised my eyes to the sky as I munched my rice. I saw a great black cloud spreading rapidly until it covered the heavens. Suddenly at the edge of the cloud a flight of snow white cranes passed over my head. The contrast was so beautiful that my spirit wandered far away. I lost consciousness and fell to the ground. The puffed rice was scattered. Somebody picked me up and carried me home in his arms. An excess of joy and emotion overcame me. . . . This was the first time that I was seized with ecstasy [Rolland, 1929, p. 22–23].

Ramakrishna's father, who had been ill for a while, died when the boy was around eight years of age. The effect of the father's death was to make him withdrawn and fond of solitude. His attendance at school became fitful. He drew closer to his mother and spent much time in helping her with her household duties and joining her in her daily prayers to the gods. He became very fond of listening to discourses on spiritual matters and spent hours at a pilgrimage house where wandering ascetics found a bed for a night or two before they resumed their wanderings. The latter activity alarmed his mother, who feared that her son might decide to leave home and embrace the renunciant's life.

The gradually deteriorating condition of the family after Khudiram's death worsened with the marriage of Ramakrishna's second brother. With the advent of the new daughter-in-law, quarrels and bickering in the household increased markedly; a situation that the family's worsening economic circumstances, driving it to the edge of subsistence, did not help improve. The daily clamor and strife, I imagine, perhaps added its own impetus in pushing the sensitive and artistic boy more and more away from the distasteful discord of everyday reality and toward transcendental, spiritual matters and religious life. The latter coursed through the village, too, in a powerful stream, as it does to a great extent even today in rural India. There were the many rituals in which everyday life was embedded, frequent recitals from the Puranas, and the religious plays and festivals in which Ramakrishna participated by singing and dancing with fervid abandon. And, above all, there were the sudden inward, abstracted states, brought on at the oddest of times by outer stimuli such as listening to a song in praise of a god or to snatches of devotional music.

The young daughter-in-law died in childbirth when Ramakrishna was 13 years old, and the burden of running the household once again fell on the aging shoulders of Ramakrishna's mother. To help alleviate the poverty, his eldest brother left for Calcutta to run a small Sanskrit school. His position as the head of the family now devolved on Ramakrishna's second brother, who was temperamentally disinclined to take over responsibilities for his siblings and was, in any case, much too busy scrounging around for work.

Thus, at the beginning of adolescence Ramakrishna was left to his own devices, without the guiding voice of his father or eldest brother. School became even more occasional. When he was not an enthusiastic participant in the village's religious life, Ramakrishna was at home with his mother, helping her with household tasks and sharing with her the rhythm of her woman's days. The village women who dropped in on his mother for a visit during the day seem to have adopted him as one of their own. They would ask him to sing—he had a very sweet singing voice—or to tell stories from the Puranas, of which he had an enormous repertoire. He performed scenes from popular plays for their amusement, playing all the parts himself. He listened to their secrets and woes and would attempt to lift the spirits of a dejected woman by acting out a rustic farce. He loved putting on women's clothes and ornaments. Dressed thus, with a pitcher under his arm to fetch water from the tank like the village women, he would pass in front of the men and felt proud that no one suspected he was not a woman. A fantasy from this period has Ramakrishna imagining that were he to be born again, he would become a beautiful child widow with long black hair who would not know anyone else except Lord Krishna as a husband.

In the meanwhile, Ramakrishna's eldest brother, Ramkumar, was doing well in Calcutta, running his small school and performing religious services for some rich families. He called the 17-year-old Ramakrishna to the city to assist him in his priestly duties. Soon after, a new opportunity opened up when a rich woman built and consecrated a temple to the goddess Kali outside Calcutta and employed Ramkumar as its full-time priest. Ramkumar, who had been ailing for some time, found the task arduous and handed over his duties to Ramakrishna; he died a year later.

Ramkumar's death was to have a profound effect on Ramakrishna. Thirty-one years older, he had looked after Ramakrishna like a father after Khudiram's death. "Who can say," Ramakrishna's disciple-biographer (Saradananda, 1983) asks, "how far his brother's death contributed to the kindling up of the fire of renunciation in the Master's pure mind, by producing in him a firm conviction about the transitoriness of the world?" (p. 156). In any case, Ramakrishna's behavior changed markedly as he became more and more engrossed in the worship of the Mother Goddess. As her priest, he had to wake her up early in the morning, bathe and dress her, make garlands of flowers for her adornment. He had to perform her worship at nine, offer her food, and escort her to her silver bed at noon, where she rested for the afternoon; then came the evening worship. For Ramakrishna, these were no longer duties but heartfelt services. He became so absorbed in each one of them that he had to be reminded when it was time to go on to the next ritual.

After the closing of temple at midday and midnight, Ramakrishna shunned all company and disconsolately roamed around in the jungle, at the edge of which the temple was located. All he yearned for with all his soul, he was to later tell us, was the personal *darshan,* "vision," of the Mother. This spiritual thirst, a clinician might have observed, was embedded in all the signs of a full-fledged depression: there was a great restlessness of the body, sleepless nights, loss of appetite (in which eating was reduced to the bare minimum), eyes that filled up often and suddenly with tears. The nephew who looked after Ramakrishna became alarmed for his sanity when he saw him sitting at night under a tree naked, having flung off his clothes and even the sacred thread of the Brahmin, or when he saw him put the leavings from leaf plates from which beggars had eaten to his mouth and to his head. But now, as we come to a culmination of his "dark night of the soul," we need Ramakrishna's own words:

> There was then an intolerable anguish in my heart because I could not have Her vision. Just as a man wrings a towel forcibly to squeeze out all the water from it, I felt as if somebody caught hold of my heart and mind and was wringing them likewise. Greatly afflicted by the thought that I might not have Mother's vision, I was in great agony. I thought that there was no use in living such a life. My eyes suddenly fell upon the sword that was in the Mother's temple. I made up my mind to put an end to my life with it at that very moment. Like one mad, I ran and caught hold of it, when suddenly I had the wonderful vision of the Mother, and fell down unconscious. I did not know what happened then in the external world—how that day and the next slipped away. But in my heart of hearts, there was flowing a current of intense bliss, never experienced before. . . . It was as if the houses, doors, temples and all other things vanished altogether; as if there was nothing anywhere! And what I saw was a boundless infinite conscious sea of light! However far and in whatever direction I looked, I found a continuous succession of effulgent waves coming forward, raging and storming from all sides with great speed. Very soon they fell on me and made me sink to the abysmal depths of infinity [Saradananda, 1983, pp. 162–163].

Unlike similar accounts of the first vision in the lives of most mystics, this particular vision, to which we'll come back later and to which all Ramakrishna's boyhood experiences seem like forerunners, was not sufficient to take him out of the "valley of the shadow of death." Its aftertaste but whetted an appetite for repeated blissful salvings. Even for the pious visitors to the temple, accustomed to a wide range in manifestation of religious fervour, Ramakrishna's behaviour appeared bizarre. He would decorate his own person with the flowers and sandalwood paste brought for the worship of the goddess. He would feel the statue of the goddess breathing, try to feed her stony mouth, and carry on playful conversations with her as to who, the goddess or her priest, should eat first. Any diminution in the sense of her presence made him throw himself on the ground and roll violently, filling the temple with loud wailing at her absence. At such times his breath would almost stop and he appeared to struggle for his very life. When he again received a vision of the goddess, he would beam with joy and become a different person altogether. The consensus of his employers and others was that he had become insane. Romain Rolland calls this a necessary period of hallucination, and even Ramakrishna referred to it as a passing phase of *unmada* (insanity), leaving it unambiguous — something he was not wont to do with respect to the visions in his later life — that the madness was not so much divine intoxication as human disintegration, however necessary it may have been as a prelude to the former. Later in life, he would wonder at some of his behavior during this phase — worshipping his own phallus as that of Shiva, being seized by ecstatic visions while he defecated, and so on.

The prescribed treatment for insanity did not have the desired effect. Finally, Ramakrishna was taken to his village home, where his worried mother had him ministered to by both an exorcist and an Ayurvedic doctor. Slowly, he regained his normal state of health. To safeguard the apparent gains, the family arranged his marriage, a step that I know from professional experience is even today considered the best antidote to threatened or actual psychic breakdown. Of course, as far as Ramakrishna was concerned, there was never any question of the marriage being consummated. From the very beginning, in relation to his girl bride he saw himself either as a woman or, in his ecstatic states, as a child. In the former case the husband and wife were both girlfriends *(sakhis)* of the Mother Goddess while in the latter the wife was envisioned as the Goddess herself.

At the age of 24 Ramakrishna, now accompanied by his wife, returned to Calcutta to resume his priestly duties at the Kali temple. There was a relapse in his condition, though in an attenuated form. Whereas his initial visions had been untutored and spontaneous, initiated by the passionate intensity of his longing for *darshan,* "a vision," of the Goddess, during the next eight years he systematically followed the prescribed practices laid down by the different schools of Hindu mysticism. The disciplines were undertaken under the guidance of different gurus who were amazed at his natural facility and speed in reaching the goal of *samadhi,* "cosmic consciousness," a capability they themselves had acquired only after decades of strenuous effort. Ramakrishna's preferred mystical style did not need ascetic practices, yogic exercises, or a succession of ever more difficult meditations. What it required of the aspirant was, first, a recovery of a childlike innocence and freshness of vision, a renunciation of most adult categories:

> To my Mother I prayed only for pure devotion. I said "Mother, here is your virtue, here is your vice. Take them both and grant me only pure devotion for you. Here is your knowledge and here is your ignorance. Take them both and grant me only pure love for you. Here is your purity and here is your impurity. Take them both Mother and grant me only pure devotion for you. Here is your *dharma* [virtue] and here is your *adharma.* Take them both, Mother, and grant me only pure devotion for you" [Gupta, 1988, vol. 1, pp. 135–136].

And at another place, "Who can ever know God? I don't even try. I only call on him as Mother. . . . My nature is that of a kitten. It only cries 'Mew, mew'. The rest it leaves to the mother" (p. 41).

Being like a child in relation to the Divinity does not mean being fearful, submissive, or meek but existing in the bright-eyed confidence of continued parental presence and *demanding* its restoration when it is felt to be lacking or insufficient. "He is our Creator. What is there to be wondered if He is kind to us? Parents bring up their children. Do you call that an act of kindness? They must act that way. Therefore we should force our demands on God. He is our Father and Mother, isn't He?" (Gupta, 1988, vol. 1, p. 41) Being a child, then, meant the joy of total trust, of being in the hands of infinitely powerful and infinitely beneficent forces. The power of this total trust is tremendous, its contribution to reaching the mystical goal vital. In one of Ramakrishna's illustrative stories Rama, who was God Himself, had to build a bridge to cross the sea to Lanka. But the devotee Hanuman, trusting only in Rama's name, cleared the sea in one jump and reached the other side. He had no need of a bridge.

But perhaps the most important requirement of devotional mysticism, in all its varieties, was the intensity of the aspirant's yearning to be with God, whether in the dyad of mother–child or as a friend, servant, or lover. The longing had to be so intense that it completely took over body and mind, eliminating any need for performing devotions, prayers, or rituals. Ramakrishna illustrated this, his own yearning, through the parable of a guru who took his disciple to a pond to show him the kind of longing that would enable him to have a vision *(darshan)* of God. On coming to the pond, the guru pushed the disciple's head under water and held it there. After a few seconds he released the disciple and asked, "How do you feel?" The disciple answered, "Oh, I felt as if I was dying! I was longing for a breath of air!" "That's exactly it," said the guru (Gupta, 1988, vol. 2, p. 241). What is this *bhava,* a term that Ramakrishna uses constantly to describe the states of consciousness that preceded his visions and ecstatic trances?

Literally translated as "feeling" or "mood," *bhava* in Vaishnava mystical thought means a state of mind (and body) pervaded with a particular emotion. Basing his illustrations on Hindu ideals, Ramakrishna lists the *bhavas* in relation to God as (1) *shanta,* the serenity of a wife's devotion to her husband; (2) *dasya,* the devoted submissiveness of the servant; (3) *sakhya,* the emotion of friendship; (4) *vatsalya,* the feeling of a mother toward her child; and (5) *madhurya,* the romantic and passionate feelings of a woman toward her lover. Ramakrishna felt that the last, symbolized in Radha's (the beloved of God Krishna) attitude toward Krishna, included all the other *bhavas.* Indeed, the discourse of passionate love is conducted in many *bhavas.* At times idealizing the lover makes one experience the loved one as an infinitely superior being who is needed outside oneself as a *telos* to which or whom one can surrender and obey in *dasya.* At other times there is the contented oneness of *vatsalya* as the lover becomes as a babe on the breast, not in quiescence, a complacence of the heart, but in voluptuous absorption and repose. At yet other times there is the serene tranquility of *shanta,* the peace of the spouses in an ineffable intimacy. Besides the compulsions of possessive desire, all these *bhavas,* too, are at the core of man's erotic being.

Vaishnava mysticism, being a mysticism of love, does not consider awe as a legitimate *bhava* in relation to the Divine. Thus, there are no feelings of reverence, of the uncanny, or of mystery. Nor are there the degrees of fear associated with awe where, in extremity, terror and dread can reign. Vaishnava devotionalism would consider awe as an obstacle in the mystical endeavor; it distances and separates rather than binds and joins.

Psychologically speaking, I would tend to see *bhavas* as more than psychic looseners that jar the soul out of the narcissistic sheath of normal, everyday, self-limiting routine. They are experiences of extreme emotional states that have a quality of irradiation wherein time and space tend to disappear. We know of these feeling states from our experience of passionate love, where, at its height, the loved one's beauty is all beauty, the love cannot be conceived as not being eternal, and memories of all past loves dim so precipitately as to almost merge into darkness. We also know *bhava* from our experience of grief, which, beginning with a finite loss, irradiates all the world at its height; the world becomes empty, and all that is good is felt to be lost forever. We even know of the quality of *bhava* from states of extreme fear, when the smallest sound, the minutest changes of light and shade, the quivering shapes of objects in the dark—all take on an air of extreme menace. The threat becomes eternal, with nary a thought that it might ever end.

Bhava, then, is a way of experiencing that is done "with all one's heart, all one's soul and all one's might." The *bhava* fills the ecstatic mystic, as it did Ramakrishna, to the brim. He is not depleted, and there is no need for that restitution in delusion and hallucination that is the prime work of insanity. *Bhava,* then, is creative experiencing or, rather, the ground for all creativity—mystical, artistic, or scientific. The capacity for *bhava* is what an ideal analysis strives for, an openness toward experiencing, a capacity for "experiencing experience," as Bion would call it. All the other gains of analysis—insight into one's conflicts, the capacity to experience pleasure without guilt, ability to tolerate anxiety without being crippled, development of a reliable reality testing, and so on—are secondary to the birth of the analytic *bhava.* Of course, the analytic *bhava,* the total openness to the analytic situation, manifested in the capacity to really free associate, is not simply a goal to be reached at the end of analysis but a state to strive for in every session.

From *bhava,* the ground of mystical creativity, let us turn to *darshan,* vision, the mystic's primary creative product, his particular nonmaterial creation or mystical art. Visions are like hallucinations in that they are images, such as flashes of light, that are visually perceived without the external stimulation of the organ of sight. They are, however, not hallucinations in that they occur during the course of an intense religious experience rather than during a psychotic episode. They are thus less bizarre and less disorganized. Visions belong more to the realm of perceptions that take place, say, during a dream, while falling asleep (hypnagogic), or when awakening (hypnopompic). None of these can be called a consequence of psychic impairment. Visions are, then, special kinds of dreams that find their way into waking life. To have a vision is in itself no more a manifestation of mental disorder than is the corresponding process of real events being drawn across the barrier of sleep into the formation of dreams. Freud (1933) recognized this special nature of visions when, in an aside on the psychology of the mystic, he remarked, "It is easy to imagine, too, that certain mystics may succeed in upsetting the normal relations between the different regions of the mind, so that, for instance, perception may be able to grasp happenings in the depths of the ego and the id which were otherwise inaccessible to it" (pp. 74–80).

Ramakrishna's visions do not constitute a unitary phenomenon, as perhaps those of other mystics do. They span the whole range from what can be fairly described as hallucinations in the psychiatric sense, through more or less conscious visions, to what I would call "unconscious visions" (or visions of the unconscious?), which cannot be described since the observing ego is absent. These are the ineffable "salt doll" visions that constitute a small, though perhaps the most striking, part of the total mystical repertoire.

Before we discuss the various kinds of visions, let us note their central common feature: the intense affect they generate, an affect that endows them with their characteristic sense of noesis. The affects are also manifested in the body, and Ramakrishna's visions had certain well-defined physical correlates. At times he would shudder while tears of joy streamed unchecked down his cheeks. At other times his eyes would become half-closed and unfocused, a faint smile would play around his mouth while his body became completely rigid and had to be supported by a disciple lest he fall and hurt himself. The accompaniment to certain other trance states was a flushed chest or a strong burning sensation all over the body. Then there was the feeling of being famished—one wonders, Does spiritual receptivity have a bodily analogue (or is it vice versa)? And there were the bouts of gluttony in which Ramakrishna consumed enormous quantities of food, generally sweets. The craving for a particular dish or a sweet would come upon him unexpectedly, at any time of night or day.

From inside the tradition, all these manifestations are some of the 19 bodily signs of the mystical experience. To the analyst, however, they are a further confirmation of the mystic's access to a period in early life—the oral stage, in the classical nomenclature—when the boundary between psyche and soma was much more porous than is the case in adulthood. His is the reclamation of a truly dialogical period wherein engendered affects were discharged through the body while physical experience found easy expression in affective states.

Coming back to the various types of visions, the hallucinations, unbidden and unwelcome, belong to Ramakrishna's period of insanity (unmada): "I would spit on the ground when I saw them. But they would follow me and obsess me like ghosts. On the day after such a vision I would have a severe attack of diarrhea and all these ecstasies would pass out through my bowels." (Gupta, 1988, vol. 3, pp. 238–239). These hallucinations—or, better, nightmarish visions—were not alien but were perhaps as much a part of Ramakrishna's personality as was his artistic sensibility or his more elevated mystical visions. Their essential linkage may be better understood if we refer to Ernst Hartmann's (1984) work on nightmares.

In his study of nonpsychiatric volunteers who suffered from night-mares since childhood, Hartmann found that these subjects were usually sensitive people with a strong artistic bent and creative potential. More important, they demonstrated what he called "thin boundaries of the mind," a permeability between self and object, waking/sleeping, fantasy/reality, adult/child, human/animal, and other such boundaries, which are relatively fixed for most people. The thin boundary of the mind, Hartmann tried to show, was at the root both of the subjects' artistic sensibility and their potential for nightmares. It is tempting to speculate that Ramakrishna, and perhaps most other mystics, had a genetic predisposition, reinforced by some early experience (to which we'll come later), to thin boundaries, which may also exist between nightmarish and ecstatic visions.

The second class of visions are the conscious ones. Welcomed by a prepared mind, they fall on a receptive ground. Conscious visions may be symbolic representations of an ongoing psychic process, the symbols taken from the mystic's religious and cultural tradition. Other conscious visions are visual insights, images full of conviction and sudden clarity, couched either in a universal-mystical or in a particular cultural-historical idiom. Some examples of the former would be seeing the universe filled with sparks of fire or glittering like a lake of quicksilver or seeing all its quarters illuminated with the light of myriad candles. Such visions of light have been reported by mystics throughout the ages; indeed, seeing the Divine light has been a central feature of many mystical cults, including 17th-century Quakerism. Other visual insights of the universal variety are seeing everything throbbing with consciousness.

The full import of the more culturally constituted visions, on the other hand, can only be appreciated if we keep in mind that Ramakrishna was a Hindu Brahmin living at a time (19th century) and place (rural Bengal) where ideas of pollution and polluting substances were strong, caste taboos strict, and the threatened loss of caste a horror of the first magnitude. Visions dissolving religious distinctions and caste taboos, such as the ones on touching forbidden substances or taking foods from forbidden persons, were thus primarily expressed in a cultural imagery relevant to Ramakrishna's community. For instance:

> Then I was shown a Muslim with a long beard who came to me with rice in an earthen plate. He fed other Muslims and also gave me some grains to eat. Mother showed me there exists only one and not two [Gupta, 1988, vol. 3, p. 109].
>
> Another day I saw excrement, urine, rice, vegetables and other foods. Suddenly the soul came out of my body and, like a flame, touched everything: excrement, urine, everything was tasted. It was

revealed that everything is one, that there is no difference [Gupta, 1988, vol. 1, p. 431].

And, finally, there are the indescribable "unconscious visions," perhaps a misnomer since there is the absence of the subject who could "have" the vision. "You see," Ramakrishna once said to his disciples,

> something goes up creeping from the feet to the head. Consciousness continues to exist as long as this power does not reach the head; but as soon as it reaches the head, all consciousness is completely lost. There is no seeing or hearing any more, much less speaking. Who can speak? The very idea of "I" and "You" vanishes. While it (the serpent power) goes up, I feel a desire to tell you everything—how many visions I experience, of their nature, etc. Until it comes to this place (showing the heart) or at most this place (showing the throat) speaking is possible, and I do speak. But the moment it goes up beyond this place (showing the throat) someone forcibly presses the mouth, as it were, and I lose all consciousness. I cannot control it. Suppose I try to describe what kind of visions I experience when it goes beyond this place (showing the throat). As soon as I begin to think of them for the purpose of description, the mind rushes immediately up, and speaking becomes impossible [Saradananda, 1983, p. 417].

Ramakrishna's feelings during these visions could then only be expressed in metaphors: — for example, "I feel like a fish released from a pot into the water of the Ganges." However, he does not seem to have been overly enamored of these states, which have been so often held as the apex of the mystical experience. He consciously tried to keep a trace of the observing ego—a little spark of the big fire—so as not to completely disappear, or disappear for a long time, into the *unio mystica* with its nondifferentiation of "I" and the "Other": "In *samadhi*, I lose outer consciousness completely but God generally keeps a little trace of the ego in me for the enjoyment (here he uses a deliberately sensual metaphor, *vilas*) of intercourse. Enjoyment is only possible when 'I' and 'You' remain." As he maintained, "I want to taste sugar, not become sugar."

The unconscious visions, irreducible to language, are different from other visions that are ineffable only in the sense that their description can never be complete. The unconscious visions are a return to the world before the existence of language; they are visions of "reality" through the destruction of language that the particular mystical act entails. As Octavio Paz (1981) puts it, "Language sinks its roots into this world but transforms its juices and reactions into signs and symbols. Language is the consequence (or the cause) of our exile from the universe, signifying the distance between things and ourselves. If our exile were to come to an end, language would come to an end" (p. 133). The salt doll ends exile, writes a finis to language.

The vicissitudes of separation have been, of course, at the heart of psychoanalytic theorizing on mysticism. The yearning to be reunited with a perfect, omnipotent being, the longing for the blissful soothing and nursing associated with the mother of earliest infancy, has been consensually deemed the core of mystical motivation. What has been controversial is the way this longing has been viewed and the value placed on it by different analysts.

The traditional view, initiated by Freud, sees this yearning as reactive, a defense against the hatred directed toward the oedipal father (Salzman, 1953). For writers influenced by Klein, the longing for the blissful "good" mother is a defensive denial of her terrifying and hated aspects (Harrison, 1975). Given the limitation that Ramakrishna did not spend any time on the couch (but, then, neither have other theorists had mystics as patients), I can only say that there is no evidence in the voluminous record of his conversations, reminiscences, and accounts of his visions that is remotely suggestive of any strong hostility toward the oedipal father. The evidence for the denial of the dreaded aspects of the mother is slightly greater, namely, through a plausible interpretation of some elements of his vision in the Kali temple when he had taken up a sword to kill himself. However, seen in the total context of a large number of visions of the Mother Goddess, the ambiguous evidence of one particular vision is not enough to compel an acceptance of the Kleinian notions on mystical motivation.

Paul Horton (1974) has advanced a more adaptive view of mystical yearning and mystical states, especially during adolescence. He sees them as a consequence of the pangs of separation in which the felt reality of being utterly and agonizingly alone is *transiently* denied. The mystical experience is, then, a transitional phenomenon that soothes and reassures much as a baby is soothed by a blanket, a child by a stuffed toy or fairy tale, an adult by a particular piece of music, all these various creations, material and nonmaterial, providing opportunities for the controlled illusion that heals.

There is much to be said for the hypothesis that experiences of separation and loss spurred Ramakrishna on to the mystical path. We know that Ramakrishna's first quasi-mystical ecstasy, when he became unconscious at the sight of white cranes flying against a background of dark clouds, took place in the last year of his father's final illness (according to one place in Ramakrishna's reminiscences, two years after his father's death), that is, at a time of an impending loss. And I have described the marked change that came over Ramakrishna—his heightened mystical yearnings with all the outward signs of a full-scale depression — at the death of his brother, at a time in his life cycle, during adolescence, when the developing ego is particularly vulnerable to stress. Here, Ramakrishna is not unlike some of the Christian mystics in whose lives, as David Aberbach (1987) has demonstrated, one could hypothesize a link between personal loss and mystical calling. Teresa of Avila's life in church began with the death of her mother when Teresa was 12 years old. The loss of a parent or parent surrogate may occur very early in life, heightening a later sense of abandonment and the subsequent search for the "eternal Thou," as perhaps in the examples of St. John of the Cross, whose father died a few months after his birth, and Martin Buber, whose mother deserted him when he was three.

The mystical path is, then, also a way of lessening the agony of separation, mitigating the grief at loss, reducing the sadness of bereavement. In my own interviews with members of a mystical cult in India (Kakar, 1982), loss was the single most important factor in their decision to seek membership. The very embarkation on the mystical path had a therapeutic effect by itself, while any experience of a mystical state had a further marked effect in altering the person's dysphoric state of mind. In contrast to the person's previous feelings of apathy and depression, the turn to mysticism had the consequence of his dealing with grief in a more orderly and more detached, though in a more transcendent, manner. Perhaps T. S. Eliot is correct in observing that "a man does not join himself with the universe so long as he has anything else to join himself with" (quoted in Aberbach, 1987, p. 409).

The motivational skein of mysticism, however, as of any other psychic phenomenon, is composed of many strands. One could speculate that the advanced age of Ramakrishna's mother at his birth; his family's poverty (and thus his mother's added preoccupations with household tasks); and the birth of another sibling when he was four may have led to the emotional unavailability of his mother at a phase of his development when his own needs were driving him closer to her. In other words, the suggestion is that in the crucial rapprochement phase, his mother was unavailable at a time when Ramakrishna's anxiety around separation, and its convergent depression, were at their apex. This would fix separation and its associated anxiety as the dominant theme of his inner life. Each feared or actual loss would reactivate separation anxiety, together with a concomitant effort at combating it by reclaiming in fantasy an adored and adoring intimacy with the maternal matrix. The unity Ramakrishna aimed for is, then, not the mergerlike states of the infant at the breast — though these, too, prefigured his trances — but the ending of separation striven for by the toddler, a state in which both mother and child have boundaries in relation to each other while another boundary encloses their "double unit" from the rest of the world. Here the enjoyment of the mother's presence is deeply sensuous, almost ecstatic, and informs Ramakrishna's selection of words, images, and metaphors to describe his experiences.

One of Ramakrishna's more "private" visions attempts to paint the issue of separation with crude yet compelling brush strokes. As Bion would say, here he is like the analyst who knows that emotional truth is ineffable, available only in intimations and approximations. Like the Bionian analyst, the mystic is compelled to use terms from sensuous experience to point to a realm beyond this experience: "Let me tell you a very secret experience. Sitting in a pine grove, I had the vision of a small, hidden [literally, thief's door] entrance to a room. I could not see what was inside the room. I tried to bore a hole with a nail file but did not succeed. As I bored the hole it would fill up again and again. And then suddenly I made a big opening." He kept quiet and then started speaking again: "These are all higher matters. I feel someone is closing my mouth. I have seen God residing in the vagina. I saw him there at the time of sexual intercourse of a dog and a bitch" (Gupta, 1988, vol. 1, p. 388).

Ramakrishna's vision, followed by an associative sequel, does not need extended analytic gloss. The small secret opening to a room into which he cannot see and that he tries to keep open and the seeing of God in the genitals of a bitch in intercourse do not encode the mystical preoccupation with opening a way back to the self–other interlocking in any complex symbolic language. This interlocking, the mystical unity, is not unitary. As we saw in Ramakrishna's case, it extends in a continuum from the mother's insides, an expulsion from her womb, through the satiated infant's flowing feelings of merger at the breast, to the toddler being pulled back to the mother as if held at one end of an invisible string. What I am emphasizing, however, is not the traditional analytic agenda of pathological defensive or compensatory uses of these various degrees of dyadic unity in mystical experiencing, but the experiencing itself—its content, context, and evolution.

Sexuality and the Mystical Experience

Ramakrishna was one with other Vaishnava mystics in his insistence that sexuality (by which he meant male sexuality, phallic desire) constituted the biggest obstacle to mystical experiencing. This is a formulation with which psychoanalysts will have no quarrel. For both male and female infants, the differentiation between self and object is achieved and ego boundaries are constituted by a gradual detachment from the mother. The presence of the father is vital for this process. Whereas the masculinity of the father makes it possible for the boy to overcome his primary femininity, the presence of the paternal phallus also helps to protect the little girl from fusional tendencies with the mother. Male sexuality and male desire may thus be viewed as obstacles in the path of fusion, the phallus being the prime symbol of boundaries the mystic seeks to transcend.

The renunciation of adult masculinity is not only a feature of Hindu devotional mysticism but is also a feature of Christian emotional mysticism of medieval and early modern Europe. Affective prayer or Bernardine mysticism, as it has often been called after the influential sermons of the 11th-century saint Bernard of Clairvaux, possesses a striking affinity to its Hindu counterpart. Femininity pervades both. In medieval Europe most of the practicing mystics were women, but even the outstanding male mystics—St. John of the Cross, François de Sales, Fenelon—showed strong feminine identifications and produced their most important ideas under the direct influence of women (Moller, 1965). The psychological stance of Christian ecstatics toward Divinity, paralleling that of the Vaishnava mystics, is either that of the infant toward a loving maternal parent or of a woman toward a youthful lover. Like the Hindus, the Christian mystics disavowed or overthrew the paternal phallus as they divested the Judeo-Christian God of much of his original masculinity and sternness, virtually relegating him to the role of a grandfather. The message of the European emotional mystics seems to be the same as that of Ramakrishna: the actual gender of the mystic is not important for his practice. It is, however, vital that the mystic accept and cultivate his or her femininity to the point that the female-self part becomes dominant in his or her inner psychic reality.

Of the many mystical disciplines, the one Ramakrishna could never practice was the "heroic" one of Tantra where, at its culmination, God as a female is to be pleased—or perhaps I should say pleasured—as a man pleases a woman through intercourse. He repeatedly warned his disciples against *kamini-kanchani* (literally, "woman and gold") and his advice to novices on the mystical path was to avoid the female sex altogether, a whirlpool in which even Brahma and Vishnu struggle for their lives. Given the fact that a vast majority of widely known mystics have been celibates, at least in the Hindu devotional and medieval Christian traditions, one wonders whether celibacy, with its profound influence on hormonal balance, is not an essential physiological technique for mystical ecstasy.

Yet though Ramakrishna constantly reiterated that he looked at the breasts of every woman as those of his mother and that he felt like a child or like another woman with women, his male awareness of women as sexual beings and of the dangers of a desire that separates and bifurcates never quite disappeared, as his biographers would have us believe. He felt uncomfortable with female devotees sitting in his room and would ask them to go and visit the temple as soon as he could decently get rid of them. Being touched by a woman was not a matter of unconcern but evoked strong physical reactions: "If a woman touches me, I fall ill. That part of my body aches as if stung by a horned fish. If I touch a woman my hand becomes numb; it aches. If in a friendly spirit I approach a woman and begin to talk to her, I feel as if a curtain has come down between us" (Gupta, 1988, vol. 3, pp. 535–536). However minimal his sexual conflict, even a great mystic seems to retain at least a vestigial entanglement with the world of desire. In his normal non-ecstatic state, Ramakrishna, too, was never quite free of the sexual *maya,* free from the delight, wisdom, beauty, and pain of the "illusion" that so beguiles the rest of us.

One possible cause for the hankering after sexual purity in his youth could be a deep feeling of shame that Ramakrishna associated with the sexual act. In a country where sexual activity has always been considered a prerogative of the young — sexual desire of older men and women occasioning derisive laughter — and at a time when women not infrequently became grandmothers in their late twenties, Ramakrishna's birth itself (followed by that of the sister) is a sign of the tainted and deeply mortifying sexuality of his old parents. We have already seen how Ramakrishna's enduring wish to be a woman, expressed variously in dressing and moving his limbs like one, his fantasy of being a girl widow who secretly trysts with Krishna every evening, fitted in well with a tenet of Vaishnava mysticism that all mankind is female while God alone is male. Ramakrishna would approvingly cite the opinion that irrespective of biological gender everyone with nipples is a female. Arjuna, the heroic warrior of the Mahabharata, and Krishna are the only exceptional males since they did not have nipples.

Ramakrishna's open espousal and expression of his feminine identifications as a boy, however, also has to do with the greater tolerance of his community and its culture toward such identifications. His urge toward femininity did not meet an unyielding opposition or strenuous attempts at suppression by an enforced participation in masculine play. A transsexual or homosexual label would obscure his sense of comfort and easy familiarity with the feminine components of his self. It hides the fact that the freeing of femininity from repression or disavowal in man, and vice versa in a woman, may be a great human achievement rather than an illness or a deviation. The deviation may actually lie, as in one view of the etiology of homosexuality (Wisdom, 1983), in the *inability* to come to terms with the opposite sexual personality in one's self.

In summarizing I would say that the male-self part of Ramakrishna's personality was split off in early childhood and tended to grow, if at all, rather slowly. In contrast, the female-self part of his personality dominated his inner psychic reality. Ramakrishna's girl-self was neither repressed nor disassociated but could mature to an extent where psychically he could even possess female sexual equipment and enjoy female sexual experience.

Yet even a celebratory avowal of secondary femininity in a male mystic may not be enough to exhaust the mystery of the link between sexuality and mysticism. For if, together with "infant-likeness," secondary femininity and female bodily experience—breast-pride, absence of male external genitalia, the presence of vulva and womb—are important for affective mysticism, then women will be seen as having a head start in this particular human enterprise. They naturally are what a male aspirant must become. This may be true, though it has yet to be demonstrated that gender makes a substantial difference in the making of a mystic. What is perhaps essential in mysticism is not the presence of secondary but of "primary" femininity—that is, in Winnicott's (1971) terms, the "pure female element."

References

Aberbach, D. (1987), Grief and mysticism. *Internat. Rev. Psychoanal.*, 14:509–26.
Freud, S. (1930a), Civilization and its discontents. *Standard Edition*, 21:64–145. London: Hogarth Press, 1961.
_____ (1930b), Letter to R. Rolland, 19 Jan. 1930. In: *The Letters of Sigmund Freud*, ed. E. Freud. New York: Basic Books, 1960, p. 392.
_____ (1933), New introductory lectures on psycho-analysis. *Standard Edition*, 22:5–182. London: Hogarth Press, 1964.
Gupta, M. (1988), *Sri Ramakrishna Vachnamrita* (3 vols.), trans. into Hindi by S. Tripathi. Nagpur: Ramakrishna Math.
Harrison, I. B. (1975), On the maternal origins of awe. *The Psychoanalytic Study of the Child*, 30:181–195. New Haven, CT: Yale University Press.
_____ (1979), On Freud's view of the infant–mother relationship and of the oceanic feeling: Some subjective influences. *J. Amer. Psychoanal. Assn.*, 27:399–421.
Hartmann, E. (1984), *The Nightmare: The Psychology and Biology of Terrifying Dreams*. New York: Basic Books.
Kakar, S. (1982), *Shamans, Mystics and Doctors*. New York: Knopf.
Moller, H. (1965), Affective mysticism in western civilization. *Psychoanal. Rev.*, 52:259–267.
Paz, O. (1981), *The Monkey Grammarian*, trans. H. Lane. New York: Seaver.
Rolland, R. (1929), *The Life of Ramakrishna*. Calcutta: Advaita Ashram, 1986.

Salzman, L. (1953), The psychology of religious and ideological conversion. *Psychiat.*, 16:177–187.

Saradananda, S. (1983), *Sri Ramakrishna, The Great Master, Vol. 1.* Mylapore: Sri Ramakrishna Math.

Winnicott, D. W. (1971), Creativity and its origins. In: *Playing and Reality.* London: Tavistock, pp. 72–85.

Wisdom, J. O. (1983), Male and female. *Internat. J. Psycho-Anal.*, 64:159–168.

Mary Tyrone's Long Day's Journey into Night

FRANK M. LACHMANN
ANNETTE LACHMANN

Eugene O'Neill's plays have been discussed as reconstructions of things past. *Desire Under the Elms* and *Mourning Becomes Electra* depicted his unconscious conflicts (Weissman, 1957; Lichtenberg and Lichtenberg, 1972). *Ah Wilderness* and *The Great God Brown* reflected his wished-for and his conflicted adolescence (Lichtenberg, 1989). But O'Neill's barely disguised autobiography formed the plot for the tragedy of the Tyrone family of *Long Day's Journey into Night.* In this play O'Neill (1955) used his father's and his brother's first names—James, Sr., and Jamie—for two of the characters but called himself Edmund, reversing names with the brother (in the play he is named Eugene) born before him who died at 18 months. Extensive criticism from both literary (e.g., Floyd, 1985; Manheim, 1982) and psychoanalytic perspectives has addressed the obvious as well as subtle parallels between O'Neill's life and the life of the Tyrone family.

In this chapter we illustrate the spiraling disintegration of the Tyrone family as archaic selfobject needs in each family member are constantly revived and disrupted by disappointment and disillusionment. Persistently unmet longings for mergerlike states and nurturance are activated in each family member, and their continuous ruptures result in increasingly desperate efforts to restore an archaic sense of bliss through drugs, alcohol, grandiose fantasies, and defensive denials (Kohut, 1984; Lachmann and Beebe, 1989). Specifically, Mary Tyrone's deterioration

An earlier version of this paper was presented at the 79th Annual Meeting of the American Psychoanalytic Association, May 9–13, 1990, New York City.

forces her husband and sons to find substitutes for the attachments they need and the gratifying responsivity they crave.

In drawing on his painful life experiences, O'Neill succeeded in depicting the Tyrone family—the parents, James and Mary, and their two sons, Jamie and Edmund—as a family with a life of its own. Mary Tyrone is at its center; the family's eyes are on her. As she fragments (under the impact of her morphine addiction), so too does each member of the family. The drama aptly portrays the family's unique interactive system and the way in which the members evoke specific characteristic responses from each other. Responses typically fall short of supplying what is sought: for the sons, parental idealizations; for James and Mary Tyrone, a feeling of being appreciated and admired. Such mirroring admiration is crucially needed to supply some sense of self-cohesion and stability. Its absence propels each family member to express rage toward the others. However, eventually that rage is expressed through self-destruction.

In following the journey of the Tyrone family as a prototype of a family in the process of disintegration, we utilize only information provided through the text of the play for our illustrative data, confining our comments to the Tyrone family as it emerges through the text. The parallels to Eugene O'Neill's life are self-evident.

Evidence for placing Mary Tyrone as the pivotal member of the family is derived from several sources. At the rise of the curtain, James and Mary are found conversing, but we soon learn that their conversation is directed toward Mary's health and state of mind. Furthermore, when Mary is offstage, she is the topic of concern for the rest of the family: toward her they feel guilty, suspicious, and protective. They argue about her morphine addiction and blame her and each other for her inability to combat it. It is Mary's deterioration that leads the family into its night.

Mary's Family and History

In bits and pieces we learn about Mary's background in the course of the play. She was a beautiful young girl, ostensibly adored and spoiled by her father, a businessman who showed his love by indulging his daughter. In mid-life he became an alcoholic and developed consumption, of which he died. Mary's mother, only briefly described, was pious and strict, a jealous competitor of her daughter. She was against Mary's marriage to James Tyrone (she had hoped Mary would become a nun) and predicted that she would not be a good wife.

Mary was sent to a convent school, where her religious devotion and diligence at the piano earned praise from the Sisters. She developed a fervent desire to become a nun and, as a second choice, a concert pianist. When James talks about this period of Mary's life in the course of the play, he describes the nuns as flattering Mary and encouraging her efforts because she was so devout. In James's opinion, Mary was a beautiful, coquettish girl with only average pianistic talent.

The dramatic contrasts between Mary's parents, the father who spoiled her and the mother who begrudged her, were sources of conflict for her. Her disparate ambitions, to become a nun or a concert pianist, can be linked to her conflicted parental loyalties. We infer that Mary's confusion was derived from conflicting selfobject needs. She felt that remaining at the convent would enable her to retain its affirming and protective support and would, simultaneously, offer her mother the mirroring affirmation that she seemed to want from her daughter. That is, in being the religious daughter her mother wished her to be she may have hoped to restore the fragile tie with her mother. In contrast, James Tyrone offered her an opportunity to retain the charismatic, idealized father she was losing to alcoholism and whose enlivening, exciting presence she wanted to recapture.

Furthermore, the disparity between Mary's parents might well have resulted in her feeling overstimulated, limited in psychological resources, and empty. It is likely that from an early age, Mary felt little ability to regulate her own affect states (Socarides and Stolorow, 1984/1985); later, she was subject to states of depression that called forth archaic, self-defensive processes. To remain at the convent promised Mary a sense of peace and calm; presumably, her inner emptiness could be replaced with religious fulfillment.

In seeking guidance Mary placed her difficult choice in the hands of Mother Elizabeth. She told her that she wanted to become a nun and described a vision; "The Blessed Virgin had smiled and blessed me with her consent" (O'Neill, 1955, p. 175). Mother Elizabeth was evidently somewhat skeptical of Mary's "imagination" and advised her to test herself for a year, to enjoy her social life and then decide if she really had a calling to be a nun. Mary obediently followed the suggestion, left the convent, and felt "all mixed up" (p. 176).

Mary's long-standing conflicts were exacerbated by the appearance of James Tyrone. To marry him promised her a feeling of aliveness, a replacement for her sense of inner emptiness, and the opportunity for fulfillment as a wife and mother. Both solutions, the convent and marriage, promised Mary temporary relief from her difficulty in managing intolerable affect states, a difficulty that provided the precondition and distal source of her later attempts to regulate her mood through morphine. Thus, Mary, unworldly and naive, entered into marriage with

James Tyrone, a union that she hoped would rescue her from her sense of emptiness but that denied her the protection she sought. Instead, she felt uprooted from her conventional home and family and was thrust into the alien, unsupportive, and unstable world of the theater.

Mary said she loved Mother Elizabeth better than her own mother "because she always understands even before you say a word" (p. 175). This attunement with Mary by Mother Elizabeth provided Mary with fulfillment of mergerlike wishes and a sense of oneness (Lachmann & Beebe, 1989); to be so exquisitely understood as to make articulation unnecessary provides an illusion of merger, an archaic selfobject tie. The desire to remain in the convent also reflected Mary's unfulfilled longing to remain with a mother who was uncritical and accepting and by whom she felt loved. In the convent Mary felt understood and valued. To leave the convent then further imperiled her sense of self, competence, and efficacy. On her own she lacked the resources with which to cope with the loneliness and rootlessness of her subsequent life.

With her sense of self so impaired, it is understandable that Mary would be drawn to James and would also resent him. He was a glamorous, romantic figure, but he abandoned her for considerable stretches of time. Feeling so depleted increased Mary's dependence on James and increased her sense of isolation when he was not with her. He failed her in the same way that she had been failed by her father earlier in her life. His alcoholism left her increasingly alone and at the mercy of her own resources, which were insufficient to sustain her. First her interest in music waned, then her ability to nurture her children diminished, and eventually her efforts at creating a home for her family deteriorated.

Mary's Marriage

At the time of their marriage James Tyrone was already a matinee idol. He was also a business friend and associate of Mary's father (and had met her through him). It was love at first sight for Mary and James. After they married, Mary found that James preferred to spend his time drinking with his cronies and expected her both to fend for herself and to await him patiently in the wings. Apparently, Mary's disillusionment began on their honeymoon when James was deposited drunk outside the door of their room. Because of James's stinginess, the Tyrones traveled in second-class trains and lived in dirty rooms in small cheap hotels during the first years of their marriage. Mary eventually became pregnant with Jamie, and five years later another son, Eugene, was born. When Eugene was two, Jamie contracted measles. James Tyrone again asked his wife to join him on the road. Conflicted though she was, she left the children under the care of her mother to join James. Jamie had been warned not to go near Eugene lest the baby catch the disease. But, after Mary left, Jamie did expose Eugene, who caught the measles and died.

The tragic loss of Eugene caused Mary to berate herself for having left her children. She accused Jamie of being murderously jealous of his brother, and he was soon sent away to boarding schools. Curiously, Mary never blamed her mother, who, after all, had been left in charge. Three years after Eugene's death, Edmund was born, but Mary felt that she had been an irresponsible mother and was undeserving of another child.

After the birth of Edmund, Mary suffered severe pains; a house doctor at the hotel where the Tyrones were staying prescribed morphine. By then, in addition to feeling guilty about the death of Eugene, Mary felt that she was a failure as a mother and wife, was disappointed in James as a husband and provider, and despaired about her unstable, not quite respectable life. Her despairs and disappointments infused her longings for a house, a symbol to her of substance and stability. These disappointments and longings were the immediate precipitants of her addiction. Her losing battle against morphine led to several stays in sanitoriums and a suicide attempt.

We presume that the distant precipitant of Mary's addiction was the sense of inner emptiness that plagued her throughout her life and that was rooted in her persistent overstimulation by her father's indulgence and her mother's restraints and criticisms. Difficulties in negotiating these extremes led to Mary's propensity toward self-fragmentation, which was based on her inability to regulate affect arousal and affect states on her own. She used the convent and, later, morphine for these regulatory purposes, since they provided her with a momentary sense of well-being. But upon leaving the convent, unable to negotiate her own affect states, Mary fell victim to the feelings of guilt and despair that quickly emerged. That is, she felt unable to rely on the support and affirmation of her parents. In her early development self-regulation was impaired, and Mary had to find alternative ways to calm, arouse, validate, and affirm herself. The convent provided her with an ideal setting in that it removed her from the sharply contrasting and apparently irreconcilable stimulation by her parents and provided her with a calming and supportive milieu. However, her life after the convent repeated the characteristics of her family. Like Mary's father, James Tyrone was quixotic; like her mother, he was penurious. Neither James nor Mary could sense or provide for the requirements of the other. Both were catapulted further and further into managing their own sense of despair: Mary, forced to regulate her affective life on her own, turned to morphine, and James, only slightly less disastrously, turned more and more to alcohol. Under the influence of morphine, Mary temporarily achieved the sense of calm that she longed for and had lost upon leaving the convent. This was Mary at the rise of the curtain in act 1 of *Long Day's Journey into Night*.

The Long Day

The play condenses Mary's deterioration and the discovery of Edmund's tuberculosis into one day. By the curtain fall in act 4, the fog that has been hovering outside the Tyrone home has enveloped the family: Mary has become inaccessible. Both her pretense and her hope that she could overcome her addiction have vanished. James, Jamie, and Edmund parallel Mary's addiction with their own alcoholism.

An indication of Mary's deterioration is the conversion of the special pride she took in her figure, hair, eyes, and hands into shame in the course of the day. As act 1 opens, James Tyrone comments about Mary's figure but notes that she has not eaten breakfast, a sign that her remission from her addiction may be over. While he enjoys her as an "armful" (p. 14), she fears that she has grown too fat.

Throughout the day, Mary refers to the condition of her hair. She strives hard to convey the appearance of being intact by keeping her hair neatly arranged. Gradually, however, her hair comes down, depicting her disarray. She is also "letting her hair down" in that she becomes more self-revealing but, simultaneously, less able to maintain the illusion that she is not an addict.

As she refers to her eyes and looks for her glasses, Mary reveals her increasing agitation as well as her inability to see herself, her family, and, especially, Edmund's illness. Her hands, now arthritic, were once able to play the piano. She frequently drums her fingers, a mannerism that is perhaps reminiscent of her more promising, now-lost past. Mary's claim that she needs the morphine to dull the pain of her arthritic hands is both a rationalization and a subjective truth. Her hands are a constant reminder of her unfulfilled promise of beauty, serenity, and efficacy. It is also the pain of this loss that the morphine must alleviate.

It is made clear that as her agitation increased, between episodes of only temporary relief, Mary became preoccupied with the management of her regrets, recriminations, and longings for calm. This, in turn, made her unavailable for her sons. Both Jamie and Edmund, like their father, took to the bottle to simulate the nurturance that they missed from their mother. Edmund also escaped to the sea, which he describes as a mergerlike experience:

I lay on the bowsprit, facing astern, with the water foaming into spume under me, the masts with every sail white in the moonlight, towering high above me. I became drunk with the beauty and singing rhythm of it, and for a moment I lost myself—actually lost myself. I was set free! I dissolved in the sea, became white sails and flying spray, became beauty and rhythm, became moonlight and the ship and the high dim-starred sky! I belonged, without past or future, within peace and unity and a wild joy, within something greater than my own life, or the life of Man, to Life itself! [p. 153]

Though Edmund describes his experience at sea in the most idyllic terms, his longings for such symbiotic-like experiences remain unsatisfied. Such experiences can indeed only be fulfilling if they are experienced in the context of an intact sense of self (Silverman, Lachmann, and Milich, 1982; Lachmann and Beebe, 1989). For Edmund, unfulfilled maternal longings persist in exercising a consistent hold so that he continues to seek symbiotic-like experiences. However, his fragmentation-prone sense of self and inability to empathize with the feelings of others preclude experiences of intimacy (Lachmann, 1991). Ironically, the mergerlike experiences that Edmund sought at sea may be parallel to the experiences his mother sought at the convent. Edmund's poetry and newspaper reporting represent hope and an opportunity to transcend the family's limitations, but Jamie's life is devoid of inspirational moments and his ambitions never surface.

Each of the men in the family sees Mary as the source of support they desperately need. They want her to be their healthy, loving, mother-wife. In order to be able to depend upon her as the mainstay of the family, they strive to maintain the illusion, in spite of evidence to the contrary, that she is not becoming addicted again. James longs for Mary to be a robust, life-affirming wife, which she probably never was but which he needs her to be to counteract his own increasing sense of failure. He needs her to replenish the vigor he is dissipating. Jamie needs his mother to absolve him from his guilt. Edmund's relationship with his mother is the most complex; their similarity in temperament and frailty is emphasized by the occurrence on the same day of Mary's reversion to morphine and Edmund's diagnosis of tuberculosis. Edmund's attachment to his mother is repeatedly shattered, for example, when he comes upon her injecting herself with morphine. Although he tries to assuage the pain of his mother's detachment by seeking solace in solitary experiences at sea, those experiences also reinforce his unsatisfied longings to feel at home somewhere and to feel a sense of belonging. Ultimately, it is consumption that may rescue Edmund by removing him from the family and thereby enabling him to assess his life and his family.

Their efforts to sustain themselves as a family become a hopeless quest for each of the Tyrones. Mary, looking to her three men for support and protection, wants to recapture the sense of her goodness that she lost when she left the convent. She attempts to regain her innocence and purity in the morphine stupors, but that path alienates her even more from her family and prompts them to view her with suspicion rather than extend to her the indulgent support she craves. Yet the Tyrone family, for all its searing confrontations, holds together throughout the individual fragmentations.

Father and Sons

Though Mary depicts James as the source of her despair and unhappiness, he, too, has been disillusioned in his marriage. Mary tends to be critical and disapproving; James is repeatedly called "cheap" and accused of making foolish investments. It is clear that he is responsible in his work but has opted for a profitable, rather than artistically satisfying, acting career. Certainly, this choice was not entirely dictated by the needs of the family: James's own financial anxieties and his obsessive dread of ending in the poorhouse have been important sources of motivation. However, his attempts to please Mary do not bring him the appreciation he longs for. For example, after her hospitalization he buys her a secondhand car and hires a chauffeur for her. She complains that the car is second-rate and the chauffeur dishonest. He wants to be proud of his summer house and wants it to be a true home but feels that Mary's addiction and her seclusion will prevent it from becoming one.

In contrast to Mary's background of affluence and indulgence, James's early life was marked by ignorance and poverty. His father deserted his mother and their six children after the family came to America from Ireland. Later, his father returned to Ireland and committed suicide. At age ten, realizing that he had to be the head of the family, James began working at menial jobs to keep the family together. He worked himself up in the machinist trade and then left a good job to become an actor. He felt he was on the verge of a successful career when Edwin Booth complimented his acting skill, but through his own anxieties and his marriage his dreams of success were shattered.

James's oldest son, Jamie, is a source of disappointment to him because, presumably, he hoped to have his own shattered dreams fulfilled by him. James pushes Jamie into acting jobs the son does not want and expresses his criticism and disappointment toward him quite directly. Although initially a good student, Jamie begins to drink when he discovers Mary with a hypodermic needle and is then kicked out of a number of colleges. His idealization of his mother precipitously ruptured, he imagines that only prostitutes take dope and lives out this fantasy by associating only with "tarts." More generally, he thinks of himself as a has-been and gives up the idea of becoming a newspaperman because he is unwilling to start at the bottom.

Jamie senses Mary's agony in her addiction but believes there is no cure for her. Yet he feels that if she could conquer her habit, he would be able to conquer his alcoholism. He finds a bond with her through their respective addictions. Having been blamed by his mother for killing his little brother by infecting him with measles and, later, witnessing his mother's addicted state, Jamie is burdened by a sense of guilt from which he can not free himself. His drinking is a source of escape as is his attempt to restore himself by creating in Edmund a better version of himself.

Jamie describes himself as Edmund's Frankenstein. He tries to "wise him up" about women and introduces him to poetry. Their relationship is characterized by Jamie's intense need to live through Edmund and his resentment and jealousy of Edmund's position as their father's favorite. For his part, Edmund idealizes his older brother. He began drinking in prep school in imitation of his brother and was later kicked out of college. This emulation of Jamie, however, occurred after a long period of poor health and unhappiness since infancy. Edmund, too, is devastated by his mother's addiction and her suicide attempt. He tries to lose himself by escaping to the sea where he lives a torturous life, often broke and hungry. He, too, has attempted suicide.

The Night

Surrounded by despair and suspicion, Mary escapes further and further into her drug-induced reminiscences. She recalls the turning point in her life, her talk with Mother Elizabeth, who "wasn't so understanding" when she told Mary she had to prove that her calling to become a nun was not a product of her own imagination. In a dreamy stupor Mary describes marrying James then and being happy for a time. And that is Mary at the fall of the curtain in act 4.

For Edmund Tyrone and Eugene O'Neill, the mother's fall coincides with the fulfillment of the son's promise. His tuberculosis and the enforced stay at a sanatorium became the turning point in the life of O'Neill; it was then that his playwriting career began.

In his dedication to *Long Day's Journey*, O'Neill refers to "this play of old sorrow, written in tears and blood." He thanks his wife, Carlotta, for her love and tenderness, "which gave [him] the faith in love that enabled [him] to face [his] dead and write this play—write it with deep pity and understanding and forgiveness for all the four haunted Tyrones" (p. 7). O'Neill was able to turn his night into an evening in which the curtain rose on a series of dramas that transformed the American theater and, at the same time, probably insured his psychological survival.

References

Floyd, V. (1985), *The Plays of Eugene O'Neill.* New York: Frederick Ungar.

Kohut, H. (1984), *How Does Analysis Cure?* ed. A. Goldberg & P. Stepansky. Chicago: University of Chicago Press.

Lachmann, F. M. (1991), On some challenges to clinical theory in the treatment of character pathology. In: *The Realities of Transference: Progress in Self Psychology, Vol. 6,* ed. A. Goldberg. Hillsdale, NJ: The Analytic Press, pp. 59–67.

_____ & Beebe, B. (1989), Oneness fantasies revisited. *Psychoanal. Psychol.,* 6:137–149.

Lichtenberg, J. D. (1989), The adolescence of the creative writer. *Psychoanal. Inq.,* 9:450–465.

Lichtenberg, J. D. & Lichtenberg, C. (1972), Eugene O'Neill and falling in love. *Psychoanal. Quart.,* 41:63–89.

Manheim, M. (1982), *Eugene O'Neill's New Language of Kinship.* Syracuse: Syracuse University Press.

O'Neill, E. (1955), *Long Day's Journey into Night.* New Haven, CT: Yale University Press.

Silverman, L., Lachmann, F. M. & Milich, R. (1982), *The Search for oneness.* New York: International Universities Press.

Socarides D. & Stolorow, R. (1984/1985), Affects and selfobjects. *The Annual of Psychoanalysis,* 12/13:105–119. New York: International Universities Press.

Weissman, P. (1957), Conscious and unconscious autobiographical dramas of Eugene O'Neill. *J. Amer. Psychoanal. Assn.,* 5:432–460.

Freud's Aesthetic Response to *Michelangelo's* Moses

GARY N. GOLDSMITH

"For no piece of statuary has ever made a stronger impression on me than this." With these words near the beginning of his anonymously published essay "The Moses of Michelangelo," Freud asserts his response to the sculpture and conveys his reason for seeking out the intentions of its maker. Stating that "some turn of mind in me rebels against being moved by a thing without knowing why I am thus affected and what it is that affects me," Freud proceeds in the essay to explore the mystery of why this statue moves him so deeply. However, he seeks the clue to his aesthetic response not in an introspective search guided by his personal reaction but externally, through an attempt to locate and define the intentions of the artist, Michelangelo, believing that

> what grips us so powerfully *can only be* the artist's intention, in so far as he has succeeded in expressing it in his work and in getting us to understand it. I realize that this cannot be merely a matter of intellectual comprehension; what he aims at is to awaken in us the same emotional attitude, the same mental constellation as that which in him produced the impetus to create [Freud, 1914a, p. 212, emphasis mine].[1]

The author wishes to thank Ana-Maria Rizzuto, M.D., Evelyne Schwaber, M.D., Axel Hoffer, M.D., and Prof. Jack J. Spector for their helpful comments on earlier drafts of this paper.

[1] I highlight "can only be" because the modern analyst will understand the constriction of meaning such an assertion places on the work of art and its multiplicity of effects.

While Freud's paper is ostensibly about this effort, his unusual statements and idiosyncratic attitude toward it, often noted by commentators, invite our curiosity. When we note that the statue exerted the greatest fascination upon him and that the essay about it was published anonymously, our interest in the essay expands beyond its content alone, impelling us to explore Freud's feeling state, much as he hoped to discern Michelangelo's "emotional attitude."

In addition, for Freud, whose great discovery it was that unconscious fantasy shapes our perception of the external world, to proceed as he does in this paper in an attempt to decipher details in a work of art (the very medium in which subjectivity of response and interpretation reigns) as if that alone would reveal an understanding of its "riddles" and the reason for his (and others') fascination is indeed a departure that claims our attention. It does so not because such iconographic scrutiny is not a valid enterprise of art criticism — it is — but because Freud does it uncharacteristically, in a manner devoid of any psychoanalytic dimension.

With these issues in mind, the following are the questions I wish to address in this chapter:

1. Why did Freud, who was so moved by this statue, feel compelled to publish his essay about it anonymously?
2. What led him to depart from a more psychoanalytic orientation toward his subject, an orientation he had begun to develop in his earlier papers on applied psychoanalysis?
3. What affects and experiences, conscious and unconscious, were at the root of his aesthetic response?
4. Can exploration of these questions illuminate other aspects of Freud's life and work, including the theoretical advances contemporary with his essay on Michelangelo's *Moses*?

To address these issues, I first describe other aspects of the essay that arouse the reader's curiosity and then explore the evidence for the work's personal meaning to Freud. After a review of the phallic-competitive themes offered as explanations for his anonymity, I argue that an exploration of Freud's experiences of preoedipal maternal disruption and loss, themes entwined with his visits to the statue, both informs the previously offered oedipal interpretations and expands the explanatory framework for understanding this episode in his life.

The Moses essay diverges from Freud's prior efforts in the application of psychoanalysis to art. Whatever their individual differences of focus may be, "Jensen's Gradiva," the Leonardo essay, or the *Hamlet* and *Oedipus Rex* references in the "Interpretation of Dreams" are all rooted at some level in a psychodynamic theory of instincts wherein symptoms and features of character can be correlated with solutions to childhood conflicts. However, in the Moses essay Freud attempts to use an aspect of psychoanalytic method—described therein as "accustomed to divine secret and concealed things from despised or unnoticed features" (1914a, p. 222)—to examine the details of a statue while his exploration of the psychology and intentions of its maker (his stated aim) receives only one superficial and anticlimactic paragraph.

The focus on "secret and concealed things," on "unnoticed features," is itself a statement that merits our regard when we consider Freud's "secret" authorship. Freud himself had insisted that the psychoanalytic method approaches its task *without preference* for features either easy or difficult of notice. It opens a neutral, unprejudiced eye to *all* details, small and large, concealed and overt. In this essay Freud's partiality for the hidden leads him into a solipsism wherein his conclusion, as we shall see, neglects major formal and historical concerns attending the conception and design of the statue.

To be sure, Freud's sleuthing in "The Moses of Michelangelo" is an impressive piece of scholarship, not the "amateurish" work he initially claimed it to be when he hesitated to publish. In it he first describes what Trosman (1986, p. 141) has aptly called the "after-pleasure" that derives from attempts to understand a work after the initial experience of its aesthetic effect. His postulating of a means to uncover Michelangelo's intentions echoes the principle of psychic determinism, and the implied separation of manifest and latent content in the art work is reminiscent of dream interpretation. Yet Freud's technique in the essay is limited by remaining outside the context of a depth psychological exploration of the sculpture's meaning to the artist (or the viewer), which causes the essay to be, as Fuller (1980, p. 51) has observed, the only one of Freud's mature works so restricted.

From the outset, Freud's colleagues were aware of the work's personal nature. Jones (1955) notes in his biography that "this essay is of special interest to students of Freud's personality. The fact alone that this statue moved him more deeply than any other of the many works of art with which he was familiar gives his essay on it a peculiar significance" (pp. 363–364). The impression of "peculiar significance" received additional support from circumstances external to the text. The paper, completed in January 1914, was conceived and written in the midst of concerns aroused by the defections of Jung and Adler. Freud's identification with Moses, the lawgiver who was enraged by the defection of *his* followers to a false idol, was apparent, and Freud's own comments about the essay support that view: he wrote to Ferenczi (Oct. 17, 1912) about his concern for the movement at the time of Stekel's withdrawal, saying, "At the moment the situation in Vienna makes me feel more like the historical Moses [who lost control] than the Michelangelo one" (quoted in Jones, 1955, p. 367).

Freud's letter refers to his conclusion in the essay that Michelangelo's *Moses* was conceived differently from the historical one. Freud identifies variously not only with the Biblical Moses but also with what he proposes is Michelangelo's deliberately altered representation of Moses for the tomb project of Pope Julius II. He notes that "the Moses of legend and tradition had a hasty temper and was subject to fits of passion" and asserts in the essay that Michelangelo

> has placed a different Moses on the tomb of the pope, one superior to the historical or traditional Moses. He has modified the theme of the Broken Tables; he does not let Moses break them in his wrath, but makes him be influenced by the danger that they will be broken and makes him calm that wrath. . . . In this way he has added something new and more than human to the figure of Moses; so that the giant frame with its tremendous physical power becomes only a concrete expression of the highest mental achievement that is possible in a man, that of struggling successfully against an inward passion for the sake of a cause to which he has devoted himself [Freud, 1914a, p. 233].

This perception of Moses is strongly consistent with a view of Freud striving to restrain his own rage and internal conflict for the "higher" aim of preserving the psychoanalytic movement at what he felt to be a vulnerable phase in its development. It implies a projection onto the work that Freud's attempt at cognitive dissection endeavors to explain, except that he ascribes the feelings to the work's creator and not to himself.

Anonymity

> Although this paper does not, strictly speaking, conform to the conditions under which contributions are accepted for publication in this Journal, the editors have decided to print it, since the author, who is personally known to them, moves in psycho-analytic circles, and since his mode of thought has in point of fact a certain resemblance to the methodology of psycho-analysis [p. 211].

What may have influenced Freud to publish "The Moses of Michelangelo" anonymously? He published only three such works, all of which share a certain personal character in which a defensive motivation for the anonymity can be discerned. Trosman (1969) underscores the personal significance of these works by noting the frankness of Freud's autobiographical references:

> However, on three occasions his disclosures were so personal as to require the special kind of distancing characterized either by anonymous publication or by referring to himself in the third person. In 1899 he described an adolescent love affair in a disguised autobiographical illustration in the paper "Screen Memories." In 1914 he published "The Moses of Michelangelo," . . . an expression of his reaction to the dissensions of Jung and Adler. And in 1920 he used the thin disguise of the signature "F" for "A Note on the Prehistory of the Technique of Analysis" . . . in order to reveal a source for the discovery of the fundamental rule of psychoanalysis [p. 232].

Mahony's (1987) view is that,

> aside from anonymity, a thread of resistance runs throughout the subject matter of the three essays: Freud's conflictual acknowledgment of a predecessor, his screening of his first experience in love, and [in the "Moses"] a taboo identification with a supreme hero [p. 161].

Trosman, by his fertile exploration of the psychology behind Freud's disguise in the "Prehistory" paper, accents the value of pursuing the reasons for the anonymity in the Moses essay. In this case he describes it as a "reaction to the dissensions of Jung and Adler," but we must look further for Freud was able to acknowledge his authorship of "On Narcissism" and "On the History of the Psychoanalytic Movement," both of which address this issue unhesitatingly. Mahony infers "a taboo identification," but this in fact runs counter to our knowledge that Freud chose for his heroes many of the great leaders of Western civilization. Wollheim (1974) offers an additional interpretation: that Freud may have had "an unconscious rivalry with Morelli," the art connoisseur whom he admired and whose methods he discussed in "The Moses of Michelangelo," comparing them to those of the psychoanalyst (p. 210). Morelli, like Freud, was a revolutionary in his own field of art criticism; his innovation was to apply scientific scholarship to determine the authorship of particular paintings, which differed from the then-current method of ascertaining "spiritual content." By introducing Morelli by way of *his* pseudonym (Lermolieff), Freud prefigures the subsequent concealment of his own identity.

The explanation Freud himself gives in regard to the essay's anonymous publication was that he doubted his conclusion and felt "shame at the evident amateurishness of the essay" (Jones, 1955, p. 366). Yet doubtfulness about his conclusions had not precluded acknowledging ownership in other instances. Jones pointed out to him that its author would be easily identifiable, "but he was adamant and even got cross with Ferenczi for persisting on the point (Jones, 1955, p. 366). To Abraham, Freud argued weakly that "it is only a joke" (quoted in Jones, 1955, p. 366). As any reader of Freud's work will surmise, no demurral could be more insubstantial than this, given the extreme seriousness of purpose we know he brought to his writing. Jones, too, felt these reasons to be rather thin and offered as a more likely explanation the problems Freud faced with Jung at that time. Given Freud's identification with Moses, Jones (1955) felt that "the back-sliding mob [upon whom Moses' 'angry scorn' is directed] were to him the many former supporters who had deserted him, and gone back on his work, in the last four years—Adler and his friends, Stekel, and now the Swiss" (p. 367). However, Jones does not look beyond contemporary influences to explain Freud's behavior, and to my knowledge no author has taken up the anonymity per se as a *compromise formation* (between wishes to reveal and to conceal) with both situational *and* genetic origins. It is my hope that such an attempt can broaden our understanding of this episode.

Moses, Michelangelo, and the Bible

In addition to Moses, Michelangelo himself was another figure of identification for Freud, who writes in the essay that Michelangelo, in his relations with Pope Julius II, suffered the pontiff's "sudden anger and his utter lack of consideration for others" (Freud, 1914a, p. 234). Freud speculates that "the artist felt the same violent force of will in himself, and as the more introspective thinker . . . carved his Moses on the Pope's tomb . . . as a warning to himself, thus, in self-criticism, rising superior to his own nature" (p. 234), concluding, "It would . . . not surprise us to find that the artist, in depicting the reaction of his hero to that painful surprise [the worshiping of the idol], had deviated from the text from inner motives" (p. 232). Although "motive" may be too suggestive of conscious intent, it is nonetheless clear that an amalgam of personal feelings lay behind Freud's essay as well. Bremer (1976) suggests the same in his study of the Biblical passages relevant to an understanding of Moses' gesture in the sculpture and proposes that "Freud projects feelings of his own onto the statue, and then proceeds to ascribe these feelings to the sculptor as well" (p. 73). Fuller (1980) adds, "Freud's 'Moses of Michelangelo' is a revealing document, revealing if not about the Moses, or Michelangelo, or 'Art,' then most certainly about the man who wrote it" (p. 38).

For Freud to have reached the conclusion he did, he had to "forget" the

Bible story with which he was familiar.[2] As the reader will recall, there were two descents from Mt. Sinai; only on the first did Moses throw the tablets. Bremer (1976, p. 65) points out that Freud, by overlooking the significance of Moses' "horns," incorrectly assumes that Michelangelo was depicting that first descent from Sinai when, actually, it was the second. (The artistic tradition of representing Moses with horns stems from a mistranslation in the Vulgate.) Liebert (1983), in his psychoanalytic study of Michelangelo's life and art, allows that Freud's theory is plausible but doubtful, given matters such as Michelangelo's style, the integration of the statue's emotional presence among the other works in the overall project, and requirements of its placement in the spatial-compositional schema. He states that "so realistic a pose as part of a specific ongoing action does not conform with Michelangelo's style in single-figure sculpture, which was generally non-specific in this respect" (p. 209). Spector (1972) reaches a similar conclusion after reviewing the evidence for the design of the Julius tomb: "We must conclude that—as in the other tomb figures ignored by Freud—he [Michelangelo] intended none of the kinds of subtleties Freud speculated about, and wished mainly to display the tables as an attribute of the law-giver. . . . Freud chose to minimize the formal consequences of the changes [in the design of the tomb], . . . clearly preferring his more dramatic interpretation, with its series of imagined stages, and with its potential for his own identification" (pp. 130–131). It is noteworthy that Freud (1914a) himself offers the possibility that he may be reading too much into the details of Moses' gesture, when he writes near the end of the essay:

> But what if [we] have strayed on to a wrong path? What if we have taken too serious and profound a view of details which were nothing to the artist, details which he had introduced quite arbitrarily or for some purely formal reasons with no hidden intention behind? What if we have shared the fate of so many interpreters who have thought they saw quite clearly things which the artist did not intend either consciously or unconsciously? I cannot tell [pp. 235–236].

Perhaps Freud was recollecting that he had earlier reached a conclusion different from the one in the essay. He wrote to Martha during his first visit to Rome (1901) that "I have come to understand the meaning of the statue by contemplating Michelangelo's intention" (quoted in Jones, 1955, p. 365). Jones (1955) notes that that interpretation must have been

---

[2]Freud quoted it correctly later, in "Group Psychology and the Analysis of the Ego." He also wrote regarding Moses, "My deep engrossment in the Bible story (almost as soon as I had learnt the art of reading) had, as I recognized much later, an enduring effect upon the direction of my interest" (Freud, 1925, p. 8).

different from his final one, since "he expected Moses to start up at any moment" (p. 365) and not restrain his rage. Since Freud's fascination never wavered but his views on the statue's narrative content did, we must conclude that it wasn't just the *content* that determined his response but also the dynamic *form* of the statue. Despite his demurral in the opening paragraph of the essay, that "the subject-matter of works of art has a stronger attraction for me than their formal . . . qualities" (p. 211), it was indeed the formal qualities distinguishing Michelangelo's style that influenced Freud's aesthetic response.

It was not until ten years later, with the publication of the Gesammelte Schriften, that Freud allowed his authorship to be revealed publicly. And many years after that, he still retained his personal feeling for this essay. He wrote to Edoardo Weiss in 1933:

> My feeling for this piece of work is rather like that towards a love-child.[3] For three lonely September weeks in 1913[4] I stood every day in the church in front of the statue, studied it, measured it, sketched it, until I captured the understanding for it which I ventured to express in the essay only anonymously. Only much later did I legitimatize this non-analytical child [quoted in Jones, 1955, p. 367].

The "Father-Complex": Review of the Literature

Most commentators have postulated that psychodynamic issues relating to Freud's "father complex" and oedipal conflict influenced his fascination with the statue, his conclusion in the essay, and the idiosyncratic behavior around its publication. Jones (1955) was the first to suggest that the *Moses* stood for the father: "[Freud] used to flinch at the angry gaze as if he were one of the disobedient mob. From that one must suppose that Moses stood for the angry father-image, with perhaps the glare of Brücke's formidable eyes" (p. 365).

Interestingly, Brücke had also written about Michelangelo and, when Freud was his student, wrote an essay on the "perception of movement through its static representations" (Fuller, 1980, p. 50), an approach that Freud borrows in his investigation of the Moses statue.

---

[3]This has been alternatively translated as "loved child" (Bergmann, 1982, p. 131; Schur, 1972, p. 466). Such a translation misses the implication of illegitimacy that Freud intended.

[4]A parapraxis. It was in 1912. The slip may have significance by virtue of the fact that in that month, September 1912, Jung left on a return trip to lecture in America. Freud was aware of this from Jung's letter of August 2 and Emma Jung's letter of September 10 (McGuire, 1974, pp. 512, 514).

Bergmann (1982), citing a suggestion of Meyer Schapiro's, considers that Freud's identification with Goethe was influential in the essay, particularly with respect to Freud's perception of Moses' self-restraint: "In the Laocoon, Goethe postulates that great works of plastic art fulfill a civilising function in that they tame and moderate the human passions for the onlooker. The great artists select a moment in which one emotion is superseding another and both are still in evidence" (p. 129). The *Laocoon* sculpture, unearthed in 1506, was a major influence on the various figures, including Moses, that compose the Julius tomb (Liebert, 1983, pp. 170–173).

Spruiell (1985) demonstrates various pertinent identifications operating in Freud as he wrote about the sculpture and the oedipal significance of the death of his younger brother Julius when Freud was just 19 months of age. The need to master the resurgence of conflict around this issue is considered by Spruiell the motivating force for the essay. He bases his conclusion on the evidence of early losses and separations, chiefly from male figures:

Michelangelo's Moses was for Freud — at once — Moses . . ., Michelangelo, Julius II . . ., Freud's Julius-brother-father, and Freud himself. All in relation to early separations; all in relation to brothers and fathers; to fratricides and patricides [p. 488].

Sigg (1990) pursues the death theme further, via the association between Julius II and Freud's brother, and highlights the fact that the tomb is actually empty: "What looms here is the shadow of Julius" (p. 208). He goes on to add that Julius was "a dead person whom [Freud] unconsciously wished to forget" (p. 209).

Fuller (1980) feels, as did Jones, that Freud's relationship to Brücke is germane to the father theme and, disagreeing with Wollheim, suggests that Freud's identification with the art critic Morelli is a *disguised* identification with Brücke and his scientific methods, consistent with Freud's effort to make psychoanalysis more "scientific" and less "speculative." When seen in this light, the identification with Moses refers mainly to the safeguarding not of the "law" but of the *scientific tradition* that was being threatened by Freud's speculative and intuitive leaps (for example, in the study of Leonardo). In addition, there was the threat to psychoanalysis stemming from the mystical (i.e., nonscientific) leanings of Jung. To support his thesis, Fuller contrasts the writing in the Moses essay to that in the Leonardo essay four years earlier, finding the latter more brilliantly intuitive and compelling, as opposed to the "stuffy, pedantic and academic" endeavor in the Moses.

As this discussion shows, paternal themes and a resurgence of oedipal conflict were operative in Freud as he sought to divine the meaning of Michelangelo's *Moses*. His identification with Moses' role as leader, and with Moses' character, seems indisputable. That this essay came at a time when Freud was having to contend with his feelings about the defection of followers strengthens this view. Jung's apostasy freed him to pursue a mystical path akin, in Freud's view, to a false psychoanalytic idol, a Golden Calf. How different was this state of affairs from Freud's initial hopes! Earlier on, during another phase of his identification with Moses, he had written to Jung: "If I am Moses, then you are Joshua and will take possession of the promised land of psychiatry, which I shall only be able to glimpse from afar" (McGuire, 1974, pp. 196–197).

The "promised land" means different things at different times for Freud. He associates it with Rome in the second dream of the "Rome series" and later connects Rome to his "hero worship" of Hannibal (who never reached Rome). That identification dated from the time of the anti-Semitic incident in which Jacob Freud responded passively to the insult of having his fur cap knocked off his head, as the following passage illustrates:

> This struck me as unheroic conduct on the part of the big, strong man who was holding the little boy by the hand. *I contrasted this situation with another which fitted my feelings better:* the scene in which Hannibal's father, Hamilcar Barca, made his boy swear before the household altar to take vengeance on the Romans. Ever since that time Hannibal had a place in my fantasies [Freud, 1900, p. 197, italics added].

It does seem that the foregoing interpretations of Freud's conflicted identification with his father and "father figures" and his coping with the resurgence of oedipal guilt involving the loss of his brother Julius do convey dynamics relevant to understanding the Moses essay's personal meaning for Freud at a time of personal strain regarding the movement he himself had fathered. However, significant maternal and preoedipal themes are also embedded in Freud's response to the *Moses* statue and its surrounds (the Julius tomb, San Pietro, and Rome itself). Their exploration is requisite to a more comprehensive view of this episode and of the essay that grew out of it.

Maternal Themes: Introduction

An arresting passage in the essay serves as a cornerstone for my investigation of the maternal theme. Its implications may have been previously overlooked, and it may yield further insight into the matrix of emotions that guided Freud's scrutiny of the statue and his experience in visiting San Pietro. Its tone is personal and quite moving, and it appears in the first part of the essay, where Freud invites us into a sympathetic view of his personal experience with art. He gives us something to which he did not refer in seeking out Michelangelo's "intentions," that is, the artist's personal feelings. Freud (1914a) writes:

> How often have I mounted the steep steps from the *unlovely* Corso Cavour to the *lonely* piazza where the *deserted* church stands, and have essayed to support the angry scorn of the hero's glance! Sometimes I have crept cautiously out of the half-gloom of the interior as though I myself belonged to the mob upon whom his eye is turned . . . [p. 213, italics added].

"Unlovely . . . lonely . . . deserted." We are confronted with Freud's affect, a projection onto architecture and cityscape of his internal state. (After the passage of time, in the letter to Weiss quoted earlier, he could write quite unambiguously and without question of literary device about his experience: "For three *lonely* weeks . . ."). With this intense affect Freud comes closest to a kinesthetic rendering of his response. The language Freud uses is depressive; it is the language of loss. Nothing in the essay has quite prepared us for it. In fact, the effect upon the reader is even more startling in that these words follow lines of a distinctively brighter, even buoyant tone, in which Freud praises the "inscrutable and wonderful" statue.

To what can we attribute Freud's experience of loneliness and isolation? As suggested earlier, maternal themes that underlie the texture of the Rome experience may hold some clues. Their omission in prior analyses of Freud's essay stands in parallel to the repression of maternal themes in Freud's self-analysis. My argument will progress from Rome, to the church, to the statue itself, as I review the literature on their links to Freud's early years.

Maternal Themes: Review of Literature

In his discussion of the Rome theme, Jones (1955) contrasts Freud's love of ancient Rome with his dislike of the destructive (Christian) Rome that had supplanted it (p. 18). However, Jones also felt that "there were formidable resistances against linking these emotions with the corresponding primordial figures whom they had come to symbolize" (p. 19) and provides those links—Ancient Rome to mother; Christian Rome to anti-Semite—in Freud's own and his family's past. In another paper, "Freud's Early Travels," he demonstrates that for Freud, much as for the larger culture, the South of Europe had feminine connotations: "That the beauty of Italy has in addition to its inherent charm and interest a pronouncedly feminine connotation is familiar knowledge" (Jones, 1954, p. 84). The North connotes "energy, hard work, and stern sense of duty," the South "pleasure, happiness, . . . phantasy and far-reaching interest that stirred the very depths" (p. 81; see also Gedo, 1968, p. 291). Schorske (1980) adds: "The Rome of [Freud's] mature dreams is clearly a love-object. He ardently loved Rome as the mother of European culture" (pp. 191–192).

Before proceeding, it will be necessary to consider the role of Freud's (Roman Catholic) Czech nursemaid, Monika Zajic.[5] She was a vital presence in his first years but was abruptly dismissed when he was 32 months of age. As Hardin (1987, 1988a, b) notes in his series of papers on Freud's early mothering, the nursemaid was "Freud's primary care-taker during much of the time she worked in the household" (Hardin, 1987, p. 632) and perhaps "his sole caretaker when Julius died, a near exclusiveness that continued to the time of her disappearance" (p. 639). Her loss must have been an indelible event, coming after the displace-ment by the birth of Julius at 11 months and Julius's death when Freud was 19 months (coupled with the mother's preoccupation with mourning not only of her *son* Julius but also of her *brother* Julius, who died one month before her son). These losses were further accentuated by Freud's loss of his mother due to her confinement with the next child, Anna, and perhaps by her tuberculosis as well. The intensity of Freud's early mothering and his specialness to his mother, Amalia—he was "Mein goldener Sigi"—would have made these losses all the more acute and painful. The first mention of the nursemaid, whom Freud called the "prime originator" of his neurosis, occurs in the same letter to Fliess (October 3, 1897) as the description of his jealousy, his "germ of self-reproach," and "adverse wishes" to his brother Julius.

Since they are comprehensively reviewed elsewhere (Grigg, 1973, and Hardin, 1987), I will briefly summarize the references to the nursemaid from Freud's self-analysis. This will convey the importance of the attachment as I proceed to expose the threads that knit together nursemaid, Rome, mother, loss, and the Moses essay.

The nursemaid figures prominently in the Rome series from "The Interpretation of Dreams." In the fourth dream of the series Freud expresses a wish to meet Fliess in Rome instead of Prague. Grinstein (1980), noting that "in the course of half a year, Freud lost his Nannie

---

[5]There is some disagreement about her identity. While most writers believe her name was Monika Zajic, Vitz's (1988) research suggests it was Resi Wittek (p. 5).

and his homeland," feels "it is likely that among the determinants of Freud's longing for Rome was his desire to attain the lost [Roman Catholic] Nannie of his childhood as well as his lost Pribor [Freiburg]" (p. 76).

Erikson (1955), addressing religious themes in the Irma dream, writes that "this old woman, then, restored to the little Freud, in a difficult period, a measure of a sense of trust" (p. 159). He, too, views Freud's longing to see Rome as an aspect of his longing for his nursemaid.

Glenn (1986) describes how the nursemaid may have influenced Freud's countertransference in the Dora case and speculates that the loss of Dora rekindled Freud's feelings about his lost nursemaid and mother. After finishing that work Freud wrote to Fliess, "I already miss a narcotic" (Masson, 1985, p. 433), and in the next letter he grieved, "In the midst of the present . . . depression I am tormented by the temptation to spend this year's Easter week in Rome" (p. 435).

We cannot disregard Rome's importance to Freud as the seat of the Catholic Church when we recall how the nursemaid took Freud to all five of the churches in Freiburg and note as well that the *Moses* statue is itself in a church. In addition, the nursemaid was considered rather superstitiously religious. This is evocative of Jung's mystical interests and connects the (past) loss of the nurse to the (contemporaneous) loss of Jung during the period in which the Moses paper was conceived and written. In fact, it was during the "three lonely weeks" visiting the statue (September 1912) that Jung left on a return trip to the United States, this time notably without Freud (see footnote 4).

Grinstein (1980) sums up the dual maternal attachment (mother and nursemaid) evident in the Rome series thus:

> The first two dreams pertain to a desire and the unattainability of its gratification. Although its reference in the manifest content is to Rome, the unconscious significance seems to refer to some infantile incestuous object — as his mother or the Catholic nurse [p. 91].

The loss of the nurse stirred a conflictual grief. Freud (1900), referring to himself in the third person, wrote: "It is reasonable to suppose that the child loved the old woman . . . in spite of her treatment of him" (p. 248). That "treatment" is reflected in the dream of "Going Up The Stairs," where the maidservant, said to be "a reincarnation of the prehistoric old nurse," is considered a target of aggressive and sexual impulses (see Grinstein, 1980, pp. 75, 198, 208). Freud's attachment to her notwithstanding, she was regarded as harsh and strict and had chided him for being "clumsy and unable to do anything" (Masson, 1985, p. 269).

Freud wrote to Fliess on October 3, 1897: "In my case the 'prime originator' [of the neurosis] was an ugly, elderly, but clever woman, who told me a great deal about God Almighty and hell and who instilled in me a high opinion of my own capacities" (pp. 268–269). He then asked his mother for her memories of the nurse and wrote Fliess of her response:

"[S]he was always carrying you off to some church; when you returned home you preached and told us all about God Almighty. During my confinement with Anna . . . it was discovered that she was a thief. . . . Your brother Philipp himself fetched the policeman; she then was given ten months in prison" [p. 271].

Freud goes on to state that "if the old woman disappeared from my life so suddenly, it must be possible to demonstrate the impression this made on me." He then relates the previously undeciphered memory of the empty cupboard in which he cryingly asks his brother to unlock a wardrobe in which he hopes to find his mother:

When I missed my mother, I was afraid she had vanished from me, just as the old woman had a short time before. So I must have heard that the old woman had been locked up and therefore must have believed that my mother had been locked up too — or rather, had been "boxed up" — for my brother Philipp . . . is still fond of using such puns [pp. 271–272].

Bernfeld (1951), in her essay "Freud and Archeology," attempts to demonstrate how "the cupboard is overdetermined as box, coffin, and symbol of pregnancy." She asks, "Is it not also possible that it stands for the altar of the Catholic church?" (p. 117). Following her lead, might not this empty tomb (coffin) in the Catholic church of San Pietro also elicit a resurgence of affects around Freud's infantile maternal trauma?

Further on in her essay Bernfeld relates Freud's interest in "*statues, vases, buildings and towns*" (emphasis mine) to symbolic representations of loved and hated persons from his past. "The golden age of civilization like the golden age of Freiburg had vanished" (p. 119). She concludes:

If my reconstruction of the role of the prehistoric old woman is correct, then Freud's interest in archeological facts and objects continues his early belief in resurrection of the dead, displaced on a different level. He can gratify the death-wishes and the preservation-wishes of his ambivalent love in aim-inhibited ways with the mechanism of symbolic substitution [pp. 121–122].

Hardin (1987) reviews Freud's various interpretations of the screen memory of the cupboard and relates them to, among other things, the missing of the mother during confinements and the viewing of the mother as an idealized figure. He also illustrates that the mother may have been, ironically, a screen for the lost nursemaid:

> Freud revealed a circumvention of memories and affects associated with the sudden loss of the nursemaid and his desperate search for her. In his analysis, the affect associated with losing the surrogate became split off from the idea and attached to a lesser fear—that of the temporary loss of his mother [p. 640].

Given the influential presence of both the nursemaid and the mother, Freud must have formed a dual, or split, maternal imago. Accordingly, Swan (1974) demonstrates the role of Freud's *two* mothers (mother and nursemaid, "Mater and Nannie") in his development, showing how the role of the mother is minimized in his metapsychology, overshadowed by the later oedipal conflict (p. 33). Harrison (1979) concurs: "With the emphasis on parricide, the infant–mother relation was eclipsed" (p. 404). We can thus assert here that part of Freud's identification with the Moses (of history) and the *Moses* (of Michelangelo), as with Leonardo da Vinci earlier—not to mention Oedipus—relates to their common experience of having had "two mothers." Furthermore, we know that Michelangelo also had two mothers, a fact undoubtedly known to Freud since it appears in Condivi's 1553 biography, to which he refers in the essay.[6]

Freud (1931) wrote later on:

> Everything in the sphere of this first attachment to the mother seemed to me so difficult to grasp in analysis—so grey with age and shadowy and almost impossible to revivify—that it was as if it has succumbed to an especially inexorable repression (p. 226).

Gedo (1968) suggests that this difficulty was due to an "infantile *depression,* caused by a presumed interruption of his original mothering, . . . [and] relieved by a close attachment to his Nannie. . . . This trauma was transcended through repression of pregenital issues" (p. 305, emphasis mine). My view is that the affects surrounding Freud's visits to the *Moses* are traceable to the threatened revival of those repressed conflicts "in the sphere of this first attachment" toward his mother and mother surrogate, from which he needed to distance himself. The writing of the essay, and the self-referential conclusion regarding Moses' gesture, had adaptive aims with respect to these preoedipal conflicts, much as they had with the oedipal ones discussed earlier in this paper.

---

[6]Michelangelo was boarded with a wet nurse for his first two years, a common procedure in 15th-century Tuscany. He then returned to his family, but his natural mother died when he was six (Liebert, 1983, pp. 13–15).

Gedo (1968), concluding that "the unresolved infantile longings for the two pregenital mothers found their expression almost exclusively in his travels to the South and in his archeological interests" (p. 298), writes that this is "an acting out in the service of mastery, i.e., an attempt to turn a passively experienced, traumatic event into an actively produced, manageable one. The travels to and from the South constituted a seeking, a finding, and a relinquishment of the object . . ." (p. 299). We may add that the travels to and from San Pietro — Schur (1972) reports Freud visited the statue on every one of his trips to Rome[7] — served the same intrapsychic purpose.

It was on his first trip, in 1901, with the relationship to Fliess on the wane, that Freud first visited Michelangelo's *Moses*. He had by then resolved certain paternal and competitive issues with Fliess, but the "feminine inclinations" in the relationship remained unresolved (Buxbaum, 1951, p. 211). The salient affects in those trips contained facets of a maternal longing, a persistence of the oral aspects of the transference to Fliess, and reflected the failure to work through issues in the (divided) maternal transference. Stolorow and Atwood (1979) take this implication further and suggest that Freud's unresolved infantile maternal conflict forced a particular stamp upon his later theoretical formulations, notably, a need "by Freud to protect an idealized image of his mother against profound unconscious ambivalence" (p. 48). Embodied in this idea is the complementary notion of the inevitable incompleteness of Freud's self-analysis.

Ruth Abraham (1982) assesses the contribution made by Freud's mother's character to the texture of his childhood experience. She reviews evidence that it was Amalia, not Jacob, who dominated and was "overwhelmingly powerful." Abraham writes:

> [Freud] adored and depended on his mother and yearned to approach her for the satisfaction of his needs, but he could not help fearing, avoiding and defying her. He was torn by his love and hatred of her. This paralyzing conflict of ambivalence forced an early splitting of his mother's image [p. 441].

The early loss of both maternal figures likely engendered a rage that was later screened by idealization and avoidance. Wangh (1988) feels that "introjection of the controlling, domineering character of the mother" is one source of "Freud's early sense of guilt" (p. 278). As discussed earlier, responding to the *Moses* as to an accusatory projection of his harsh

---

[7]Freud had seen the copy of the sculpture in the Vienna Academy of Art but didn't have the response to it that he had to the original in Rome. Perhaps the interest generated by his viewing of the copy formed one part of his initial longing for Rome.

superego was central to Freud's experience of the statue: "Sometimes I have crept cautiously out of the half-gloom as though I myself belonged to the mob upon whom his eye is turned. . . ." (Freud, 1914a, p. 213). Wangh, paraphrasing Abraham, states that the "patriarchal dread is in large part defensive. It serves to hide the recognition of the matriarchal dread" (1988, p. 276). That is, it conceals the role of preoedipal aggression in the later development of the superego.

The Androgynous Statue

Looking at Michelangelo's sculpture in general, Liebert (1983) demonstrates how the "void left by maternal disappearances" influenced Michelangelo's artistic imagery (p. 416). He concludes in his book that the sculptor's male figures (chiefly, but not exclusively, the nude) contain the "imago of the archaic mother" (p. 417).

Kavka (1980) extends this theme to the *Moses* specifically. Though it is manifestly a portrayal of a powerful male figure, Kavka has cogently argued for the presence of "a hidden *pregenital* aspect to the Moses statue" (p. 295, italics added). He considers this to be an elaboration of unconscious fantasy elements in Michelangelo, an outgrowth of the artist's ambivalence to maternal figures. Reviewing Michelangelo's iconography as far back as the early *Madonna of the Stairs,* Kavka adduces the presence of androgynous features in the *Moses* — such as the (flowing) beard as a symbol for breast milk, the white marble tablets as representations of the breast, and the fact of Moses' unusual seated position (the nursing position) — and Michelangelo's lifelong use of the forefinger to indent a soft mass, such as the breast. All of these features (beard, tablets, seated position, and forefinger) are mentioned by Freud in the essay, but he sought only for their narrative significance and did not pursue latent meanings (as he had earlier, for example, with Leonardo). Kavka calls the *Moses* an "androgynous madonna" and believes it derives from Michelangelo's "identification with an *ambivalently loved and hated maternal figure* who could be projected into the statue" (p. 299, italics added). He adds that "the ambiguity . . . might help to explain the unusual fascination of this work" (p. 300). This accords with my thesis that his visits to the *Moses* rekindled conflicts in Freud's own life pertaining to maternal experiences and that such early conflict was prematurely funneled to an interest in the father or, in this case, to father substitutes.

These findings contribute to the notion that Freud may indeed have been responding to an aspect of the artist's "mental constellation," but not solely to the "intention" of Michelangelo he believed he had discerned (i.e., the artist's self-restraint). Michelangelo's successful creative adaptation, synthesized in the *Moses,* elicited in Freud (for whom current circumstance added an important readiness) a compelling absorption with a statue that resonated with themes from his own unconscious.

Synthesis

We may now posit another "archaeological" layer of meaning to Freud's daily pilgrimages to the statue of *Moses* by suggesting that the desertion and gloom that he experienced there reflect a return of the repressed. Beneath the manifest "transference" of fascination to Michelangelo's portrayal of Moses lay deeper currents of a conflicted maternal imago, complicated by the interweaving of two different mother figures, and the affects of yearning, rage, and guilt related to them. The *Moses* in the foreground against a backdrop of ancient Rome, Catholic Church, and the tomb of Julius II was a "sculptural-architectural" analogue of the oedipal conflicts fronting for the more elusive and unresolved preoedipal ones persisting in Freud due to the incompleteness of his self-analysis in the maternal sphere. Early disruption — the loving, threatening, and disappearing preoedipal mother(s) — led to a premature escape to and intensification of oedipal themes (with the resultant magnification of the superego and an ultimate tendency toward serial idealizations of task-appropriate male figures) and eclipsed the deeper exploration of preoedipal loss and conflict (in his life and his theory). It remained for later students to build upon Freud's "foundation."

We are also in a better position to elucidate Freud's feelings about his essay. In addition to oedipal issues, it appears that conflicts engendered by the *Moses* hearkened back to the early and repeated losses (Julius, mother, nursemaid) in the second and third years of life, the separation–individuation phase. Mastery of conflict over separation was impeded, with the resulting persistence of repressed affects of rage and guilt (and depression). Therefore, it is likely that *Freud's restiveness and doubts about the essay lay not so much in the validity of his conclusions but in whether or not he was asking himself the pertinent questions.* Unable to apprehend or work through the deepest of the conflicts generating his fascination with the statue, he could release the essay for publication only ambivalently. In addressing only the more accessible part of his aesthetic response he avoided the deeper issue of the unresolved constellation of feelings stemming from his separation from highly conflicted maternal figures.

I believe that this avoidance allows us to see the nonpsychoanalytic style of the Moses essay as a derivative of Freud's early conflict, manifested by a preference for the narrative over the aesthetic, for the explanatory over the inchoate. This view is echoed by Wangh (1988) in his description of Freud's differences with Romain Rolland on the matter of religious feeling. He writes that Freud disclaimed Rolland's "oceanic feeling [as] alien to his experience," which I see as similar to Freud's disavowal regarding his response to artistic form in the Moses essay. Wangh draws attention to "the *emotionality* of Freud's disclaimer, as well as his *intellectual* attempts to wrestle with the 'obscurity' of the oceanic feeling" (p. 265, emphasis mine) and demonstrates how the emotional derivatives of early maternal disruption in Freud's childhood, particularly the rage at his "mystifying, destructive mother-figure" and the fear of regressive fusion, can account for Freud's stress on the paternal origins of religious feeling.

Hide-and-Seek

There is a teasing, playful quality in the anonymous attribution of authorship of the Moses essay, drafted by Freud himself (quoted earlier in this chapter under the heading Anonymity). To publish anonymously is, indeed, to play a game of hide-and-seek; by doing so, Freud was able to reenact his rapprochement task. So fixed was he upon this (unconsciously) that he also played it inside the essay, by first acquainting us with Morelli via his pseudonym.[8] And, Freud states, both he and Morelli were engaged in efforts "to divine *secret* and *concealed* things from despised and unnoticed features" (Freud, 1914a, p. 222, emphasis mine). (Ironically, Morelli's innovation was aimed at deducing the identity of a work's creator.) Freud also suggests that Michelangelo has secretly placed in the *Moses* a reproach to Pope Julius II.

It is therefore notable that in his essay Freud has obscured the richness of the psychoanalytic concept of "latent" meanings by focusing on a pre-analytic and less fertile notion of "secret" meanings. The former deepens the aesthetic ambiguity; the latter is simply an effort at decoding. This shift is significant, coming at a time of otherwise increasing theoretical sophistication. One must therefore conclude that while the essay's manifest content pertains to Michelangelo's statue, its latent program is an intricate exercise on the subject of concealment, carried even into the act of publication. On the surface it may address the meaning of Moses' gesture, but its psychological origins lie in Freud's

---

[8]Morelli was playing too. His pseudonym, Lermolieff, is an anagram of the letters of his name: *Ler/mo/li*-eff.

biography.[9]

"The earlier phases of development continue to exist alongside the latest one," said Freud (1930) in an analogy between the archaeology of Rome and the psyche. So, too, for him—Freud's repressed childhood conflict led him to replay, in an adult context, this childhood game of hiding and discovery.

Gedo (1968) concurs:

> Freud's self-analysis . . . remained interminable because of the impossibility of mastering separation conflicts in the absence of an interpretable transference neurosis. Freud was quite successful in his adaptation *at the price of compulsive repetition of attempts to master the trauma* [p. 300, italics added].

On Narcissism

The writing of "On Narcissism" was interlaced with that of "The Moses of Michelangelo." (The latter was written in December 1913; the former was drafted in September 1913 and completed in March 1914). Along with "On the History of the Psychoanalytic Movement," the essay on narcissism addresses directly what was only implicit in the Moses essay, namely, the reproach to Jung and Adler for their defection from psychoanalytic orthodoxy (the Moses essay focuses not on the betrayers but on the leader's mastery of his rage). All are outgrowths of the creative thrust that followed the rupture with Jung. In addition, "On Narcissism" introduces the concept of the "ego ideal," a formulation that embodies dynamics inherent in Freud's conclusion to the Moses essay. Freud felt that the interpretation offered by others ("We . . . are brought to believe that Moses is . . . about to start up in wrath") inaccurately probed the statue's inscrutability. He believed his reinterpretation conformed better to its details—and we may note, to his own ego ideal as well: "struggling successfully against an inward passion for the sake of a cause." It is therefore possible to view "On Narcissism" in certain particulars as a metapsychological concordance to affects experienced by Freud in his response to Michelangelo's *Moses*.

Bergmann's observations support this. He notes that the Freudian Moses' renunciation of "an immediate satisfaction . . . for the sake of a delayed, more lasting and valuable one . . . [is an] emphasis . . . on ego-control, on the primacy of reality. In this sense . . . Freud's . . . interpretation appears as an early signpost pointing to the advent of Ego

---

[9]For a further exploration of the meaning of secrecy in Freud's life and work, see Rizzuto, A-M. et al. (1991).

Psychology" (in Kavka, 1980, p. 294, n. 4). It is "On Narcissism" that contains the early theoretical assumptions leading ultimately to the structural theory.

By a reinterpretation of Moses' actions, Freud resolves, or better, *allays,* his crisis of that period—the loss of Jung and the anger, pain, and loneliness it entailed. He fashions an external support on the model of his own ego ideal. The episode does not result in structural change; rather, it is closer to the phenomenon of loss offset by symbolic restitution, or to a model of "transference cure through art," if you will. Freud has formulated a solution in a manner similar to his earlier reaction when he felt his father's passive reactions to be unsuitable for him and thus "contrasted [the] situation with another which fitted [his] feelings better: the scene in which Hannibal's father . . . made his boy swear to take vengeance on the Romans" (Freud, 1900, p. 197). At that time the solution was accomplished by a ready-made story; with the Moses essay Freud *invents,* or proposes that Michelangelo has invented, a figure different from the one provided by the Bible story. But the end result is the same.

This also suggests that the nature of Freud's ego ideal had shifted.[10] Whereas Freud was earlier disillusioned by his father's lack of an aggressive response, in the Moses essay Freud, displeased with interpretations of Moses as too aggressive and ready to unleash his fury, has him restrain his feelings. An internal reconciliation had likely also occurred in Freud, enabling a revised view regarding the wisdom of his father's earlier reaction in a situation where he was outnumbered and faced with a senseless and gratuitous anti-Semitic provocation.

The dynamics of the ego ideal and of narcissism provide not only a view of Freud's conclusion in the Moses essay but also offer a further perspective upon its anonymous publication. If one considers Freud's loneliness as a consequence of the withdrawal of narcissistic libido following signs of the rift with Jung, then the writing of the paper can be seen as part of an attempt at restoration of his narcissistic equilibrium. Thus, Freud would have needed the essay itself to achieve sufficient perfection to serve that restorative function (already hinted at in its theme). Given his doubts (more, he describes a feeling of shame about it), the essay did not serve that purpose satisfactorily, that is, it failed to meet the standards of his ego ideal. To put it in the terms of self

---

[10]This idea is touched upon by Bergmann (1982, p. 131). He refers to a shift toward a milder superego, where "a less destructive father figure is created of Freud, . . . [one that] is a shade closer to Jacob Freud." The related notion of identification with an altered *ego ideal* may have more explanatory value in terms of the affects at play in the essay, an idea first advanced by Sachs (1942, pp. 132–134) and discussed by Bergmann.

psychology, it could not serve as an acceptable expression of his grandiose self, and therefore a de-linkage, or disavowal, by way of removing his name, was necessary. Freud's irritability at the argument that his authorship would still be obvious could then be seen as guarding this defensive stance. Since psychologically the essay no longer belonged to him, those arguments were futile and annoying.

A further link to "On Narcissism" pertains to a central theme in that essay regarding the differentiation of ego-libido from object-libido in the male's state of being in love: "sexual overvaluation is the origin of the peculiar state of being in love, a state suggestive of a neurotic compulsion, which is thus traceable to an *impoverishment of the ego* as regards libido in favour of the love-object" (Freud, 1914b, p. 88, italics added).

This is not a description of a mature love, in which satisfaction or expansion of the ego is more likely. Yet it may pertain to the reactivation of archaic derivatives of maternal loss in Freud, where disruptions in rapprochement could have led to an instability of the ego in states of love. Abraham (1982) has noted this instability in Freud's adolescent love experience with Gisela Flüss and in his engagement and subsequent marriage to Martha Bernays. Jones (1955) speaks of Freud's "inordinate demand for exclusive possession of the loved one" during his engagement (p. 433). Freud showed similar feelings for Jung following Jung's three weeks of military service: "My personality was *impoverished* by the interruption in our correspondence" (McGuire, 1974, p. 76, emphasis mine). His want of a "narcotic" after completing the writing of the Dora case is also suggestive of such "impoverishment." Freud's avowed loneliness in Rome and his daily visits to the statue until he reached his salutary conclusion about it are another reflection of this dynamic, exacerbated by the pressure of intercurrent losses.

Conclusion: Freud's Loss Sensitivity

The theme of loss, as well as the variety of Freud's efforts to protect against its affective restimulation, runs through my analysis of Freud's experience with the statue of Moses. As many have noted, it is probable that early loss is important in setting the conditions for certain intense aesthetic experiences. For Freud, by virtue of his experiences in his second and third years, the conditions were set for a sensitivity to loss and a depressive diathesis in later life, for a tendency toward sublimatory ambitions and restitutive idealizations, and for a discernible amplification of his affective response to those works of art that resonated with these dynamics. Placed in its unique setting, Michelangelo's androgynous portrayal of Moses' action amidst restraint effectively embodied this conflict for Freud.

Rose (1987) has suggested that "the creative artist is loss-sensitive and separation-prone" (p. 127). I would venture to add that at times a reciprocal dynamic occurs in certain viewers (filtered by the viewer's ability to regulate psychological distance), the specificity of whose aesthetic responses can be subjected to analytic exploration. Freud's loneliness reflects that loss sensitivity. His daily visits to the statue (like the "seeking, finding and relinquishing of the object" in his trips to Italy) reflect a resurgent separation crisis, one in which the essay itself became embroiled when publication and acknowledgment of authorship were expected.

The statue captured Freud's feelings regarding the circumstance of Jung's contemporaneous defection, his past experiences of loss, and his quest for an idealized figure as restitution. By virtue of its very materiality and durability (like that of his beloved antiquities or of transitional objects in general), the statue could endure the intense affects projected by its viewer and thus provide a measure of both fascination and security.

Freud set out to discover the intentions of Michelangelo. What he found was a personal solution to the question of the inscrutability of the *Moses* that served him ingeniously, even if it did run counter to conventional iconographic interpretation. Despite this, he has given us, through an account of his personal reaction (buttressed by copious biographical detail and his legacy of psychoanalytic theory), a window into the deeper meaning of his own aesthetic response. Ironically, like the dynamic interplay between transference love and transference resistance, what drew Freud to the statue with such beguilement may also have hindered his exploration of that complex response in a self-analytic way. Nevertheless, as always, Freud has proven himself instructive, this time by imparting a value to the investigation of aesthetic response, an inquiry for which psychoanalysis is particularly well suited.

Summary

Idiosyncrasies in the style and content of Freud's essay "The Moses of Michelangelo" and in his comments about it have heretofore been attributed to personal meanings of the statue for Freud at the critical time of Jung's defection from the psychoanalytic movement and to paternal conflict rekindled by the figure of Moses. While these explanations are undoubtedly significant, this chapter seeks to expand the potential field for interpretation beyond the exploration of phallic/competitive issues by demonstrating that it is the resurgence of affects relating predominantly to preoedipal maternal loss and conflict, and defenses against those affects, that can most harmoniously account for the essay's unusual features, its anonymous publication, and for Freud's beguilement with Michelangelo's statue.

Freud's loss sensitivity and his attempts to master it are evident in his aesthetic response. Aspects of the contemporaneous "On Narcissism" are found to be correlated with the derivatives of this struggle as seen in the Moses essay and suggest further dynamics for its understanding. In addition, the theme of secrecy in Freud's essay is explored.

References

Abraham, R. (1982), Freud's mother conflict and the formulation of the oedipal father. *Psychoanal. Rev.,* 69:441–453.

Bergmann, M. S. (1982), Freud and Jewish marginality: Moses and the evolution of Freud's Jewish identity. In: *Judaism and Psychoanalysis,* ed. M. Ostow. New York: Ktav, pp. 111–142.

Bernfeld, S. C. (1951), Freud and archeology. *Amer. Imago,* 8:107–128.

Bremer, R. (1976), Freud and Michelangelo's Moses. *Amer. Imago,* 33:60–75.

Buxbaum, E. (1951), Freud's dream interpretation in the light of his letters to Fliess. *Bull. Menn. Clin.,* 15:197–212.

Erikson, E. H. (1955), Freud's "The Origins of Psycho-Analysis." *Internat. J. Psycho-Anal.,* 36:1–15.

Freud, S. (1900), *The Interpretation of dreams, Standard Edition* 4 & 5. London: Hogarth Press, 1953.

———— (1914a), The Moses of Michelangelo. *Standard Edition* 13:211–236. London: Hogarth Press, 1955.

———— (1914b), On narcissism: An introduction. *Standard Edition* 14:73–102. London: Hogarth Press, 1957.

———— (1925), An autobiographical study. *Standard Edition* 20:7–74. London: Hogarth Press, 1959.

———— (1930), Civilization and its discontents. *Standard Edition* 21. London: Hogarth Press, 1961.

———— (1931), Female sexuality. *Standard Edition* 21:225–243. London: Hogarth Press, 1961.

Fuller, P. (1980), *Art and Psychoanalysis.* London: Writers & Readers Publ. Coop.

Gedo, J. E. (1968), Freud's self-analysis and his scientific ideas. In: *Freud: The Fusion of Science and Humanism,* ed. J. E. Gedo & G. H. Pollock. New York: International Universities Press, 1976, pp. 286–306.

Glenn, J. (1986), Freud, Dora and the maid: A study of countertransference. *J. Amer. Psychoanal. Assn.,* 34:591–606.

Grigg, K. A. (1973), "All roads lead to Rome": The role of the nursemaid in Freud's dreams. *J. Amer. Psychoanal. Assn.,* 21:108–126.

Grinstein, A. (1980), *Sigmund Freud's Dreams.* New York: International Universities Press.

Hardin, H. T. (1987), On the vicissitudes of Freud's early mothering: I. Early environment and loss. *Psychoanal. Quart.,* 56:628–644.

_____ (1988a), On the vicissitudes of Freud's early mothering: II. Alienation from his biological mother. *Psychoanal. Quart.*, 57:72–86.

_____ (1988b), On the vicissitudes of Freud's early mothering: III. Freiburg, screen memories, and loss. *Psychoanal. Quart.*, 57:209–223.

Harrison, I. B. (1979), On Freud's view of the infant–mother relationship and of the oceanic feeling: Some subjective influences. *J. Amer. Psychoanal. Assn.*, 27:399–421.

Jones, E. (1954), Freud's early travels. *Internat. J. Psycho-Anal.*, 35:81–84.

_____ (1955), *The Life and Work of Sigmund Freud, Vol. 2.* New York: Basic Books.

Kavka, J. (1980), Michelangelo's *Moses:* "Madonna androgyna." *The Annual of Psychoanalysis,* 8:291–316. New York: International Universities Press.

Liebert, R. S. (1983), *Michelangelo: A Psychoanalytic Study of His Life and Images.* New Haven: Yale University Press.

Mahony, P. J. (1987), *Freud as a Writer.* New Haven: Yale University Press.

Masson, J. M. (1985), ed. & trans. *The Complete Letters of Sigmund Freud to Wilhelm Fliess, 1887–1904.* Cambridge, MA: Harvard University Press.

McGuire, W., ed. (1974), *The Freud/Jung Letters.* Princeton, NJ: Princeton University Press.

Rizzuto, A.-M., Barron, J. W., Beaumont, R., Goldsmith, G. N., Good, M. I., Pyles, R. L., & Smith, H. F. (1991), Sigmund Freud: The secrets of nature and the nature of secrets. *Internat. J. Psycho-Anal.*, 18:143–163.

Rose, G. J. (1987), *Trauma and Mastery in Life and Art.* New Haven, CN: Yale University Press.

Sachs, H. (1942), The man Moses and the man Freud. In: *The Creative Unconscious.* Boston, Sci-Art Publishing.

Schorske, C. E. (1980), *Fin-de-Siècle Vienna: Politics and Culture.* New York: Knopf.

Schur, M. (1972), *Freud: Living and Dying.* New York: International Universities Press.

Sigg, B. W. (1990), Moses hiding the empty tomb. *Internat. Rev. Psycho-Anal.*, 17:205–226.

Spector, J. (1972), *The Aesthetics of Freud.* New York: Praeger.

Spruiell, V. (1985), The joke in "The Moses of Michelangelo": Imagination and creativity. *The Psychoanalytic Study of the Child,* 40:473–492. New Haven, CN: Yale University Press.

Stolorow, R. D. & Atwood, G. E. (1979), *Faces in a Cloud: Subjectivity in Personality Theory.* New York: Aronson.

Swan, J. (1974), Mater and Nannie: Freud's two mothers and the discovery of the Oedipus complex. *Amer. Imago,* 31:1–64.

Trosman, H. (1969), The cryptomnesic fragment in the discovery of free association. In: *Freud: The Fusion of Science and Humanism,* ed. J. E. Gedo and George H. Pollock. New York: International Universities Press, pp. 229–253.

_____ (1986), Toward a psychoanalytic iconography. *Psychoanal. Quart.,* 60:130–167.

Vitz, P. C. (1988), *Sigmund Freud's Christian Unconscious.* New York: Guilford Press.

Wangh, M. (1988), The genetic sources of Freud's difference with Romain Rolland on the matter of religious feelings. In *Fantasy, Myth and Reality,* ed. H. P. Blum, Y. Kramer, A. K. Richards, and A. D. Richards. Madison, CN: International Universities Press, pp. 259–285.

Wollheim, R. (1974), *On Art and the Mind.* Cambridge, MA: Harvard University Press.

IV

PSYCHOANALYSIS AND PHILOSOPHY

Psychoanalysis and Commonsense Psychology

ANDREW BROOK

In addition to its unique, highly specialized theories, clinical psychoanalysis depends on and makes use of a good deal of nonpsychoanalytic knowledge. Knowledge of language is the most obvious example, but one could also cite knowledge of the physical world, of human biology, of the use and effect of body language and tone of voice, and so on. So far, few would disagree. It is more controversial to suggest that psychoanalysis also depends on nonpsychoanalytic *psychological* knowledge. And it would be even more controversial to urge that, as well as depending on nonpsychoanalytic psychological knowledge, psychoanalysis is also an extension of it. Let us call the first claim the *dependency hypothesis,* the second, the *extension hypothesis.* Both have had their advocates, including Edelson (1988) in the United States and Hopkins (1986) in England. The nonpsychoanalytic psychology in question is the commonsense psychological knowledge of everyday life, the knowledge that allows us to interpret others' noises as expressions of ideas, attitudes, intentions; others' facial gestures and body language as expressions of affects, desires, and so on. In the last decade, this commonsense psychology has sometimes been referred to as folk psychology (Stich, 1983; Churchland, 1984; Dennett, 1987a), but this term is misleading. We are not talking about something on a par with folk art; we are talking about the stuff of great novels, the raw material of Shakespeare. Even the term *commonsense psychology* is too weak for this store of interpretive skill and wisdom, but it is the term I will use.

By commonsense psychology, I do not have in mind primarily the conscious beliefs of everyday psychological life. Psychoanalysis has shown many of these to be false. Indeed, at this level, if common sense and psychoanalysis coincide, it is probably by accident, as a colleague once said to me. Rather, I mean the interpretive, sense-making apparatus that commonsense psychology provides — the vast resource of largely unconscious principles, precepts, rules, and skills for recognizing and inferring psychological states from behavior and other psychological states, the body of knowledge every competent language user has available to make sense of him- or herself and others. This resource is what allows us to infer that someone is angry when we observe him or her shouting and red in the face, that someone wants to be comforted when he or she cries or moans, that someone is experiencing pleasure when he or she laughs, becomes animated, and so on. We have many thousands of such recognitional and inferential tools at our disposal. Given how adept even very young babies are at recognizing forms as human and at inferring humans' emotional states, probably at least part of this resource is innate.

To illustrate both the kind of thing on which psychoanalysis depends and how this material enters clinical work, let me give a couple of brief clinical examples. The first is from the analysis of Mr. S, a 26-year-old graduate student. Near the end of a session during which he had anguished over his socially isolated childhood, I made the following interpretation:

> *AB:* It's a long way from that fringe kid hanging out with socially inadequate people to the young man with an honors degree in graduate school.
>
> *S:*   I can't fit my image of myself and my life now together.

That is to say, Mr. S took my interpretation to be about his feeling marginalized now. His reaction told me a number of things; how he saw himself, what the transference was like at that moment, and so on. But this is not what interests me here. What interests me is that I was able to make these inferences. Though I made them instantly and effortlessly, I did not use anything specifically psychoanalytic to do so. To spot the understanding, I used semantic and pragmatic knowledge ("pragmatic" in the linguistic sense). To spot the implications for how he saw himself, I used precepts for inferring representations of self from utterances and their contexts. I did not use anything specifically psychoanalytic.

Let us now consider a second example, from the analysis of Ms. A, a 38-year-old government manager. Early in her analysis, the way leisure time and even the simplest pleasures caused her to feel uneasy and distracted from something more important became a point of urgency. Knowing by then something of her deprived, traumatized, and intensely religious childhood, I once said, "One reason ordinary happiness leaves you feeling uneasy may be that it strikes you as shallow, a betrayal of the high mission of your childhood." This example has clear connections to a specifically psychoanalytic theory, of course, the theory of the superego. But how was I able to make the inferential jump from pleasure leaving her feeling uneasy and distracted—from information I had about her childhood (as she experienced it, of course)—to the conclusion that she was feeling an unconscious sense of betrayal? Not, I think, by applying distinctively psychoanalytic knowledge.

Examples like these illustrate how clinical practice depends on commonsense psychology. They could be multiplied endlessly; indeed, new ones can be found in virtually every session. How do we spot that a patient raised by a depressed mother feels that he will never have the strength he needs until someone gives him what he feels he did not get from his mother? How do we spot in another patient that she always experiences a disappointment as proof of her inferiority? Or, to take a more "classical" example, how do we suddenly infer that a patient is immobilized by feelings of fear, anger, and concern for a damaged mother, feelings that are of roughly equal strength and pulling in different directions? That some of these examples are narcissistic and some to do with classical conflicts is not significant here. Indeed, that these conclusions make contact with psychoanalysis at all is not what interests me. What interests me is the inferential processes by which we reach them. So far as I can see, they are not based on much that is specifically psychoanalytic.

In addition to its intrinsic interest, the kind of relationship between psychoanalysis and commonsense psychology just introduced may be important for another reason. As is well known, the last two decades have seen some far-reaching critiques of the scientific credentials of psychoanalysis, both by the hermeneutic reinterpretation of it as a kind of narrative art and by philosophers of science, Adolf Grünbaum (1984, 1988, 1990) in particular. The relation between psychoanalysis and commonsense psychology may allow us to answer these charges from an unexpected direction. Commonsense psychology consists largely of factual claims and inference rules about human psychological states, claims and rules that allow us to make and test predictions about future human behavior, utterances, and the like. Thus, even if these claims generate narratives, as the hermeneutical critics claim, they are also something more than narratives. They are factual claims about a particular kind of thing in the world, namely human beings. By factual claims, I do not mean the old empiricist idea of perceptions unsullied by any conceptualization. It is now generally recognized that every factual claim is saturated with theory and concepts. I mean claims that can be supported or disconfirmed by observation, even though these observations will also be theory- and concept-saturated. It is factual claims in this sense that I contrast with the view advanced in some quarters that psychoanalysis is in the business of constructing internally coherent narratives, not making and testing factual claims about events and causes. This view of the relation of the factual underpinnings of psychoanalysis to its concepts and theory has been receiving increasing attention. (Goldberg, 1988, gives a good account of it.) I, however, want to explore a different idea.

One of the most important features of commonsense psychology is that we know it works, in everyday contexts at least. Our great success in interpreting one another's noises as expressions of intentions, affects, wishes, and so on is proof of that. (Here I am talking about the interpretive apparatus of commonsense psychology, not its explicit beliefs.) Moreover, commonsense psychology has been massively tested over the course of human history, so we can consider it exceedingly well confirmed. That raises an interesting possibility. Could we use the relationship of psychoanalysis to this body of well-tested commonsense knowledge to answer the skeptics? I think we can. I take up this idea in the last section of this chapter. Interestingly, Grünbaum flatly rejects this approach. "I no more think that psychoanalytic theory is an extension of commonsense psychology that I think theoretical physics is an extension of commonsense 'physics' " (quoted in Edelson, 1988, p. 330); this stance may be connected to his skepticism.

The idea that psychoanalysis is dependent on or, even worse, is an extension of commonsense psychology can threaten our sense that, as analysts, we see further, indeed, may even seem bizarre. Clearly, psychoanalysis contradicts much in commonsense psychology and contains much that the latter could never have dreamed of. In general, I see the relationship between the two of them this way. The psychoanalytic theories of instincts, development, dreams, psychic structure (topographical and structural), defense, interpersonal relations (transference, countertransference, projective identification), and psychopathology all go far beyond anything in commonsense psychology. The same is true of that most basic of psychoanalytic concepts, the concept of the unconscious, the concept of motives, beliefs, and fantasies, which cannot be introspected and are governed by a strange primary process. When we add ideas contained in the newer theories, such as the concepts of unconscious fantasies of infantile helplessness, murderous aggression, and uninhibited lust, fantasies populated by infantile "internal objects," various part-objects, one-sided preambivalent affects, and so on in object relations theory, and the concepts of selfobject, narcissistic deficit, the developmental line of the self, empathy connection, selfobject transferences, transmuting internalizations, and the like of self psychology, we end up with something very remote from commonsense psychology.

In addition to these claims, which run directly counter to commonsense psychology, psychoanalysis has also proposed causal connections quite unlike anything it contains, notably those between infantile sexuality and narcissistic development and the vicissitudes of adult life; and it has rejected some of commonsense psychology's dearest beliefs, for example, the belief that conscious ideas largely control one's life. It also has a method, free association, that at the very least vastly expands the range of phenomena that can be interpreted in terms of reasons, and it has a whole range of special techniques to assist it in doing so. Clearly, psychoanalysis contains much that commonsense psychology has never dreamed of, indeed that is flatly inconsistent with it. That is why Grünbaum rejects the idea that psychoanalysis could possibly be an extension of commonsense psychology. Nevertheless, the two have a close relationship. (A further question, which I cannot go into, is how far the various theories of psychoanalysis are consistent or even comparable with themselves; on this, see Goldberg, 1988, Ch. 3.)

Like all psychological theories, psychoanalysis began with and grew out of commonsense psychology. Some psychologies grew by way of rejection. Freud tried to do this in the 1890s with his mechanistic metapsychology (a term he actually coined only later) and behaviorism tried the same thing in a different way much later. What the two theories have in common is the attempt to replace the vocabulary and explanatory style of intentionality with something else. Despite officially beginning in mechanism, psychoanalysis did not follow this course; it grew by way of development, not rejection. For the most part, it has not replaced commonsense psychology but extended it. The same is true of practically all psychological theories: all the various "dynamic" psychologies, most clinical psychologies and most of contemporary experimental cognitive psychology are all extensions of commonsense psychology. The failure of Grünbaum and others to see that psychoanalysis has roots in commonsense psychology is a serious one.

It is important to understand that psychoanalysis is in no way diminished by having been built on a foundation of commonsense psychology. What it has taken over is extremely basic and in no way detracts from what it has gone on to add. In any case, it had no alternative. Virtually all the inferences made by anyone from any point of view about people's psychological states and behavior must rely in some way on the resources of commonsense psychology. We could no more give up our psychological vocabulary and interpretive resources than we could give up our ability to speak. And we have no more reason to want to do so. Moreover, as Morton (1982) points out, the traffic has been anything but one way. If psychoanalysis grew out of commonsense psychology, it has also had a deep structural effect on the latter. For example, morally loaded character terms ("rigid," "self-absorbed") have largely disappeared, in favor of more neutral terms of personality ("obsessive," "narcissistic"). Let us now turn to the first of the two hypotheses about the relationship between the two introduced earlier, the *dependency hypothesis*.

The Dependency Hypothesis

The resources of commonsense psychology, and similar ones contained in our commonsense physics and biology, have a special relationship to psychoanalysis. Though they are not themselves psychoanalytic, psychoanalytic thinking cannot take place without them. Edelson (1984, p. 83; 1988, pp. 245, 254–255) calls them nontheoretic with respect to psychoanalysis. The nontheoretic for a given discipline is everything (1) that the discipline takes for granted in order to proceed and (2) that we do not need the discipline to understand. Thus, for example, physics is nontheoretic in biology. In just the same way, much of commonsense psychology and virtually the whole of its mundane apparatus of psychological inference is nontheoretic for psychoanalysis. Psychoanalytic reasoning takes it for granted. Just as biology relies on chemistry and astronomy relies on physics, so psychoanalysis relies on commonsense psychology. As we shall see, it also relies on commonsense syntax, semantics, physics, biology, and perhaps even sociology.

In some measure, Freud himself was aware of this dependency. As he said repeatedly (though perhaps ambivalently), psychoanalysis is not a general psychology (Freud, 1914, preface to 1905a, 130; 1912, p. 99 n2; 1914, p. 50 ("psychoanalysis has never claimed to provide a complete theory of human mentality in general"); 1924, 209; 1937, p. 226, n2). It is a psychology of a special class of phenomena (Edelson discusses the grander ambitions of Hartmann and others in 1986a and 1988). If so, in addition to distinctively psychoanalytic ideas, psychoanalysis has no choice but to use a lot of nonpsychoanalytic psychology, too. As Freud knew, psychoanalysts have to rely on their store of "latent memories," as he sometimes called them, of people and their feelings and behavior as much as anyone else does.

A psychoanalyst uses the resources of commonsense psychology in many places. One crucial one is in establishing and maintaining the intersubjective, communicative field between analyst and analysand.

When we interpret another's words and understand the simple, immediate intentions they are trying to communicate, we do not use anything specifically psychoanalytic to do so. Yet if we could not rely on this communicative field's being there and quietly working away, we could not bring the special knowledge of psychoanalysis to bear at all. Consider cases where this field is not secure, where the analyst is not sure an analysand understands him or her and communication is uncertain and insecure. In these cases the analytic experience is totally different from what it is in cases where analyst and analysand are both secure in the conviction that they understand each other's other immediate, conscious communications. What makes this understanding possible is mutual interpretation of the words each utters. This work of interpretation could not be using anything particular to psychoanalysis because, for one thing, the analysand has no such knowledge. What makes it work is the commonsense psychology knowledge analyst and analysand share.

Indeed, a good deal of other commonsense knowledge is involved, too. Before we can interpret one another's communicative intentions, we must interpret the noises being made. This in itself is a multistage process of extraordinary complexity. First we must interpret the noises as phonemes and words. Next we have to interpret the syntactic structure of the words. Then we have to find a semantic interpretation, an interpretation of the linguistic meaning, that fits the syntactic structure (and everything else we know that is relevant to the situation). Only then are we in a position to begin to interpret the communicative intentions behind the linguistic meaning.

Of these various stages, the only one that has been studied at all well is the syntactic one, by Chomsky (1959) and his followers. The following is one of Chomsky's standard examples of syntactic interpretation. Compare the sentence, "John is easy to please." with the sentence, "John is eager to please." Physically, these sentences could hardly be more similar. The only difference is that for the letters *sy* in the first, we find *ger* in the second. Yet their syntactic structure is totally different, and this is intuitively obvious to anyone who knows English. Indeed, most three-year-old children would respond to these sentences in a way that recognizes the difference. To the first, the response might be, "So I don't have to be so good, then?" To the second, the response might be, "I'll ask him to buy me something, then." Given the great physical similarity between these two sentences, clearly the rules that allow us to react to them as totally different must be complex and highly discriminating. They are also entirely unconscious. It seems clear that they have nothing to do with anything specifically psychoanalytic, yet we rely on rules like these by the thousands in every session.

Communication with patients in the course of any kind of therapy makes use of our ability to interpret one another's speech and therefore makes use of the commonsense syntactic, semantic, and psychological knowledge that underlies this ability. Unlike many other therapies, however, psychoanalysis does not immediately ignore or implicitly deny the special knowledge and skills that its intersubjective communicative practices presuppose. From the mechanistic neurology of the 19th century to the behaviorism of today, psychological treatments have ignored or denied in their theories what they assume and take for granted in their communicative practices. Not psychoanalysis. Since it freed itself of 19th-century mechanism and energetics its theory has been of a piece, most of the time, with its communicative practices.

Another place where commonsense psychology looms large is in the area of technique (Edelson, 1988, p. 335). How are we able, by acts of inference, to conclude that unconscious psychic causes are at work behind what we see and hear? Although training can make analysts better at it, there is also much that is not specifically psychoanalytic in inference-making of this kind. One indication of this is that being good at inference is in part a matter of talent; if talent is lacking, any amount of training may not make up for the lack. Another indication is that there are people who are good at psychological inference and yet have never had psychoanalytic training, novelists for example.

To see how commonsense psychological skills enter the activity of psychological understanding, think of the huge difference between reading a transcript of a therapeutic encounter and hearing a tape of the same encounter. Where the affects and transference are often quite opaque in the transcript, they become clear when we hear the tape. The reason, I think, is that we have a richly discriminating capacity to "read" psychological states in tone of voice. In the transcript, we no longer have the voices of the participants. The skills we are using here are complex in the extreme and pervade all interpersonal life, psychoanalysis included. Yet there is little that is distinctively psychoanalytic about interpreting tone of voice, even though being able to do so is essential to psychoanalytic practice.

Such illustrations of the role of background commonsense psychology in psychoanalysis could be multiplied endlessly. Inferences from the manifest to the latent content of a dream, for example, bear some resemblance to those used to decode the real structure of a sentence from its often misleading surface structure. Inferences about how environment or interpersonal situation has affected someone rely very heavily on our commonsense knowledge about how people are affected by their environment and by other people. So does the ability, as essential in everyday life as in psychoanalysis, to form a picture of a whole narrative from the briefest sketch of it and a few bits of personal history. Perhaps the clearest example of the role of commonsense psychology in psychoanalysis is the ability analysts have to reconstruct the role of significant figures in an analysand's childhood from the briefest, most fleeting bits of transference. In all these cases, commonsense psychological knowledge plays an essential role.

Certain striking clinical abilities may also have commonsense psychology at their root. I have empathic insight particularly in mind. Empathic insight is an activity, obviously, of grasping an analysand's psychological states on the basis of his or her words and actions (and sometimes our reactions to them); yet the competences that allow us to do so are not contained in any explicit theory, psychoanalytic or otherwise. (Some theories may give us the beginnings of an explanation of the phenomenon, but none of them are detailed enough to give us any guidance as to how to do it.) If the competences that allow empathic insight do not come from commonsense psychology, I do not know where else they could come from. Having commonsense psychological ability to an unusually penetrating degree may also be what allows an analyst "to turn his unconscious to the unconscious of the patient." That people differ in the sensitivity and insight required to do so and differ to a striking degree is no argument against the idea that these clinical skills rely on common sense psychological knowledge; people differ in commonsense psychological talent just as they do in everything else.

If empathic insight and unconscious understanding use more commonsense than specifically psychoanalytic psychology, that is to be expected. Commonsense psychology has not been well explored yet, but even our commonsense ability to use language, which has been explored by Chomsky and his followers, is vastly richer and more complicated than anything in any explicit body of theoretical knowledge. The complexity of the unconscious system that allows us to decipher the syntax and the semantics of the words we hear is truly staggering. A child as young as three can recognize and produce, if Chomsky (1972) is right, about 90 million well-formed sentences. Even in the earliest days of speaking, children make very few grammatical mistakes, and only of certain sharply limited kinds. There is every reason to expect that commonsense psychology will turn out to be far more complicated than language. Certainly the corpus of our commonsense psychological beliefs and competences is orders of magnitude larger and more sensitive than anything we have ever come close to capturing in conscious psychological theory, psychoanalytic or otherwise. Great novelists, most of whom had no access to psychology at all except for commonsense psychology, attest to that. Nor do we need to look to novelists and poets to see its richness. Even young children have an astonishing capacity to identify complicated patterns of intentionality. Given the richness and subtlety of our background commonsense psychology, it is not surprising that the discriminations it allows us to make are much, much finer than those that any conscious psychological theory could generate. Indeed, the superior sensitivity of commonsense psychology may be one reason why it is better to listen to analysands with evenly hovering attention, rather than with specific theories in mind, psychoanalytic or otherwise. Any adequate critique of psychoanalysis must take into account the role of commonsense psychology in it.

This idea that commonsense psychology plays a central role in psychoanalysis has been greeted with skepticism, even hostility. Freud would probably have been appalled by the idea (though, as we shall see, he himself made extensive use of it). As we have seen, however, the idea is not very radical. Nor are commonsense syntax, semantics, and psychology our only stores of commonsense knowledge. We depend on a great variety of commonsense beliefs and competences. Every time we ascribe a psychological state to someone, conscious or unconscious, we must use not just commonsense psychology but also commonsense physics, to pick out and locate the body, and commonsense biology, to recognize that it is living, conscious, and of our species. Only then do we get to the point where we can even begin to apply our commonsense syntax and semantics, to interpret the noises the body is making, and our commonsense psychology, to interpret the psychological states behind the noises. Only then does the specialized knowledge of psychoanalysis get a chance to go to work. If there is anything to the work of Lévi-Strauss, Lacan, and their followers, we may even have a store of shared, commonsense social and cultural beliefs and competencies, too, what Lacan called the Symbolic.

The philosopher Daniel Dennett (1987a) has described the role of commonsense or what he calls folk knowledge in our lives this way:

> Thanks to folk physics we stay warm and well fed and avoid collisions, and thanks to folk psychology we cooperate on multiperson projects, learn from each other, and enjoy periods of local peace. These benefits would be unattainable without extraordinarily efficient and reliable systems of expectation-generation [p. 11; see also pp. 17–18].

In short, commonsense psychology is not only ubiquitous in almost all psychological thought, psychoanalysis included, but it also works.

The Extension Hypothesis

To understand the extension hypothesis, the crucial point is that commonsense psychology is an intentional psychology. An intentional psychology is a psychology about states and events that are about something, that is to say, that have intentionality. Clearly, as it has in fact developed, psychoanalysis ended up as an intentional psychology, too, whatever Freud may have originally intended. (We will return to this point.) Since commonsense psychology is the ultimate ground out of which all intentional psychologies grew, this alone is enough to show that the two are closely related. What defines an intentional psychology is its vocabulary, which is utterly unlike the vocabulary of any other explanatory activity. First, psychological vocabulary is a language of representations: of perception, belief, desire, affect, and psychic reality (dreaming and imagination). Second, psychological vocabulary ascribes intentionality to whatever it describes. This makes it unique. Intentionality here does not mean "intention," although intentions do have intentionality. (The etymological link between intentionality and intention can be misleading because many other psychological states have this property of being about something, too.) Intentionality means to have an object, to be about something (Searle, 1983; Dennett, 1987b). A belief is about whatever is believed; a desire is about whatever is desired; a fantasy is about whatever is imagined in it; an affect is about whatever it is directed at. The technical term for what a mental state is about is *intentional object*. In this usage, events and states of affairs, including psychological events and states, can just as well be intentional objects as objects strictly defined. Moreover, intentional objects need not exist or correspond to anything real. Some psychoanalysts and philosophers also refer to intentional objects, what a psychological state is about, as *content*.

Contrary to the dreams of the metapsychologists, the working vocabulary of psychoanalysis is and always has been intentional in this way. The psychological vocabulary of beliefs, desires, emotions, attitudes, motives, fantasies — the language of representations in psychic reality — is also the language of psychoanalysis (see Edelson, 1988, pp. xxii–xxiii, 102–109, Ch. 7). Psychoanalysis has supplemented our common psychological vocabulary in various ways, of course, introducing such terms as repression, superego, identification, and selfobject. But nothing has ever come close to eliminating or replacing it. In fact, there have only been two serious attempts to eliminate psychological vocabulary from psychology. One was 19th-century quantitative mechanism as expressed in metapsychology; the other was modern behaviorism. Neither was able to do the job. (On the failure of mechanistic metapsychology, see Schafer, 1976, Gill and Holzman, 1976. On the failure of behaviorism, see Dennett, 1978).[1] If psychoanalysis is an intentional psychology, that is enough by itself to show that psychoanalysis is an extension of commonsense psychology, at least in respect of its vocabulary.

In a slightly different way, all the theorists who see psychoanalysis as an interpretationist, hermeneutic activity advance the same idea. They see procedures for interpreting "meanings," procedures for interpreting people's motives for thinking, feeling, and acting as they do, as central to psychoanalysis. These procedures use intentional psychology and are direct descendants of the everyday activity of making sense of ourselves; interpreting "meanings" is a direct descendant and extension of interpreting one another in everyday life. If psychoanalysis is an activity of interpretation of "meanings," then it is also an extension of commonsense psychology. For at least 25 years, a debate has raged over these issues. On one side are those who think that any adequate theory of the human psyche must be developed in purely nonintentional terms, so that psychoanalysis either is or should become a nonintentional science. At the very least, anything intentional in it could make no special contribution to its status as science. Freud's metapsychology, the psychological theory built out of such notions as psychoenergetics, cathexes, barriers, and discharges (economics, dynamics, and topography/structure), is the best worked-out example of this point of view. On the other side are the interpretationists. Taking their inspiration from Dilthey, Weber, and Jaspers, they argue that psychoanalysis is an activity of psychological interpretation. It aims to uncover the often unconscious meanings (motives and other reasons) behind patients' perceiving and believing and feeling and wishing and fantasizing and dreaming and acting as they do. (Rycroft, 1966, was the first; after him came G. S. Klein, 1969, 1976; Gill and Holzman, 1976; Ricoeur, 1970, 1981; Schafer, 1976, 1978; Spence, 1982; Wollheim, 1984; Hopkins, 1986; Edelson, 1988; and Goldberg, 1988.) Edelson, Goldberg and others argue that being interpretive does not preclude being scientific, indeed that all science is interpretive, a point Goldberg particularly emphasizes. Among the many points that make this debate interesting is that Freud's work richly represents both sides of it.

In his official pronouncements, Freud usually advocated the stance of

---

[1]Schafer's (1976, 1978) attempt to do analysis in the language of action may seem to some like a third attempt, but it is not so much an attempt to replace psychological vocabulary with something else as to force a part of that vocabulary (action language) to serve for the whole (the full range of psychological terms for belief, desire, affect, and so on).

nonintentional science; but his actual reasoning, as we will see, was often pure intentional psychological, both in vocabulary and in the kind of explanations he gave. This duality in Freud may have had something to do with his feelings about Brentano (1874) the father of modern intentionality theory. Although Freud had attended his lectures for two years, at exactly the time Brentano was writing the famous 1874 book that reintroduced intentionality theory into modern thought, Freud shut him out of his work completely (so far as the explicit text is concerned, at any rate) and talked as though the only respectable scientific vocabulary for psychoanalysis was mechanistic metapsychology (energy, energy discharge). (There is only one reference to Brentano in the whole *Standard Edition* (Freud, 1905b, pp. 31 n. 6 and App.), and it is to a riddle Brentano devised, not to intentionality. In contrast, Freud referred to Plato, Aristotle, Kant, and Nietzsche dozens of times each.) Yet, at the same time, Freud not only used intentional psychological language constantly, he also modeled the special concepts of psychoanalysis on it. Indeed, Freud was as clear as he could possibly have been about the crucial concepts of psychoanalysis being extensions of related concepts in commonsense psychology.

Extensions of Commonsense Vocabulary

Consider Freud's favorite argument for the existence of the unconscious, an argument he used repeatedly and over a period stretching from 1909 (pp. 175–176) through 1915 (pp. 166ff.) and 1923 (pp. 14–18), to 1938 (pp. 196–197). In that argument, Freud explicitly models this central notion of psychoanalysis on consciousness. In outline, the argument goes as follows. Our inferences about the psychic states that caused a person to behave in a certain way usually correspond, Freud begins, to what the person him- or herself is conscious of and believes to be the cause. But sometimes a person either grossly misidentifies what seems to us to be the clear cause of some behavior or is just now aware of any cause at all. Either way, there is a gap. At this point, Freud adds something new. In these cases too, he tells us, the cause of the behavior is something psychological. This thought almost instantly generates the concept of the unconscious: since there is nothing conscious to be the cause, Freud (1923) infers, the cause must be some psychological state that is unconscious. As he put it, "we have found—that is, we have been obliged to assume—that very powerful mental processes or ideas exist . . . which can produce all the effects in mental life that ordinary ideas do (including effects that can in their turn become conscious as ideas), though they

themselves do not become conscious" (p. 14). This momentous conclusion, of course, changed forever both psychology and the way we view
ourselves. Momentous as it was, Freud's new concept of the unconscious
is entirely modeled on the standard concept of consciousness. The latter
is a concept, in fact the central concept, of commonsense psychology.

Indeed, this argument relates the concept of the unconscious to our
standard concept of consciousness in more ways than one. Freud says that
unconscious mental processes are like ordinary ideas; ideas have intentionality. Unconscious states, Freud (1938) says, are a way of "filling up
the gaps in the phenomena of our consciousness" (pp. 1976–197). "All the
categories that we employ to describe conscious mental acts, such as
ideas, purposes, resolutions and so on, can be applied to them" (Freud,
1915, p. 168). For Freud, unconscious mental processes are also quite
different from conscious ones in some ways. In particular, they are
largely governed by the primary process. But the concept for them is still
a concept for an intentional phenomenon.[2] In short, Freud's derivation of
the unconscious depends essentially on commonsense psychology, indeed
on commonsense psychology's being correct as far as it goes. The idea of
the unconscious does not replace commonsense psychology; it extends it.
If even the most distinctive of psychoanalytic concept of the unconscious,
is such a close kin of a concept of commonsense psychology, surely the
same will be true of many of the others.

In addition—and this is a point of fundamental importance—when
psychoanalysis is through extending intentional vocabulary into its own
special concepts, it does not discard this vocabulary. Quite the reverse.
Psychoanalysts continue to use such concepts as belief, desire, perception, imagination (or cognates), dream, memory, thought, feeling,
effort, trying, anger, and longing, just as much as any lay person.
Freud's dream of a nonintentional vocabulary for psychoanalysis notwithstanding, it is hard to see how psychoanalysis could even begin to
dispense with its vocabulary of representations in psychic reality. To say
that psychoanalysis has extended and supplemented this vocabulary in
various ways is very different from saying that it could do without it, as
Freud may have dreamed.

Extensions of Commonsense Doctrines

In addition, and appearances perhaps to the contrary, a number of the
most central doctrines of psychoanalysis are also extensions of

---

[2]Edelson (1988, Chs. 6 and 7) gives a good account of the idea that the concept of the
unconscious, indeed psychoanalysis in general, is based on filling causal gaps in
consciousness with unconscious psychological states.

commonsense psychology, extensions of some of its precepts (see Hopkins, 1986; Edelson, 1988). We can find a number of examples in the theory of defense. The concept of repression seems to be an extension of the precept that people tend to forget or distort their recollection of troubling experiences (Edelson, 1988, p. 337). The theory of splitting representations seems to extend the precept that people tend not to integrate feelings, motives, fantasies, or the like when they conflict or are inconsistent. The theory of the splitting of the ego, that people will isolate inconsistent attitudes to something (Brook, in press), seems to extend the commonsense notion that we can have inconsistent attitudes to things without being aware of it. The theory of resistance seems to extend the commonsense idea that we will try to avoid thinking about things that trouble us. Although the various parts of the theory of defense have been a signal contribution to intentional psychology, many of them are also fairly clear extensions of what we already know from commonsense.

The theory of transference is another example. The concept of transference is an extension of the precept that people tend to repeat ways of reacting to people learned in childhood. There is much more to the doctrine of transference than that, of course. It also reflects the fact that in psychological beings causes from the distant past can continue to operate in the present, through both memories and dispositions (Wollheim, 1984). And it is tied to theory of neurosis by the idea that neurotic pathogens inevitably appear in the transference. Grünbaum (1990) finds this last idea both far removed from our normal intuitions and particularly badly supported. I think he is wrong on both counts. He seems to think that Freud's only reason for thinking that the causes of neurosis will be recapitulated in the transference was that earlier ways of reacting to people are recapitulated in the transference. This would indeed be grossly invalid reasoning. I think, however, that Freud's reasoning was more subtle. His conviction that pathogens will appear in the transference relies on a general background conviction, as much a part of commonsense psychology as of psychoanalysis, that what is troubling people will appear in their relationships to significant others. This idea is intuitively plausible. The extension that psychoanalysis introduces is the idea that the repetition of childhood patterns will be particularly relevant, and it creates a setting that maximizes the chances that this repetition will occur. Thus, even the doctrine that pathogens appear in the transference is an extension of commonsense psychology. Clinically, transference is generally held to be the most important field of events to which analysts apply their interpretive and explanatory skills, but that does not mean that it is unrelated to commonsense psychology.

Psychoanalysis has also made many contributions to intentional psychology that go far beyond commonsense psychology. The innovative parts of the theory of defense and the theory of transference are two; it would take us too far afield to explore the many others. Methodological contributions have been particularly rich. Much psychoanalytic work, as I will argue shortly, is concerned with restoring the real intentionality of affects, fantasies, and the like. The methods of free association, evenly hovering attention, and empathy are probably the first and only tools ever discovered for dealing with pathologies of intentionality. Other important contributions include the theory of drives as the biological basis of intentional reactivity, the theory of the developmental stages, the theory of interpersonal intentionality (transference, countertransference, projective identification), the theory of the real content of dreams and how to uncover it, and so on. A complete list of psychoanalysis's extensions of commonsense psychology and contributions to intentional psychology in general would be very long.

Let me close this section with a look at the opposition. As we saw earlier, Grünbaum argues vociferously that psychoanalysis is no more an extension of commonsense psychology than theoretical physics in an extension of commonsense "physics." If psychoanalytic theory is an extension of commonsense psychology, why, he asks, did it encounter so much disbelief? Many of its doctrines are quite counterintuitive. Indeed, the idea that horror dreams should be wish fulfilling is "utterly incredible common-sensically" (quoted in Edelson, 1988, p. 330). Well, maybe there is also more to commonsense physics than Grünbaum thinks! But the real point is that he is failing to make a distinction. That psychoanalysis ends up with results that are counterintuitive to commonsense psychology does not mean that it does not use, model itself on, and extend the methods and vocabulary of commonsense psychology (Edelson, 1988, p. 330). Moreover, as I will argue later, it is very good that psychoanalysis does so, because the methods and vocabulary of commonsense psychology contain powerful scientific tools.

Extensions of Psychological Explanation

What makes it important that the phenomena of interest to psychoanalysis have intentionality and are extensions of commonsense vocabulary and precepts is that psychoanalysis can thereby use a distinctive kind of interpretation and explanation. Usually called *psychological explanation,* it is the methodology of interpreting and explaining actions and psychological states in terms of the reasons for them. Unlike phenomena that do not have intentionality (such as energies and neurons), intentional phenom-

ena can be explained by reasons. This feature of psychological explanation is unique to them. As I mentioned earlier, Edelson, Goldberg, and
others are now making the point that all science is interpretive. The
observation that psychological explanation interprets reasons allows us to
carry this point one step further. In interpreting people's reasons,
psychoanalysis and psychological explanation in general are different
from other sciences. (That does not mean that they are not science at all,
but I will have to take that issue up elsewhere.)

It is almost impossible to fit interpretive explanations in terms of
reasons and meanings into nonintentional metapsychology. Nevertheless,
Freud made psychological explanation, and its central idea that people
generally do what they do for a reason, one of the cornerstones of
psychoanalysis. It is the basis of the crucial claim that when there is
nothing conscious to be the cause of some behaviour, the cause will often
still be psychological; there will often still be reason, but they will not be
introspectible. This idea was one of Freud's most important contributions. Thus, his official preference for metapsychology notwithstanding,
psychological explanation as I have just defined it is the heart and soul of
his work. So far as I know, he never tried to reconcile the two.

To illustrate just how central psychological explanation is in his work,
consider this comment from the Rat Man case study:

> When there is a mésalliance . . . between an affect and its ideational
> content (in this instance, between the intensity of the [Rat Man's]
> self-reproach and the occasion for it) . . . the analytic physician says
> "The affect is justified. The sense of guilt is not in itself open to further
> criticism. But it belongs to some other content, which is unknown
> (unconscious), and which requires to be looked for" [Freud, 1909, pp.
> 175–176].

Though Freud did not use the term, this is a remark about how
psychological explanation works. It is clear from the way Freud writes
that he saw this kind of explanation as central to psychoanalysis (Sachs,
1982; for a marvellous example of Freud giving an explanation of this
kind, see Freud, 1926, p. 117). Note that Freud did not argue that the
Rat Man had reasons for feeling guilt; he took that for granted. So
automatic was his recourse to psychological explanation, he did not even
feel a need to justify the assumption. His innovation was to see that often
people's reasons are unconscious. That is what made the very ordinary
precept that there are reasons for what people feel and do such a powerful
tool in his hands. Suddenly there could be reasons for vast ranges of
thought, feeling, motive, and behavior that until then had seemed
completely senseless.

The Alternative Theories of Hopkins and Edelson

To get a more detailed idea of how psychoanalysis makes use of and extends the basic principles of psychological explanation, we might examine the alternative accounts of this process given by Hopkins (1986) and Edelson (1988). To orient ourselves, let me begin with a brief clinical vignette.

> When Ms. B, a 50-year-old divorced counselor, was seven years old, she witnessed her mother having an almost fatal miscarriage. The miscarriage was quite possibly self-induced, and the baby was probably not her father's. Ms. B witnessed much of the scene, which was extremely bloody. Mother was then hospitalized for a month. Ms. B's mother was difficult, and Ms. B enjoyed having her father to herself during that month. As soon as the mother returned home, she cut off Ms. B's beautiful long hair. I suggested to Ms. B that the bloody scene, followed by sinful pleasure and humiliating punishment, had become her model of sexual pleasure.

This vignette contains material that is clearly psychoanalytic, material that we probably could not have seen before the advent of psychoanalytic theory gave us the lens through which to see it. Nevertheless, the type of explanation it gives for Ms. B's adult ways of reacting to sexual pleasure, that the memories and fantasies she carried away from her earlier traumatic experiences contain her reasons for reacting as she does, is an extension of a pattern of explanation intrinsic to commonsense, intentional psychology. Hopkins and Edelson give different accounts of how this extension occurs and what it is like.

In outline, Hopkins begins with one of the basic interpretative patterns of commonsense psychology, inferring a pattern of desires (or other motives) and beliefs (or other cognitive states) such that, given what we infer a person to desire and believe, it would have been rational to act as he or she did. This pattern was first articulated by Aristotle and has been much studied by philosophers and cognitive scientists of late (Davidson, 1970, 1974; Dennett, 1978, 1987a; Fodor, 1988). Freud took over the pattern, argues Hopkins, but extended it in two important ways. First, Freud was primarily interested, not in actions, but in psychological states, especially states that do not issue directly in intended actions, such as dreams, fantasies and parapraxes. Second, parallel to the way that actions are explained when we see how the person doing them could have done them to satisfy a desire, these psychological states are explained when we see how they could have been a way of imagining the fulfilment of a wish. (Hopkins, following Wollheim, carefully distinguishes wishes from desires, but we need not follow him in that here.) Thus, psychoanalysis is not a direct application of the commonsense psychological principle that, all other things being equal, people will act to get what they believe will satisfy their desires. It is, however, an extension of that principle. To be sure, there are also important differences. If a wish causes a dream, fantasy, or parapraxis, there need be no belief that any of the latter will be a means to satisfying the former, for example. But the lineage is still clear.

Hopkins puts this argument to good use, and it certainly seems to have merit. For example, he uses it to show that an interesting observation of Grünbaum's does not mean what it seems to mean. The observation (Grünbaum, 1984, p. 75) is that important classes of psychoanalytic explanation cannot be assimilated to the desire/belief/action pattern. Grünbaum is right about this, Hopkins (1986, p. 55) argues, but he draws the wrong conclusion from it. Contrary to Grünbaum, these explanations are still psychological explanations. But the pattern they follow is an extension of the belief/desire/action pattern, not the pattern in its original form. However, Hopkin's account also faces a fairly obvious problem. Contrary to Hopkins, explanations of fantasies, day-dreams, and the like as wish-fulfilling fantasies are not an extension of commonsense psychology — they are part of it. Our everyday activities of making sense of our own and others' psychological states use the wish/imaginary wish-fulfillment pattern of explanation just as much as the belief/desire/action pattern.

Edelson's (1988) approach to the extensionist argument avoids this problem. Unlike Hopkins, he does not argue that psychoanalysis picked one form of commonsense psychological explanation and extended its logic. Rather, he argues that psychoanalysis extended all the forms of explanation found in commonsense psychology. It did not, however, extend their logic; it extended their range of application by applying them to new areas — infantile sexuality and stages of psychosexual development as well as adolescent and adult ones; unconscious wishes and fantasies as well as conscious ones; primary as well as secondary processes; latent as well as manifest content; bizarre as well as acceptable wishes, desires and affects (pp. 327–338).

In my view, as well as allowing Edelson to avoid the objection just mentioned, this difference gives his approach two further advantages over Hopkins's. First, it allows for a more realistic picture of the richness and diversity of the explanatory strategies of commonsense, everyday psychological interpretation. Explanations of actions in terms of beliefs and desires hardly scratch the surface. Second, Edelson's approach presents a more accurate picture of how psychoanalysis grew out of and now relates to commonsense psychology. It grew out of many forms of everyday psychological discourse and many interpretive patterns of commonsense psychology, not just one of them. It is as closely related to our fictional and mythological activities, to poetic speculations about sexual love, to all the products of the human imagination, as it is to our everyday activities of explaining our own and others' actions. (Freud refers to Shakespeare far more often than to Herbart!) Psychoanalysis grew out of many different forms of human activity and reflection on it, not just one of them.

Nevertheless, Edelson's account has a weakness, too; it contains far too little detail. Nowhere does he attempt to lay out how many kinds of interpretive patterns there are in commonsense psychology, and nowhere does he explore just how psychoanalysis extends them. In fact, his account is more like a suggestion for where a theory might be developed than a completed theory. Edelson's (1988) basic idea is that psychoanalysis uses as an analogy what is confidently known in commonsense intentional psychology "as a homely model" (p. 329). He sees commonsense psychology as providing useful analogies at two or more levels. At the most general level, most, if not all, of the explanatory patterns of commonsense psychology find the causes of psychological states by studying how content has been conveyed down a causal chain. A desire for x, a belief that doing y will secure x, an intention to secure x, and an action that attempts to secure x by doing y, all have x as their common content. Likewise, a wish for x, a wish-fulfilling fantasy of getting x, and a guilty feeling of not being entitled to x, all have the same content. This process of conveying content results in what has come to be called *thematic affinities* between cause and effect, affinities sometimes spanning many years or even whole lifetimes. Edelson emphasizes that "reasoning by appeal to thematic affinities is . . . central in the explanatory strategies of psychoanalysis" (p. 332). This claim plays an important role in the final section of this chapter because Grünbaum has argued that such appeals to thematic affinities are "unavailing" as a way of establishing causal connections.

At a slightly less general level, commonsense psychology provides two analogies, one far more useful than the other. The less useful one is its way of finding the causes of actions (also intentions) by finding beliefs and desires that would have made it rational to do them. This pattern is not very important in psychoanalysis, Edelson (1988) believes. Far more usefully, commonsense psychology has a pattern of explanation in which various imaginings, dreams, etc., are explained as expressions of wishes. In Edelson's view, the latter pattern is also the distinctive explanatory pattern of psychoanalysis.

In my view, all this is an extremely good start. However, these two points of contact between the explanatory patterns of psychoanalysis and commonsense psychology do not exhaust the field. Recall the vignette with which I began this section. Explanations in terms of wishes are forward looking: we explain the fantasy as a surrogate for going out and getting something. However, the psychological states displayed in the vignette were backward looking: Ms. B's way of experiencing sexual pleasure is really about, or partly about, the bloody scene she witnessed as a child and the feelings she felt then. The same was true in the vignette about Ms. A presented much earlier: Ms. A felt that she was betraying an ideal — an ideal she had held for a very long time. Likewise, the interpretations I offered appeal to past psychological states in both cases: retained memories (or repressed, memorylike states), and retained ideals. Many of the psychological states of most interest to psychoanalysis have this character. To explain them, we must refer to earlier psychological states — to retained dispositions, to memories (and repressed memories) and, of course, to fantasies that are really about earlier experiences (including earlier fantasized experiences).

Yet Hopkins and Edelson deal only with forward-looking psychic states such as desires and wishes, states aimed at securing or avoiding something, and the imagined, wish-fulfilling surrogates for action they generate. The examples of psychoanalytic explanations we have examined are not like this. They do not work from wish fulfillments to the wishes they fulfil in fantasies or dreams, but back from fantasies, anxiety, and ways of experiencing to earlier experiences that the fantasies, etc., are really about. As I put it elsewhere (Brook, in progress), many psychoanalytic explanations surround restoring the intentionality of psychological states where processes of defense have rendered their true intentionality obscure or invisible, not forward looking and in terms of desire satisfaction or wish fulfillment. Fortunately, adding the restoring of the intentionality of psychological states to our list of types of psychoanalytic explanation is no problem for the extensionist hypothesis about psychological explanation. Backward-looking explanations in terms of earlier traumatic memories and fantasies are just as much part of commonsense psychology as forward-looking ones in terms of desire satisfaction and wish fulfillments. Put another way, the explanatory direction of thematic affinity can run either way.

In short, Edelson's suggestions about how the explanatory patterns of psychoanalysis extend those to be found in commonsense psychology is promising, but there is still work to be done. In addition to extending the explanatory patterns of commonsense psychology, we have also seen that psychoanalysis has extended and continues to use its vocabulary, and that some of the most distinctive doctrines of psychoanalysis are extensions of precepts of commonsense psychology. Furthermore, as we saw even earlier, specifically psychoanalytic interpretations and explanations require a substructure of ordinary, commonsense psychological interpretations before they can even get started. (We must first interpret the direct, literal meaning of an expression or report, for example, before we can interpret its unconscious meaning.) Neither Hopkins nor Edelson has much to say about any of these other connections.

Commonsense Psychology in Case Studies

Let us now apply the results of our investigation to one of the great skeptics about the possibility of establishing psychoanalytic hypotheses, Adolf Grünbaum. Grünbaum thinks that the primary method of investigation in psychoanalysis, the case study, cannot establish claims about either fact or cause. As we saw earlier, he also rejects the idea that psychoanalysis is an extension of commonsense psychology. Yet, as we have seen, it extends commonsense psychology in no less than three different ways: in vocabulary, doctrines, and type of explanation. In addition, psychoanalysis uses a good deal of commonsense psychology that it does not incorporate into its own corpus at all. In my view, Grünbaum's skepticism about case studies as a method of uncovering causal connections and his rejection of the idea that psychoanalysis is an extension of commonsense psychology are connected. Commonsense psychology gives psychoanalysis a special power to uncover fact and cause that Grünbaum completely overlooks.

The distinctive home of psychoanalytic thinking is the case study built out of psychological explanations. Grünbaum's (1984, 1988, 1990) reservations about the extent to which case studies can identify causes and establish causal claims, claims like the big hypotheses of psychoanalysis at any rate, are far reaching. Because of the possibility of suggestion, confusion of fantasy with memory, and the like, he argues, case studies cannot establish what happened, that is, the facts about such things as temporal sequences, correlations, and thematic affinities in content. Even if they could do that, however, they could not uncover the causal relations in what happened. To find out what caused what in these data, we need to find out what made a difference to the occurrence of what. But a case study, he argues, could never tell us when a prior or correlated event, or something with a similar thematic content, made a causal difference, changed the probability of something occurring. According to Grünbaum (1984, p. 280), a main reason for this is that claims about causal difference must be tested against a control, and case studies provide no independent control. Grünbaum's charges cannot be sustained (Edelson, 1988, agrees). Grünbaum is particularly interested in the ability of case studies to establish the big theses of psychoanalysis: the generalizations meant to hold true of everyone, such as that repression is a central factor in neurosis; or that neurotic pathogens will appear in the transference; and especially the more counterintuitive ones, such as that paranoia in males has a homosexual etiology.[3] But it seems to me that if his charges apply anywhere, they ought to apply just as much to other uses of case studies, too.

Most of the time, analysts use case studies to figure out individual lives, not to uncover or test general hypotheses. However, we can see immediately that Grünbaum's critique of case studies cannot be entirely right. The problem he identifies, lack of a control, for example, would vitiate the use of case studies to understand individual lives just as much as it would vitiate their use to establish big, generalized hypotheses. Yet it could not possibly be right to claim that case studies are impotent to establish causal claims about individual lives. We are doing case studies practically every waking moment in our lives. When I understand even something so simple as the words a person utters, I have to interpret what the person means by the noises he or she makes—a miniature case study. Similarly, every time I judge what a person is believing, desiring, feeling, or hoping on the basis of what the person is saying and doing, I have done a miniature case study. (The theory behind the points I am making here was first developed by Davidson, 1984, in the 1970s.) These little case studies involve psychological interpretation and explanation just as much as big, psychoanalytic studies of a life do.

Moreover, the small case studies and psychological explanations of everyday life work. We do understand one another, and we do assess each other's thoughts and feelings correctly, most of the time and in simple situations, at least. Or if we do not understand one another completely, we come close enough for practical purposes. It is a simple matter of fact that not just psychoanalysts but everyone can establish fact and cause using case studies. We can all judge when something prior to a given phenomenon might or might not have been causally relevant to its coming to be. We can decide when the probability that a thematic affinity is the result of a causal connection is high or low. And we do these things by interpreting reasons. Whether case studies can establish the more complicated and generalized hypotheses of psychoanalysis is another

---

[3]The only big hypotheses Grünbaum considers are the ones Freud offered. However, the question of whether analysts hold these views in any unqualified form nowadays is not important for present purposes.

matter, to which we will return. It is also true that people sometimes render some of their thoughts, feelings, and actions pretty opaque by defensive, ideological or other distortion. But any suggestion that in principle case studies cannot reveal causes of behavior would have to be wrong; for vast reaches of ordinary human existence and most of the time, they can. If untutored commonsense can do this well, surely psychoanalytic case studies will often do much better.

I am not maintaining, of course, that case studies relying on psychological explanations can do everything. Clearly, they cannot. A lot of the causal substructure of any thought, feeling, or action has nothing directly to do with psychological factors at all (appropriate processing of oxygen, for example). Freud (1920) was well aware of this limitation:

> So long as we trace . . . development from its final outcome backwards, . . . we feel we have gained an insight which is completely satisfactory or even exhaustive. But if we proceed the reverse way, . . . we notice at once that there might have been another result, and that we might have been just as well able to understand and explain the latter [pp. 167–168].

But the fact that case studies using psychological explanations cannot do everything does not mean that they can do nothing.

For an example of how commonsense psychological explanation enters a psychoanalytic case study, go back to the vignette from Ms. B's analysis. In the context of Grünbaum's critique, this vignette is particularly interesting; it is centered on a thematic affinity of just the sort to which Grünbaum has given special attention, in this case the similarity between Ms. B's early experience of a bloody miscarriage followed by oedipal guilt and punishment, and her current way of experiencing sexual pleasure. As I related earlier, I inferred that we could find the reasons for the current reaction in the earlier experience. In making this connection, I was relying on commonsense psychology, and specifically on its widely instantiated and well-supported precept that such earlier experiences would give a person, in particular a female, good reason to react to later experiences that are thematically related in just the way Ms. B now reacts.

As we will see shortly, Grünbaum accuses Freud of making inferences like this on the basis of the thematic affinity alone. As a charge against analytic reasoning in general, that could not be right. Rather, when analysts come across a striking thematic affinity of the sort I found in Ms. B and interpret a causal connection, I think, following Hopkins and, by implication, Edelson (1988, pp. 332–333), that their reasoning is both more complicated and more plausible than Grünbaum allows. To reach a conclusion about a causal connection, they call on the background psychological knowledge of how a normal person would probably react in a simulation. At any rate, that is what I think I did. I referred, as I said, to a widely shared belief that early experiences such as Ms. B had would live on and give any normal female excellent reason to view later experiences having a similar thematic content in the way Ms. B now views sexual activity. This belief, it seems to me, is widely instantiated in ordinary human experience.

Note that in my inference to the cause, the thematic affinity played no direct role. It merely alerted me to the possibility of a connection. What allowed me to infer that a connection actually existed was my background commonsense psychological knowledge of the conditions under which thematic affinities are apt to be the result of causal connections in normal persons. It is this background that allows "reasoning by appeal to thematic affinities [to be] . . . central in the explanatory strategies of psychoanalysis" (Edelson, 1988, p. 332; see also pp. 331–335 and Hopkins, 1986, p. 50 for related arguments). Let me pursue this point a bit further. Grünbaum thinks that Freud repeatedly made the error of inferring causal connections from thematic affinities alone. I am not convinced. To the contrary, I am inclined to think that what this criticism provides, rather, is an unwitting example of what Grünbaum is over-looking. Take his critiques of Freud's case studies of the Rat Man and the Wolfman. Repeatedly, Grünbaum (1988) accuses Freud of drawing causal conclusions from mere thematic affinities. Here is part of what Freud (1909) had to say about the Rat Man.

> The notion of a rat is inseparably bound up with the fact that it has sharp teeth with which it gnaws and bites. . . . [They] are cruelly persecuted and mercilessly put to death by man. . . . But he himself had been just such a nasty, dirty little wretch, who was apt to bite people when he was in a rage, and had been fearfully punished for doing so. . . . It was almost as though Fate, when the captain told him [of the anal rat punishment], had been putting him through a . . . test: . . . he had reacted to it with his obsessional idea [that his dead father was to undergo the same punishment] [pp. 215–216].

Now consider Grünbaum's response. He suggests that Freud, *on the basis of a mere thematic affinity* (p. 631), drew an etiologic inference connecting the Rat Man's experience of himself as ratlike when a child and his current obsession with the idea of his father undergoing the monstrous punishment of anal rat penetration.

As I said, I am not convinced. When Freud reasoned from affinity to cause, as he seems to have been doing here, I think it was always, though perhaps not explicitly, by way of a reference to some background principles about how human beings act. In this case, the principle might be something like this: "Feeling that one is like a rat in early childhood makes one susceptible to obsessions about rats doing evil things to loved ones in adulthood, especially if one would like to do such evil things oneself but is not aware of it." I am not saying that such a principle is true, only that Freud was appealing to some such principle, not to a bare thematic affinity, when he drew his etiological conclusion. I have not been able to find a single place where Freud clearly and unambiguously used nothing but a thematic affinity as his grounds for inferring a causal connection.

In general, Freud's evidence for his claims concerning the Rat Man and the Wolf Man in his case studies of them does indeed often look weak, as Grünbaum reconstructs them. But perhaps Grünbaum has missed something, for Freud's own claims may not be questioned, his own words have an interest, and sometimes even a plausibility, that is lost in Grünbaum's reconstructions. What seems to make the difference is this: Freud weaves a whole web of inferences connecting behavior in the present to reasons for that behavior from deep in the past. When he does not actually weave such a web, he creates in us a sense of what the web might have been like. These inferences are drawn from both commonsense and psychoanalysis. All that remains of them in Grünbaum's reconstructions are the bare bones of the claims themselves, starkly isolated from their context, and the strictest construal of Freud's representation of the evidence on which he made them (Fine and Forbes, 1986, p. 238). Grünbaum misses what really gives Freud's conclusion their appeal, namely, the implicit web of background psychology, both commonsense and psychoanalytic, that was Freud's real basis for his inferences.

I would make the same response concerning the other false principle of causal inference that Grünbaum claims to find in Freud's work, the tally principle, or NCT (necessary condition thesis). This is the thesis that improvement in a patient is evidence for correctness of interpretation because only correct interpretations can cure. Again, to the extent that Freud did reason from improvement to causal accuracy, he did so, I think, through implicit reference back to his general knowledge of the conditions under which change occurs in analytic patients. He may not always have been entirely clear about this, and he did say things inconsistent with this reading (e.g., Freud, 1916–17, p. 452, justly quoted by Grünbaum, 1984, p. 138, and Grünbaum et al., 1986, p. 222), but I know of nothing in his actual causal practices that is inconsistent with this reading. Moreover, as Grünbaum (1984, p. 152; Grünbaum et al., 1986, p. 222) relates, Freud (1926, p. 134) himself came to harbor reservations about the principle and said things inconsistent with it (on his final view of the general relation between insight and cure, see Freud, 1937).

Nothing I have said so far touches Grünbaum's most important objection, that case studies lack an independent control. Without a control, we cannot distinguish the merely "post hoc" from the truly "proper hoc," so we cannot distinguish causal connections from mere coincidences. Edelson and Hopkins both respond to this argument by urging that in normal psychological reasoning, no such controls are required. Edelson (1988) thinks we can do the job they do, and more, with causal mechanisms. Hopkins (1986, p. 37) argues that inferring motive from action or wish-fulfilling fantasy by coincidence of content needs no control. By contrast, I think that Grünbaum is right; case studies do need an independent control. I also think we have one.

The control we have is our background commonsense psychological knowledge of how people think, feel, and behave. The whole of a psychoanalyst's psychological competence and experience is the control against which he or she tests causal judgments. This is not a formal control, consisting as it does of the collective knowledge of human causality built up over human history, but what has been called a historical control (Lasagna, 1982). Nevertheless, it is a control. Far from being negligible, these background beliefs, principles, precepts, rules, and skills for recognizing and inferring psychological states are a huge control and one that has been thoroughly tested. It is against this that we assess observed correlations, sequences and thematic affinities for their causal content.

To be worth much, this body of background psychological knowledge and the special knowledge that psychoanalysis has added must (1) generate generally good predictions and explanations; (2) allow principled generation and resolution of disagreements (Putnam, 1983); and (3) do so by using its own method of interpretation and explanation in terms of reasons, in terms of meaning in psychic reality. Both commonsense psychology in general and psychoanalysis in particular usually meet these tests. The explanations they generate yield fairly accurate predictions, we can generally recognize when they are apt to be good and when they are not, and we are able to do so without straying outside psychological interpretation and explanation.

As accounts of individual lives, I have been arguing, case studies not only can but do work fairly well. Let us now turn to the applications where Grünbaum's skepticism is higher, namely, the general hypotheses of psychoanalysis, such as that unconscious fantasies exist and repressed conflicts are pathogenic, and especially the counterintuitive ones, such as that paranoia in males has a homosexual ethiology. Can case studies using commonsense psychology and its psychoanalytic extensions give us what we need to scale up from accounts of individual lives to hypotheses applicable to whole classes of lives? As a science, psychoanalysis has to be able to do so. I call this the problem of scale.

The Problem of Scale

At first blush, Grünbaum's concern here appears to be easy to meet. Surely, case studies relying on psychological explanation can address the big these as well as the small ones. Indeed, the only obvious way to test the big theses is by reducing them to several smaller theses about individual patients. Each case study of an individual may yield results with some degree of uncertainty, but so long as the uncertainty has a different source in each case and yet the results they yield are consilient, progress can be made. In short, at this level of abstraction, the idea that the big theses of psychoanalysis can be tested by case studies seems, in principle at least, untroubled. If case studies work for individuals, the usual canons of induction should be able to scale up their results to classes of individuals without too much difficulty.

These points, however, only touch the surface. Not just psychoanalysis but all forms of intentional psychology have signally failed to achieve the theoretical unity, breadth, and depth of even the most modest natural science. An increasingly influential school of thought in cognitive science now argues that they are unlikely ever to do so (Churchland, 1984, p. 46; Churchland, 1986). For one thing, no one has ever succeeded in quantifying phenomena described in the language of intentional psychology. Yet quantified relationships are the hallmark of science. Moreover, despite attempts to get rid of the economic point of view, it is hard to see how we could do without quantified relationships in psychology. Surely, for example, we will always need to compare desires by their strength: "he did it because he wanted x more than he wanted to stay out of trouble." It is hard to see how cases studies — or anything else — could help us with this problem of quantifying psychological states.[4] Note that the problem I am raising here is not just a problem of "reducing" intentional

---

[4]In an excellent discussion of the relation of psychoanalysis to the neurosciences Edelson (1988) agrees that intentional psychology will not reduce to neuroscience. Following Fodor, he thinks that this is because psychological concepts group things so differently from the neurosciences that they will not usefully reduce (cf. Davidson's, 1970, 1974, anomalous monism). The argument we are examining claims that the concepts are so flawed that they are empirically useless in the first place.

psychology to some nonintentional discourse such as metapsychology or neuroscience. It is a problem of organizing psychological observations and inferences into any kind of unified general theory—even a unified general theory in the language of intentional psychology!

The problems I have just sketched are extremely serious so far as the hopes of any intentional psychology to become a mature science are concerned. Will psychoanalysis ever be able to arrive at and justify quantified, unified theories? Will it ever generate long-term, detailed predictions and retrodictions that are as successful as its explanations and predictions about individual lives? At this point, we do not know. However, two points should be made. First, the problems just discussed apply to all intentional psychology, not just psychoanalysis. Second, there is nothing specific to case studies behind them.

If case studies relying on commonsense psychological explanations can do so well, why has psychoanalysis had such a hard time marshalling convincing evidence for its larger theses? Here I will make just two points. Historically, psychoanalysis has gotten into the most trouble when it has veered farthest from the vocabulary and methods special to psychology. Think of the quantitative mechanistic notions Freud played with in the 1890s and their residue in metapsychology. The legacy of psychic energies and "cathexes" of energy and energy barriers persisted and interfered with scientific progress in psychoanalysis for a long time. Where psychoanalysis has stuck to intentional psychology, it has done much better. Second, psychoanalysis has often paid too little attention to evidence. A recent study by psychoanalysts of 60 often-cited papers from major psychoanalytic journals found that not one of them offered any direct evidence for the claims they were making (Klumpner, 1989). Sometimes ideas become influential in psychoanalysis not because of the strength of the evidence for them but because they capture the imagination. Psychoanalytic research does not have to be like this.

REFERENCES

Brentano, F. (1874), *Psychology from an Empirical Point of View* (trans. D. B. Terrell). London: Routledge & Kegan Paul, 1971.
Brook, J. A. (1992), Freud and splitting. *Internat. Rev. Psycho-Anal.*
Chomsky, N. (1972), *Language and Mind.* New York: Harcourt.
Churchland, P. M. (1984), *Matter and Consciousness.* Cambridge, MA: MIT Press.
Churchland, P. S. (1986), *Neurophilosophy.* Cambridge, MA: MIT Press.
Davidson, D. (1970), Mental events. In: *Essays on Actions and Events.* London: Oxford University Press, 1980.
_____ (1974), Psychology as philosophy. In: *Essays on Actions and Events.* London: Oxford University Press, 1980.

_____ (1984), *Inquiries into Truth and Interpretation*. London: Oxford University Press.
Dennett, D. (1978), *Brainstorms*. Montgomery, VT: Bradford Books.
_____ (1987a), *The Intentional Stance*. Cambridge, MA: MIT Press.
_____ (1987b), Intentionality. In: *The Oxford Companion to the Mind*, ed. R. Gregory. Oxford: Oxford University Press.
Edelson, M. (1986a), Heinz Hartmann's influence on psychoanalysis as a science. *Psychoanal. Inq.*, 6:575–599.
_____ (1988), *Psychoanalysis: A Theory in Crisis*. Chicago: University of Chicago Press.
Fine, A. & Forbes, M. (1986), Commentary on Grünbaum (1984). *Behav. & Brain Sciences*, 9:237–8.
Fodor, J. (1988), *Psychosemantics*. Cambridge, MA: MIT Press.
Freud, S. (1905a), Three essays on sexuality. *Standard Edition*, 7:125–248. London: Hogarth Press, 1953.
_____ (1905b), Jokes and their relation to the unconscious. *Standard Edition*, 8. London: Hogarth Press, 1960.
_____ (1909), Notes upon a case of obsessional neurosis. *Standard Edition*, 10:153–318. London: Hogarth Press, 1955.
_____ (1912), The dynamics of transference. *Standard Edition*, 12:97–108. London: Hogarth Press, 1958.
_____ (1914), On the history of the psychoanalytic movement. *Standard Edition*, 14:3–66. London: Hogarth Press, 1957.
_____ (1915), The unconscious. *Standard Edition*, 14:159–216. London: Hogarth Press, 1957.
_____ (1916–17), Introductory lectures on psychoanalysis. *Standard Edition*, 15 & 16. London: Hogarth Press, 1963.
_____ (1920), The psychogenesis of a case of homosexuality in a woman. *Standard Edition*, 18:145–174. London: Hogarth Press, 1955.
_____ (1923), The ego and the id. *Standard Edition*, 19:3–68. London: Hogarth Press, 1961.
_____ (1924), A short account of psychoanalysis. *Standard Edition*, 19:191–212. London: Hogarth Press, 1961.
_____ (1926), Inhibitions, symptoms and anxiety. *Standard Edition*, 20:77–178. London: Hogarth Press, 1959.
_____ (1937), Analysis terminable and interminable. *Standard Edition*, 23:209–270. London: Hogarth Press, 1964.
_____ (1938), An outline of psychoanalysis. *Standard Edition*, 23:141–204. London: Hogarth Press, 1964.
Gill, M. & Holzman, P. (1976), *Psychology versus Metapsychology. Psychological Issues*, Monogr. 36. New York: International Universities Press.
Goldberg, A. (1988), *A Fresh Look at Psychoanalysis: The View from Self Psychology*. Hillsdale, NJ: The Analytic Press.
Grünbaum, A. (1984), *The Foundations of Psychoanalysis*. Berkeley: University of California Press.
_____ (1988), The role of the case study method in the foundations of psychoanalysis. *Canadian J. Philos.*, 18:623–658.
_____ (1990), "Meaning" connections and causal connections in the human sciences: The poverty of hermeneutic philosophy. *J. Amer. Psychoanal. Assn.*, 38:559–578.
_____ et al. (1986), Précis of *The Foundations of Psychoanalysis*, with peer commentary (including by analysts and analytic writers such as Eagle, Holt, Edelson, Luborsky, Marmor, Pollock, Reiser, Spence, and Storr). *Behav. & Brain Sciences*, 9:217–284.

Hopkins, J. (1986), Epistemiology and depth psychology: Critical notes on *The Foundations of Psychoanalysis*. In: *Psychoanalysis, Mind and Science,* ed. S. Clark & C. Wright. Oxford: Basil Blackwell.

Klein, G. S. (1969), Freud's two theories of sexuality. In: *Psychology Versus Metapsychology,* ed. M. M. Gill & P. S. Holzman. *Psychological Issues,* Monogr. 36. New York: International Universities Press.

_____ (1976), *Psychoanalytic Theory.* New York: International Universities Press.

Klumpner, G. (1989), Interview with Chair, Committee on Scientific Activities. *Amer. Psychoanal. Assn. Newsl.,* 22:13.

Lasagna, L. (1982), Historical controls. *New Engl. J. Med.,* 307:1339–1340.

Morton, A. (1982), Freudian commonsense. In: *Philosophical Essays on Freud,* ed. R. Wolheim & J. Hopkins. Cambridge: Cambridge University Press.

Putnam, H. (1983), *Realism and Reason.* Cambridge: Cambridge University Press.

Ricoeur, P. (1970), *Freud and Philosophy.* New Haven, CT: Yale University Press.

_____ (1981), *Hermeneutics and the Human Sciences.* New York: Cambridge University Press.

Rycroft, C. (1966), *Psychoanalysis Observed.* London: Constable.

Sachs, D. (1982), On Freud's doctrine of emotions. In: *Philosophical Essays on Freud,* ed. R. Wolheim & J. Hopkins. Cambridge: Cambridge University Press.

Schafer, R. (1976), *A New Language for Psychoanalysis.* New Haven, CT: Yale University Press.

_____ (1978), *Language and Insight.* New Haven, CT: Yale University Press.

Searle, J. (1983), *Intentionality.* Cambridge: Cambridge University Press.

Spence, D. (1982), *Narrative Truth and Historical Truth.* New York: Norton.

Stich, S. (1983), *From Folk Psychology to Cognitive Science: The Case Against Belief.* Cambridge, MA: MIT Press.

Wollheim, R. (1984), *The Thread of Life.* Cambridge, MA: Harvard University Press.

Author Index

Subject Index

311